THE JEWISH LAW ANNUAL

The Institute of Jewish Law
Boston University School of Law
765 Commonwealth Avenue
Boston, MA 02215
Publication No. 7

THE JEWISH LAW ANNUAL

VOLUME SIX

THE INSTITUTE OF JEWISH LAW
BOSTON UNIVERSITY SCHOOL OF LAW

Routledge
Taylor & Francis Group
LONDON AND NEW YORK

First published 1987 by Harwood Academic Publishers

2 Park Square, Milton Park, Abingdon, Oxfordshire OX14 4RN
52 Vanderbilt Avenue, New York, NY 10017

Routledge is an imprint of the Taylor & Francis Group, an informa business

First issued in paperback 2020

Library of Congress Catalogue Card No. 79-648405

ISBN 13: 978-3-7186-0466-1 (hbk)
ISBN 13: 978-0-367-60583-4 (pbk)

We express our appreciation to Irwin and Ruth Shapiro
through whose generosity this volume has been published.

The Annual is published under the auspices of The Institute of Jewish Law, Boston University School of Law, in conjunction with the Oxford Centre for Postgraduate Hebrew Studies and the International Association of Jewish Lawyers and Jurists.

Editorial communications should be addressed to Prof. B. S. Jackson, Keynes College, The University, Canterbury, Kent CT2 7NP, England. Intending contributors are asked to request a stylesheet before their contribution is typed. The Annual enjoys complete editorial independence. Contributors are welcome from all, irrespective of religious faith or denomination. Neither the Editor nor the members of the Editorial Advisory Board are to be associated with the views expressed by the contributors.

ISSN: 0169-8354
This book is part of a series. The publisher will accept continuation orders which may be cancelled at any time and which provide for automatic billing and shipping of each title in the series upon publication. Please write for details.

CONTENTS

PART ONE

THE PHILOSOPHY OF JEWISH LAW (I)

PART TWO

CHRONICLE

PART THREE

FROM THE EDITOR

This issue is the first to be published exclusively by the Institute of Jewish Law of the Boston University School of Law, and represents a substantial demonstration of support. At the same time, it is fitting to record with gratitude the commitment to the *Annual* showed by the original publisher, E.J. Brill of Leiden, without whom the venture would not have been born. Thanks are due, in particular, to Dr. F. Th. Dijkema, whose friendly co-operation sustained the publication in this first phase of its history.

The symposium on the Philosophy of Jewish Law, which forms the main content of both this and the next issue, represents a major contribution to an area of investigation which has attracted increasing interest in recent years. Most of the articles have been awaiting publication for longer than is usual; nevertheless, their effect remains timely. The second part of this two-part symposium, which includes a substantial reply to the debate by the late Julius Stone, will appear volume VII, production of which has already commenced.

As from volume VIII (1988), most issues will include an open section, not confined to a particular symposium topic. Intending authors are invited to contact me in advance of sending a typescript; style-sheets and advice on the possibility of submitting material on disc are available by writing to me at Keynes College, The University, Canterbury, Kent CT2 7NP, England.

PART ONE

THE PHILOSOPHY OF JEWISH LAW (I)

SECULAR JURISPRUDENCE AND THE PHILOSOPHY OF JEWISH LAW: A COMMENTARY ON SOME RECENT LITERATURE*

by

BERNARD S. JACKSON**

1.0 Much modern writing on the theory of Jewish law is informed, sometimes but not always explicitly, by the views of modern schools of jurisprudence. A wide range of such views is represented (1.1-1.5), and there is considerable variation in the thoroughness and sensitivity of the applications. After a survey of the principal stances we encounter, this article seeks to elucidate the underlying philosophical issues necessarily involved in any attempt to match the secular and religious corpora of theory, with a view to clarifying the nature and significance of the substantive issues themselves.

1.1 Jurisprudential positivism has recently attracted influential support amongst writers on Jewish Law. Menahem Elon bases the whole structure of his magnum opus, *Hamishpat Ha'ivri,* on a classification of sources into historical, legal and literary, and identifies the legal sources as the sole test of validity. Following Salmond, he defines the "legal sources" as "the sources of law and means of creating law recognised by the legal system itself as conferring binding force on the norms of that system",[1] and his language implies an equation of "binding force" with "validity". But whence do these sources of law which confer such validity on the substantive norms themselves derive their validity? Elon again follows Salmond (but in reality and importantly Kelsen) in asserting the existence of a "basic norm" which gives authority to the sources of law. This "basic norm", referred to in both Kelsenian and Hartian terms as a "*Grundnorm*" or "basic rule of recognition", is identified by Elon with "the rule that everything stated in the Written Law is of binding authority for the Jewish legal system". We may note that if Kelsenian analysis is to be applied, this rule is *not* to be

* This article was written in 1980, and sent to contributors to the symposium in order to indicate a range of issues which might appropriately be considered. Since a number of contributors have addressed themselves to it directly, I have left it in its original form, rather than revise and update it.

** Professor of Law, University of Kent at Canterbury.

1 M. Elon, ed., *The Principles of Jewish Law* (Jerusalem: Keter, 1975), 10.

identified with the *Grundnorm,* but rather with the "historically first constitution",[2] since something further, taken from outside the system itself, is required to give authority to it. The need for such a step is accepted by Elon: "The source of authority of this basic norm itself is the basic tenet of Judaism that the source of authority of the Torah is divine command."[3] This, for Elon, is the real *Grundnorm.*[4] This view of Jewish law, in terms of a hierarchy of authority deriving ultimately from God, may appear natural and unsurprising. There is, however, one aspect of positivism increasingly stressed by legal theorists - particularly by Kelsen and Hart, though in different ways - that has proved particularly attractive to modern Jewish law scholars. It is the degree of discretion, exercised quite legitimately under a power conferred by this very hierarchy of authority of the system, which positivism claims is (and in some versions is necessarily) exercised by the legitimate institutions of the system for the purposes of legal clarification and development. Elon has stressed this factor in terms of the "legislative" sources of Jewish law;[5] Lamm and Kirschenbaum have more recently done the same in respect of judicial discretion.[6] The attractiveness of this model for modern Jewish Orthodoxy lies in its explanation of the legitimacy of legal *development.* The argument can be presented that Jewish law, just because it is a system of law, may be expected to possess such institutions; and it is not difficult to proceed from that point to illustrate their existence from the treasure-house of data of the history of Jewish law.[7] Legal

2 H. Kelsen, *The Pure Theory of Law,* trld. M. Knight (Berkeley and Los Angeles: University of California Press, 1967), 200.

3 *Supra* n.1, at 15.

4 But see Kelsen, *supra* n.2, at 193f. See also H. Kelsen, *General Theory of Law and State,* trld. Wedberg (Cambridge: Harvard University Press, 1946), 115: "The basic norm of a religious system says that one ought to behave as God and the authorities instituted by Him command."

5 M. Elon, *Hamishpat Ha'ivri* {Engl. title: *Jewish Law* } (Jerusalem: The Magnes Press, 1973, 3 vols.).

6 N. Lamm and A. Kirschenbaum, "Freedom and Constraint in the Jewish Juridical Process", *Cardozo Law Review* 1 (1979), 99-133.

7 Interestingly, this is denied by M. Silberg, *Talmudic Law and the Modern State,* trld. B. Z. Bokser (New York: Burning Bush Press, 1973), 51, who claims that Jewish law, being a system of religious law, "does not define norms for deciding the law, but norms of behaviour" - thus apparently reducing Jewish law (in Hartian terms) to a system of primary rules only. He also denies (at 57) that there is any recognised competence to effect change in Jewish law. It may be noted that Silberg was a Justice of the Supreme Court of the State of Israel, and an early advocate and exponent of the application of Jewish law in Israel. His views were not, therefore, reflections of the conservative approach described later in this paragraph of the text.

development is itself regarded as a positive value, in the context of debates with ultra-conservatives who deny the *moral* authority of the current generation to initiate change. The debate then becomes centrally relevant to the issue of incorporation of Jewish law into the law of the State of Israel, since few would deny that a necessary precondition of such incorporation is a degree of clarification, restatement and development.

There are, however, at least two important flaws in the attempt to apply these positivist models to the Jewish legal system. The first lies in the temporal status of the historically first constitution (Kelsen) or ultimate rule of recognition (Hart). Both theories accept that such a basic norm, identified for Jewish law by Elon as the rule that everything stated in the Written Law is of binding authority, may indeed be changed by unilateral, revolutionary action of the subjects of the law. Secular jurisprudence thus accords the current constitution a merely contingent validity, until and unless a revolution occurs and succeeds; but such a possibility can hardly be accepted for Jewish law, wherein the basic law is eternal, or at least (even if we think of notions of *berit hadashah* or concepts of *Torah* in the messianic age) is not susceptible to change by unilateral action by its subjects. The covenant may be broken, but it cannot be unilaterally revoked. This theoretical dissonance raises an important methodological question: how legitimate is it, or what ends are served, by importing part of a theory while neglecting some other part that according to that theory may represent a central or crucial aspect?

A second flaw relates to the manner in which Elon derives the "exclusive authority (of the halakhic scholars of each and every succeeding generation) to interpret the Written Law and ensure its continuing evolution". It was, he says, "derived from a number of Pentateuchal passages". But this is a circular argument. There could be no legitimate derivation of authority from the Pentateuchal passages on the part of the scholars unless they already possessed authority to interpret.[8] I have suggested elsewhere that the (uncontested) invocation of a *bat kol* in the context of the establishment of rabbinic authority in *Erub. 13b* may be viewed as a response to this logical

---

8 Dr. Dov I. Frimer, in private correspondence, defends Elon's argument as non-circular, on the grounds that *Deut*. 17: 8-11 confers the necessary authority, directly, without involving any act of interpretation on the part of those to whom authority is to be given. This contention rests upon the assumption of an identity between rabbinic judicial authority, specifically the High Court of Jerusalem and its successors, with the "Levitical Priests and the judge (N.B. singular) who is in office in those days". To me, that identification necessarily involves an act of interpretation.

difficulty.[9] Yet even so, the extent of power conferred on rabbinic authorities according to the positivist understanding of the legal system may appear rather different, and very much restricted, if we do seek to avoid the circular argument by basing such authority on such sources only as do not themselves rely upon rabbinic interpretation. The only alternative, if this model of the Jewish legal system is to be maintained, is to adopt a version of it which ignores this internal viewpoint: one which claims that rabbinic authority is in fact conferred by the written law independently of the rabbinic view as to how this is done. Any rabbinic derivation of rabbinic authority from scriptural verses would then stand as a kind of expostfacto rationalisation or *asmakhta*. It is not every jurisprudential theory, however, which would accept such a bypassing of the internal viewpoint, and we may wonder, in particular, whether Jewish law would countenance it.

A similar problem of partial correspondence between the data of Jewish law and positivist legal theory is encountered by Otto Bondy, who views Jewish law in predominantly Kelsenian terms.[10] The sticking point, for Bondy, is the problem of sanctions. Kelsen maintained that sanctions were essential to law, indeed that a sanction was built into the structure of every individual legal norm. Bondy appears to regard Jewish law as affording a falsification of this particular aspect of Kelsenian theory.[11] But this explanation of the mismatch is only one possible alternative. The other, which cannot be discounted simply by ignoring it, is that Kelsen is right and therefore "Jewish law" is not, in part or in whole, "law". In order to decide which alternative explanation of the mismatch is preferable, we have to arrive at a view of the nature of the Kelsenian theory - what, in particular, it claims to be. This is but one example of an essential methodological problem which has been virtually ignored thus far in the literature. As in so many types of comparative research, the material with which the researcher attempts to compare his primary subject area is taken to be unproblematic.

9 "The Concept of Religious Law in Judaism", *Aufstieg und Niedergang der römischen Welt* II.19.1 (1979), 33-52.

10 O. Bondy, "The Validity Problem in Hebrew Law", *Archiv für Rechts-und Sozialphilosophie* 54 (1968), 217-232. For comparison of Englard's approach with that of Kelsen, see B. S. Jackson, "Modern Research in Jewish Law - Some Theoretical Issues", in *Modern Research in Jewish Law*, ed. B. S. Jackson (Leiden: Brill, 1980), 136-157, at 157. See further Yuter in this volume.

11 *Ibid.* at 222f.

1.2 Natural law theory is an area where the student of Jewish law must be especially careful before making comparisons.[12] The long history and variety of natural law theory is such as to tempt us to use the term in almost any context where the source of a rule or obligation appears to be other than a recognised authority in a particular legal system. A famous talmudic passage, *Yoma* 67b, interprets *Lev.* 18:4 *et mishpatay ta'asu* as referring to commandments which "if they were not written, they should by right have been written" (referring to the prohibitions of idolatry, immorality, bloodshed, robbery and blasphemy). Lamm and Kirschenbaum refer to this as "the major talmudic passage which may serve as a source for a theory of natural law".[13] But it does not follow that the talmudic passage had in mind, as a source of obligation other than the written law, any "laws ... issue(ing) from a primordial and eternal order...(which entail the existence of) certain moral notions (as) indigenous to man and nature and discoverable by unaided reason".[14] The talmudic passage, without more, simply does not tell us (a) whether the alternative source (to the written law) issued from a primordial order or represented an order contemporary with Sinai; (b) whether that source was indigenous to man (i.e. universal) or communicated to Jews alone; and (c) whether its discovery other than through the Written Law could be accomplished by "unaided reason". It is tempting to us to read such passages in the light of debates which possess contemporary heat. But even though the classical naturalist assertions were in the philosophical air in the time of the talmudic Rabbis, one might suspect that (especially in the light of Jewish-Christian debate) the problem of the range of recognised forms of revelation was (for them, if not for us) by far the hotter potato.

Julius Stone captured a number of important facets of the natural law comparison in the following remarks: "Jewish theory of law has some of the marks of natural law, in so far as man, his position, rights and duties are held within a transcending order revealed by the divine word as interpreted by man's reason. But it did not proceed from this to admit that mark of natural law which ... consists of the juxtaposition of positive and natural legal orders".[15] The latter assertion would command, perhaps, more general assent

---

12 Recent contributions to the literature include S. Atlas, *Netivim bemishpat ha'ivri* (New York: American Academy for Jewish Research, 1978), 17-21; Z. W. Falk, *Arkhe mishpat veyahadut* (Jerusalem: The Magnes Press, 1980), 57-65. See also S. Freehof, "Natural Law in the Jewish Tradition", *Natural Law Institute Proceedings* 5 (1951), 15-26.

13 *Supra* n.6, at 110.

14 Extracted from their own definition, at 106.

15 J. Stone, *Human Law and Human Justice* (London: Stevens, 1965), 26.

than the former. Yet even the latter may admit of qualification. Lichtenstein has argued that Jewish law recognises the existence of a universal, intuitive human morality, which may serve as a minimum standard in the interpretation of Jewish law itself.[16] In all such debates over the Jewish attitude to natural law, the status of Noahide law and the views of Maimonides have predictably played a major role. Here modern writers have displayed commendable caution. Neither universalism not rationalism necessarily entail naturalism. And while Lamm and Kirschenbaum[17] may be correct in accusing Fox[18] and Faur[19] of going too far in suggesting that *Yoma* 67b implies only a capacity, *resulting from* revelation, to recognise the rationality and desirability of prohibitions such as bloodshed and robbery, that latter argument may at least serve to remind us of the need to take account of the relationship between revelation and reason, and to warn against any simple equation of reason with natural law thinking. Jurisprudential positivism similarly admits of the possibility that a particular legal system may, through its authorised institutions, allow for the incorporation of a standard of morality or reason as a criterion of validity of lower-order norms.[20] What positivism denies is that legal systems in general must of their nature apply such criteria, irrespective of express incorporation.

1.3 Social contract theories have been used in support of both positivist and naturalist views of the legal system. The important issue as between these two uses is whether the sovereign, whose creation is justified in terms of an (historical or supposed) social contract, is thereafter necessarily limited by natural rights which survive in the subjects. The Jewish concept of *berit*, covenant, seems to parallel at least that form of social contract theory in which the contract is between subjects and sovereign (rather than merely

16 A. Lichtenstein, "Does Jewish Tradition Recognize an Ethic Independent of Halakah?", in *Modern Jewish Ethics*, ed. M. Fox (Ohio State University Press, 1975), 62-88. A similar viewpoint seems to be held by Shalom Albeck, who sees universal principles of justice, which represent a fixed and unchangeable element in human nature, as inherent in the *halakhah* itself. See his "Law and History in Halakhic Research", in *Modern Research in Jewish Law*, ed. B. S. Jackson (Leiden: Brill, 1980), 1-20 (translated from *Dine Hamamonot batalmud* (Tel- Aviv: Dvir, 1976), 13-31), at 5f., 16, and my comments in the same volume, at 140f.

17 *Supra* n. 6, at 110f.

18 M. Fox, "Maimonides and Aquinas on Natural Law", *Diné Israel* 3 (1972), v-xxxvi.

19 J. Faur, "Law and Justice in Rabbinic Jurisprudence", in *Samuel K. Mirsky Memorial Volume* (New York: Yeshiva University, 1970), 13-20.

20 Hart has always allowed for such incorporation.

between the subjects *inter se),* and the parallel has attracted considerable support as a basis for the philosophy of Jewish law. Thus Helen Silving has claimed that the covenant between God and Israel is "in every way comparable to Rousseau's *"contrat social"*,[21] and a similar emphasis has been placed by Orlinsky.[22] Most commonly, the *berit* is given a function comparable to the social contract in positivist versions. Even the sovereignty of God cannot be accepted without a validating act of popular assent. Both Faur[23] and Dorff[24] see the covenant as the basis of validity of a positivist system of Jewish law. Yet Faur at the same time maintains that the sovereign authority is limited by law, and that the basic rights of man are guaranteed by the covenant.[25] We may note how closely this conception follows the model of the theory of the American constitution: a social contract may validate a positive legal order; a positive legal order does not necessarily entrench basic rights; but the constitution of a particular legal order - such as that of the U.S.A. and, according to this argument, Jewish law - may choose to do so. Indeed this approach to the philosophy of Jewish law has proved particularly attractive to American writers.

Once again one must observe that the parallel is only partial, and that the significance of the discrepancies falls to be assessed. Can the transition be so lightly made from a human, secular sovereign to a sovereign claimed to be divine? Are statements that God is bound by the terms of the covenant anything more than figures of speech? How do they relate to theological conceptions of the nature of God? Can God unilaterally revoke the covenant? May divine sovereignty be rejected if God is conceived to have broken the covenant - a question which has indeed been posed after Auschwitz? It is hardly of assistance, in this context, to reply that breach of the covenant by God is inconceivable. Such a response would merely underline the fact that the equation of God with the sovereign in a social contract theory is little more than a metaphor. In other respects, too, the theory runs into difficulties on closer inspection. The social contract theory purports to explain the very creation of the sovereign, but God's existence and indeed his legitimate power over man must certainly precede the covenant in Jewish thought. Finally,

---

21 H. Silving, "The Jurisprudence of the Old Testament", *New York University Law Review* 28 (1953), 1129-1148, at 1130.

22 H. M. Orlinsky, *The Bible as Law: God and Israel under Contract* (New York: Horace M. Kallen Press, 1978) (The Horace M. Kallen Annual Lecture, 1976).

23 *Supra* n.19.

24 E. Dorff, "Judaism as a Religious Legal System", *The Hastings Law Journal* 29 (1978), 1331-1360.

25 *Supra* n.19, at 18f.

we may note that there appears to have existed at least a body of rabbinic opinion directly opposed to contractarian validation of Jewish law. A view reported in the Talmud[26] stresses that such consent as was given at Sinai was procured by duress,[27] and elsewhere the election of Israel is explained in terms of its *unconditional* surrender to the divine will.[28] Indeed, the conception of God's being bound by any law in exercising divine justice has also met with a direct denial in the recent literature.[29]

The viewpoints of the historical school of jurisprudence are strongly reflected in the thinking of the American Conservative movement, for which "historical Judaism" is a motto and the progressive development of Jewish law in the past is a value and a model for contemporary action.[30] This is hardly surprising. The *wissenschaftliche* tradition on which Conservative thought was nurtured goes back to a Germany still much influenced by Savigny and his pupils. Thus Boaz Cohen, citing Böcking and Maine, writes that "students of legal history ... will readily recognize that the same agencies and instrumentalities that operated in the development of the legal institutions of the civilised peoples of bygone days, played a dominant role in the evolution of our system of Law."[31] Even without the explicit reference to Maine, and the subsequent attempt to apply his sequence of fiction-equity-legislation, one would know from the terminology alone how much Cohen was indebted to Maine. The influence of the Historical school is apparent also at a more sophisticated theoretical level. When Max

26 *Shab*. 88a.

27 *Cf.* Silberg, *supra* n.7, at 2.

28 *Cf.* H. H. Cohn, "Prolegomena to the theory and History of Jewish Law", in *Essays in Jurisprudence in Honor of Roscoe Pound* (Indianapolis and New York: Bobbs-Merrill, 1962), 44-81, at 44f., largely reprinted in Cohn, *Jewish Law in Ancient and Modern Israel* (New York: Ktav, 1971), vii-xxxiv.

29 H. H. Cohn, "The Concept of Justice in Jewish Law", in *The Jewish Tradition and its Relevance to Contemporary Life* (New York: Center for the Study of Democratic Institutions, 1973), 1-13, at 2. See R. Gordis, "A Dynamic Halakhah: Principles and Procedures of Jewish Law", *Judaism* 28/111 (1979), 263-282; idem, "The Halakhah, Past, Present and Future: A Reply to the Responses", *Judaism* 29/113 (1980), 85-109; *idem*, "Authority in Jewish Law", in *Conservative Judaism and Jewish Law*, ed. S. Siegel (New York: Rabbinical Assembly, 1977), 47-78 (reprinted from *Proceedings of the Rabbinical Assembly* (1944), 41-44, 64-93). See also L. Jacobs, *A Tree of Life* (Oxford: Oxford University Press for The Littman Library, 1984), and my review article in *Legal Studies* 5/2 (1985), 233-238.

30 See, for example, the work of Robert Gordis, cited n. 29, *supra*.

31 B. Cohen, "Towards a Philosophy of Jewish Law", *Conservative Judaism* 6/1 (1949), 1-31, at 14f., reprinted in Cohen, *Law and Tradition in Judaism* (New York: Ktav, 1969).

Kadushin argues that *aggadah* and *halakhah* are both concretizations of the value-complex embedded in the psyche of the Jewish people, but that *halakhah* is the more precise form of concretization, requiring therefore the Sages to act as representatives of the people in its development,[32] he reflects at every point - the correlation between the forms of expression of values and the respective capacities of people and scholars to express it; the attribution of law to the common consciousness of a particular people; and the role of the scholars, at a certain stage of development, as the representatives of the people - the thinking of Savigny.[33]

Here too one must be aware of what is entailed in the adoption of particular aspects of the thinking of the school. The supreme value in this system is the social psychology of each particular *volk*. There is little room here for the doctrine of election, or for transcendent values. Indeed, Maine saw the chief jurisprudential significance of his work as lying in the destruction of the basis of natural law theory. Even if the historical school provides models of legal development which may be useful in describing Jewish legal history, this does not necessarily assist us in the search for a philosophy of Jewish law. Even Maine appears to have regarded the results of his research as providing only a test of value of modern law; as regards validity, he was content to support and popularise the views of Austin. Yet we must ask what justifies the adoption of the course of history even as a criterion of value. As Novak has recognised, this would appear, without more, to breach the logical rule, adhered to by the vast majority of analytical philosophers, that one may not derive an "ought" from an "is".[34] Unless one has grounds for the claim that development in the past has reflected a value existent in the social psychology of the people[35] (a stance which may well have been the viewpoint of Savigny, if not Maine", one does not avoid the question: by virtue of what was such historical development in the past

32 M. Kadushin, "Halakhah and Haggadah", in *Conservative Judaism and Jewish Law*, ed. S. Siegel (New York: Rabbinical Assembly, 1977), 217-236, reprinted from Kadushin, *The Rabbinic Mind* (3rd ed., New York: Bloch, 1972).

33 F. K. von Savigny, *System of Modern Roman Law*, trld. W. Holloway, quoted in Lord Lloyd of Hampstead, *Jurisprudence*, 4th ed. by Lloyd and M. D. A. Freeman (London: Stevens, 1979), at 654; discussed in B. S. Jackson, "The Ceremonial and the Judicial: Biblical Law as Sign and Symbol", *Journal for the Study of the Old Testament* 30 (1984), 25-50, at 46f., and in "Structuralism and the notion of Religious Law", *Investigaciones Semióticas* (IS), 2/3 (1982-83), 1-43, at 17f.

34 D. Novak, "Change and Status Quo", *Judaism* 29/113 (1980), 38-42, at 42 n.12.

35 This may be what Novak means when he defends the use of Jewish legal history by saying that it contains a "normative continuum, which already contains prescriptions which themselves call for future applications", *ibid.*

legitimate in terms of the Jewish legal system? This is why a scholar like Elon, most of whose magnum opus is concerned with the description of the use of the sources of Jewish law at successive periods of time, has to commence with an attempt to develop a theory justifying the use of such sources. We may observe that the choice of means to accord normative status to historical development and its instrumentalities is of great theoretical importance. If, following Savigny, we do identify the historic consciousness of the people with the ultimate source of values (as Gordis seems close to doing), we may risk a conflict with theological claims of the transcendence of moral values and the sovereignty of God. This accounts for the radical difference of opinion in a recent symposium between Gordis and Bleich - the only point of agreement being that they believe in different Gods![36]

1.5 The viewpoint of the Realist legal thinkers, with their anti-conceptual stance and insistence on attention to policy issues, is reflected in or paralleled by that of the Reconstructionist movement. Thus Eisenstein rejects the reification of the *Halakhah*. It should be regarded not as a living entity but rather as a description of the norms of behaviour accepted by the Jewish people in a given place at a given time.[37] Similarly, the realists rejected the equation of legal doctrine, or law in the books, with law, and identified it with what judges actually do, or may be predicted to do. We may note that this stance, which entails a rejection of the positivist conception of law based on sources and has been largely rejected as a result, would therefore encounter no difficulty with the circular argument we observed in discussing Elon's attempt to account for the authority of rabbinic reasoning. For realists, normative justification can only be grounded in an ethical relativism which is anyway a dead end. We should therefore not detain ourselves with questions of what justifies rabbinic interpretation; rather, we should observe it in action, use it as a predictor of future behaviour, and seek to influence it in conformity with modern policy aspirations wherever possible. So stated, the position of Reconstructionism can readily be seen to conflict with the mainstream of Jewish theological thinking: it is based upon a secular ethical relativism which Judaism would simply not accept. Yet we shall see that the conclusion from ethical relativism that modern positivism has drawn, namely

36 J. D. Bleich, "Halakhah as an Absolute", *Judaism* 29/113 (1980), 30-37, at 37; Gordis, "The Halakhah, Past, Present and Future", *supra* n.30, at 92.

37 I. Eisenstein, "There is no "One" Halakhah", *Judaism* 29/113 (1980), 64-65, at 64.

that there is no necessary connection between law and morality, has been surprisingly influential amongst recent Orthodox writers.

We may also observe significant differences amongst orthodox scholars on the role of policy argument in modern halakhic development. While Bleich is in all respects the antithesis of a realist, stressing the objectivity of halakhic doctrine and seeking to exclude "volitional inclinations" (= policy),[38] there are examples of a quite contrary practice, as may be seen from a recent exchange between R. Moshe Feinstein and R. Eliezer Waldenberg over abortion.[39] The question of whether policy arguments may rightly be developed in judicial reasoning has recently been hotly debated also in secular jurisprudence, with Ronald Dworkin attacking the positivist view that such policy argument is legitimate at least in cases of ambiguity or lacunae in the legal system.[40] But here too, the debate cannot be readily transferred to the sphere of Jewish law, this time for structural as well as theological reasons. Dworkin's rejection of the legitimacy of policy argument is based upon a democratic political philosophy which claims that policy argument is the exclusive preserve of the elected legislature. Jewish theorists cannot rely upon such an alternative source of policy-making. Nevertheless, there remains a question of whether policy is reserved for institutions which may be revived in the future, or whether, indeed, policy is an unchanging, transcendent matter that is already coded into the Jewish *Grundnorm*. These are issues which may be resolved only on the basis of Jewish theology.

Even amongst those who do, unlike the realists, take normativity seriously, there has been a body of opinion, often associated with existentialists or situation ethicists, which stresses that values are to be found in action, not in doctrine.[41] An attempt to apply this view to the theological sphere itself is made by Jacques Ellul, who identifies divine justice with the divine act of judgment rather than the divine statement of legal doctrine.[42]

38 "*Yikov hadin et hahar* ... and let the chips fall as they may": *Contemporary Halakhic Problems* (New York: Ktav, 1977), xv.

39 See D. B. Sinclair, "Law and Morality in Halakhic Bioethics", in *The Jerusalem Conference Volume*, ed. B. S. Jackson (Atlanta: Scholars Press, 1986, Jewish Law Association Studies II), forthcoming.

40 Most recently in *A Matter of Principle* (Cambridge: Harvard University Press, 1985).

41 See my "On the Tyranny of the Law", *Israel Law Review* 18/3-4 (1983), 327-347, at 330f., on Joseph Fletcher and George Cohn.

42 *The Theological Foundation of Law*, trld. M. Wieser (London: SCM Press, 1961), 46.

It is not difficult to locate the specifically Christian pattern of theological beliefs into which this claim fits and in which context it must be understood.[43] Nevertheless, a question is here posed, on the one hand by realists and on the other by many Christian moral philosophers, as to whether there is a difference in kind between statement of legal doctrine and judicial application of law.[44] We shall consider presently whether a Jewish answer to this problem can be detected.

2.0 The effect of the above survey has been to identify various points of partial correspondence between theories of secular jurisprudence and theorising about Jewish law, but to deny systematic correspondence of the latter with any of the former. Indeed, on a number of points it has seemed probable that Jewish theology would press its own exclusive claims, in contradiction of aspects of secular theory.[45] We may now note that some forms of secular jurisprudence have recognised this very claim of the exclusivity of theological jurisprudence. Nineteenth century positivism, in particular, denied that religious law properly fell within the ambit of jurisprudence[46] This point is made explicitly by John Austin, who accepts that "laws set by God to his human creatures" may properly ("without extension by metaphor or analogy") be termed "law", being rules "laid down for the guidance of an intelligent being by an intelligent being having power over him", but excludes them from "positive law", which is restricted to laws set by men as political superiors to men as political inferiors, and which (alone) is "the matter of jurisprudence". The result of this classification was that religious law shared some but not all its features with secular law. Specifically, religious law was, like all law "properly so called", to be understood as a species of command, thus entailing the intimation of a wish to do or forbear from some act together with the power and intention to inflict evil in the event of non-compliance with that wish. On the other hand, only positive law required the further test of the existence of a

---

43 See my "Legalism", *Journal of Jewish Studies* 30/1 (1979), 1-22, esp. at 6f.

44 This has been a theme of my more recent work: see my *Semiotics and Legal Theory* (London: Routledge & Kegan Paul, 1985), esp. section 11.3; "Legalism and Spirituality: Historical, Philosophical and Semiotic Notes on Legislators and Judges", Proceedings of Conference on "Religion and Law: Middle Eastern Influences on the West", University of Utah and Brigham Young University, March 1985.

45 For a strong statement to this effect, see A. H. Rabinowitz, *The Jewish Mind in its halachic talmudic expression* (Jerusalem: Hillel Press, 1978), ch.1. I am indebted to my friend Dr. Frimer for this reference.

46 See further my "Structuralism and the notion of Religious Law", *supra* n.33, at 1-5.

relationship of political sovereignty between the law giver and the subject.[47] Bentham earlier had put the relationship rather differently. For him there was only one definition of law, itself including the concept of sovereignty in a political community, but religious law could qualify if it was "adopted" by such a sovereign, and even though the sanctions on which the expression of will relied for its accomplishment were merely religious in nature.[48]

These partially exclusive stances may be explicable in terms of the historical conditions attending the rise of modern positivism (quite apart from the very different personal attitudes to religion of Bentham and Austin). As Lloyd has put it: "the rise of new national states anxious to assert their total independence in a new age of economic expansion and to reject all feudal notions of overlordship or papal interference" was one of the major lines of development towards the modern doctrine of sovereignty.[49] Nevertheless, we see clearly from them, and from Austin's formulation especially, that the delimitation of the concerns of jurisprudence - its "appropriate matter" - reflects (properly and inevitably) a value judgment.

Thus before we can assess the competing claims of secular jurisprudence and Jewish legal theory, we are obliged to try to identify the value judgments which their respective classifications reflect. We must not, as scholars, accept at face value either claims of exclusivity or claims of exclusion. Both reflect value judgments. It is only when these value judgments have been identified that we may be in a position either to choose between them or to distinguish the different purposes for which they may severally be suited.

3.0 One essential element in an assessment of the values underlying any jurisprudential theory is attention to the nature of the claims that theory makes. That will provide a clue not only to the values implicit in the theory, but also to the significance of dissonance as between the theory and the phenomena of Jewish law.

3.1 For these purposes, a distinction may be drawn between analytical and descriptive theories of law. The chief example of the former is Kelsen's "pure theory", which claims to be an analysis of the concept of legal normativity rather than a description of legal systems. It follows that

---

47 *The Province of Jurisprudence Determined* (London: Weidenfeld and Nicolson, 1954), 9-14.

48 J. Bentham, *Of Laws in General,* ed. H. L. A. Hart (London: The Athlone Press, 1970), 1, 133f.; *cf. An Introduction to the Principles of Morals and Legislation,* ed. J. H. Burns and H. L. A. Hart (London: The Athlone Press, 1970), 34f.

49 *Supra* n.33, at 170.

Kelsen's theory cannot be falsified by proof that actual legal systems operate differently, even less so by evidence that the subjects of those systems perceive them differently from Kelsenian theory. A striking example of such a conflict was provided by the late Abraham Harari, who argued that since Kelsenian theory requires legal systems to have an institution of desuetude, English law (being a legal system) must have such a theory, and the fact that the judges deny it merely shows that the judges are wrong.[50] The same analysis, according to the claims of Kelsenian theory, must apply where there is dissonance between Jewish law and the pure theory - unless the claim of Jewish law to be a "legal system" is withdrawn. Of course, if it were proved that a majority or even a major number of the actual systems operating in the world which are commonly regarded as "legal" failed to satisfy Kelsen's criteria, very few people would continue to take an interest in the theory. But that, in logic, would demonstrate only that the theory lacked usefulness or practical application; it would not threaten its status as an analysis of the concept of legal normativity.

What, then, is the status of such an analytical theory? There are three possibilities. The first is that the theory is semantic, that it purports to report either the definition of the word law most in accord with linguistic usage (unlikely, if it turns out that actual legal systems tend not to fall within its terms) or the personal, stipulative definition of Kelsen himself (arbitrary, and in the contingency we are considering, unhelpful). The second is that the theory is metaphysical, that it claims the external existence of a concept of law (external, that is, to the mind and language of the observer) in a manner comparable to the platonic *eidos,* so that actual legal systems (as in the Platonic system) are but imperfect shadows of this existent, metaphysical concept. Such metaphysical theories of law are today unpopular (even in natural law circles), and it was certainly not Kelsen's intention to purpose one. The third possibility is that the analytical theory defines a concept of law in terms of a cluster of characteristics which are regarded as *significant,* significant especially in the distinction they draw between phenomena which meet the conditions of the cluster and those which do not. In this way, the theory is indeed value-based. Kelsen claims for his theory that it is the only means by which legal rules may be distinguished from moral rules and (merely) social rules; moreover, he regards that distinction as useful, helpful and important.[51] This, indeed, may be said to

---

50 "Desuetude", in *Studies in Jewish Legal History, Essays in Honour of David Daube,* ed. B. S. Jackson (London: Jewish Chronicle Publications, 1974), 101-103 (= *Journal of Jewish Studies* 25 (1974)).

51 *Pure Theory, supra* n.2, at ch. II.

be Kelsen's purpose in constructing an analytical, rather than a merely descriptive legal theory. And it follows that anyone who does not attach value to these distinctions has no business following or applying Kelsen's theory. For such a person, the status of the theory must be either semantic or metaphysical (both unsatisfactory), unless it is possible to propose some alternative value which its adherent is able to propose in justification of it, Legal theories are not objects on a supermarket display, designed to be picked up on the strength of their packaging, often by the impulse buyer.

3.2 Descriptive theories of law, on the other hand, claim to describe the essential characteristics of actual legal systems, what counts as a legal system for these purposes normally being ascertained by linguistic usage. Such theories therefore purport to identify the central features of those normative systems we call "legal". Hart's legal theory is of this kind: he himself describes it as "an essay in descriptive sociology". Descriptive theories of law may differ in scope. They may purport to be universal or to apply to a more or less restricted class of legal systems. Hart's claims to be universal for the legal systems of advanced, as opposed to primitive, societies. For these purposes, the *halakhah* would certainly count as the legal system (for we refer to it as "Jewish law") of an advanced society.[52] It should follow, therefore, that if we find that the *halakhah* does not possess any of the central elements of the concept of law (in fact equated by Hart with the "distinctive structure of a *municipal* legal system"[53]) the claimed universality of the theory should be falsified. The theory being merely descriptive, that should be the end of the matter.

In fact, the relationship is less simple. There is a strong temptation to reverse the conclusion and to argue that if the *halakhah* lacks any of these central features, it is not a legal system (even though we may refer to it as "Jewish law"). But once we take this step, we are importing an analytical element into the claims of the theory. We are saying that all normative systems to which the appellation "legal" is applied *should* possess a certain combination of characteristics - or else the appellation "legal" is not *properly* applied to them.. Once we take this step, we are driven back to the three possible justifications sketched in 3.1. In practice, we are claiming that these central features represent a *significant* cluster in terms of some value or other. One of the persistent problems of jurisprudence is the ambiguity of many of its theories in terms of such claims. While Kelsen's position seems

52 *Cf.* R. Unger, *Law in Modern Society* (London: MacMillan, 1976), 119.
53 H. L. A. Hart, *The Concept of Law* (Oxford: The Clarendon Press, 1961), 17.

unequivocally analytical, Hart's position is less clear. With Dworkin the position is even more complex. He claims that his account of the judicial process is descriptively true (though for what range of legal systems the claim is made is not clear); at the same time, he argues that it is normatively valid in terms of political morality.[54]

Descriptive theories may or may not take account of the viewpoint of the subjects of the systems to which they are applied; analytical theories regard such subjective viewpoints as entirely irrelevant, unless merely for purposes of comparison. One descriptive theory that does take account of the subjective viewpoint is that of Hart. For him, the "internal aspect" - the reasons the subjects themselves give for following a norm, is itself a necessary element in the determination of whether "rules" exist.[55] In such a theory, therefore, even secular jurisprudence itself requires recourse to the religious viewpoint, if the theory is to be applied to the norms of a religious community. This does not, however, mean that such values as the secular theory reflects will be replaced by those of the religious system concerned. Clearly, in this context, the secular theory requires recourse to the internal, religious viewpoint for its own, secular purposes.

4.0 The argument thus far might appear to be wholly negative: secular jurisprudence is imperfectly applied in the literature on Jewish law, and the very attempt to apply it would seem to involve the often unwitting endorsement of unascertained, foreign values. But these are criticisms of a genre and a methodology. It has not yet been suggested that secular jurisprudence can only be imperfectly applied and/or that such foreign values must remain unascertained and must inevitably be alien. It is to this last question which must now briefly turn. What justification may be offered for the application of jurisprudential theories based on secular values?

There are two possible answers. The first would be that Judaism itself *endorses* such secular values. Here, I suggest, the very interesting and important concept of Noahide Law[56] may be of crucial significance. We conventionally address this issue in terms of Jewish endorsement of gentile *law*, i.e. the rules of gentile law, whether for purposes of Jewish validation

54 R. Dworkin, *Taking Rights Seriously* (new impression, London: Duckworth, 1978), 84.

55 *Supra* n. 53, at 86-88.

56 D. Novak, *The Image of the Non-Jew in Judaism* (New York and Toronto: The Edwin Mellen Press, 1983); D. I. Frimer, "Israel, The Noahide Laws and Maimonides: Jewish-Gentile Legal Relations in Maimonidean Thought", in *The Jerusalem Conference Volume, supra* n. 39.

of gentile systems or conflict of law situations or indeed as a means to fill gaps or interpret difficulties in the *halakhah* itself. It would surely be no illegitimate extension of such enquires to ask to what extent Judaism thereby also endorses the underlying values of secular theories *about* law?

A second possible answer is that Judaism, while not endorsing such secular values, does not exclude them. If we conclude this to be the case, then the application of secular jurisprudence to Jewish law may be regarded as useful (in terms of the secular values underlying such jurisprudential theories), but the results cannot be regarded as part of Jewish legal theory or of (in one sense of the term) the philosophy of Jewish law.

It is only if this second possible answer is rejected a priori that the application of secular jurisprudence to Jewish law becomes, in Jewish terms, not only un-Jewish but also illegitimate. This radical, negative conclusion is, however, reached *only* if *torah* is regarded, for Jews, as the *exclusive* source of both substantive and epistemological categories. There are, no doubt, some thinkers (and many non-thinkers) who would take this view. If they have read this far, they need continue no further.

5.0 I turn now to more detailed consideration of the possible application to Jewish law of the major debate currently exercising jurisprudence in the English-speaking world, that provoked by Ronald Dworkin's attack upon modern positivism. This will serve, in part, to illustrate the general relationships outlined in sections 3 and 4 above.

5.1 As a preliminary, it is necessary to define the senses in which a number of terms will be used in what follows.

I use the term *legitimacy* to mean the acceptability as law of norms and decisions in terms of the criteria of a particular legal system.

I use the term *validity* to refer to production of a norm or decision in conformity with authorised *procedures* of decision-making and norm-creation of a particular legal system. Validity in this sense thus has no relation to the content of a decision or norm: in principle, a decision or norm of *any* content may be valid.

I use the term *authenticity* to refer to conformity with a criterion of *content* required by a particular legal system.

5.2 The modern debate between positivists and natural lawyers may now be described in terms of the above three concepts. *Positivism* holds that legitimacy conceptually entails only validity and not authenticity, while accepting that particular legal systems may choose to add a criterion of authenticity to criteria of validity, as has occurred in the case of the constitution of the U.S.A. Expressed differently, there is no necessary connection between law and morality, but a criterion of morality may be incorporated by particular legal systems. *Natural law,* on the other hand, claims that legitimacy does entail some element of authenticity (apart from criteria of validity), whether this is explicitly recognised by a particular legal system or not.

5.3 There is a degree of correlation between stances on the issue as defined in 5.2 and attitudes to the nature of judicial discretion. According to positivism, a system whose criteria of legitimacy are restricted to matters of validity will thereby impose no fetters as regards the content of a decision or norm, where the criteria of validity indicate that there is no existing norm but that the judge has power to fill the lacuna. Since such a system has not incorporated criteria of authenticity, the judge may adopt a rule of any content, since there are no criteria as to content which restrict his choice. In principle he may decide on grounds of policy or even on arbitrary grounds. Dworkin refers to such discretion as "strong". Where, on the other hand, a particular legal system (such as the U.S.A.) has adopted criteria of authenticity, judicial discretion will be fettered thereby in the content of the rule or decision enunciated. Thus the U.S. Supreme Court may not (according to positivism, if not realism) decide a case in conflict with any of the Amendments of the U.S. Constitution, with their guarantees of basic human rights.[57] But positivism claims that such a situation, where the discretion of the judge is "weak", is a contingent fact about particular legal systems, not a necessary characteristic of legal systems in general. Modern positivism has denied the possibility of a third alternative, namely that the judge has no discretion at all. But this follows not from its equation of legitimacy with validity (for conceptually it is possible that through the authorised procedures of the system an answer should be produced to every legal problem, thus leaving the judge with nothing more than mechanical application); it follows rather from a linguistic theory that claims that interpretation (hence judgment, hence at least "weak" discretion) will

[57] The one positivist who would qualify this statement is Kelsen,with his theory of "normative alternatives" in relation to the "unconstitutional statute". See *Pure Theory, supra* n.2, at 267-76; further, Jackson, "Kelsen between Formalism and Realism", *Liverpool Law Review* VII (1)(1985), 79-93.

inevitably be required of the judge so long as rules are expressed in language, which possesses an "open texture".[58]

For natural lawyers, the position is different. Since legitimacy is held to require an element of authenticity,[59] there will always be some criterion of content guiding the judge in his decisions or norm-creation. Discretion, therefore, can never be "strong". At most it may be "weak". The third possibility, that discretion may be non-existent, is not pressed.

5.4 Modern positivism is best represented by Hart, who conceives of law in terms of a positivist concept of legitimacy as described above. In principle, therefore he accepts that in some legal systems the judge may have an unrestricted, legislative discretion to fill gaps and resolve ambiguities, even though other legal systems, by adopting some criterion of authenticity as part of the test of legitimacy, may restrict the judge to a choice within the range of authentic solutions.

A major attack upon this view has been mounted by Dworkin, who claims that both descriptively and as a matter of political morality legitimacy requires satisfaction of a criterion of authenticity (in his view, deriving from "community morality").[60] He is not satisfied with the positivist view that such criteria of authenticity as he illustrates (from judicial argument on the basis of application of legal principles) are sufficiently explained by the fact of contingent incorporation under the positivist model. Even if every legal system had explicitly incorporated such criteria, Dworkin would not be satisfied with the positivist account of law as based upon sources which are ascertainable by criteria of validity. The reason for Dworkin's steadfast refusal to have his theory subsumed beneath the positivist model reveals the contrast between the underlying values of positivism and natural law. It is not merely an unwillingness to depend, in any particular legal system, upon an act of will explicitly or tacitly incorporating the values of community morality. More importantly, he points out, the positivist model seeks above all else demonstrability, the capacity of the system to know, in advance of litigation, where there exists clear law and what that law is, so that citizens

58 Hart, *Concept, supra* n.53, at 121-32 (the section, VII.I, is entitled "The Open Texture of Law"); see further my *Semiotics, supra* n. 44, at 155-66.

59 For Aquinas, will creates law only when regulated by reason: *Summa Theoogiae* 1a2ae, 90.1, 4.

60 For an analysis of the differences between them, see my "Hart and Dworkin on Discretion: Some Semiotic Perspectives", in *Semiotics, Law and Social Science,* ed. D. Carzo and B. S. Jackson (Reggio and Rome: Gangemi Editore and The Liverpool Law Review, 1985), 145-67.

may plan their lives in reliance thereon.[61] Such demonstrability is best achieved by use primarily of procedural tests of legitimacy, thus avoiding controversy and ambiguity as regards contentual conformity. This value would inevitably be sacrificed, according to Dworkin, if positivism were to be modified by the wholesale incorporation of the kind of criteria of authenticity which Dworkin claims both in actuality and in morality apply. In preference to demonstrability, Dworkin's legal theory attaches supreme importance to the value of rationality in the form of consistent application of the morality of the community, and thus implementation of the rights which that community morality confers. Dworkin accepts that while such rationality entails the view that in principle there is almost always[62] one correct answer to a legal problem, in practice that right answer is not demonstrable in the positivist sense. Indeed, Dworkin accepts that only a judge of superhuman ability would be able to reach such perfect solutions. Nevertheless, the value of rationality is so important that we must strive as far as possible for the right answer, even at the cost of demonstrability. Clearly, therefore, Dworkin prefers the satisfaction of moral criteria to the utilitarian preference for clarity and a greater capacity to plan, irrespective of the content of the law.

Nevertheless, Dworkin falls short of a full-blooded natural law stance in a number of respects. First, he equivocates about the situation where a later judge considers that a rule laid down earlier, which in terms of the validity criteria of the system concerned constitutes a precedent binding on him, conflicts with his own view of the requirements of the authenticity criteria. Only in extreme cases does Dworkin allow a judge in such a situation to prefer his own view of what is the one correct answer, and then, says Dworkin, the judge should lie and misreport the law[63] - a formulation clearly conceding that the earlier, inauthentic rule is still conceived to be "the law". Second, he remains wedded to a theory of judicial "weak" discretion, even though the logic of "one right answer" might suggest that in reality there is no discretion, but only a privilege to fall short of the standards of Hercules (Dworkin's judge of superhuman abilities) while still being entitled to insist on having one's judgments enforced. Third, his conception of the community morality which generates the principles and rights which the

---

61 On this aspect, see my *Semiotics, supra* n.44, at 211-221. For Dworkin's emphasis upon "demonstrability", see especially his "No Right Answer?", in *Law, Morality and Society,* ed. P. M. S. Hacker and J. Raz (Oxford: The Clarendon Press, 1977), 58-84.

62 For the nature of the qualification, see my *Semiotics, supra* n.44, at 208-211.

63 *Supra* n. 54, at 326f.

judge is to apply (even though they may exist below the surface, and thus may fail to be revealed, or at least be rendered demonstrable, by positivist criteria of validity) is a dynamic one: such values are likely to change, and the judges must echo such changes. Thus we find that alongside the value of rationality - which in itself might be expected to lead to a static and conservative view of the judicial role - Dworkin would still adhere to an ideal of judicial creativity in the application of the shifting principles (though not policies) of the community. Llewellyn's "Grand Style"[64] clearly maintains its appeal.

5.5 The competing values of a positivism which says that validity is conceptually independent of authenticity and of a naturalism that says that authenticity is conceptually independent of validity are both attractive. Is there any way in which we can resolve their apparent conflict?

I believe that the inner logic of Dworkin's theory suggests such a resolution. It is clear that as regards judicial decision-making, authenticity is *not,* in Dworkin's view, an absolute (or even a common) criterion of legitimacy. In hard cases, Dworkin says, the judge must have superhuman ability to reach the one correct answer, even though he must believe (and we must believe) that such a uniquely correct answer does exist in principle. It follows that for Dworkin every decision in a hard case is liable to be less-than-perfect, since no judge in the legal system is in fact superhuman. (Dworkin is not a polytheist.) Yet Dworkin nowhere concludes - and it would be absurd to do so - that every such less-than-perfect decision is illegitimate.[65] Authenticity cannot therefore be for Dworkin an absolute criterion of legitimacy. At most, it is a matter of degree; only in cases of extreme dissonance should a judge refuse to follow a valid norm. However, this in no way challenges the claim of Dworkin that there does exist in principle such a thing as absolute authenticity. Rather, it requires us to locate the role of such authenticity *outside* the judicial process. For some positivists and realists such a conclusion would remove the issue from the proper sphere of jurisprudence altogether. Jurisprudence, they would say, is concerned with validity within the functioning legal system. Once one departs from the functioning legal system, and asks questions of authenticity independently of questions of validity, one is no longer concerned with legitimacy but rather with moral philosophy. In common (I believe) with

64 K. N. Llewellyn, *The Common Law Tradition* (Boston: Little, Brown & Co., 1960), 36-38.

65 In his later writings, this formulation is toned down to the "best possible solution".

Dworkin, I would reject such a view. The concept of legitimacy cannot be reserved for legislation and the judicial process, to the exclusion of legal scholarship. When scholars debate a difficult legal problem, and one says "The Law is X" while another says "The Law is Y", these statements are (even in terms of linguistic usage and popular understanding) on their merits either legitimate or illegitimate statements *of law* no less than the formulation by judges or legislature of propositions accorded binding authority because of the validity criteria of the system.[66]

There are also positive arguments in favour of a concept of the legitimacy of legal propositions, advanced outside the legislative or judicial processes, in terms of their authenticity. Although the scholar is just as human, and thus fallible, as the judge, the notion of the one correct answer is far more credible and useful in the context of legal scholarship than it is in the law in action.[67] Legal scholarship differs materially in its nature from judicial decision-making. The latter has a human situational context where the variables cannot be controlled in advance, and where one case cannot without distortion be fully assimilated to another. The scholar on the other hand operates in a theoretical context where variables can be controlled and exact comparisons made. It follows that at the level of generality at which the scholar operates, a higher degree of authenticity can be anticipated. In terms of logic, the scholar can ensure that the minor premises of his syllogisms (his theoretical legal problems) contain no terms not accorded a place in his major premises (his theoretical apparatus for problem solving, consisting of his legal principles and their inter-relationships). He is thus in a position to make syllogistic deductions (provided only that he has correctly

66 The semiotic study of law is making a notable contribution to the analysis of such comparisons. Thus, F. E. Oppenheim, "Outline of a Logical Analysis of Law", *Philosophy of Science* 11 (1944), 142-160, distinguishes between the "correctness", "truth" and "official quality" of legal propositions (corresponding to their syntactic, semantic and pragmatic decisions), so that it is possible to conceive of (in my terms) authentic propositions (being correctly formulated, and true in that they do not contradict any other legal proposition) which lack "official quality", not being stated by a legislator or judge. Conversely, a proposition may have "official quality" even though it lacks either correctness or truth (Kelsen's case of the "wrong" judicial decision or the "unconstitutional" statute). Oppenheim reserves the term "validity" for legal propositions where all three characteristics are present, but agrees that a proposition may be "enforceable", even if it lacks correctness and/or truth, provided that it has "official quality". G. Kalinowski has taken such analysis considerably further, in distinguishing the syntactic, semantic and pragmatic levels of different languages within law. For an introduction, see R. Carrión-Wam, "Semiotica Juridica", in Carzo and Jackson, *supra* n. 60, at 11-67, esp. 24-43.

67 See my articles cited *supra*, nn. 41, 44.

matched up his minor and major premises). The judge, on the other hand, is never in a position to make such syllogistic deductions. The case before him always contains elements not accorded a place in the judge's major premises. It may be that those elements may therefore be described as non-legally significant. But their non-legal-significance is merely contingent; the judge's task is to consider whether they should remain non-legally-significant.

6.0 The problem has been considered thus far in purely secular jurisprudential terms. When we turn to the attitudes encountered in Jewish tradition, I believe that we find significant support for a dualist approach such as that described in 5.5 above. In line with the argument of the earlier part of this paper, however, it will not suffice to start with this last problem and to consider its possible application in isolation. Rather, we must consider the problem in the context of the nature of the claims of the relevant jurisprudential theory, its underlying values, and the relationship of those to Jewish thought.

6.1.0 Let us commence with the problem described in 5.2 above. What is the relationship between Jewish legal thought and the jurisprudential debates between positivists and natural lawyers as to whether legitimacy necessarily entails criteria of authenticity?

6.1.1 If we wish to view the jurisprudential positions in the light of the phenomena of Jewish law, we must first ask what claims the jurisprudential theories are making. If they are making universal descriptive claims, then Jewish law - unless excluded, as by John Austin, from the "appropriate matter of jurisprudence" (2.0) - may provide falsification; specifically, Jewish law might be cited in falsification of a natural law claim that legitimacy necessarily entails authenticity, if it is shown that legitimacy does not entail authenticity in Jewish law. Conversely, Jewish law might be cited in falsification of the positivist position if it is shown that such criteria of authenticity as are applied by Jewish law owe their place in the Jewish legal system *not* to some act of incorporation, but rather are there, in some sense, as being of the essence of the Jewish legal system. In assessing such questions, we will be obliged to decide whether the viewpoint of traditional Jewish thought is to be taken into account (this thought, no doubt, requiring to be translated from a theological mode - such as, for example, the concept of the pre-existence of *torah*). Some descriptive theories (such as Hart's) will take account of that internal viewpoint; others will not.

If the claims of the jurisprudental theory are analytical, they cannot be falsified merely by showing that Jewish law does not fit the analytical model. Any such finding will mean, rather, that the values or claims being made by Jewish law differ from those of the analytical theory concerned. In this context, a comprehensive study is much needed of the viewpoints of Jewish thought on general jurisprudence, i.e. on the characteristics of legal systems in general in contradistinction to its viewpoints on the nature of Jewish law itself (conceived, a priori, to be peculiar). A starting point would, no doubt, be the controversy regarding the status of the gentile who observes Noahide law. Does the Maimonidean preference (putting the matter at its lowest[68]) for the observance of Noahide law in virtue of its divine revelation rather than in virtue of its evident moral quality indicate a Maimonidean view that all law must be commanded, or rather that consciousness of divine command is the highest form of moral sensitivity? And if, indeed, it is the latter, what does this tell us about the Jewish values underlying the stress on *ius divinum positivum* ? Does it suggest that validity in such a religious legal system reflects values different from validity in secular legal systems? We may note that one of the values underlying the positivist position is that the separation of law and morality is to be encouraged not only because in a liberal, democratic society values may differ and morality should not be imposed, but rather because such separation is thought to *promote* moral sensitivity. Just because there is no necessary connection between law and morality, the morality of any particular law is not presumed, and the individual is put to an autonomous decision as to whether that law is or is not moral (and whether, therefore, he has a moral obligation to obey it[69]). In comparing positivism with Jewish legal thought, we must decide whether the conception of *torah* admits of such moral pluralism and such autonomous moral decisions.

6.1.2. When we reverse the relationship, and consider what is involved in viewing the phenomena of Jewish law in the light of jurisprudential theories, we must pose, in addition, the question raised in 4.0. Since jurisprudential theories usually reflect secular values, to what extent does Jewish thought either endorse or tolerate or exclude those values? Here again, specific answers must await further work on the Jewish attitude to gentile values, both in general and in particular. But it may be useful to state what values

68 I allude to the textual difficulty in Maimonides, discussed in Lamm and Kirschenbaum, *supra* n. 6, at 117-119, and elsewhere in this volume.

69 This is the position of Hart, in his famous debate with Fuller. See H.L. A. Hart, "Positivism and the Separation of Law and Morals", *Harvard Law Review* 71 (1958), 593-629.

(in addition to those referred to in 6.1.1) are involved in the jurisprudential positivism which is currently enjoying a surge of popularity amongst Jewish writers.

One value derives from the denial of the transcendence of morality. Since there is no, or at least no ascertainable transcendent source of morality,[70] moral legitimacy may be obtained for particular moral values only by virtue of agreement. All morality is thus conventional morality; hence the need in a positivist theory for incorporation if any such values are to play a part in the legal system. A second value lies in the notion of identity. It must be clear (demonstrable) whether a particular norm does or does not belong to the legal (rather than social or moral) system. The reason for this need is that law alone regularly applies measures of coercion, and these may be justified only in terms of the demonstrable measure of consent obtained through the legal system. A third value is also related to demonstrability. In many situations utilitarian considerations make it important to have a clear legal rule, irrespective of its content, for the purposes of forward planning. The maximum capacity should be given to the citizen to plan his life in reliance on his understanding of the legal consequences of each possible course of action. Such freedom reflects the belief (receding, no doubt) that each individual is ultimately master of his own fate, or at least should be.[71]

Most modern writers on the theory of Jewish law live in liberal, democratic states which endorse the above values. They imbibe these value from childhood, and naturally are disposed to regard them as universal and to anticipate that they are equally endorsed by Judaism. It is not my purpose here to deny that they are so endorsed; any such claim would invoke work of an extent and complexity not here possible. My purpose is simply to warn against the assumption that these values are endorsed by Judaism. For there are a number of Jewish concepts which would seem, prima facie, to point in the opposite direction: revelation, pre-existence of Torah, the status of Torah as divine wisdom, divine reward and punishment, providence.

Even if we accept that Jewish law may indeed endorse the underlying values of foreign legal systems, on the basis perhaps of an extended understanding of *dina demalkhuta dina*, we must still attend to the restrictions which would be applied to such incorporation (as *dina demalkhuta*

---

70 Secular jurisprudence *not* adhering to a theory of divine revelation; the point even about Dworkin's Hercules is that he will *not* be available for consultation.

71 This value also underlies the theory of Lon Fuller of the "internal morality of law". See L.L. Fuller, *The Morality of Law* (New Haven and London: Yale University Press, 1964), esp. 162-167 ("The View of Man Implicit in Legal Morality").

dina itself shows). And so we must ask how we may draw the line between foreign values that Judaism may tolerate (while not endorsing as Jewish) and foreign values that it will regard as intolerable. An example of such a distinction may be found in the attitude of Aquinas to the various categories of Biblical law. Aquinas held that there were three such divisions: the moral law (still binding on gentiles), the judicial law (being the *ius divinum positivum* laid down for the Jews, which may be adopted by gentiles insofar as it is considered an appropriate concretization of moral law), and the ceremonial law. Controversy raged over the status of this last, the ritual law. Clearly, it was no longer binding on Christians, but was it now prohibited? Aquinas took the view that it was. The primary purpose of the ceremonial law was to act as a symbol of the coming of Christ: the sacrifices, in particular, prefigured that of Jesus. Hence the continued observance of that law would constitute a denial of a basic Christian dogma, namely that the prophecy had now been fulfilled. Observance of the ceremonial law would therefore be mortal sin.[72] I would suggest that a similar methodology be employed in assessing the attitude of Judaism to secular legal values. Some (reversing the relationship perceived by Aquinas between the judicial law and non-Jewish civil law) may be tolerable, given the different conditions (including the lack of revelation) in which gentiles and Jews live; others must be deemed intolerable, insofar as they entail denials of basic Jewish dogmas. I shall not be tempted further into the methodological and substantive problems of Jewish dogmatics, except to suggest that prima facie there may be a distinction to be drawn between the need to justify the imposition of coercive measures by human courts or the need to provide citizens with a predictable framework on which to base future action, on the one hand, and the denial of the transcendence of morality on the other. It would seem to me that this last is as incompatible with the revealed status of Torah for the Jew as the continued observance of the ritual law was with the divine status of Jesus for Aquinas.[73] If this distinction is sound, then positivism reflects a value complex whose components are of varying moral status in the eyes of Jewish thought. Those who would describe Jewish law in positivist terms may perhaps defend their endeavour in terms of a Jewishly-tolerated value that demonstrability is required to preserve the identity of the Jewish legal system (in gentile and secularly-educated Jewish eyes or to facilitate planning); but they risk thereby appearing to endorse a

72 *Summa Theologiae*, qu.103.4; *cf.* Jackson, "Legalism", *supra* n.43, at 11.

73 *Contra*, I. Englard, "Isaiah Leibowitz at Eighty", *The Jerusalem Quarterly* 29 (1983), 112f.

denial of the transcendence of Torah morality. For if the Torah (or any part of it) is believed to be divinely revealed, why propound a theory which, by requiring criteria of authenticity (in this context the substantive moral content of Torah) to be humanly incorporated, appears to deny Torah morality that transcendent moral quality? No doubt the response may be made that man is given moral autonomy by God, and that he is therefore not bound by any morality, however transcendent, unless he has freely adopted it. But does such moral autonomy really entail freedom from obligation to a pre-existent *Torah* ? And are such *midrashim* as stress the capacity of Israel to accept the Torah to be understood in dogmatic terms, or rather perhaps as rabbinic reactions to the positivist conceptions of law and conventionalist views of morality of their own times?

Even when we consider the possible application of jurisprudential positivism to Jewish law at a level closer to the surface, in terms of the content of the theory rather than the underlying values it reflects, we find that some of the apparent resemblances become weaker on closer examination. Consider the following argument of Elliot Dorff.[74] In seeking to explain the dilemma (his term) of the relationship between the rabbinic claim "that human judges in each generation have the authority to make decisions in Jewish law" and the belief that all interpretations and new applications are divine, he refers to the belief in Sinaitic revelation of the Oral Law. But all the same "how is it possible that everything was revealed at Sinai and yet new things are revealed each day?" Dorff points to the changing and varying interpretations of the U.S. Constitution by the Supreme Court as a similar phenomenon: all of the later developments were inherent in the original Constitution because they are all derived from the governmental bodies that it created and the general principles that it established. Similarly every rabbinic interpretation "comes directly or indirectly from the procedures and principles embodied in the Jewish constitution, the *Torah.* Even revisions that Rabbis have made over the centuries are based upon the authority the Torah gives the judges to act on behalf of Jewish law in every generation. The revisions may represent a change in the content of the law, but they are nevertheless part of Jewish law because they were enacted by its duly authorized representatives."

But the similarity must be qualified on closer inspection. I would point to three significant differences. First, the *Torah* does not limit itself to procedures and principles (the latter bring generalised statements, capable of varying but equally conformable concretizations); the *torah* - or more correctly, if we are to use the constitutional analogy, that which is *de'orayta* -

---

74 *Supra* n.24, at 1339.

consists primarily of rules. And while there is nothing in positivist theory which excludes the incorporation in a particular constitution of any amount of specific rules, in order to entrench their moral status, this is certainly not the kind of extensive and specific incorporation which it is in the spirit of positivism to endorse. Second, the constitution in positivist theories itself depends for its validity upon continued acceptance. Not only may it be amended in accordance with procedures which are themselves constitutionally provided; it may also lose its validity entirely as a result of revolution. There is, to my knowledge, no counterpart in Jewish law to this basis of validity of the constitution. Third, positivism in requiring procedures for the creation of law in accordance with the constitution (criteria of validity, in the terminology used earlier), thereby requires explicit acts of promulgation.[75] But the Jewish category of *de'orayta*, as Faur has pointed out,[76] does not require promulgation. It includes rabbinic interpretation of biblical law,[77] even when transmitted orally and not yet committed to writing. The acceptance of a category of law which enjoys that status despite the absence of promulgation is the very antithesis of positivism. Indeed, the immutability and permanence of *de'orayta* is frequently stressed,[78] and may possess dogmatic status even if the historical reality may be different.

6.2 What, then, of discretion? Is it true to say, of Jewish law, that it imposes *no* fetters as regards the content of a decision or norm, where the criteria of validity indicate that there is no existing norm that the judge has power to fill the lacuna? Is it true to say that in such cases "the judge may adopt a rule of any content", that "he may decide on grounds of policy or even on arbitrary grounds" (5.3, above)? Does this provide a satisfactory account of Jewish law, even granting the massive importance of the incorporation within the system of controlling norms in the form of *de'orayta* ? And if so, for what purpose is such an account satisfactory?

The question, then, is the nature and status of judicial discretion, not its existence. Even on the positivist account, there must be some discretion in the interpretation of incorporated *principles*, as Dorff's comparison with the interpretation of the U.S. Constitution shows. In practice, then, there will be little difference between such accounts and other, apparently naturalist,

---

75 This custom, according to Austin, becomes law only when endorsed by the judge, although Hart has attacked this view.

76 *Supra* n.19, at 17.

77 *I.e. Torah Shebeal peh* - following the preferred view of Nahmanides; see Elon, *Principles, supra* n.11, at 9f.

78 E.g. Bleich, *supra* n.36, at 31.

views such as those of Albeck.[79] The issue will be confined to discretion in matters classified as *derabbanan.*

The positivist view has, indeed, been advanced by recent writers on the theory of Jewish law, though not always, one suspects, with full appreciation of all the implications of such a position. Thus Bleich, while adopting a declaratory view of the role of the judge in matters which are *de'orayta* (thus lining up with Dworkin rather than the positivists), says in relation to *derabbanan* that "the Sages clearly have the right to temper their own legislation *in any way they deem proper.*"[80] Englard perhaps goes further in denying the normativity of "principles" in Jewish law, and restricting the notion of Jewish law to binding *halakhot.* Englard rejects the notion that the content of the *halakhah* reflects anything specifically Jewish; norm-creation *(derabbanan)* reflects conscious policy decisions based on socio-economic considerations, rather than principles of Jewish law.[81] And in a recent study of discretion in Jewish legal thought in the light of the jurisprudential debate initiated by Dworkin, Lamm and Kirschenbaum conclude that while there are Jewish views favouring the Dworkinian approach, the balance of opinion is in favour of a positivist (in their terms, pluralistic rather than monistic) view.[82] We may note that the realist position, which goes further than modern positivism in denying any distinction between "hard" and "easy" cases, and which asserts unfettered judicial discretion even in cases which appear to be clear by virtue of the existence of an unequivocal binding rule, is echoed from the Reconstructionist viewpoint by Herberg, who argues that no commandment (not even *de'orayta*) is absolute in the sense of being automatically applicable without regard to circumstances.[83] And Siegel appears to deny the autonomy of *de'orayta* with the general claim that *aggadah* should control *halakhah.*[84]

---

79 *Supra* n.16.

80 *Supra* n.36, at 31, emphasis supplied.

81 I. Englard, "Research in Jewish Law, Its Nature and Function", in *Modern Research in Jewish Law,* ed. B.S. Jackson (Leiden: Brill, 1980), 21-65 (translated from *Mishpatim* 7 (1975-6), 34-65); see also my response in the same volume, 136-157.

82 *Supra* n.6.

83 W. Herberg, "Torah: Teaching, Law and Way", in *Conservative Judaism and Jewish Law,* ed. S. Siegel (New York: Rabbinical Assembly, 1977), 153-173, reprinted from Herberg, *Judaism and Modern Man* (Philadelphia: J.P.S.A., 1951).

84 S. Siegel, "Ethics and the Halakhah", in *Conservative Judaism and Jewish Law,* ed. S. Siegel (New York: Rabbinical Assembly, 1977), 123-132, reprinted from *Conservative Judaism* 25/3 (1971), 33-40.

The anti-positivist view would maintain that, even in hard cases, judicial discretion is limited by the legal-moral principles[85] of the system, and that these, to the exclusion of policy considerations, are the only legitimate guides to a decision. There is, indeed, a considerable body of support for such a position. Writers of Jewish legal theory commonly refer to the statements of general principle and value found in the *torah shebiktav,* and their role as arguments in rabbinic literature. Lamm and Kirschenbaum themselves cite *kedoshim tiheyu*[86] and *va'asita hayashar vehatov,*[87] and list 13 (mainly rabbinic) such "values and ideals which serve as constant antidotes to excessive formalism".[88] Others note the importance of *tsedek* and *shalom,*[89] and *imitatio del.* Indeed, Novak rightly points out, in a discussion of the use of analogy in the *halakhah,* that theological or philosophical criteria taken from beyond the strict precedents of the law itself are necessary, unless analogy is to be purely subjective and arbitrary. These views draw attention, in addition, to the substantive differences between the values of Jewish law and those of contemporary, secular systems.

Before leaving this issue, we may note that the literature also contains hints of a more extreme anti-positivist stance, which comes close to denying discretion altogether (even "weak" discretion in the Dworkinian sense). Silberg argues that the religious nature of Jewish law has such consequences even in the area of civil law. Whereas secular law can allow itself principles such as "reasonable care" or "proximate cause", leaving the task of concretization to the judge in each individual case, "Jewish law ... does not define norms for deciding the law, but norms of behavior. The one who owes payment, who evaded paying what is due from him without justification, is not forgiven by paying damages which he caused by his action for the claimant. He must know at the outset how to act, and for this kind of precise knowledge there is no other source but a law[90] which is clear[91] and explicit."[92]

85 This awkward formulation is adopted to take account of the claim of Dworkin that such principles are part of the legal system itself, distinguishable (on criteria he states) from purely moral or political principles.

86 *Lev.* 19:2.

87 *Deut.* 6:18.

88 *Supra* n.6, at 132f.

89 Faur, *supra* n.19, at 20. Note the incorporation of such values (specifically as "principles") by the Foundations of Law Act, 1980, s.1.

90 See G. Appel, *A Philosophy of Mizvot* (New York: Ktav, 1975), 103f., 116f.

91 D. Novak, "Judaism and Contemporary Bioethics', *Journal of Medicine and Philosophy* 4 (1979), 347-366, at 358.

92 *Supra* n.7, at 51f.

6.3 Does the anti-positivist position entail the further claim, made by Dworkin, that there exists in principle one correct answer to every legal problem? Restricting ourselves here to the approach of Jewish law, a distinction may have to be drawn between correctness in terms of the practical unchallengeability of a particular judicial decision and its substantive correctness. A decision in Jewish law is not open to challenge on the grounds that although there was no previously binding rule, the decision actually arrived at is wrong. But this is no argument against the Dworkinian model; there too the validity of a decision is not threatened by the inability of the judge to arrive at, or at least demonstrate, the one correct answer (5.4, above). Nevertheless, there is good reason to claim, both as a consequence of the general tenets of Jewish theology and with the support of particular sources, that there does exist a concept of absolute correctness in Jewish thought.

Positivists may deny this position only by denying the concept of authenticity in Jewish law altogether, or assigning it a function outside the sphere of jurisprudence. Englard (6.2) seems to me to be doing the former. The latter approach was reflected recently in the discussion of Dr. Ben Menahem's paper "Is there always one correct answer to a legal problem in the Talmud?"[93] The discussion centered upon the famous passage in *Erub.* 13b where a dispute between the Schools is resolved by the dictum of a *bat kol,* that *elu ve'elu divre elohim hayyim,* but that the *halakhah* follows Bet Hillel. I had suggested that *elu ve'elu* represents a claim of authenticity, resolvable at the level of divine cognition (the source is a *bat kol*) despite the human perception of contradiction, and that this contrasts with the claim of validity, represented by the preference (always) for the view of Bet Hillel, which is relevant to the sphere of *halakhah lema'aseh.* Ben Menahem denied that such a claim to substantive authenticity was in contemplation; the purpose of *elu ve'elu* was functional, to ensure that whatever decision *was* ultimately accepted should not be challenged as unrevealed (in the light, especially, of views that only unanimous opinions could claim the status of *torah shebe'al peh).* [94] No doubt that functional interpretation assists us in understanding the historical background to *elu ve'elu,* but it does not appear to me to diminish its dogmatic importance. One can hardly assert that any

93 When presented at the First International Conference of The Jewish Law Association, Jerusalem, August 1980. For the paper, see *infra.*

94. See Lamm and Kirschenbaum, *supra* n.6, at 121 n.87, on the components of the Oral Law according to Maimonides, in his Introduction to the Commentary on the Mishnah.

proposition is the word of the living God, without thereby attaching to it a claim to authenticity.

6.4 Nevertheless, I have suggested, in commenting on Dworkin's theory, that it has a more appropriate sphere in legal scholarship (5.5, above) than in the judicial process. Because of the nature of judicial decision-making (*halakhah lema'aseh*), I would argue (contrary to Dworkin) that the judge ought not to be restricted to legal principles in arriving at his decision, even though he should be guided by the recognition that there is, in principle, one correct answer to the theoretical problem reflected in, but not wholly accounting for, the case before him.[95] There is certainly support for such a position in both the classical and the modern literature on the theory of Jewish law. Lamm and Kirschenbaum have themselves cited a number of relevant sources.[96] R. Nissim Gerondi, in commenting on the oven of Okhnai passage, suggested that the sages realised that R. Eliezer came closer to the truth than they, but felt bound nevertheless to follow the reason of the majority. R. Solomon Luria explained the variety of judicial opinions in terms of the variability of perception of the one true revelation, which all had personally (through the presence of their souls at Sinai) received. R. Mosheh Feinstein and others have maintained the distinction between absolute halakhic truth and truth for purposes of decision-making. Indeed, the rationale for such a distinction offered by Abarbanel is essentially the same as that argued above: "divine law is formulated in objectively true, just and equitable generalizations, which of necessity disregard individual circumstances".[97]

It may be objected that this conclusion sells out to the positivist position. But it does so only if we regard decision-making as co-terminus with law. It may well be that jurisprudential positivism does conceive of law in this restricted sense: its alliance with philosophical utilitarianism leads to a conception of law in terms of social control, in terms of order, and for this the functioning judicial process is clearly central. To the extent that Jewish law endorses such values, we may regard the positivist model as

---

95 This is closer to the position of D.N. MacCormick, *Legal Reasoning and Legal Theory* (Oxford: Clarendon Press, 1978), although MacCormick, like Dworkin, assumes a unified legal system, in which judicial decision-making and legal doctrine refer to one and the same phenomenon.

96 *Supra* n.6, at 103-105.

97 See Lamm and Kirschenbaum, *supra* n.6, at 124. This is close to the classical distinction between speculative and practical reasoning, as found, for example, in the Thomist treatment of natural law. See *Summa,* qu.94,4.

capable of making a contribution to the philosophy of Jewish law; to the extent that Jewish law merely tolerates those values, we may say that positivism is useful for the external analysis of Jewish law. But one thing must surely be clear. Even if Judaism endorses those values, it does not endorse them to the exclusion of the values inherent in legal scholarship - in Jewish terms, of *Torah* study.[98] We need not here enter into the question of a hierarchy of values as between torah study and following a rule binding by a criterion of validity, although it would not be difficult to cite sources which accord priority to the former over the latter.[99] But we may affirm with every confidence that any philosophy of Jewish law which omits to reflect the value and underlying assumptions of *Torah* study must be defective. Hart teaches us to attend in our jurisprudence to the core concepts of a system; *torah* study can hardly be detached from the concept of Jewish law.

7.0 The attempt made above to treat the relationship between secular jurisprudence and the philosophy of Jewish law systematically has necessarily entailed reflection on the underlying values of these various thought systems. I conclude with some comments and questions on the explicit theoretical basis of Jewish law (s.7) and the relationship between jurisprudential issues and more general ontological assumptions in Jewish thought (s.8), and finally suggest that we have an opportunity to apply a very different external theoretical viewpoint (s.9).

7.1 At the beginning of this paper (1.1), the need to base an hierarchical system of normative validity ultimately upon some phenomenon taken from outside that system was noted in commenting upon Elon's application of the sources theory. This need is, indeed, not restricted to positivists. It is of interest to compare the content, status and consequences of the ultimate bases in our various thought systems.

98 Lamm and Kirschenbaum, *supra* n.6, at 114, note that the Maharal of Prague considered Maimonidean rationalism to lead to a preference for the *via contemplativa* rather than the *via activa,* but this criticism appears to have been directed to the idea that natural law serves as a source of right and wrong, rather than at the activity of study through divinely revealed channels. Contrast the view of the Vilna Gaon, recounted by L. Jacobs, *Jewish Values* (London: Vallentine and Mitchell, 1960), 24, who said that if he were offered infallible instruction by an angel he would refuse, since he wanted to arrive at the truth by his own efforts.

99 See N.L. Rabinovitch, "Halakha and Other Systems of Ethics: Attitudes and Interactions", in *Modern Jewish Ethics* , ed. M. Fox (Ohio State University Press, 1975), 89-102, at 97, quoting Maharal.

For Kelsen, the content of the *Grundnorm* is either the proposition that coercive acts ought to be performed only in accordance with the historically first constitution, or (in a monistic international order) that states ought to behave as they have customarily behaved. For Hart, the content of the ultimate rule of recognition is the view of officials that they ought to make the constitution the ultimate reason for action, in the interests of social solidarity. Social contract theory may be seen as providing an alternative ultimate base for normativity, the acceptability of the normative order here being attributed to the community as a whole rather than (as in Hart's system) the officials. Dworkin too has an ultimate basis for the view that the judge should strive for the one correct answer, namely the view one ought in a democratic society to follow community morality. We have seen the view expressed that the equivalent basis of normativity in Jewish law resides in the proposition that the source of the Torah is divine.

7.2 We must ask how far this parallel extends. Consider the status of these various bases. For Kelsen, the *Grundnorm* does *not* depend on conscious acceptance by the community or officials, or even conscious knowledge of it on their part. It is, in his view, a logical presupposition of which they may be wholly unaware. As a logical presupposition, it cannot be falsified in terms of fact. Hart's ultimate rule of recognition, on the other hand, is a psychological fact. It may therefore be falsified by evidence that the officials of the system do not, in fact, think in that way. I would regard Dworkin's ultimate basis as closer in status to Kelsen's; the existence of a correct answer is a presupposition of judicial discourse rather than a psychological fact which must be consciously accepted. Social contract theories fall into both camps. Some make historical assertions, that there was in fact an original agreement between individuals to establish a society and a sovereign within it; others disclaim any such historical claim (which may be falsified) in favour of according the proposition the status of a necessary presupposition.

When we speak of a necessary presupposition, we are bound to ask "necessary for what?" On this, Kelsen is quite explicit. The *Grundnorm* is a necessary presupposition *if* you want to operate an objective system of normative validity, and thereby justify the exercise of coercive power by the state. The theory is thus based ultimately on the assumption that such a system is in itself a value or desideratum; the *Grundnorm* functions as a *means* to achieve that objective. Similarly with Dworkin. The presupposition[100] of the existence in principle of one correct answer is necessary *if* one wishes to operate a system of normative authenticity - if, in other words, one adopts rationality as a value, as Dworkin argues we should. Again, the presupposition is a means to an end. Even fact-based ultimate bases such as Hart's presuppose that the psychological fact is accepted for a purpose: social order or solidarity.

7.3 Does the status of the Jewish basis follow a similar pattern? I do not wish to commit myself to any answer to this question. But it would seem that there are some grounds for suspecting that it does not. We must ask first of all whether the basis of the Jewish *Grundnorm* is the mere proposition that the *Torah* is divine, or rather acceptance of the proposition that the *Torah* is divine. If it is the former, we must ask what status that proposition has. For if the divinity of the *Torah* is not a means to some value-end but rather a primary dogma, we would, in my view, have encountered a very important difference between secular jurisprudence and the philosophy of Jewish law, one whose consequences would require to be very carefully assessed.

7.4 What kind of issues might turn on this last question? If the doctrine of the divinity of the *Torah* is a means towards the achievement of some other value-end, rather than an end in itself, the question will naturally arise as to whether it is a merely sufficient means (thus not excluding the existence of alternative sufficient means) or a necessary and sufficient means (thus excluding the existence of alternative sufficient means). The Christian view of the basic controversy between Judaism and Christianity may be put in these terms. The divine law is seen as a means to salvation; with the coming of Jesus, the divine law either ceases to be a means at all (complete rejection of "justification by works") or at least ceases to be the exclusive means ("justification by works *or* faith"). Debates within Judaism as to the function of revelation may be similarly described. If the divine law is viewed as a means towards justice or goodness, the argument may be proposed that there are alternative routes to justice or goodness - perhaps through the autonomous conscience of the existential self.

If we reverse the relationship between the divinity of *Torah* and justice/goodness, and treat the former as primary and the latter as an inevitable consequence of the former, we are, I suspect, in a better position to

100 A semiotic, not a logical, presupposition, as I argue by comparing Dworkin to Blanché's logic on the one hand, and Greimasian semiotics on the other (*supra* n.60).

appreciate some traditional Jewish positions. The dogma of the unchangeability of *de'orayta*, for example, would seem more acceptable on the theoretical plane if viewed in this context;[101] perhaps also the virtual inconceivability to the talmudic rabbis of a conflict between law and morality.[102] Above all, the issue may affect our view of the nature and status of the rabbinic modes of reasoning. If the divinity of the Torah is an end rather than a means, the justifiability of value-orientated or policy-based argument (except insofar as those policies are clearly indicated in the Torah itself) becomes questionable; if the Torah is indeed a means rather than an end, then interpretation in the light of the presumed end (which is or may be external to the Torah itself) becomes legitimate.[103] In the same way, our view of the status of the detail of *halakhah* may be affected by this issue. We may recall that Maimonides declined to seek reasons for the *peratim* of the *mitsvot;* beyond a certain level of specificity, reasons were not to be sought.[104] Thus even for Maimonides, the supreme Jewish rationalist, the reasons for the law (*ta'ame hamitsvot*) cannot have constituted the ends towards which the *halakhah* provided the means: for some elements of *halakhah* did not serve (at least in their content) in this way (and yet God did nothing in vain)[105]. It would seem to follow that the detail of the *halakhah* is an end in itself, which entails (amongst other things) what we describe as *ta'ame hamitsvot* as inevitable consequences.

Here as elsewhere, determination of which is the authentic Jewish view (if such a thing can be demonstrated) does not exclude consideration of the issues from any other vantage point. If we conclude that Judaism regards the divinity of the Torah as an end rather than a means, our perception of a

---

101 See L. Jacobs, "The Talmud as the Final Authority", *Judaism* 29/113 (1980), 45-48, at 47.

102 See D.W. Halivni, "Can Religious Law be Immoral?", in *Perspectives on Jews and Judaism*, ed. A.A. Chiel (New York: Rabbinical Assembly, 1978), 165-170 (Essays in Honor of Wolfe Kelman).

103 Somewhat along these lines is the distinction drawn by B.Z. Wacholder, *Messianism and Mishnah: Time and Place in the Early Halakhah* (Cincinnati: Hebrew Union College Press, 1979) (The Louis Caplan Lecture on Jewish Law), at 42-47, between rabbinic *midrash* (reflecting "an insatiable appetite to study words of God as such, even ignoring the present altogether and living in the past") and sectarian *pesher*, viewed as serving contemporary, apologetic purposes.

104 *Guide* III.26.

105 Otherwise expressed, Maimonides does not regard the reasons as the basis of legitimacy of the *mitsvot:* their legitimacy derives from that validity, from the fact of divine command. Nevertheless, reasons should be sought for the sake of justifiability. Cf. A. Chill, *The Mitzvot* (Jerusalem: Keter Books, 1974), ixx, on Soloveitchik.

variety of issues *as part of the philosophy of Jewish law* may thereby be affected. But this does not preclude our continuing to view that doctrine as a means rather than an end, in the light of secular jurisprudence, and constructing alternative analyses accordingly. These analyses will reflect the values of secular jurisprudence - values which, as we have seen, may in turn be either endorsed, tolerated or rejected by Judaism. Indeed, much profit may be had from the application of such external viewpoints, as long as we realise what we are doing and do not make internal claims on the basis of external criteria.

8.0 The reference made in the preceding section to the relationship between law and salvation may serve to remind us that we have been considering the relationship between secular jurisprudence and the philosophy of Jewish law almost exclusively through the eyes of the methods and agenda of the former. Our question has been: to what extent may secular jurisprudence be applied to the phenomena of Jewish law? This approach necessarily selects from the "phenomena of Jewish law" those elements most cognate to the issues as defined by secular jurisprudence. Clearly, such an approach cannot provide a balanced view; it inevitably (and for appropriate purposes legitimately) excludes phenomena which Judaism itself may regard as related and even central. (This is one reason why Austin may have considered religious law outside the proper sphere of jurisprudence.) Even if we confine our concern to jurisprudential (i.e. excluding theological) issues, the underlying ontological assumptions of Jewish thought may still impinge upon the problem, and the differences between these ontological assumptions and those of secular jurisprudence may again make comparison and application difficult. A few examples must suffice to illustrate this difficulty.

8.1 In jurisprudential theories, the concept of time is taken to be unproblematic. However that may be, Wacholder's recent study[106] suggests that it would be rash to assume that the conception of time of the Rabbis of the Mishnah was comparable. For them, past present and future correspond to value-laden epochs in the history of Israel, with the result that the present was conceived as a somewhat unsatisfactory interim between an ideal past and its revival in an eschatological future. In other words, the present was downgraded. Wacholder suggests that this explains the character of much of

---

106 *Supra* n.103.

the law of the Mishnah.[107] Much of it would be regarded, in secular terms, as ineffective: because of the loss of the Solomonic temple and associated first commonwealth institutions, much of the law of the Mishnah could not be put into practice in the present. Yet the Rabbis themselves clearly regarded it as no less important (we might even use the terms "valid" or "binding") for that reason: the present was not the exclusive or even overriding time-reference of the *halakhah.*

To the extent that this attitude persisted, we thus encounter a conflict between the ontological (and value) assumptions of *halakhah* and modern jurisprudence. If, then, we seek to apply such jurisprudential theories as those of Hart or Kelsen, for both of whom overall effectiveness is a necessary (though not a sufficient) condition of legitimacy (in their terminology, validity), we must recognise that we are indeed using an external viewpoint for the purposes of values which may also be external. It may, of course, be countered that Jewish law distinguishes here between ritual and civil matters; that as regards the latter, the Jerusalem Talmud even recognises a limited institution of desuetude - *haminhag mevatel et hahalakhah.*[108] Yet it is surely significant - even if we take a broad view of the normativity of the *yerushalmi* source - that ritual and civil norms are presented side by side in the Mishnah, with no explicit distinction being made as to the manner of their effectiveness or its significance. Moreover, both Wacholder's study and other considerations show that there is no complete correlation between the ritual-civil and the eschatological-presently effective distinctions: much of the ritual was still presently effective, and some of the civil was not.[109]

8.2 Ontological assumptions regarding the nature and capacities of man are also relevant to the interrelationship of jurisprudential theory and Jewish thought. Dworkin's distinction between Superhuman Hercules and the merely human judge is, indeed, entirely consonant with the Jewish view of the ultimately limited capacity of the human mind.[110] But what of the

---

107 Compare Jacob Neusner's frequently-expressed view about the ahistorical character of the Mishnah. See his *Judaism, The Evidence of the Mishnah* (Chicago and London: The University of Chicago Press, 1981).

108 See, e.g., Dorff, *supra* n.24, at 1345f.; Harari, *supra* n.50, at 109. See especially B. Lifschitz, "Minhag mevatel halakhah", *Sinai* 86 (5740), 8-13.

109 On the ritual/civil distinction, see further my "The Ceremonial and the Judicial: Biblical Law as Sign and Symbol", *Journal for the Study of the Old Testament* 30 (1984), 25-50.

110 For reflections of this in Biblical and early rabbinic sources, see Jackson, *supra* n.9.

jurisprudential assumption - most prominent in the nineteenth century Historical School but still of some importance - of the progress of man? There is strong evidence for a rabbinic view of the decline of man,[111] even though it may have been opposed in significant respects by Maimonides.[112] Clearly these ideas will be in conflict where historical interpretation of jurisprudential theory seeks explanations in terms of increasing rationality. A number of writers have so interpreted the substitution of "rational" methods of proof for the few examples of the use of oracles, ordeals and the like in the Bible.[113] But we may have to recognise that such interpretations reflect an external viewpoint. The traditional Jewish approach is one consistent with both an ontology of the decline of man and a refusal to separate spiritual from intellectual capacities.[114] That view holds that prophecy and Urim and Thummim (a form of oracular decision probably through a sacred set of lots) disappeared because of the spiritual decline of man, but will be revived in the messianic age.

9.0 Elsewhere I have argued for the usefulness of a structuralist approach to questions of legal theory, both in general and with particular reference to Jewish law.[115] Why should such an external approach fare better than the jurisprudential approaches examined in this paper?

First, let me concede that the application of a structuralist approach is just as much "external" in terms of Jewish thought as are the jurisprudential

---

111 See Wacholder, *supra* n.103, at 9, 29ff.

112 Dr. A. Fuss, in a paper presented at the First International Conference of The Jewish Law Association in Jerusalem, August 1980, noted that Maimonides accepted that there had been a decline only in Torah study. See further my report of the conference, "Some Current Studies in Jewish Law", *The Jewish Quarterly* 29/1 (1981), 26-29, at 28.

113 See H.H. Cohn, "Secularisation of Divine Law" *Scripta Hierosolymitana* 16 (1966), reprinted in Cohn, *Jewish Law in Ancient and Modern Israel supra* n.28, at 1-49.

114 For a Christian refusal to separate such capacities, *cf.* H.J. Berman *The Interaction of Law and Religion* (London: SCM Press, 1974), 136f.: "At the highest level, surely, the just and the holy are one - or else not only all men but the whole universe, and God himself, are condemned to eternal schizophrenia."

115 "Towards a Structuralist Theory of Law", *The Liverpool Law Review* 2 (1980), 5-30; "Structuralisme et "sources du droit"", *Archives de Philosophie du Droit* 27 (1982), 147-160; "Modern Research in Jewish Law", *supra* n.10; "History, Dogmatics and Halakhah", in *Jewish Law in Legal History and the Modern World,* ed. B.S. Jackson (Leiden: Brill, 1980), 1-26; "Some Semiotic Questions for Biblical Law", in *The Oxford Conference Volume,* ed. A. Fuss (Atlanta: Scholars Press, forthcoming; Jewish Law Association Studies III).

theories considered above. Questions of comparability must thus be posed in a systematic fashion, and underlying values also compared. This is not the place to undertake such an Inquiry. Instead, a number of points where a structuralist approach would differ from those of traditional jurisprudence will be briefly noted, and preliminary comments made on the extent to which they may be endorsed, tolerated or rejected from the internal point of view.

9.1 First, structuralism would adopt a different approach to the scope of the subject matter. Although Raz has argued that legal systems are (even from the positivist point of view) conceptually comprehensive, in that they claim authority to regulate any type of behaviour,[116] analytical jurisprudence has in practice restricted the scope of the norms to which it attends both by virtue of a restricted (utilitarian or libertarian) view of the proper role of law and (in some versions) by tests of enforceability through sanctions. Structuralism, on the other hand, would apply no such restrictive tests. Focusing upon the communicative function of law, and the underlying rationality of all forms of human culture, it would not accord preference to the civil as opposed to the ritual. This matches the approach of Jewish sources. No doubt, both structuralism and Jewish law would find the distinction between civil and ritual useful for some purposes (as did Aquinas). But these purposes would not include the proposal of an essential difference, such as to justify restriction of the scope of the enquiry. We may note, in this context, that even Elon himself notes that *mishpat ivri* is a purely conventional concept, and stresses the common features of "religious" and "legal" *halakhah*, while noting the existence of important practical differences between the spheres of *mamona* and *issura*. [117]

9.2 Related to the question of scope is that of function. As opposed to the utilitarian view of the function of law[118] which today still dominates jurisprudential thought, both structuralism and Jewish thought stress the communicative function of law. Both seek, as against analytical jurisprudence, to break the exclusive concentration on normative phenomena. Norms may function to communicate facts, beliefs, relative status, etc., according to structuralism; there is a classical Jewish (Maimonidean) view

116 J. Raz, *Practical Reason and Norms* (London: Hutchinson, 1975), 150f.

117 *Supra* n.1, at 5-7.

118 In this respect, much sociology of law, in recognising the symbolic dimensions of law, stands closer to structuralism than to analytical jurisprudence. In this, it builds on some early insights of the historical school, such as that of Savigny, noted *supra*, at n.33.

that the *halakhah* functions not only to promote order but also to effect moral and intellectual improvement - to influence opinion as well as action.

9.3 Also related is the structuralist stress on the form of expression of culture, as a phenomenon worthy of as much attention as its content. Both grammatical form and larger-scale arrangement are forms of communication in themselves. Neusner has rightly paid particular attention to this in his studies of mishnaic literature, and has, in my view, revealed genuine internal perspectives. This concern also possesses a diachronic dimension. Jean Piaget has brought to light evolutionary progressions in cognitive development, reflected inter alia in the development of language and reasoning powers.[119] I have suggested elsewhere that such theories may be applied also to the development of the cognitive capacities of legal systems.[120] There is also a body of thought which sees the same progressions as reflected in the growth and progressive forms of moral consciousness,[121] though here the cognitive sequences would seem to be at best necessary but certainly not sufficient conditions of the development. At any rate, such insights seem quite compatible with Jewish thought. Rabinovitch has recently spoken of the *halakhah* as a moral code for which the ethical theory is as yet imperfectly known, although parts of it are being progressively discovered.[122]

9.4 A final perspective of structuralism which may assist our theoretical approach to Jewish law better than traditional approaches (although in this particular respect it may be viewed as a development of the natural law tradition) is the light it throws upon the distinction between universal human traits and culturally-contingent expressions. Our developing knowledge of

119 E.g. *Six Psychological Studies* (repr. Brighton: Harvester Press, 1980).

120 "Historical Aspects of Legal Drafting in the Light of Modern Theories of Cognitive Development", *International Journal of Law and Psychiatry* 3 (1980), 349-369; "Legal Drafting in the Ancient Near East in the Light of Modern Theories of Cognitive Development", *Mélanges à la mémoire de Marcel-Henri Prévost* (Paris: Presses Universitaires de France, 1982), 49-66.

121 For a preliminary comparison of L. Kohlberg's theory of moral development with the historical development of rabbinic modes of legal reasoning, see N. Solomon, "Extensive and Restrictive Interpretation in Rabbinic Hermeneutic", *The Touro Conference Volume,* ed. B.S. Jackson (Chico: Scholars Press, 1985), 125-139. (Jewish Law Association Studies, 1).

122 N.L. Rabinovitch, "Halakha and Other Systems of Ethics: Attitudes and Interactions", in *Modern Jewish Ethics,* ed. M. Fox (Ohio State University Press, 1975), 89-102, at 90.

the universals of the human mind assists us in drawing the borderline between these two immensely important categories. This may seem, at first sight, to match ill the particularist Jewish legal tradition. Indeed, the specificity of the Sinaitic Torah to Jewish history and the Jewish people has been stressed in a manner more reminiscent of the teachings of the Historical school.[123] Yet even here we find, in Jewish thought about the relationship between Noahide and Sinaitic law, echoes of this same, modern concern. Indeed, the view that the Noahide (level of) law is more general than the (culturally specific) Sinaitic *halakhah* is fully in accordance with such conclusions as structuralist and other modern research has been able to draw as to the character of universals of human mind.[124]

123 Appel. *supra* n.90, at 39, on Halevi.

124 I am indebted to four good friends - Dov Frimer, Lionel Kochan, Oliver Leaman and Neil MacCormick - for critical comments and suggestions. The usual *caveat* against guilt by association applies. I was privileged to present this paper to a Faculty Seminar of the Faculty of the Hebrew University of Jerusalem in December 1981, and am grateful to those who commented on it on that occasion.

The Jewish Law Annual, Vol.VI

SECULAR JURISPRUDENCE AND *HALAKHAH*[*]

by

EMANUEL RACKMAN[**]

In halakhic literature one can find support for virtually every theory of legal philosophy known to secular jurisprudence. No one theory by itself dominates the scene. This is true of many other legal systems. Indeed, in many a jurisdiction, members of the same judicial tribunal can agree on a specific decision but arrive at it from diverse stances in legal philosophy. One judge may be a positivist; another may favour natural law theories; and a third may be partial to social needs; but all might arrive at the same conclusion. However, many are surprised that this can happen in a legal system whose basic norm is that God is the ultimate source of authority. They ask: How can a God-given law yield to social needs? Did He not anticipate them in His divine commands? Or how can His mandates be reviewed and interpreted in the light of natural law? Is He limited by that law? And if positivism is the proper approach, what can Jews do to get legislative relief when the Legislator is so inaccessible? Is rejection of the Covenant the only way out?

These challenges are not really as serious as they sound. It is conceivable that the Jewish people will reject their Covenant with God. The legal order based upon that Covenant will then be no more, precisely as in the case of Hobbes' social contract when the people reject the sovereign because he no longer affords them with the protection for which they committed themselves to him without reserving any rights to themselves. Hobbes' system is positivistic but eternal until rejected. And some halakhic authorities deal with Jewish law the same way. The Jews who reject the Covenant are outside the pale while those who are loyal to it are bound by the Law without regard to any considerations other than the Law itself and that which logically can be deduced from it. Tradition has furnished the exegesis by which there can be some development from existing rules and texts but without reference to ideal ends or social facts. For these Jews there can be no legislation for there is but one Legislator - God himself. Yet,

---

* With only a few changes, this essay was the inaugural lecture of the Jack D. Weiler Chair in the Philosophy of Halacha at Bar-Ilan University.

** President of Bar-Ilan University, Ramat Gan, Israel.

there are many halakhic authorities who differ and reckon very often both with demands of justice and human needs, individual and social.

Furthermore, there is Biblical authority for the proposition that God respects natural law. It is, therefore, part of the Covenant. It was the patriarch Abraham himself who challenged God on the basis of an assumption of natural lawyers - that the Judge of all the earth must be just and not punish the righteous with the wicked.[1] If Abraham could do it, why should Jewish judges of a later date be precluded from pondering mandates that appear to offend against natural law and why should they not arrive at interpretations that do not offend? In this connection the American experience is relevant. The power to declare legislative or executive action in the United States unconstitutional - very often because of natural law - resides in the judiciary but not because the federal constitution so states. It was assumed that this power is, of necessity, a judicial function.[2] Historians have complained about this usurper of power but others have regarded it as a blessing. At least for the judiciary to exercise this power in Judaism there are explicit verses in Deuteronomy.[3] Pursuant to them, the Supreme Covenantor approved that human judges shall resolve questions which arise in the future. He anticipated that such questions would arise and He vested authority in those who in fact have been exercising it. And they may reckon with natural law as indeed they have.

Thus when the schools of Shammai and Hillel debated the status of a person who is half slave and half free - owned by one partner and emancipated by the other - the school of Shammai convinced the school of Hillel with an argument from natural law.[4] The school of Hillel had thought that it would be possible for such a person to work for himself one day and for his half owner the next. The rejoinder of the school of Shammai is a classic. "You have have taken good care of the master but have you taken care of the slave himself? He cannot marry a female slave because he is half free and he cannot marry a free woman because he is half slave. How will he fulfill God's will to populate the earth?" Needless to say, if his status does not allow him - because of God's law - to populate the earth, then he is under no obligation to do it. It is God's law that stops him. But the school of Shammai was concerned with the slave's natural right, though that term is not used. The slave is not to be denied his humanity.

1 *Gen.* 18:23-25.
2 Marbury v. Madison, 1 Cranch 137.
3 17:8-11.
4 *M. Gitt.* 4:5.

One must also reckon with the fact that Moses himself appealed to the people of Israel to appreciate the law given unto them because of its justice-content by comparison with other legal systems.[5] Apparently human beings have the capacity to evaluate and pass judgment on God's prescriptions. On what do they rely if not on standards which are very much a part of natural law?

There are scholars who hold that Maimonides recognized only divine commandments as the basis for morality and justice.[6] It is their view that Maimonides did not believe that moral principles could be derived autonomously.

Crucial to their argument is the manner of reading one paragraph in Maimonides' *Mishneh Torah.*[7]

> A heathen who accepts the seven commandments and observes them scrupulously is a 'righteous heathen', and will have a position in the world to come, provided that he accepts them and performs them because the Holy One, blessed be He, commanded them in the Law and made known through Moses our Teacher that the observance thereof had been enjoined on the descendants of Noah even before the Law was given. But if his observance thereof is based upon a reasoned conclusion he is not deemed a resident alien, or one of the pious of the Gentiles, but one of their wise men.

These scholars substitute for the word "but" in the very last phrase the words "and not" and in that way justify their conclusion that Maimonides was not committed to any principles of natural law.

However, Maimonides in a passage dealing with a revealed law - the banning of witchcraft - says the following:

> These practices are false and deceptive ... It is not proper for Israelites who are highly intelligent to suffer themselves to be deluded by such inanities ... Whoever believes in these and similar things and, in his heart, holds them to be true and scientific and only forbidden by the Torah, is nothing but a fool, deficient in understanding ... Sensible people, however, who possess sound mental faculties, know by clear proofs that all these practices which the Torah prohibited have no scientific basis but are chimerical and inane ... [8]

---

5 *Deut.* 4:7.

6 M. Fox, "Maimonides and Aquinas on Natural Law", *Diné Israel* III (1972), V-XXXV.

7 *Hilkhot Melakhim* 8:11.

8 *Hilkhot Avodat Kokhavim* 11:16. See also N. Lamm and A. Kirschenbaum, "Freedom and Constraint in The Jewish Judicial Process", *Cardozo Law Review* I:1 (1979), 99, 109-120.

Now, if Maimonides holds that with respect to witchcraft no divine commandment was necessary, and by virtue of the exercise of reason alone one must abhor it, then is it conceivable that he would say that with respect to murder one must desist from homicide only because God revealed that it was wrong? Perhaps Maimonides did not conceive of, or define, natural law as Aristotle did before, and Aquinas after, him. But no Jewish philosopher could justify God's punishment of Cain for his fratricide unless there are moral imperatives which require no divine revelation but are derived either a priori from man's nature or reason, or a posteriori from the nature of society.

Yet, one may ask, even if the authorities reckoned with what we now call natural law, how did they dare consider social ends? Is God's legislation not for eternity and is it subject to change because of change in human circumstance? One may expect human law to be defective, requiring constant replenishment from ever advancing conceptions of morality and justice, but God's law one expects to be perfect *ab initio*.

To all of this, a religiously committed sociologist might reply that since God endowed man with free will, it is inevitable that there will always be changes in man's political, social, and economic institutions. The unexpected is to be expected. And to cope with such changes the revealed law provides for the exercise of equity and other rules for autonomous action by executives, legislators, and judges. Jewish theology affords an even simpler reply. God made man His partner in continuous creation. He also made the Jew His partner in the continuous process called Torah. In the process, the Jew is more than God's obedient servant. He participates in the discovery of God's word for every situation and, therefore, his own needs must enter into the dialogue. One of those needs is the fulfillment of justice in society for man's own self-fulfillment.

Yet, does the Torah provide for rabbinic regulation of society through judicial action which reckons with social needs? Again an affirmative answer is available. The Torah contains not only specific rules of law but also general rules by whose terms one may properly consider social needs. Such a general rule is the rule not to oppress strangers, widows, and orphans.[9] Oppression is not defined. Therefore, it is by no means unreasonable for halakhic authorities to deal with social and economic conditions that are oppressive. They may also follow Moses' pattern and in an emergency break the Law as he broke the tablets. Sometimes they justified action which ran

9 *Ex.* 22:20-21.

counter to Biblical prescriptions by reference to a verse in the Psalms[10] but Moses' precedent is at least as good.

One impressive but little known argument for reckoning with individual needs (in addition to all the specific commands that stress the Torah's concern for human happiness) is the manner in which Moses handled four cases for which he did not have God's mandate. Two cases involved sinners - a man who cursed God[11] and one who desecrated the Sabbath.[12] The other two involved persons who felt disadvantaged, one group that could not observe the Passover because they were ritually unclean[13] and the other group, the daughters of Zelafhad who feared that they might be denied the right to inherit their father.[14] Moses dealt quite differently with the two sinners than he did with the groups who complained that they were being disadvantaged. It appears that he was in no hurry to ascertain the penalty that was to be meted out to the former, while he countenanced no delay whatever in obtaining relief for the latter. The *Targum Yerushalmi* explains why. It is to teach us how alert one must be when persons' rights are in jeopardy or when they suffer feelings of deprivation but how slow one may be when one has to punish the wicked.

Thus, not only rabbinic literature but even the Bible sensitizes us to be mindful of individual and social needs in the judicial process and thus the so-called sociological jurisprudence also has its place in the development of Jewish law with Biblical warrant and support.

II

There is diversity among halakhic authorities not only in legal philosophical positions but also with regard to the rules. Two factors contribute to the inordinate diversity with regard to rules.

First, there is the fact that the law was given not only to specified authorities but to all who joined in the Covenant. The inevitable consequence of such an agreement with God is that all who are covenanted have a voice in the development of the Law and will decide many issues for themselves. There would be anarchy if in all matters such autonomy prevailed. As a general rule, therefore, in most matters affecting others, or

10 119:126.
11 *Lev*. 24:10-16.
12 *Num*. 15:32-36.
13 *Num*. 9:6-12.
14 *Num*. 27:1-18.

the group as a whole, the duly chosen authorities have the last word but in matters affecting one's self the individual has considerable freedom of interpretation and action.

Second, although the term *halakhah* is generally used to describe the literature of Jewish law, in contradistinction to the *aggadah*, which comprises the non-legal literature of Judaism, Jewish law in fact comprises much more than is generally deemed law by modern states. It is important to bear this in mind when trying to understand why there is so much diversity and why there are so many different approaches to its development, even among those fervently committed to it.

In modern states one of the most important characteristics of law is its enforceability. A law without sanctions is not regarded as law at all, but as mere exhortation. Yet a very substantial portion of the *Halakhah* is only exhortation, directed only to the conscience of individuals. No action by courts was ever contemplated in such matters. Disobedience often entails no punishment by human tribunals. Moreover, the *Halakhah* does not hesitate to prohibit action of which no one other than the actor is aware. It enjoins the mind with regard to beliefs and attitudes. Thus *Halakhah* is much more than law insofar as it encompasses almost all the behavior and thought of those who live by it.

Recently, one halakhic authority[15] dealt with the problem whether a prisoner of war may commit suicide to spare himself the torture that was likely to be inflicted upon him to compel him to reveal military secrets and also whether one may give him the wherewithal to commit suicide. As for the prisoner himself, the conclusion was that he may kill himself but as for the accessory before the fact - the person providing the means for suicide - there was a difference of opinion. According to Jewish law it is clear that he would not be punished as a murderer though he made possible the death of a human being. Therefore, no court would ever be involved and the question involved only the action of individuals who may opt to obey the *Halakhah* or ignore it. Nonetheless, the issue is debated as a very serious halakhic one.

In a system in which the scope of law is limited in that it deals only with matters that can be brought to court for final resolution, there must be an ultimate authority that hands down decisions binding on all the courts within that judicial system. No judicial system could tolerate for long a situation wherein different courts in the same jurisdiction apply the law differently. That would in effect mean that all citizens are not subject to the same law, a denial of the basic ideal of equality before the law. In the United

15 Y. Gershuni, *Kol Tsofayikh* (Jerusalem: Gershuni, 1980), 216-220.

States, for example, the United States Supreme Court is frequently called upon to make the final decision when lower courts in different regions arrive at contradictory rulings. The Supreme Court makes the decision which then binds all the judges in the land. However, since the *Halakhah* - even when ideally there is a Sanhedrin and a system of lower and appellate courts - pertains so overwhelmingly to matters that never come before courts for resolution - matters pertaining principally to personal behavior, with no sanctions attached - there is no way to impose the will of an ultimate authority on the diversity of opinions that are advanced. It is virtually impossible to create regimentation. There are differences with regard to almost every new issue that arises. In addition, in matters of religious observance there is a plethora of local custom. In matters of creed there is hardly ever a precise formulation. And with respect to almost all matters that do not evoke the resistance of another, an applicant is practically always autonomous both with regard to the choice of an authority as well as whether to obey or not.

Thus, for example, in connection with medical ethics, one finds that a distinguished halakhic authority in Israel allows abortion when it is likely that the foetus will be afflicted with Tay-Sachs disease.[16] Another authority, in the United States, disapproves.[17] The pregnant woman may consult a rabbi who will recommend one view or the other.

With respect to a very pressing public issue, one finds similarly polar positions. On the one hand, you have in Israel a very respectable group of halakhic authorities who argue that Jews may not give back an inch of sacred soil on obvious halakhic grounds. This land is ours, they say, given to us by God. God ordered us to take it and to hold it by risking our lives for it. We were told to engage in war - in violence - for that purpose, and war *ipso facto* means the loss of life. Therefore, Chief Rabbi Yitshak Nissim, and Rabbi Zevi Yehuda Kook, the son of the former chief rabbi, are unequivocally opposed to the return of any part of the land.[18]

The "doves", on the other hand, include Rabbi Joseph B. Soloveitchik, whose public statements on the subject have received attention all over the

---

16 E.J. Waldenberg, cited in J.D. Bleich and F. Rosner, *Jewish Bioethics* (London and New York: Sanhedrin Press, 1978), 186.

17 J.D. Bleich, "Sexuality and Procreation", *Biomedical Ethics in Perspective of Jewish Teaching and Tradition,* ed. I. Franck (Washington, D.C.: College of Jewish Studies of Greater Washington, 1980). 1, 9-10.

18 Their names are not mentioned but all their arguments and sources are dealt with in O. Yosef, "Hahzarat Shetahim Me'eretz Yisra'el Bimkom Pikuah Nefesh", *Torah She-Be'al Peh* 21 (1980), 12-20.

world.[19] To him the issue is whether the sanctity of life is not so great that if Jews can buy peace with the return of some of the soil it is not more important to save life. Yet how do these authorities answer the question of Rabbi Nissim, which on its face is such a logical one. The answer is simple: Jews were told to go to war only when victory was something that was likely. It is a halakhic requirement that one does not engage in violence or war unless victory is probable. When God told the Jews to conquer the Holy Land He was on their side. Today victory is not necessarily something of which Israel can be assured, and thus the problem is whether on the basis of the present situation *Halakhah* would dictate the return of the territories. Which view the people of Israel will adopt remains to be seen.

Yet, in many matters it is necessary for the rabbinical courts to make a decision in the face of a diversity of rulings. It was long held by some halakhic authorities that a corporation has no legal personality independent of the persons who create it and own its shares.[20] They are partners and no more. The rabbinical courts, however, now subscribe to the view that a corporation has legal personality on its own.[21] That ruling is now binding on all rabbinical courts in Israel.

It thus appears that the presumably totalitarian character of the *Halakhah* contains a paradox. Because the *Halakhah* affects almost everything that a person thinks, says, or does, his personal freedom is radically proscribed. Yet, precisely because its scope is so extensive and most of it is beyond the possibility of enforcement, the diversity in rules and opinions that it contains defies description and makes it the least monolithic system of law known to legal scholars in the west.

It has been suggested that the existence of so much diversity of opinion in the halakhic system is not intrinsic, nor ideal, but rather one of the unfortunate consequences of the Jewish dispersion. "Ideally", it is said, the *Halakhah* "envisages some ultimate authority in which there is vested the final responsibility for the determination of all questions which fall within the purview of problems to be settled by reference to halakhic standards."[22] This is simply not true unless the ultimate authority meant is God Himself. So long as it is only men who exercise the authority, not even a unanimous

---

19 It might be that his views are derived from his grandfather's position as described in the footnote, *ibid* ; p.18.

20 S. Miron, "Ma'amad ha-Hevrah, B.E.M. bemishpat Ivri", *Sinai* 59 (1966), 228-245.

21 *Piske Din, Rabbaniyim* Vol.10, p.278, at 285-291.

22 W.S. Wurzburger, "Plural Modes and the Authority of the Halakhah", *Judaism* 20/4 (1971), 391.

Sanhedrin relieves the Jew of his obligation to ignore its decision when he knows it has erred.[23] He must obey the Sanhedrin if he is acting as a judge in a lower court; without such a rule, there would be anarchy in the judicial system. Moreover, if the Sanhedrin is trying to establish its authority in a period when there is the threat of chaos, it is the moral obligation of the dissenter to make his contribution to the establishment of order. In addition, when the decision affects persons other than himself, he cannot, of course, use his dissent as an excuse for disobedience. However, when the mandate pertains to his religious observance, and he is certain that he is right and the Sanhedrin is wrong, he must express himself and act accordingly. Thus even ideally neither a majority nor a unanimous Sanhedrin becomes a surrogate for personal commitment to the Covenant and the will of God that must be fulfilled because of it.

Furthermore, the halakhic system prescribes much that can never fall within the purview of problems that enter the jurisdiction of the Sanhedrin. For example there is a wide range of prohibitions the flouting of which draws neither divine nor human punishment. Of these prohibitions the individual Jew can, if he so wishes, be critical, and he can disobey them with impunity. Insofar as such matters are concerned, even the *Halakhah's* highest tribunal engages in nothing more than exhortation. And surely if, in the exercise of personal autonomy, the will of the Sanhedrin can be flouted in matters involving biblical mandates, all the more can this pertain when the prohibitions are only rabbinic ordinances!

What, then, unites all who are committed to the *Halakhah*, those presently called "Orthodox"? It is simply the belief that from the Covenant between God and Israel there emerged the obligation to obey His Law, which is subject to change and development only as that Law - Written and Oral - made such change and development possible. The dissenter, or the champion of a new rule, must base his dissent or his effort at legislation on these fundamental norms and the methodology they prescribe.

III

It might appear, at first glance, that the difference between enforceable and non-enforceable *Halakhah* resembles Kant's differentiation between law and ethics and Hart's differentiation between law and morality. However, in the *Halakhah* the two are totally integrated and one cannot study or understand the one without the other.

---

23 *Hor.* 2a and 3b.

For example, the halakhic source material pertaining to usury is voluminous and covers almost every type of loan transaction imaginable even in modern times. Yet the instances in which the transactions are voidable or in which a borrower may retrieve the money he paid as interest on the loan are notably few. But that does not mean that all the other forms of loan which are prohibited but not voidable are to be relegated to the domains of ethics and morality. The fact is that a lender who lends money in any manner disapproved by the *Halakhah* may never be required to make restitution but he may forfeit his competency as a witness before a court because he engaged in transactions upon which the *Halakhah* frowns.[24] Thus, for the law of evidence one requires knowledge of all the halakhic rules on usury because one who offends against any of the rules may lose his credibility. Indeed, he may suffer other disabilities as well.

A man who was presumed dishonest could not take an oath. This was a disability of major consequence. According to Jewish law, most oaths were taken by parties to relieve themselves of liability.[25]

Thus, for example, if the creditor claimed money from the alleged debtor and had but one witness instead of two, the alleged debtor could take an oath that he owed nothing and that was the end of the case. Or if the creditor claimed more money than the debtor admitted owing, then the debtor took an oath that his obligation was less than that alleged. However, if the debtor was disqualified from taking the oath, his adversary could take it and collect his full claim.[26] Dishonest men were, therefore, at the mercy of claimants, and thus the *Halakhah* created a very meaningful legal sanction for men to seek to retain their reputations as presumptively honest.

Furthermore, a man who was known to the judge to be dishonest or even suspect in the matter of oaths might be denied the right to take an oath to clear himself, and his adversary could take the oath as plaintiff and recover. It was simply dangerous for any man to forfeit his claim to a good name.[27]

Another example involves the legal personality of a corporation to which reference has already been made. One important source to support this conclusion is a text involving religious vows. One man can adjure another and prohibit him from deriving any benefit from property owned by the person making the declaration (which is regarded as a vow). The prohibition also applies to property in which the person making the declaration has an undivided partnership interest. And this includes property which belongs to

24 *M. Sahn.* 3:3.
25 *M. Shebu.* 7:1.
26 *Ibid;* and 7:4.
27 Maimonides, *Mishneh Torah*, *Hilkhot Sanhedrin* 24:1.

all the inhabitants of the city since they are deemed partners in the assets of their municipality. However, the vow does not apply to the assets of the Jewish people as a whole. Of no individual Jew can it be said that he has property in those assets.[28] They belong to the Jewish people as such, independently of the individuals who constitute the Jewish people. And this entity with an independent existence is comparable to a corporation.

Presently this problem is under discussion with regard to the property of a Kibbutz.[29] Are its members partners or is the Kibbutz like a corporation? Rabbi Joseph B. Soloveitchik in a volume on "Penitence"[30] derives the corporate character of the Jewish people from texts dealing with animal offerings and liturgy. He holds that in addition to the sins of individual Jews, and the sins of the group for collective conduct that is sinful, there are sins of the eternal House of Israel - unconnected with any individual or group of individuals. It is the guilt of the entity which has an independent existence and comprises the dead, the living, and the still unborn, and makes of them a metaphysical reality for which there must be atonement. To such an extent are religious and legal thought interwoven in halakhic thought and enterprise!

The *Halakhah* also describes many situations in which one person harms another but no liability attaches. The conduct is immoral but punishable only by God - "by the laws of Heaven".[31] Thus a man who places fire in the hands of a child or an incompetent in order to burn his neighbour's property is not liable by the Jewish law of tort because it was the act of the intervening agent, the child or the incompetent, that caused the damage (*Gerama*). Similarly, he who places poison near his neighbour's animal is not liable because it was the animal's own act that killed it. Even a man whose testimony could have availed another in a lawsuit is not liable for his failure to testify though he violated a Biblical injunction. These are only a few of the instances of malfeasance and misfeasance in which a human tribunal awards no damages. In the eyes of Heaven, however, there is liability. From the point of view of morality, a wrong has been committed.

---

28 *M.Ned.* 5:4 and 5.

29 N. Bar-Ilan, "Hakibuts Keshutafut vekekehilah behalakhah", *Tehumin* I (1980), 414-422: Y. Cohen, "The Kibbutz as a Legal Entity", in N. Rakover, ed., *Jewish Law and Current Legal Problems* (Jerusalem: The Library of Jewish Law, 1984), 55-65.

30 *Al hateshuvah* (Jewish Agency: Jerusalem, 1974), 78.

31 *B.K.* 55b and 56a. On this *sugya,* see further B.S. Jackson, *Essays in Jewish and Comparative Legal History* (Leiden: E.J. Brill, 1975), ch.10; L. Jacobs, *The Talmudic Argument* (Cambridge: Cambridge University Press, 1984), ch.20.

Could the rabbis leave it at that? No, they provided legal sanctions for what they deemed morally reprehensible behavior.

Rashi suggests that liability by "the laws of Heaven" is of a punitive character rather than compensatory - and the tortfeasor is only encouraged to pay to avoid punishment by God.[32] *Rashi* apparently does not regard the liability as liability to compensate so that failure to compensate might be deemed theft - withholding from another man what is his due. The *Meiri* holds differently.[33] For him, it becomes the duty of the court to tell the defendant that he ought to pay, and for.failure to pay he is presumed a thief and, therefore, incompetent to testify in other litigation or to take oaths in lawsuits against him, with all the dangers described above in connection with usurious transactions.[34] Again, what "Heaven" forbade has practical legal consequences.

In modern times no one has done more to articulate the total unity of the *Halakhah* and the interdependence of all its parts than Dr. Soloveitchik.

Given the premise that all the Law is God's revealed will, it follows logically that all of it will have theological significance. The totality of the Law is taken by Soloveitchik as a realm of ideas in the Platonic sense, given by God for application to the realm. Just as the mathematician creates an internally logical and coherent fabric of formulas with which he interprets and integrates the appearance of the visible world, so the Jew, the "Man of *Halakhah*", has the Torah as the divine idea that vests all of human life with direction and sanctity. Legislative change is irreconcilable with *Halakhah*, yet creativity is of its very essence. "The Halakhah is a multi-dimensional ever-expanding continuum which cuts through all levels of human existence from the most primitive and intimate to the most complex relationships" (from an unpublished lecture by Dr. Soloveitchik). Thus, though *Halakhah* refers to the ideal, its creativity must be affected by the real.

Halakhic creativity is not an ingenious academic exercise. The man who would bridge the distance between the ideal and the real, who would discover what is the intent of divine will in a new and unprecedented situation, must employ the dialectic of reason in "fear and trembling" - his thinking must be part of a religious agony. God willed that man obey his Law. God also willed man's welfare. Sometimes the Law and man's welfare come into seeming conflict. The pious jurist must then probe the sources and the

---

32 On *B.K.* 104a.

33 *Meiri* on *B.K.* 56a. (See also *Ketsot hahoshen*, 32a.)

34 *Ibid.*, and *Rabbenu Meshulam, Hahashlamah, B.K.* 6:1.

commentaries of the saints, and descend into that same crucible of pain out of which the right way was originally revealed.

A modern case in *Halakhah* involved the armed forces of the United States. These were, and still are, in need of Jewish chaplains. The three largest rabbinic groups in America - Orthodox, Conservative, and Reform - instituted drafts. Rabbis were to be drafted compulsorily by their own rabbinic groups. For Orthodox rabbis, there was a significant halakhic problem. Could rabbis undertake to place any colleague in jeopardy? Futhermore, could they undertake to place their colleague in such a position that he might some day have to desecrate the Sabbath or another holy festival?

To this query Rabbi Soloveitchik gave an affirmative reply.[35] In a magnificent responsum based on a keen analysis of talmudic sources, he upheld the action of Yeshiva University in calling for the drafting of its alumni for the military chaplaincy. He cited a text[36] permitting one to embark upon a voyage to fulfill a *mitsvah* - a religious commandment - though it was possible that in the course of the voyage one might have to desecrate the Sabbath in order to save one's own life for the life of another. Rabbi Soloveitchik admitted that he had not approached the sources with complete objectivity; that he had had certain intuitive feelings and held certain basic values that prejudiced him in favour of the decision rendered by Yeshiva University and guided him in his exploration of the various aspects and facets of the problem. But this lack of objectivity is merely a fundamental avowal of inevitable human limitation, and is not to be confused with arbitrariness. As anyone who has studied the Talmud knows, the *Halakhah* is too objective a discipline to permit an approach based on transient moods. Nevertheless, in the deepest strata of halakhic thinking, logical judgment is preceded by value judgment, and intuitive insight gives impetus to the logic of argument.

Two other responsa by Rabbi Soloveitchik reveal the vitality of the *Halakhah* for the resolution of uniquely modern problems. For many years it was the practice in New York City for all foundlings to be turned over to Catholic and Protestant adoption agencies. Recently the city's Jewish adoption agency made a request for its share - since a third of New York's inhabitants are Jewish. Was the request halakhically proper, since there was no way of identifying the faith of the foundlings' parents and the greater

35 The responsa herein quoted and reported were never published by Dr. Soloveitchik but the author of this essay has seen and studied them. The two pertaining to foundlings and icons may still be in the archives of the American Jewish Congress in New York.

36 *Shab*. 19a.

mathematical probability in the case of each child was that it was non-Jewish? Could foundlings be reared as Jews and converted to Judaism by foster parents?

Dr. Soloveitchik sustained the propriety of the agency's request, in a responsum that cited halakhic sources but also referred to mathematical formulas of probability. The Jewish Law frowns upon the use of mathematical probabilities in capital cases. On complex philosophical grounds,[37] Dr. Soloveitchik placed cases involving religious identity in the same category. Hence the fact that the majority of foundlings may be non-Jewish becomes inconsequential; if only one foundling may be Jewish, the Jewish community must assert its claim.

On another occasion he was asked about the use of anthropomorphic symbols in the stained-glass windows of an interfaith chapel on a college campus. He opposed their use, and his responsum revealed how the historical method may be used in solving halakhic problems. Since talmudic law, which was developed principally in Babylon, did not support him, he relied upon later medieval Jewish law, which had been developed in Christian Europe. His responsum explains why, in a Christian society, it was more imperative to expand, rather than restrict, the prohibition against icons that suggest the Christological idea of God-man. "To what our sages in a non-Christian Babylonia did not object, our forefathers in Christian countries were very sensitive."

In these decisions one can see how laws pertaining to the Sabbath have a bearing on the right to draft personnel for war and the right of a Jewish community to demand a share of the foundlings for adoption. Furthermore, one can see that Soloveitchik also reckons with history and sociology in the

---

37 The following may serve as a sample: "One school sees, in a naturalistic fashion, life and death on a biological level exclusively and identifies *Pikuah Nefesh* (the obligation to conserve life) with the saving of a carnal existence from extinction. The other school introduces an idealistic motif. It maintains that the law of *Pikuah Nefesh* which is based upon a value judgment - the appraisal of life as the highest good - transcends the bounds of biological fact and extends into the domain of spiritual activity. Life is not only a *factum* but also an *actus*, not only a tangible reality but also an abstract ethical value to be attained. Death is both a biological and ethical-spiritual phenomenon. The failure of an individual to realize his own personality in a manner decreed by his creator at birth is as tragic as his physical disintegration. One may save a life not only through medical skill but also by extending moral help. Hence, whenever man's inner life, his unique relationship to God, and the mode of his existence as an individual and social being are to be determined, we encounter the problem of *Pikuah Nefesh*, which means here the preservation of a spiritual identity .. Hence (the concept of) majority finds no application in this case."

case of anthropomorphic symbols in a chapel and with teleology in his analysis of what one means when one says that the saving of a life includes saving a person from being raised in a faith different from the one in which he was born.

Thus, halakhic development involves much more than logic. It also involves man's sense of justice and all his needs as an animal and a creature with a unique relationship to God.

If the *Halakhah,* whose basic norm is the Covenant or Revelation, can be developed not only by the exercise of logic but also in response to man's sense of justice and man's social and personal needs, what is the measure of God's input and man's input?

The late Justice Benjamin Cardozo once essayed to describe what it is that a judge does when he engages in the judicial process creatively. The conclusion is inescapable that one can acquire the art only after years of preoccupation with the law, its history, its ideals, its methodology, its philosophy. So it is with Torah - until one has studied long and much from earlier masters, one does not learn how to balance one's commitment to authority with one's obligation to be master instead of the obedient servant. Both imitation and originality play their part in the process. Modesty coupled with respect for forebears commingles with self-reliance.

Thus, the halakhic authority faces on the one hand the authorities: revealed texts, revealed norms, and the dicta of sages whose prescriptions are almost as sacred as the revealed data (because what the sages of each generation ordain becomes part of the tradition which the revealed texts enjoin us to obey). On the other hand, the Law's doctors are themselves partners in the development of the Law. Indeed God abdicated in their favor when He bequeathed the Law to them. He thereby restrained Himself from any further revelations.[38] The Talmud tells us that Rabbis are not to rely upon heavenly voices or miracles. They are to act as sovereigns in the sphere of halakhic creativity allocated to them. Can one conceive a more difficult equilibrium than this - subservience to mountains of authority coupled with a well-nigh arrogant usurpation of legislative and judicial power over the divine legacy? Yet both poles play their necessary roles in halakhic development.

If not for *Halakhah's* theocentric character, it would be no different from other legal systems that are rooted only in history and economics. Because its students are committed to the divine origin of the Law, their creative achievement in the law is ever oriented to the fulfillment of God's Will. In

---

38 *B.M.* 59b.

order that we never lose sight of this commitment, the Law includes mandates that are also supra-rational - inexplicable in terms of human values and interests. Thus Dr. Samuel Belkin, the late President of Yeshiva University, maintains that even the suprarational commandments of the Torah have a purpose although we may not fathom their reason.[39] These mandates are to be obeyed solely because God decreed them. Such mandates are to be found in every branch of the Law. Obedience to them is of the essence of one's religious experience - one obeys not because one understands but rather because one believes. As children sometimes obey parents not because they comprehend but because they trust, so are we to obey God. It was to conserve this attitude that our Sages hesitated to make too explicit their own analysis of the Law in terms of human values and interests. Such analyses might prompt students to embrace a completely humanistic approach to the Law which would thus lose its theocentric character altogether. In a general way they did explore the rationale of most of the *mitsvot* , but in the articulation of specific rules they did not presume that they completely fathomed the teleology of all the revealed texts.

Yet God gave the Law to the Jewish people who alone were responsible for its development. As humans they crave to understand what they are commanded to perform. Moreover, their needs are not the same in every age or clime. The Torah itself takes note of these factors. It appeals to man to comprehend the justice-content of the law. It also bids him to live by the law, and not perish because of it. Moses' successors were vested with authority not only to interpret the Law but to constitute themselves as authorities in every generation. The Rabbis often undertook not only to rationalize the presumptively suprarational, but also to suspend, even overrule, the revealed words of God.

Furthermore, the halakhic authority must not only veer between what God mandated and what man requires, but he must also veer frequently between antithetical values found in the basic norm, the Covenant itself, such as universalism and particularism, freedom and self-control, the needs of society and the needs of the self, this worldliness and other worldliness.

It is in this connection that the principle of polarity of Morris Raphael Cohen can be so helpful. In virtually all of life he saw "necessary opposition in determinate effects" as a "heuristic principle directing our inquiry in the search for adequate explanations."[40] Professor Cohen

---

39 S. Belkin, "Philosophy of Purpose", in *Studies in Torah Judaism,* ed. L.D. Stitskin (New York: Yeshiva University Press & Ktav Publishing House Inc., 1969), 1-29.

40 *Studies in Philosophy and Science* (New York: H. Holt & Co, 1949), 12.

mentions as an excellent example of polarity Professor Felix Adler's use of the opposing action of the blades of scissors "to denote the fact the mind never operates effectively except by using both unity and plurality.[41] It would appear that Dr. Soloveitchik uses a similar approach. He rejects Hegel's idea of thesis, antithesis and synthesis, as suitable for the dialectic of the *Halakhah* simply because the revealed antinomies never lose their validity. Forever they remain poles. However, the halakhic authority veers between them in making decisions.

One example to illustrate this approach is the attitude of most halakhic authorities to the status of women in modern times. The status of women in Jewish law unmistakably involves some deeply entrenched ideas which are in conflict with each other and veering between them is not an easy task for the creative halakhic expert. One finds, on the one hand, a Biblical command with regard to the equality of males and females. All have the divine image. All are equally responsible to the civil and criminal code and are equally protected by it. Yet, one finds on the other hand that in Rabbinic literature there is a deep-seated distrust of males in the matter of sex. They are easily stimulated - even a woman's voice can be the cause. And the only safeguard against sexual immorality is separation - as total as it can be. Between husbands and wives many a rabbi so encouraged the practice of the art of love that even the passion of the most virile of men is gratified. But, as between men and forbidden women, no one is to be trusted. It was not easy even to permit fathers and their daughters to be together unchaperoned. When the taboo of incest became well established, parents and their offspring were not expected to abide by the strict rules forbidding a male and a female to be together alone. However, it is because of this pole - call it a "fixation" if you will - pertaining to the weakness of the male and his uncontrollable sexual drive (it is difficult to deny that they knew whereof they spoke - they, themselves, were male!) that halakhic authorities insisted on separation of the sexes in the synagogue and domestic careers for women. From this there derive separate seating in the synagogue, the exclusion of women from most civic, communal, and religious functioning, and much else that makes the tradition offensive to many modern women.

Now, a Jewish legislator today, confronted by the two poles, somehow finds it easier to decide, as did several halakhic giants in Israel, that women can be involved in the political process as voters,[42] and in the judicial

41 *Reason and Nature* (2nd ed., Glencoe: Free Press, 1949), 165 n.4.
42 B.Z.M. Uziel, *Piske Uziel* (Mossad Rav Kook: Jerusalem, 1977), 228-234.

process as witnesses and judges,[43] but not in synagogue procedures and leadership. So to interpret the law that the disability of women to be judges and witnesses is removed is a fulfillment of the Biblical pole of equality, and if it impinges upon the purity of thought of males, at least the sanctity of a synagogue is not thereby affected, nor is the meditation of any worshipper. Quite different is the situation where the synagogue is concerned. In that connection the other pole comes into play. And the reluctance to change the rules is great.

Yet, the debates among halakhic authorities may involve not only the measure of the "veering between antinomies" when the poles are well defined, but also the very existence of the pole and its definition. As an example, in one instance Dr. Soloveitchik reacted quite strongly to this writer's suggestion that an important presumption in Jewish family law no longer be valid and if this could be proved, it might be possible to annul many marriages and dispense with the need for a *Get* (divorce). The Talmud asks[44] why a woman betrothed to a man who died before consummation of the marriage - and thus in need of a release from a surviving brother-in-law (*halitsah*) before being permitted to remarry - cannot obtain annulment of the betrothal on the ground that her husband's untimely death was a circumstance that would have deterred her from entering upon the marital relationship. The answer is that there is a presumption that every woman prefers any kind of a marriage, even a bad one, to living alone, and therefore when she married she was prepared to do so unconditionally and without regard to any future developments. But this presumption cannot be said to reflect modern conditions. In today's society, which has witnessed the "Woman's Liberation" movement, it can be said unequivocally that the overwhelming majority of women would prefer to be single and cope very well as such, rather than be bound in any way to dead men or their kin. One might readily object that the challenge to the presumption may not help in cases where the marriage was fully consummated, for all conditions are presumed waived once the spouses cohabit. There may be ways to overcome this objection but that was not the basis of Dr. Soloveitchik's demurrer. He argued that the talmudic statement to the effect that every woman prefers any kind of marriage, even a bad one, to living alone is a metaphysical pronouncement and not subject to rebuttal. Perhaps the Biblical statement that in God's view it is not good for man to be alone is the basis for it.[45] Thus one would here

43 M. Bar-Ilan, "Tazkir", *Yavneh* III (Nisan, 5709, April 1949), 32.

44 *B.K.* 110b and 111a.

45 *Gen.* 2:18.

find a "pole" whose existence this writer would challenge especially since God's pronouncement that man should not be alone was interpreted by the Rabbis[46] to have no reference to the misery of loneliness but rather to the fact that if, unlike other animals, males had no mates they might think they are equal of God - He is alone and they too are alone. (Echoes of Plotinus!).

The Talmud is regarded by its lovers as a sea. Perhaps the metaphor is meant to suggest not only the matter of size but also the image of waves. And perhaps even the phenomenon of winds and storms. These storms will also rage with regard to the philosophy of law that a study of the folios can and ought generate.

---

46 See *Rashi's* commentary.

NATURAL LAW IN MAIMONIDEAN THOUGHT AND SCHOLARSHIP (On *Mishneh Torah, Kings*, VIII. 11)

by

JACOB I. DIENSTAG*

Whether or not the old rabbinic concept of Noahide Commandments,[1] which bears some resemblance to the idea of natural law, really fits that juristic category, Maimonides' formulation of this concept has been the subject of considerable discussion in Jewish thought and scholarship.[2]

Unlike other themes in Jewish law and theology, the interest in the Noahide Commandments extended, however, beyond its intrinsic halakhic and

* Former Professor of Bibliography and Chief of the Judaica Division, Yeshiva University Library (retired).

1 For a general discussion of the Noahide Commandments, see David Solomon Shapiro, *Yesode hadat ha'universalit* (New York: Bloch, 1936); Aaron Lichtenstein, *The Seven Laws of Noah* (New York: Rabbi Jacob Joseph School Press/Z. Berman, 1981); David Novak, "The Origin of the Noahide Laws", in *Perspectives on Jews and Judaism; Essays in Honor of Wolfe Kelman* (New York: Ktav, 1980), 301-310; *idem, The Image of the Non-Jew in Judaism* (New York & Toronto: Edwin Mellen Press, 1983). The strictly halakhic aspects of the Noahide laws according to Maimonides are analyzed by R. Hirsch Chajes, *Tiferet leMosheh* (Zolkiew: S. Meyerhoffer, 1840); reprinted in *Kol Kitve Maharaz Chajes* (Jerusalem: Divre Hakhamim, vol.1, 1958), end of chapter 5; R. Meir Dan Plocki, *Hemdat Yisrael* (Piotrkow: N. Kronenberg, 1903), leaves 86a-116b; Michael Guttman, *Behinat Kiyyum hamitsvot* (Breslau: T. Shatzky, 1931; repr. Jerusalem: Mekor, 1978), 69-75: Gerald J. Blidstein, *Political Concepts in Maimonidean Halakha* (Ramat Gan: Bar Ilan University Press, 1983), 130-134, 240-241 (Hebrew).

2 On natural law in Maimonides, see H.A. Wolfson, *Philo*, vol.II (Harvard University Press, 1962), 310-312; Steven S. Schwarzschild, "Do Noahites Have to Believe In Revelation?", *JQR* n.s. 52 (1962), 297-309; 53 (1962), 30-65; José Faur, "La Doctrina de la ley natural en el pensamiento judio del medioevo," *Sefarad* 27 (1967), 239-268 (pp. 258-265: Maimonides); *idem, Studies in the Mishneh Torah; Book of Knowledge* (Jerusalem: Mosad Ha-Rav Kook, 1978), 61-65; 161-176 (Hebrew); Marvin Fox, "Maimonides and Aquinas on Natural Law", *Diné Israel* III (1972), V-XXXVI; reprinted in Jacob I. Dienstag, ed., *Studies in Maimonides and St. Thomas Aquinas* (New York: Ktav, 1975), 75-106; Amos Funkenstein, "Maimonides; political theory and realistic messianism", in Albert Zimmerman, ed., *Die mächte des Guten und Bösen; Vorstellungen im XII. und XIII. Jahrhundert über ihr Wirken in der Heilsgeschichte* (Berlin: W. de Gruyter, 1977), 81-103; Norman Lamm & Aaron Kirschenbaum, "Freedom and constraint in the Jewish judicial process", *Cardozo Law Review* 1, no.1 (Spring 1979), 99-133; S. Atlas, *Pathways in Hebrew Law* (New York: American Academy for Jewish Research, 1978), 21-40 (Hebrew).

theological aspects. The political and social conditions of the Jews in Europe were due for review as a result of the new thinking expounded by the champions of Enlightenment on the eve of the French Revolution.[3]

Jewish thinkers, who yearned to break out of the ghetto walls and be accepted as equals with the rest of the non-Jewish population, naturally desired to see in Judaism a reciprocal attitude. How can one demand a humanistic approach to Jews and Judaism on the part of one's gentile neighbours without extending the same to the latter? In an age in which theological discussions dominated the intellectual scene, the question whether Judaism accepts unconditionally the talmudic principle, "All the righteous men of the nations of the world have a share in the world to come," is a very crucial one in the struggle for emancipation. Is it a wonder then that much of the discussion borders around scholarship and apologetics or theology and political science?[4]

Before we begin this survey, let us first cite Maimonides' succinct wording of the above mentioned talmudic principles:

> A heathen who accepts the seven commandments and observes them scrupulously is a "righteous heathen," and will have a portion in the world to come, provided that he accepts them and performs them because the Holy One, blessed be He, commanded them in the Law and made known through Moses, our teacher, that the observance thereof had been enjoined upon the descendants of Noah even before the Law was given. But if his observance thereof is based upon a reasoned conclusion he is not deemed a resident alien, or one of the pious of the Gentiles, but one of their wise men.[5]

It is Maimonides' last condition, that it is not enough to observe the seven Noahide Commandments in order to be counted among the righteous of

---

3 Jacob Katz, *Exclusiveness and Tolerance* (Oxford University Press, 1961); Yehezkel Kaufmann, *Golah Venekhar,* II (Tel Aviv: Dvir, 1932; reprinted 1961), 55-110.

4 Jacob Katz, "The Vicissitudes of Three Apologetic Passages", *Zion* 23-24 (1958-59), 174-193 (Hebrew).

5 *Mishneh Torah, H. Melakhim,* VIII:11;= A.M. Hershman translation, *Yale Judaica Series* (Yale University Press, 1949), 230.

On Maimonides' use of the terms "wise" and "righteous" in this ruling and the parallel use in *H. Deot* and *Moreh Nebukim,* see Norman Lamm, "The Sage and Saint in the Writings of Maimonides", *Samuel Belkin Memorial Volume* (New York: Yeshiva University, 1981), 27 (Hebrew); *Cf.* L. V. Berman, "Maimonides on Political Leadership", in D.J. Elazar, ed., *Kinship and Consent* (Ramat Gan: Turtledove Publishing, 1981; reprint: Washington, D.C.: University Press of America, 1983), 124 note 20. He was unaware of Lamm's study.

the gentile nations and to acquire a share in the world to come, which agitated some thinkers. According to the Sage, only those who fulfill the seven Noahide Commandments because they were divinely revealed are to acquire a share in the world to come. Apart from this stipulation there is also a textual problem: did Maimonides say "nor one of their sages" *("velo")* or "but one of their sages" *("ela")* ?[6]

It is ironic that "on the eve of modern times there stands out one opponent of Maimonides, to whom he was very much indebted, against whom he rebelled so vehemently .... Baruch Spinoza."[7] Spinoza, who had the reading, *"velo"*, opened his attack on Maimonides for his alleged illiberal view. His critique of Judaism through his attack on Maimonides is worth quoting:

> The Jews are of a directly contrary way of thinking for they hold that true opinions and a true plan of life are of no service in attaining blessedness, if their possessors have arrived at them by light of reason only, and not like the documents prophetically revealed to Moses. Maimonides ventures openly to make this assertion: "Every man who takes to heart the seven precepts and diligently follows them, is counted with the pious among the nations, and an heir of the world to come; that is to say, if he takes to heart and follows them because God ordained them in the law, and revealed them to us by Moses, because they were of aforetime precepts to the sons of Noah: but he who follows them as led thereto by reason, is not counted as a dweller among the pious, nor among the wise of the nations."[8]

6 For the references to the literature on the variants of this passage, see the last part of our survey below.

7 Simon Rawidowicz, "On Interpretation," *PAAJR* 26 (1957), 106-107; reprinted in his *Studies in Jewish Thought* (Philadelphia: Jewish Publication Society of America, 1974), 64.

8 *The Chief Works of Benedict de Spinoza,* trld. R.M.H. Elwes, Vol.1: *Tractatus Theologico-Politicus,* ch. 5 (London: George Bell & Sons, 1900), 79-80. On Spinoza's critique of Maimonides, see Leo Strauss, *Die Religionskritik Spinozas* (Berlin: Akademie Verlag, 1930), 129-181; Eng. tr. (by E.M. Sinclair), *Spinoza's Critique of Religion* (New York: Schocken, 1965), 147-192; N. Porges, "Das Wort Pharisäer bei Spinoza", *MGWJ* 61 (1917), 154-55; Hermann Cohen, "Spinoza über Staat und Religion, Judentum und Christentum", in his *Jüdische Schriften,* III (Berlin: C.A. Schwetschke, 1924), 346-55; *idem,* "Ein ungedruckter Vortrag Hermann Cohens über Spinozas Verhältnis zum Judentum", *Festgabe zum Zehn-Jährigen Bestehen der Akademie für die Wissenschaft des Judentums,* 1919-1929 (Berlin: Akademie Verlag, 1929), 42-68; S. Zac, "Spinoza, critique de Maïmonide", *Les Etudes Philosophiques* (Juillet-Sept. 1972), 411-28; reprinted in his *Philosophie, Théologie, Politique dans l'oeuvre de Spinoza* (Paris: J. Vrin, 1979), 85-95; J.I. Dienstag, "Biblical Exegesis of Maimonides in Jewish Scholarship" in *Samuel K. Mirsky Memorial Volume* (New York: Yeshiva University, 1970), 180-82.

Was it a corrupt version of the Maimonidean passage which misled Spinoza? The corrected version stipulated that those who kept the seven Noachide Commandments merely on rational grounds, namely, as basic ethical precepts following from human reasoning, could be called "wise" but not "pious" and were, therefore, not entitled to bliss of the hereafter.

But Hermann Cohen (Coswig, Germany, 1842 - Berlin. 1918) was not so sure that it was a corrupt version that misled Spinoza, for Joseph ben Shem Tob (Spain, c. 1400-1460), who is referred to by Spinoza in the above context, cites the corrected version.[9] Did, then, Spinoza deliberately quote the corrupted version in the heat of his attack on the Jewish religion?

Cohen saw in Maimonides' teachings of the doctrine of the state its highest and purest expression of humanity."[10] "For Spinoza's polemic has become the source of a fundamental misunderstanding of the Jewish religion. As such it has affected the most noble ages of German literature, and even today has not exhausted itself. Kant obtained from Spinoza his knowledge and his judgment of Judaism.[11] While Leibniz (1646-1716), like the middle ages and modern times, still knew and valued Maimonides,[12] Kant came to know Maimonides only through Spinoza. It seemed to Kant, through Spinoza, that in Maimonides Judaism is rightly condemned. It is, therefore, important to refute Spinoza on this point and to justify Maimonides."[13]

Unlike Spinoza, who was out to defame Judaism through his attack on Maimonides, Mendelssohn was an admirer of the Sage of Fostat and

---

9 Cohen learned of Shem Tob's correct reading from M. Joël's *Spinoza's Theologisch-Politischer Traktat* (Breslau: H. Skutsch, 1870), 56. See note 50.

10 Hermann Cohen, *Religion der Vernunft* (Frankfurt a. M: J. Kauffmann, 1929), 385; English tr. (by S. Kaplan) *Religion of Reason* (New York: F. Ungar, 1972), 331.

11 On Kant and Maimonides, see Friedrich Niewöhner, "Maimonides und Kant", *Israel Forum* 4 (1976), 11-19; *idem,* "Primat der Ethik oder erkenntnistheoretische Begründung der Ethik? Thesen zur Kant-Rezeption in der Jüdischen Philosophie", *Wolfenbütteler Studien zur Aufklärung* IV (1977), 119-61; S. Zac, "Kant et le problème du Judaïsme", *Le Nouveaux Cahiers* 49 (1977), 32-49.

12 Leibniz's comments on Maimonides' *Guide for the Perplexed* have been the subject of studies by Jacob Guttman, "Der Einfluss der maimonidischen Philosophie auf das christliche Abendland", *Moses ben Maimon* (ed. W. Bacher, M. Brann, D. Simonsen), Band I (Leipzig: G. Fock, 1908), 224-230; Nicole Ulman, "Leibniz Lecteur de Maimonide",*Le Nouveaux Cahiers* 24 (1971), 13-17: Lenn E. Goodman, "Maimonides and Leibniz", *Journal of Jewish Studies* XXXI no.2 (Autumn 1980), 214-236.

13 Hermann Cohen, *Religion of Reason, supra* n.10, at 331. *Cf.* also his *Jüdische Schriften,* III, *supra* n.8, at 347. A penetrating analysis of Spinoza's relation to Maimonides on this point and Cohen's critique is presented by Schwarzschild (see note 2). See now, Franz Nauen, "Hermann Cohen's Perception of Spinoza: a Reappraisal", *AJS Review* 4 (1979), 111-124.

commentator on the latter's *Treatise on Logic*[14] and *Guide for the Perplexed.*[15] In his famous polemic with the theologian, Johann Caspar Lavater, Mendelssohn summed up his *confessio Judaica* and continuously emphasized his conviction of the truth of Judaism.[16]

When he was challenged by Lavater to either contradict Charles Bonnet's proofs for the truth of Christianity or accept the Christian religion, Mendelssohn, in his defense of Judaism also emphasized the rabbinic dictum that assigns to the "righteous" or "pious" of the Gentiles a share in the world-to-come. It was, however, Maimonides' stipulation (in its corrupt text available to him) which contradicted his own views on the Noahide Commandments as identical with the essence of natural law.[17]

It is Maimonides' alleged idea of restricted tolerance which compelled Mendelssohn to address R. Jacob Emden: "Should all inhabitants of the earth except ourselves be doomed to perdition unless they believed in the Torah, which was given as an inheritance to the congregation of Jacob alone; especially as it [viz. the Noachian law] is something not even expressly written down in the Torah but is transmitted only through the tradition of the chosen people or exegetically derived by its sages from the words of the Torah? .... What, then, shall the nations do who are not recipients of the light of the Torah and who received no tradition except from untrustworthy and unreliable ancestors? Does God, then treat his creatures in the way of a tyrant, annihilating them and blotting out their names [by denying them a share in the world-to-come], though they committed no injustice?"[18]

---

14 J.I. Dienstag, "[Maimonides'] *Treatise on Logic* during the Haskalah", *Hadoar* vol.34 no.22 (Aprill, 1955), 420-422 (Hebrew); *idem*, "Maimonides' *Treatise on Logic*; an annotated bibliography", *Aresheth* II (1960), 10-14.

15 Simon Rawidowicz, "Mendelssohns handscriftliche Glossen zum More Nebukim", *MGWJ* 78 (1934), 195-202; reprinted without introduction in Moses Mendelssohn, *Gesammelte Schriften, Jubilaeumsausgabe,* 14. Band (Breslau: Stefan Muenz, 1938), 271.

16 Alexander Altmann, *Moses Mendelssohn* (University of Alabama Press, 1973), 215; Julius Guttmann, *Philosophies of Judaism* (New York: Rinehart & Wiston, 1964), 294-95. On Mendelssohn as a critic of Spinoza, see Julius Guttmann, "Mendelssohns *Jerusalem* und Spinozas *Theologisch-Politischer Traktat*"", 48. *Bericht der Hochschule für die Wissenschaft des Judentums* (Berlin: [Hochschule], 1931), 33-67; Engl. translation in Alfred Jospe, ed., *Studies in Jewish Thought; an Anthology of German Jewish Scholarship* (Detroit: Wayne State University Press, 1981), 361-86.

17 Altmann, *supra* n.16, at 217.

18 Altmann, *supra* n.16, at 217-218.

To Mendelsohn's great disappointment, Emden, in his reply, justified Maimonides' verdict as coinciding with the rabbinic sources.[19] This German Jew, sensing the new winds which were blowing through Europe, in his correspondence with Lavater, explicitly identified the Noahide Commandments with the law of nature.[20] Mendelssohn, according to Marvin Fox, "understands correctly that Maimonides makes the ruling because he holds that moral principles are not subject to any kind of rational demonstration and that, in fact, they have no truth-value. Consequently, unless one can depend on revelation, there is no source for morality except social convention."[21]

Mendelssohn's response is that, contrary to Maimonides, he has "clear and sound demonstrations concerning good and evil, right and wrong, beautiful and ugly, showing that they are all truly rational principles."[22] "To our sorrow," Fox concludes, "neither in this letter, nor elsewhere in his writings, does he set forth for us these demonstrative principles..."[23]

A most penetrating analysis of the Maimonides passage in the light of Mendelssohn's polemic against R. Jacob Emden and Cohen's sharp critique of Spinoza is given by Steven S. Schwarzschild.[24] After reviewing the textual problems in the Maimonides passage referred to above, Schwarzschild is not satisfied with the attempt to substitute the corrected version: "This emendation of the text does not relieve us of the difficulties that arise from Maimonides' statement, however. It still remains true that he excludes what [he] might call the philosophical rather than the religious Noachites from the class of the righteous men of the gentile nations of the world and thus also

19 Altmann, *supra* n.16, at 217, 294-295. Of interest is Theodore Dreyfuss, "Moses Mendelssohn's Attitude Towards R. Jacob Emden", in M. Hallamish and M. Schwarcz, eds., *Revelation, Faith, Reason; A Collection of Papers* (Ramat-Gan: Bar Ilan University, 1967), 99-112 (Hebrew).

20 Besides his definitive biography of Mendelssohn in which he analyzed the philosopher's struggle for the promotion of the civil rights of his coreligionists (at 421-552), Altmann has written an additional study on this subject: "The Philosophical Roots of Moses Mendelssohns's Plea for Emancipation", *Jewish Social Studies* 36 (1974), 191-202; reprinted in his *Jewish Intellectual History* (Hanover, N.H.: University Press of New England, 1981), 154-169.

21 Marvin Fox, "Law and Ethics in Modern Jewish Philosophy: The Case of Moses Mendelssohn", *PAAJR* 43 (1976), 8-9.

22 Fox, *supra* n.21, at 9.

23 Fox, *ibid.* Mendelssohn's dichotomy "of a natural law without revelation or he will make all religion superfluous" is further analyzed by Fox, *ibid.*, at 10-12.

24 Schwarzschild. *supra* n.2.

from the world-to-come. All questions which were previously raised with respect to this dictum, therefore, retain their validity."[25]

The attempt to point to *The Mishnah of R. Eliezer*[26] as the source for Maimonides' position is also irrelevant. Quoting a personal communication from the late Dr. Samuel Atlas that he does "not think that Maimonides would take it as a source for a *halacha* if he did not have a weighty reason for it .... Consequently, the source in *Mishnat R. Eliezer* does not help matters if we cannot explain Maimonides' view logically and rationally ... My considered opinion is that this passage has been added by some commentator on the basis of Maimonides' passage in *Hilchot Melachim*."[27]

Schwarzschild dismisses R. Jacob Emden's attempt "to buttress Maimonides' position" without coming up with a talmudic source as requested by Mendelssohn.[28] He sharply argues against Hermann Cohen in his polemic contra Spinoza. Cohen, in his opinion, is an "interested party" for "he had unbounded admiration for Maimonides." He "knew very well that Spinoza used that passage in the *Mishneh Torah* "in one of his most virulent attacks on Judaism. And Spinoza was the arch-enemy to Hermann Cohen ... Spinoza's attack on Maimonides and through Maimonides on Judaism as a whole had to be annihilated at all costs." Schwarzschild, too, opposes Spinoza, "but Cohen's refutation by vindicating Maimonides ... does not succeed." [29]

Schwarzschild reviews Spinoza's vitriolic attack on Maimonides. By willfully citing the incorrect version of the Sage's ruling in *H. Melakim*, Spinoza aimed to incriminate Judaism and to give the general non-Jewish public the impression that Maimonides' view authoritatively represented the consensus of the Jewish opinion on the subject.[30] Spinoza, continues Schwarzschild, intentionally misrepresented Judaism by ascribing Maimonides' view on this question to all of Jewish law.[31]

In Schwarzschild's view both Maimonides and Spinoza subscribed to the concept of natural law, whereas "Cohen's first main objection to the doctrine

---

25 Schwarzschild, *supra* n.2, at 302.

26 *Mishnat R. Eliezer*, ed. H.G.E. Enelow (New York: Bloch, 1933), 121.

27 Schwarzschild, *supra* n.2, at 306.

28 Schwarzschild, *supra* n.2, at 32.

29 Schwarzschild, *supra* n.2, at 38. See now, Friedrich W. Niewöhner, "Ein Schwieriges Maimonides-Zitat im *Tractus Theologico-Politicus* und Hermann Cohens Kritik an Spinoza", *Zeitschrift für Philosophische Forschung*, Band 31, Heft 4 (Oct-Dez. 1977), 618-626.

30 Schwarzschild, *supra* n.2, at 46-47.

31 Schwarzschild, *supra* n.2, at 48-49.

of natural law is that it identifies ethics with physiology ...; it assumes that morality is something that exists rather than something that is to be achieved. A subsidiary weakness of the doctrine which results from this fundamental fault is that it leads to chaos, for all ethical programs have... invoked the warrant of nature for their particular theses."[32]

A complete turn-about in the scholarship on this theme was inaugurated by the young scholar, José Faur, who completely negated the idea of natural law in Jewish thought. Uninhibited by apologetic considerations which may have coloured Central European thought and scholarship, in a series of studies in various periodicals culminating in his *Studies in the Mishneh Torah,* dedicated to the first part of *The Book of Knowledge,* Faur surveyed the various theories of natural law from ancient Rome through the Christian Church Fathers and the Moslem Middle Ages including Jewish medieval philosophers and the Karaites.[33]

In Faur's view the entire concept of natural law is totally foreign to rabbinic literature. In particular is this true of Maimonides who held that the divine commandments are imperative on the basis of revelation alone. In stressing Maimonides' opposition to those medieval Jewish theologians who distinguished between 'divine', i.e. 'ceremonial', and 'rational', i.e. 'moral', commandments, Faur severely criticized those scholars who attempted to stress the rationalistic or so-called humanistic element in Jewish theology.

Faur, therefore, considers the entire discussion of the so-called corrupt reading in Maimonides ruling on the Noahide laws to be irrelevant. In fact, he goes out of his way to state that the correct reading is the conventional version "nor of their wise men." All other evidences to the contrary ("but of their wise men") found in some manuscripts were merely doctored to suit the rational or humanistic approach of some copyists. According to Faur, this emendation is contrary to Maimonides' entire outlook.

Marvin Fox held, too, that there is no natural law doctrine in Judaism. "It is through God's revelation, mediated by the prophets, that men know what is right and wrong. Moreover, the vast majority of biblical commandments are addressed specifically to the Jews. Only the smallest part of biblical legislation is universal law intended for the rest of mankind."[34]

---

32 Schwarzschild, *supra* n.2, at 59.

33 José Faur, *supra* n.2; *idem,* "The Origin and Classification of Rational and Divine Commandments in Mediaeval Jewish Philosophy", *Augustinianum* 9 (1969), 299-304; *idem,* "The Basis for the Authority of the Divine Commandments according to Maimonides", *Tarbiz* 38 (1968), 43-54; 301 (Hebrew); *idem, Studies in the Mishne Torah, Book of Knowledge* (Jerusalem: Mossad Harav Kook, 1978 [Hebrew]).

34 Fox, *supra* n.2, at vi-vii; reprinted in Dienstag, *supra* n.2, at 76-77.

After introducing this reservation, Fox attempts to analyze the views of Maimonides, the "complete rationalist", who turns out to be the "most extreme in his rejection of all claims concerning a natural law based on right reason. However wide the extent of reason's dominance may be, it never, in Maimonides' teaching, extends to the realm of morals."[35] Contrary to those scholars who accept the revised reading in Maimonides' ruling *("ela")* to suit their rational outlook, Fox held that "a correct understanding of Maimonides will show why he could not affirm a theory of natural law, why he denied salvation to those who believed that they could have moral knowledge on purely rational grounds, and why he considered the latter neither pious nor wise."[36]

SOURCE FOR MAIMONIDES' STIPULATION

One of the major trends in classical rabbinic scholarship is the identificaton of the sources which Maimonides used for decisions and rulings in the *Mishneh Torah.*[37] Even though R. Joseph Karo in his *Kesef Mishnah* concedes that there is no source for Maimonides' stipulation and is convinced that "our teacher [Maimonides] made this statement as a result of his own independent thinking (*savara denafsheh*)", with which he completely agrees, attempts have been made to find some source.

The first reference to an unknown *midrash* is given by R. Solomon ben Isaac of Wolosin (brother of R. Hayyim of Volozin, disciple of R. Elijah Gaon), as quoted by his biographer, Ezekiel Feivel ben Zev, in his *Toledot Adam* where the following *midrash* is reported:

> R. Chassidi said: I have heard that the righteous of the nations of the world have a share in the world to come; we have, however, not been taught that the wise men of the nations of the world are in this position. Who is a righteous man from among the nations of the world? He who accepts the seven commandments because they are written in the Torah. A wise man from among nations of the world, on

35 Fox, *supra* n.2, at xii (reprint 82).

36 Fox, *supra* n.2, at xiv (reprint 84).

37 J.I. Dienstag, "The Relationship of Maimonides to his Predecessors", *Jewish Law Annual* 1 (1978), 42-43.

the other hand, is one who fulfills them because his own reason induces him to do so.[38]

R. Solomon of Wolosin, it may be added, has the reading: "but from their sages." R. Hirsch Chajes bluntly rebutted the entire story of Ezekiel about such a *midrash* and accused him of forgery.[39] Schwarzschild also informs us of Prof. I. Sonne's skepticism about the authenticity of this unknown *midrash* and dismisses its value as a possible source for Maimonides' ruling.[40]

It was Professor Michael Guttmann who first called attention to *The Mishnah of R. Eliezer (The Midrash of Thirty-two Hermeneutic Rules)*[41] which contains a passage that reflects Maimonides' thought and could have inspired his controversial ruling: "... but if they [the pious of the nations of the world] observe the seven Noahide laws saying 'we have learned these from somebody or other' - or as a result of their own intellectual reasoning - even if they observe the entire Torah, they will only be rewarded in this world."

Guttmann, however, has his reservations: Didn't a later hand interpolate a passage from Maimonides? He, therefore, compared the style of this *Midrash* with that of the *Mishneh Torah* in order to detect such a possibility.[42] Guttmann's revelation of this passage in the *Mishnat R. Eliezer* was picked

38 Translation in Schwarzschild, *supra* n.2, at 305, who states that the first edition of the *Toledot Adam*, Dyrenfurth, 1801, omits the name of the rabbi who states the *Midrash*. He also cites the second edition in Danzig, 1845. The Wilna, 1884 edition, available to me, (Photo-offset, Bnai Brak, 1962), part II, leaf 25, also omits the name of the rabbi.

39 R. Hirsch Chajes, *Minhat Kena'ot, Kuntres Ahron*, in *Kol Kitve Maharaz Chajes*, vol. II (Jerusalem: Divre Hakhamim, 1958), 1,035a; cited also by R. Wolf Leiter, "Kavod HaKhamim", in *Mishneh Torah*, vol.5, (New York: Shulsinger, 1947), 4a (end of volume) and S. Abramson in his notes on Maimonides' *Responsa*, ed. J. Blau, vol. III (Jerusalem: Mekize Nirdamim, 1961), 163-164.

40 Schwarzschild, *supra* n.2, at 305-306.

41 Michael Guttman, "Zur Quellenkritik des Mischneh Thora", MGWJ 79 (1935), 148-159; *idem*, "Maimonides sur l'universalité de la Morale Religieuse", *REJ* 99 (1935), 34-43; *idem*, "A Misné Tóra Forráskritik á Jához", *Magyar Zsido Szemle* 52 (1953), 101-110; *idem*, "Maimonides a Valláselmeteti Ethika egyetmmességérol", *Országos Egyétertes* XI (1935), no. 14-15. These last two Hungarian items I received from secondary sources.

42 M. Guttmann, "Zur Quellenkritik ...", *supra* n.41, at 153.

up by later scholars.[43] As stated above, S. Atlas suspects that this passage has been added by some commentator on the basis of Maimonides' passage in *Hilkhot Melakhim*. It probably escaped Atlas that Maimonides himself cites the *Mishnat R. Eliezer* in his *Sefer hamitsvot* [44] and *Responsa*.[45]

43 B.M. Lewin in J.L. Fishman [Maimon], ed., *Rabbenu Moshe Ben Maimon* (Jerusalem: World Mizrachi Organization, 1935), part I, p.102 (second pagination), citing R. Saul Lieberman; H. Revel, "Towards a clarification of Maimonides' View on Reward and Punishment", *Horeb* II (April 1935), 114 note 10 (Hebrew), citing Prof. Louis Ginzberg.

44 *Sefer hamitsvot*, Pos. Comm. no.5. See R. Hayyim Heller's note in his edition (New York & Jerusalem: Mossard Harav Kook, 1946), 36 note 20.

45 Miamonides' *Responsa*, ed. A. Freimann (Jerusalem: Mekize Nirdamim, 1934), 117, 370; Maimonides' *Responsa*, ed. J. Blau, vol I (Jerusalem: Mekize Nirdamin, 1957), no.148, p.282-84 and notes by Shraga Abramson, *ibid.* vol.III (1961), 163-4.

APPENDIX

THE VARIANT "NOT EVEN ONE OF THEIR WISE MEN" OR "BUT ONE OF THEIR WISE MEN"

The scholarship of *variae lectiones* in rabbinic literature is, relatively speaking, of recent date. The *Mishneh Torah* has only recently been subjected to the study of its variant readings.[46] The fact that Maimonides' ruling in the printed editions of his Code[47] which have the reading *"velo"* ... ("not even one of their wise men") was not supported by rabbinical sources, had, naturally, aroused the interest, if not suspicion, of scholars. This led not only to the consultation of *Mishneh Torah* manuscripts[48] but also to the tracing of this passage in the early medieval Jewish works predating the first edition of the Code in Rome, 1480.

Profiat Duran (died c.1414) seems to have been the first scholar to cite the corrected version, "*ela* ... " ("but one of their wise men") without any reservation.[49] He was followed by Joseph ben Shem Tob (c.1400-c.1460)[50] and R. Moses Alashkar (1466-1542).[51] Alashkar, who could have made use

---

46 We shall limit ourselves to two references: [B. Feigenbaum], *Abweichungen des gedruckten Textes der Jad Hachasaka* (Amsterdamer Ausgabe 1702), von *einer Handschrift aus Anfang des XIV. Jahrhunderts* (Frankfurt a. M.: J. Kauffmann, 1889); *Mishneh Torah* ... according to the [1509] *Constantinople Edition with Variae Lectiones from Unpublished and Early Editions* [by Moshe Hayyim Katzenelenbogen] *and Annotations of Sources* [by Jacob Cohen], ed. Saul Lieberman (Jerusalem: Mossad Harav Kook, 1964). Thus far only *Sefer hamadda* appeared.

47 More than sixty editions have appeared of the *Mishneh Torah*, between 1480 and 1970. See J.I. Dienstag, "Mishneh Torah; bibliography of editions", *Studies in Jewish Bibliography, History and Literature in Honor of I. Edward Kiev* (New York: Ktav, 1977), 21-108.

48 The *Ets Hayyim* manuscript in Amsterdam, of 1282, and Kaufmann manuscript in Budapest, of 1295-6, have the reading *"ela"* (see Jacob Levinger, "Maimonides on Prophecy amongst the Gentiles" (Heb.), *Hamayyan* vol.12, no.1 (Sept.-Oct. 1971), 16-17); the Bodleian and British Museum manuscripts also have the reading " *ela* " (F. Niewöhner, *supra* note 29. at 622). I. Twersky, *Introduction to the Code of Maimonides* (Yale University Press, 1980), 455, claims that practically all texts support the reading "*ela*".

49 Profiat Duran, *Ma'aseh Efod* (Vienna: J. Holzwarth, 1865), Introduction, p.3.

50 Joseph ben Shem-Tob, *Kebod Elohim*, Ferrara, 1555 (unpaged), last leaf. The reading is "*aval*" ("but"), which carries the same meaning. See Schwarzschild, *supra* n.2, at 302.

51 R. Moses Alashkar, *Responsa*, no.117.

of several printed editions of the *Mishneh Torah*,[52] nevertheless cited the reading "but one of their wise men" without pausing for an explanation for his choice of this variant.

It is very ironic that neither R. Jacob Emden nor Mendelssohn who were very agitated by Maimonides' stipulation as cited in the printed editions of the *Mishneh Torah* knew of the correct version as cited by Shem Tob and Alashkar.

During the nineteenth century we find that R. Hirsch Chajes (1805-1855), who knew of Shem Tob's and Alashkar's corrected variant, followed their reading: "but of their wise men."[53] Likewise, Manuel Joel (1826-1890) alluded to Shem Tob's corrected reading[54] and was cited by Hermann Cohen in his polemic against Spinoza in which he accused him of deliberately choosing the less tolerant reading, "*velo* ", of Maimonides' stipulation.[55]

Contrary to the above, David Rosin (1823-1894)[56] insisted on the authenticity of the printed reading: "*velo* ", and was refuted by S. Halberstam (1832-1900).[57] In reply to Halberstam, Rosin reiterated his view on the subject.[58]

The first attempt to draw up a complete list of departures and discrepancies appearing in a fourteenth century manuscript of the *Mishneh Torah* was accomplished by J. Feigenbaum.[59] This manuscript, which was supposed to have belonged to Don Isaac Abravanel, does have the reading "*ela*".

52 The following editions of the *Mishneh Torah* could have been available to R. Moses Alashkar: Rome, 1480; Soncino, 1490; Spain or Portugal, 1491; Spain, 1500?; Constantinople, 1509; Venice, 1524.

53 R. Hirsh Chajes, *supra* note 39.

54 Joël, *supra* n.9, at 56.

55 Cohen, "Spinoza ...", *supra* n.8, at 347-349.

56 D. Rosin, "Maimonides über die Tugendhaften und Weisen unter den Völkern", *Magazin für die Wissenschaft des Judentums* 3 (1876), 206-215.

57 S. Halberstam, *MWJ* 4 (1877), 57-58.

58 D. Rosin, *MWJ* 4 (1897), 111-113.

59 See note 46.

This survey is concluded with an examination of the *Mishneh Torah* manuscript in the Landeskirchl. Archiv in Nuremberg, Germany, which was written in 1389.[60] The reading is "*ela* ."

60 Photocopy listed in State of Israel, Ministry of Education and Culture, The Institute of Hebrew Manuscripts, *List of Photocopies in the Institute,* Part I: *Hebrew Manuscripts in the libraries of Austria and Germany,* by N. Allony and D.S. Loewinger (Jerusalem: Ministry of Education and Culture, Institute of Hebrew Manuscripts, 1957), p.50, no.671.

MAIMONIDES AND NATURAL LAW*

by

OLIVER LEAMAN**

In loving memory of Zoe Ruth Marks

It is not difficult to see why Maimonides is generally credited with hostility towards doctrines of natural law. He frequently comments upon the necessity of basing law upon revelation and disparages the notion of finding out what we ought to do by merely using reason. Yet at the same time it is recognized that he was a fervent advocate of the project of seeking rational explanations for law, explanations which show how such law is directed towards achieving a worthwhile end. As a recent commentator puts it: "For Maimonides, laws are true by divine sanction, but reason discovers their wisdom and intelligibility."[1] This is indeed a tempting conclusion to reach, but it will be argued here that this temptation should be resisted in order that a more accurate view of Maimonides' thought may be established.

Any such attempted reinterpretation would immediately seem to founder on Maimonides' approach to the problem of accounting for the Noahides. Human beings as a whole, the descendants of Noah, are obliged according to the Talmud to adhere to a minimum of seven laws. These involve not indulging in idolatry, blasphemy, murder, adultery, robbery and eating a limb from a living animal, plus the positive injunction to establish courts of justice.[2] The traditional Jewish position seems to be that anyone who conscientiously carries out such instructions is potentially righteous, and "All the righteous men of the nations of the world have a share in the world

* The argument here is developed in more detail in my *Introduction to medieval Islamic philosophy* (Cambridge University Press, 1985).

** Lecturer, Department of Education, Liverpool Polytechnic. I should like to thank Professor Bernard Jackson for his very helpful comments upon an earlier draft and Ms. Jill Stothard for her great bibliographical assistance.

1 I. Twersky, *Introduction to the Code of Maimonides (Mishneh Torah),* (Yale University Press, 1980), 457. The description of laws as true is not a happy one, given that laws are norms, but it does capture the notion that what gives the laws their force is divine authority quite well.

2 *Sanhedrin* 56a.

to come."[3] Any Jewish philosopher interested in expounding a natural law doctrine could be expected to make much of this talmudic discussion, since it appears to claim that one might know what the right course of action is, and moreover follow that course of action, without the benefit of *any*, and certainly without the benefit of the Jewish, revelation at all. It would not matter for a natural law theorist that righteous gentiles felt themselves bound to observe the seven laws as a result of some intrinsically rational features of those laws, while knowing that these laws are part and parcel of the revelation of a particular religious group. Nor does it matter if the righteous gentiles base their adherence to these laws on something other than reason (instinct, perhaps). What *is* important is that they do not base their adherence to the laws on a revelation. This is the case, for instance, for Aquinas. He argues that the essence of law is that "... it is nothing else than an ordinance of reason for the common good, made by him who has care of the community, and promulgated."[4] It would be possible for a righteous gentile to adhere to the seven laws because he sees by the use of reason that they serve the common good while at the same time he may, or may not, believe that those laws have as their source some individual, whether human or divine. As is well known, Maimonides rejects any such option by adding another condition to the Talmudic doctrine. He claims that "Any man who accepts the seven commandments and is meticulous in observing them is thereby one of the righteous of the nations of the world, and he has a portion in the world to come. This is only the case if he accepts them and observes them because God commanded them in the Torah, and taught us through our teacher, Moses, that the children of Noah were commanded to observe them even before the Torah was given. But if he observes them because of his own conclusions based on reason, then he is not a resident-alien and is not one of the righteous of the nations of the world, nor is he one of their wise men."[5]

Maimonides seems to be making two separate points in this passage. He is clearly in no sympathy with the idea that it would be possible for a person to acquire his moral beliefs by the application of reason as such. It may well be that the object of Maimonides' criticism is Saadia Gaon and the latter's attempt at proving the logical necessity of religious prescriptions. Perhaps he is being referred to in the passage "Some of our later sages, who

3 *Sanhedrin* 13:2; 105a.

4 *Summa Theologica* Ia2ae, 90.4.

5 *Mishneh Torah, Melakhim* VIII,11. The translation is taken from M. Fox, "Maimonides and Aquinas on Natural Law", *Diné Israel* III (1972), V-XXXVI.

were infected with the unsound principles of the Mutakallimun, called these rational laws".[6] Saadia's account of the objectivity of moral principles borrows heavily on the rationalism of the Mu'tazilites and is unconvincing.[7] Maimonides may have thought that not only is such an account unconvincing, but that someone who became aware of the weakness of the argument might think that it is only arguments of that sort which justify religious commandments. Such a person might then conclude either (a) that we should acknowledge the bindingness of the commandments but abandon the attempt to find any non-religious reasons for them, or (b) that we should abandon the commandments themselves. Clearly Maimonides would not support either (a) or (b). The other, and more controversial, point which Maimonides has been taken to have made is that anyone who even considers that moral rules are attainable by the use of unaided reason is not just unfit for salvation but not wise either. There has been much discussion over the textual issue of whether the conclusion of the passage above from *Melakhim* should read "... but he is one of their wise men" or "... nor is he one of their wise men", centering on the similarity of the Hebrew terms *velo/ela*. Faur[8] and Fox are in favour of the translation "not" while Katz[9], Lamm and Kirschenbaum,[10] Schwarzchild[11] and Twersky[12] support "but". Both sides make a valid point that the copyists who have produced the manuscripts with the differing Hebrew terms may have decided on which term to use by referring to their understanding of what Maimonides must have meant in that passage. Thus copyists impressed by his "rationalism" would read it as "but" and those otherwise inclined would read it as "not", and so textual arguments about which texts are preferable are unlikely to be profitable. The texts themselves seem to bear evidence of the same sort of argument with which modern commentators are involved.

Let us then consider on non-textual grounds which rendering of the conclusion of the passage would be more likely. Is it the case that

6 *The Eight Chapters of Maimonides on Ethics*, ed. and tr. J. Gorfinkle (New York: AMS Press, 1912), 77.

7 For an acute analysis of Saadia's position on the Mu'tazilites, see M. Fox, "On the Rational Commandments in Saadia's Philosophy: a Reexamination", in *Modern Jewish Ethics*, ed. M. Fox (Ohio State University Press, 1975), 174-87.

8 J. Faur, "La doctrina de la Ley Natural", *Sefarad* XXVII (1967), 239-68, at 259.

9 J. Katz, *Exclusiveness and Tolerance* (New York: Schocken, 1962), 175ff.

10 N. Lamm and A. Kirschenbaum, "Freedom and constraint in the Jewish judicial process", *Cardozo Law Review* I (1979), 99-133.

11 S. Schwarzchild, "Do Noachites have to believe in revelation?", *Jewish Quarterly Review* LII (1962), 297-308; LIII (1962), 30-65.

12 Twersky, *supra* n.1, at 455 n.239, for additional bibliography.

Maimonides thought that any attempt to answer the question "How are we to behave?" by the use of reason alone is evidence not only of unrighteousness but also of a lack of wisdom? Fox is an ardent supporter of this interpretation and it is with his account that this article wishes to take exception. He argues persuasively that Maimonides held the philosophical view that moral rules are conventions which are incapable of being either true or false, and so it would be a mistake to try to establish their truth. An important aspect of Fox's argument is that Maimonides follows Aristotle on this point - "As a follower of the Aristotelian teaching, he quite properly would refuse to recognize a man as wise who could be so confused that he would treat matters of convention or taste as if they were capable of rational demonstrations" (p.XVII). In support of this interpretation Fox cites the well-known passage from the *Nicomachean Ethics* in which Aristotle argues that each universe of discourse has its own criteria of validity and precision, so that it is an error to suppose that one way of thinking (i.e. demonstrative thinking) is applicable to the language of moral rules (NE I ii 1094b 12-28). Fox suggests that for Aristotle it is the mark of the wise person that he is able to distinguish between the different universes of discourse and the differing criteria which are relevant to them. If morality is based upon convention, upon the joint activities of a community, then it might be regarded as a mistake to try to derive morality by the use of demonstrative reason (although Fox ignores the possibility, to which we shall return later, that Maimonides could be arguing that moral rules are demonstrable but demonstration is not their ground of acceptance). Fox's approach to Aristotle's thinking on this issue is not very acute, however. What Aristotle actually says is that we must be subtle in our discussions about the many varieties of moral reaction - "Now fine and just actions, which political science investigates, admit of much variety and fluctuation of opinion, so that they may be thought to exist only by convention, and not by nature" (1094b 14-17). It would be curious to take this passage as showing that Aristotle believes that moral rules are (just) conventions; he is merely pointing out that people often disagree about which actions are good. It does not follow that there is no rational answer to the question of who is right. Aristotle does in fact think that there is an answer, and that many of the objects which people call "good" are only instrumentally so called in reality, because people mistake them for the end of practical action, *eudaimonía* or happiness. We do ordinarily recognize, on Aristotle's account, that some things are, and some things are not, proper objects of pleasure. What we count as pleasant or painful is in terms of the standard of the good man, in exactly the same way as the healthy man is the measure of what is sweet or bitter and of similar matters of taste (NE III3a 25 - bI). Aristotle's entire moral philosophy is constructed around the idea that it is a mistake to separate the uses of reason and desire in explaining the nature of moral choice. In fact, the characteristically Aristotelian virtue of *phronesis* involves both reason (NE II39a 35) and a disposition towards certain realisable types of activity (NE II46a 8). Fox is thus quite mistaken in thinking that Maimonides could have correctly obtained the doctrine that moral rules are not demonstrable from Aristotle.

Of course, it may well be that Maimonides does not follow Aristotle on this, but Fox might be correct in thinking that Maimonides held it to be foolish to try to derive morality by the use of just reason. And there can be no question but that Maimonides does make a distinction between claims which are accepted as a result of reason and those which are based upon tradition. He claims that the first two of the Ten Commandments concerning the existence and unity of God are apprehensible by reason and not through prophecy. But "As for the other commandments, they belong to the class of generally accepted opinions and those adopted in virtue of tradition, not to the class of intellecta" (MN II,33 p.364).[13] Fox thinks that this is a "categorical rejection of natural law theory" (p.xx). Maimonides puts his point even stronger in the second chapter of Part I of the *Guide of the Perplexed* where he discusses the nature of Adam's and Eve's punishment. Adam had achieved the true perfection of human beings in the development of his intellect, and yet he did not know that it is shameful to be naked. How could Adam not know that if his intellect was so fully developed? The answer seems to be that the question of how, if at all, Adam ought to dress is not the sort of question which would be asked by someone at the summit of human intellectual powers, since it is not a question which has a determinate answer:[14] "Through the intellect one distinguishes between truth and falsehood, and that was found in Adam in its perfection and integrity. Beautiful and ugly, on the other hand, belong to the things generally accepted as known, not to those cognized by intellect" (MN I, 2 p.24). It was only when Adam and Eve were toppled from the pinnacle of intellectual achievement that they considered it ugly to expose their genitals. The use of reason could not by itself discover that such a practice is ugly. Maimonides seems to be making a very strong point here, namely, that not only *would*

13 Maimonides, *Guide of the Perplexed*, tr. S. Pines (University of Chicago Press, 1963). All page references are to this translation (abbreviated MN).

14 For a full account of this passage see L.V. Berman, "Maimonides on the Fall of Man", *AJS Review* 5 (1980), 1-15.

we not arrive at such conventions by the use of reason alone, but also we *could* not.

To conclude, though, that Maimonides thought that there is no way in which moral attitudes and practices can be justified by the use of reason would be to go too far. Maimonides does think that reasons can be provided for a great many religious commandments and that it is incumbent upon us, in so far as we are capable of the enterprise, to seek those reasons. He explicitly states that " ... all the statutes (*hukkim*) will show to all the nations that they have been given with wisdom and understanding. Now, if there is a thing for which no reason is known and that does not either procure something useful or ward off something harmful, why should one say of one who believes in it or practises it that he is wise and understanding and of great worth?" (MN III,3I p.524). It is not sufficient to discover that people on the whole find nakedness repellent, or do not approve of murder; although both these propositions may be true, they do not of themselves justify injunctions against nakedness or murder. Maimonides seeks to provide a rational basis for moral practices and religious commandments, a basis which shows why God devised rules of such-and-such a form and what *end* such rules serve. So on the one hand we find Maimonides apparently rejecting the idea that we can use reason to justify moral practices (as in the discussion of Adam and Eve), while on the other hand he insists that religious statutes would not be valuable if they could not be shown rationally to have some important function. Indeed, the leitmotiv of the whole third part of the *Guide* is the necessity of rationally accounting for the different kinds of statutes which are found in Jewish law. One way of resolving this apparent contradiction is by looking more closely at the way in which the term "reason" is being used by Maimonides.

Why does Maimonides think that the ethical and aesthetic features of objects of thought debar those objects from being the objects of demonstrative reasoning? This doctrine really follows from Maimonides' interpretation of Aristotle. For the latter contemplation is the real end of human life, of those human beings who are able by their intellectual attributes to realise it. It is the self-sufficiency of a contemplative existence which makes it the ultimate end. Such an existence has no further end and is productive of a type of happiness not available by those limited to the happiness derivable from virtuous behaviour (NE X viii II78a, 20-23). Not to involve oneself in this "divine" activity is to deny one's true self and to live the life of someone other than oneself (NE X vii). These Aristotelian points are worth making because they emphasize how for Maimonides the ethical virtues are largely instrumental to the end of preparing someone to set up for a contemplative life; they are doubtless one step up from the virtues of a healthy régime as a stepping stone to the *autarchia* of the contemplative life. Aristotle contrasts the life of man in society with the life of man outside society, in a state of abstraction from the world of matter and everyday communal activities. In such a condition of separateness the moral rules which control our social behaviour have no purchase.[15] That is why Adam before the Fall did not consider nakedness an objectionable thing. The latter eight of the Ten Commandments are social regulations and so are not appropriate objects of thought for the asocial contemplative person. Maimonides expresses his position clearly in this passage: "It has already been demonstrated that man has two perfections: a first perfection, which is the perfection of the body, and an ultimate perfection, which is the perfection of the soul. The first perfection consists in being healthy and in the very best bodily state, and this is only possible through his finding the things necessary for him whenever he seeks them. These are his food and all the other things needed for the governance of his body ... This cannot be achieved in any way by one isolated individual. For an individual can only attain all this through a political association .. His ultimate perfection is to become rational in actu ... this would consist in knowing everything concerning all the beings that it is within the capacity of man to know in accordance with his ultimate perfection. It is clear that to this ultimate perfection there do not belong either actions or moral qualities and that it consists only of opinions toward which speculation has led and that investigation has rendered compulsory" (MN III,27 pp.510-11). Why cannot one use reason to determine issues in the field of moral conduct, on Maimonides' account? Is it because moral propositions are subjective, matters of opinion and taste, conventions, as Fox and the anti-natural law school of interpreters have it? Must we agree with Berman's account of the fall of Adam where he asserts that "Maimonides ends this section with a verse from Psalms, 'Adam, unable to dwell in dignity, is like the beasts that speak not.' Adam finally ends up an irrational animal"?[16] An affirmative answer is not inevitable. Those who support an affirmative answer are usually operating with a crude rational/irrational dichotomy with reference to the making of judgments which is foreign to the Aristotelian flavour of Maimonides' thinking here. For Maimonides moral reasoning is not of the category of scientific or

---

15 It is clear that Maimonides is closely following in the steps of his Muslim predecessors, al-Fārābī and ibn Bājja. See A. Altmann, "Maimonides' 'four perfections'", *Israel Oriental Studies* 2 (1972), 15-24. The notion of having duties to oneself, outside society, was not considered by those philosophers.

16 Berman, *supra* n.14, at 12.

demonstrative reasoning, proceeding from necessarily true propositions to a necessarily true conclusion. It is rather probable or dialectical, since it takes as its premisses the nature of a particular society and of the people in it, and then derives conclusions concerning how they might best live together in such conditions. Such reasoning would be pointless were there to be no objects in existence which such concepts of society and its citizens could successfully describe. In contrast, purely demonstrative reasoning is uninterested in whether any objects in fact instantiate the concepts involved, since it works at a level of abstraction where no such considerations have any force. The contemplative thinker, given the opportunity to choose between these two different subject matters, necessary propositions as premisses or merely probable premisses, would choose the former since he will then be dealing with a much higher level of truth than if he thinks about propositions which describe the contingent features of the world.[17]

Let us give an example to show how Maimonides distinguishes between dialectical and demonstrative reasoning. In his account of the features of a *nomos* as opposed to divine law he argues: "Accordingly, if you find a law the whole end of which [is] directed exclusively towards the ordering of the city and of its circumstances and the abolition in it of injustice and oppression; and if in that law attention is not at all directed toward speculative matters, no heed is given to the perfecting of the rational faculty, and no regard is accorded to the opinions being correct or faulty - the whole purpose of that law being, on the contrary, the arrangement, in whatever this may be brought about, of the circumstances of people in their relations with one another and provision for their obtaining ... happiness - you must know that that law is a *nomos* ... If, on the other hand, you find a law all of whose ordinances are due to attention being paid ... to the soundness of the circumstances pertaining to the body and also to the soundness of belief ... this law is divine" (MN II,40 pp.383-4). The laws of the Greeks, the *nomoi*, had as their end the proper regulation of society, namely, the ordering of a great number of citizens of widely different characteristics and perceived ends. Given the possible variety of human behaviour and yet the necessity for human beings to live in society (MN II,40 pp.381-2) it is no mean feat to arrive even at a *nomos*, limited though such a law is in its contribution to

17 By "contingent" Maimonides includes much less than a contemporary philosopher would.

the development of our contemplative potential.[18] The devising of such a law will clearly be a rational process and will take into account the individuals who are to be covered by it, and the sorts of happiness which are consequently possible for them. The constitution of such a law is by no means a matter for arbitrary choice or taste; it is not subjective or arational or irrational. Legislators who are not prophets are obliged to reconcile differing civil interests in order to preserve, or establish, social harmony, and clearly such legislation involves the use of reasoning, albeit not its application to necessarily true propositions. Such a *nomos* accepts the unsophisticated and restricted account of happiness as the end of human action and does not lead those subject to it to any higher knowledge of God or the nature of reality. It is based upon dealing with people as they are rather than with them as they might become.

The relevance of this discussion to the argument over the *ela* as against *velo* reading to describe Noahides who use reason to determine how they are to behave should be evident. Maimonides does think that reason plays an important part in determining what form our actions ought to take, and even if we are without a revelation, or if we do not accept one when offered it, we are still in a position to accept "second best" in the form of a *nomos* instead of the *Torah*. The acceptance and design of this law involves the use of reason, and it is a step on the route to the paradigmatically reasonable existence, the contemplative life. Maimonides would not deny the possibility of someone being a wise man *(hakham)* without being righteous *(hasid)*.[19] He famously argues that it is desirable for the reasons for the commandments to be sought. He makes a distinction here: "Those commandments whose utility is clear to the multitude are called *mishpatim*, while those whose utility is not clear to the multitude are called *hukkim*" (MN III, 26 p.507). The contrast here is between those religious commandments whose utility is not clear because they deal with aspects of ritual which seem to bear no relation to anything worthy of legislation, and those commandments which seem to have an obvious point. As is well-known, Maimonides provides a remarkable anthropological argument based upon the relative stability of human nature to account for the usefulness of the *hukkim* in weaning people away from idolatrous beliefs and practices.

18 In the translation "*nomos* " is read for *nāmūs* and *shari'a nāmūsiyya*. See Pines p.383. For an excellent account of the *nomos/Torah* distinction, see E. Rosenthal, "Torah and nomos in medieval Jewish philosophy", *Studies in Rationalism, Judaism and Universalism*, ed. R. Loewe (London: Routledge & Kegan Paul, 1966), 215-31.

19 For more examples suggesting that Maimonides held this position throughout his works, see Lamm and Kirschenbaum, *supra* n.10, at 118.

He suggests that the statutes surrounding the practice of sacrifice are a divine ruse which oppose the previous point of such practices by stealthily undermining them. In the third part of the *Guide* Maimonides spends a lot of effort in explaining the point of many apparently obscure statutes by appealing to the tardiness involved in any change in human behaviour from its primitive Sabian past to a future level of Jewish sophistication. It is important to note that he does not think that it is thus possible to defend the *detail* of all the statutes; whether it is a ram or a lamb which is to be sacrificed, for instance, cannot be justified in the general way that sacrifices as such can be (MN III, 26 p.509).[20] We might be sceptical of the need for such statutes, but this is because "... the doctrines of the Sabians are remote from us today, the chronicles of those times are likewise hidden from us today. Hence if we knew them and were cognizant of the events that happened in those days, we would know in detail the reasons of many things mentioned in the Torah" (MN III,50 p.615).

It might be suggested, though, that there is in that case nothing wrong in sacrificing one type of animal instead of the legally specified type, since there is no a priori reason why the legally specified type of animal was selected instead of some animal rather similar. Further, it might also be suggested that if one is a person who has eradicated all vestiges of polytheism from his mentality, then it is not necessary for such a person to obey the rather tiresome ceremonial and antique laws specified by religious law. There should be no argument that Maimonides himself would not accept such a view; in fact, one of the criteria which he lays down as evidence of a false messiah is of a person who suggests that even tiny changes in the law are desirable.[21] A defence of Maimonides' position here on philosophical lines would take the position that the development of personal virtue depends upon the training of one's personal traits in the direction of ultimate perfection such that rigorously following the divine law in every little particular is to tend to inculcate in oneself the habit of obedience to God. But could it not be, one might ask, that a person could achieve ultimate perfection, or at least the secondary perfection of moral virtue,

20 One of the best accounts of Maimonides' approach is to be found in A. Funkenstein, "Gesetz und Geschichte. Zur historisierenden Hermeneutik bei Moses Maimonides und Thomas von Aquin", *Viator* I (1970), 147-78.

21 Maimonides, *'Iggeret Teman*, ed. A. Hankin (New York: American Academy for Jewish Research, 1952), Chapter 4. It is worth noting, though, that Maimonides suggests that were Moses to appear in his time there would not be a need for a sacrificial cult (MN III,32 p.526) since most people did not require it at that point in time (MN III,47 p.592).

without following all these rules and regulations? Take an example which was at one time popular with British moral philosophers. Suppose that there is a general rule that no-one should cross the lawn in the quad, because if everyone does so then the grass will suffer. It would not affect the quality of the lawn if just one person (like me) occasionally crosses it, provided that my behaviour does not encourage others to infringe the rule (as would be the case if my crossing took place under the cover of darkness, for instance). The point which Maimonides would want to make is that what is also of importance in this case is the effect that the flouting of the rule has on *me*, on my disposition to keep rules which are on the whole well worth keeping. What is of importance is not the precise *content* of the divine laws (i.e. the *hukkim*) but the *form* of such regulations is designed, according to Maimonides, to bring about a virtuous character, strengthening the tendency to do right and weakening the contrary disposition. It is obvious to anyone, according to Maimonides, how some *mitsvot* serve this end; these are the *mishpatim*. Such laws have no non-rational details, they outline the form which any civilized form of social life must take. These laws do not require the historical rationales which are provided for the *hukkim*, dealing e.g. with laws of uncleanness and sacrifices, since these laws are replete with non-rational details which themselves cannot be grounded in the same way as the form of such laws can. But although the content is not logically determined by the form to be exactly as it is in law, it is immutable: "... governance of the law ought to be absolute and universal, including everyone, even if it is suitable only for certain individuals and not suitable for others; for if it were made to fit individuals, the whole would be corrupted and you would make of it something that varies" (MN III,34 p.535). That is, it is of greatest benefit to have universal laws which are designed to be of utility to the largest number of people; everyone is then obliged to obey such laws even if a particular individual on a certain occasion finds that such an obligation is undesirable. Such an individual might be capable of doing the right action and adopting the correct opinion (the two aspects of divine law) without on a particular occasion obeying a religious statute, yet he would be at fault were he to reject the statute on that occasion. For "... all the practices of the worship, such as reading the Torah, prayer, and the performance of the other commandments, have only the end of training you to occupy yourself with His commandments ... rather than with matters pertaining to this world" (MN III,51 p.622).

It might be thought that Maimonides comes out quite clearly against a natural law position by his insistence that we base our obedience to law on divine authority rather than the use of reason. The very minimum that a natural law theory entails is that it is possible to observe nature and determine the form of legislation accordingly without any appeal to the character of the supernatural authority. Indeed, we may conclude by the use of reason that a particular aspect of the law was not devised with us in mind, and yet we would nevertheless be obliged to obey it, given that it is of the nature of law to be entirely general and without exceptions in terms of place, time and person. And in Maimonides' comments on the problem of the Noahides he clearly asserted that people can acquire no obligations by the use of reason alone. So the conclusion that he was antagonistic to the natural law tradition, in common with the general body of Jewish medieval philosophers, appears to be well founded. But if we compare him with one of his Islamic predecessors who definitely took an anti-natural law position, such as al-Ghazāli, we can see how different Maimonides' position is from that of the anti-natural law theorist. In classical Islam the notion of obligatory acts (acts which are *wājib)* is equivalent to whatever is commanded by God and rewarded or punished accordingly; this was the doctrine of the main Sunnite legal traditions established by Shāfi'ī and ibn Hanbal and supported by the theology of Ash'arī. They were strongly opposed to the Mu'tazilite idea that certain acts just were obligatory as a result of their properties, and God laid them down as requisite because they are the sorts of acts which they are. The notion that there is anything objective in acts which necessarily makes them obligatory is a doctrine which al-Ghazāli attacked constantly. He also had no time for the idea that God has ends, and that one of these ends is human welfare. But the Mu'tazilite position which particularly angered him, and remarkably so considering the paucity of Mu'tazilite influence in the Eastern Mediterranean at that time, was that we can know some of our obligations by the independent use of reason, regardless of the aid of revelation. This is because some moral properties of actions are objective and really apply to certain kinds of phenomena in the world. Clearly the Mu'tazilite doctrine comes nearer to natural law theory than doctrines of ethical subjectivism, and there is no doubt that Maimonides distances himself from some of the beliefs of the Mu'tazila (e.g. see MN III,17 pp.469-71). It is also true that Maimonides seems to share al-Ghazāli's view of the nature of moral propositions as subjective and only really obligatory if commanded by God.

Nevertheless, Maimonides is upholding very different philosophical principles than al-Ghazāli, in spite of the superficial resemblance between their views. As we argued earlier, interpretations of Maimonides which make him out to think that moral propositions are non-cognitive are mistaken. The final end of human beings is the life of contemplation, but the acquisition of moral virtues is a sine qua non for such a life. In the introduction to *Seder Zera'im* from the *Commentary on the Mishnah* Maimonides compares the philosopher who has no control over his passions with the unlearned man who possesses the moral virtues, and claims that the latter does not achieve perfection and yet is more perfect than the former.[22] Moral opinions are opinions which are generally accepted (Aristotle's *endoxa)* and which regulate political life at the same time as preparing for our final perfection, theoretical knowledge of things as they really are Moral opinions have as their function the regulation of our political life on harmonious lines, and there is no reason to think that ratiocination plays no part in the discovery of such opinions and their application to our lives. To be sure, the reasoning involved would be of a lower order than the reasoning which characterizes pure contemplation, but it would still qualify as reasoning. The results of the reasoning, the moral opinions, would be objective in the sense that they would accurately describe how people could live together successfully; that is all that we can expect from a law which is not divine. That is the point of the passage from *Melakhim* which was quoted right at the beginning. People who use reason to work out how they ought to live are no doubt more perfect than people who do not even establish a system of accepted moral opinions, yet their law is entirely at the level of *nomos* and is not divine, and so they do not merit a divine reward. They might merit such a reward were they to realize that the *nomos* which they accept is a part of a divine system, i.e. if they have correct opinions about the *nomoi* which they use. But they regard the law as entirely a vehicle for prudential reasoning, for reconciling interests in a mutually agreeable manner, and so they have a merely superficial view of how they ought to live. Maimonides' criticism of such legislators and their obligations is not that they have tried to discover how they ought to behave by the use of their reason. It is that after they have discovered how they ought to act by the use of their reason they stop and feel satisfied that at that stage they have discovered all that there is to be discovered. And yet, from an Aristotelian point of view, they have still to achieve the greater perfection of the contemplative life, and from the Jewish point of view, they have yet to appreciate the religious nature of the world and its maker. Maimonides, who incorporated both these points of view, was clearly very unhappy at the prospect of people feeling that they had come to their limit at the level of ethical existence; this is why he stresses the necessity for them to appreciate the divine nature of their

22 *Perush Ha-Mishna le-Rabbi Moshe b. Maimon*, ed. S. Sassoon (Copenhagen, 1956), Plate 31.

existence if they are to hold correct opinions and merit divine reward. He is not suggesting that reason is not capable of discovering how we ought to act, but rather that this discovery can only give us partial information about our nature as human beings and the world in which we live.

Maimonides is scathing towards the doctrine, popular with al-Ghazāli and his followers, that it is not possible to find a rational explanation for God's creation of the world taking a particular form (MN III,31 pp.523-4). Maimonides is convinced that all the commandments have utility which we should attempt to grasp. Of course, the way in which he explains these rules does not always allow for a perspicuous explanation of each iota of the law. As we have seen, only general reasons can be given for rules having certain forms. Given his theory that many rules are based on the effectiveness of slowly changing idolatrous practices by pretending to incorporate some of their features, he can always appeal to the fact that we do not now know enough about the idolatrous practices to see in detail the justification for the present law (see again MN III,50 p.615). This is an important point. Maimonides makes clear his opinion that there is no reason *in principle* why we should not know the rationale for the *form* of every regulation in the law. As it happens, we are too distant from the events which led God to construct laws in the way he did to appreciate all the precise causes, yet we may obtain some glimmering of their foundations by considering the principles which have been used in the divine legislation. Al-Ghazāli argues that we are obliged to base law on tradition *(nakl)* rather than on reason *('akl)* since the latter is no guide at all in deciding which laws are to be obeyed.[23] Maimonides' view is very different. Reason is a guide, but an insufficient one, not because of any limitations inherent in that mode of thinking, but rather because of the limitations in the data which that mode of thought can have as its objects from a human point of view. We are told by Maimonides to seek the causes of the commandments because we are entitled to assume that every commandment has a cause and that in principle we can establish the general nature of that cause, and that we can derive the cause from our knowledge of God as a wise and purposive ruler. This latter piece of information can be used to see how reasons may be provided for the detail of the law: "It is through ... wisdom, in an unrestricted sense, that the rational matter we receive from the law through tradition, is demonstrated" (MN III,54 p.633).

[23] For an account of al-Ghazali's ethical thought see his *al-Iktisād fi al-i'tik ād,* ed. I. Çubukçu and H. Atay (Ankara, 1962).

This point, that the law is demonstrable, is highly significant. It might be argued, though, that since Maimonides insists upon the importance of tradition and revelation as the first steps in our acquisition of understanding, he cannot then go on to adhere to a natural law doctrine. That is, such a doctrine has as its main feature the idea that reason can unaided observe nature and then discover what form legislation ought to take. It is true that some natural law doctrines take this form, in particular those adopted by the Stoics and Cicero which are commonly contrasted with Maimonides. But there is considerable variety in what could count as a natural law doctrine. It has been argued that Maimonides cannot hold such a doctrine because of his account of the subjectivity and arationality of moral judgments. This argument has been shown to be false. It has been argued that Maimonides cannot hold a natural law doctrine because he insists that tradition is a more complete and perfect source of knowledge about ourselves and the world than demonstrative reason (see his account of the order of explanation of the law at MN III,54, pp.633-4). But a natural law doctrine does not have to accept that every significant fact is attainable by us through reason alone. If we as finite creatures are limited to a particular point of view, then we must rely upon something other than reason to acquire knowledge concerning what lies beyond our horizon. There is no reason why this doctrine should not become part of a natural law theory: "In so far as any common core can be found to the principal versions of the natural law theory, it seems to amount to the statement that the basic principles of morals and legislation are, *in some sense or other,* objective, accessible to reason and based on human nature."[24]

Maimonides account of divine law satisfies all these requirements. It is because human beings have such a constant nature which takes a great deal of time to alter that the law takes the conservative form it does. The law is then based upon human nature, and it would be strange if it were not thus based since both the law and human nature are presumably divine artifacts. Now, it might be suggested that practically all Jewish law is meant to apply exclusively to Jews and so there is no point in appealing to the universality of a common "human nature" in analysing this law. Yet Maimonides in the *Guide* describes his conception of human nature as such, not just the characteristics of human beings who happen to be Jews. He certainly did not hold that: "... one eternal unchangeable law will be valid for all nations and all times."[25] Ciceronian natural law doctrine is not, however, the only

24 D.J. O'Connor, *Aquinas and Natural Law* (London: Macmillan, 1967), 57.
25 Cicero, *De re publica* III xxii, 33.

available variety of that doctrine. For Maimonides, given a notion of a common human nature, people who accept the Jewish revelation are in a position to reap divine reward as a result of obeying a system of regulations designed to perfect them in so far as their particular characteristics make this attainable. It is worth emphasizing that Maimonides' account of human nature makes possible his account of seeking reasons for the regulations which encompass the lives of Jews; i.e. it is because human beings share certain common characteristics that *Jewish* human beings are obliged to obey a certain sort of law.

It is necessary to face the question yet again of why so many of the commentators on Maimonides are convinced that he is a great opponent of natural law theory. There are no doubt many explanations in terms of the emphasis upon Stoic natural law theory, upon the conventional rather than objective theory of ethical judgments which he is taken to have held, and upon his denial of religious merit to the beliefs and actions of the Noahides who base their moral principles solely upon reason. But the main source of this mistaken view of Maimonides lies in a lack of understanding of how Aristotle influenced his thinking. In his account of human perfection and the moral virtues Maimonides was adhering to an orthodox Aristotelian position. An Aristotelian would tend to think of the world exhibiting teleological properties which we can discover, and such properties would be equally observable in human beings. The answer to the question of how we ought to live is found by considering what our nature or function is and then determining which actions are appropriate to the realization of our end, the end of human beings who, in principle at least, are capable of moral behaviour and the "divine" application of contemplative understanding to our existence. Given this sort of intellectual background, it was "natural" for Maimonides to hold a natural law doctrine. It may well be the case that the rest of the body of Jewish medieval philosophers did not hold such a doctrine; this would be explicable in terms of their general lack of adherence to Aristotle. It is time to reassess radically Maimonides' position on natural law.

TUR, PREFACE TO *HOSHEN MISHPAT* - TRANSLATION AND COMMENTARY

by

LOUIS JACOBS*

Jacob b. Asher (d. 1340), compiler of the *Tur*, prefaces the section of this Code which deals with jurisprudence, *Hoshen Mishpat*, with a statement on the importance of justice for the social order and the nature of the authority vested in the judges. As a summary of the forms and attitudes which prevailed in the middle ages, influencing Jewish life in subsequent ages down to the present, this statement is important for a study of traditional Jewish legal philosophy. The section is here translated into English for the first time (the words in parenthesis, including the source references, are explanatory and are not in the original). The translation is followed by annotations.

The section *Hoshen Mishpat* of the *Tur* (and the *Shulhan Arukh)* is different from the other three sections (*Orah Hayyim; Yoreh De'ah* and *Even ha-'Ezer)* not only in the subject matter itself (this naturally differs from section to section) but also in the approach to this subject matter. Although in a general sense all four sections can be said to belong to Jewish law *(Halakhah)*, jurisprudence, the topic with which *Hoshen Mishpat* deals, is in a category of its own, that of *dine mamonot* (laws of property, 'civil law') and kindred subjects. If the analogy of the tree is allowed , one can say that *dine mamonot* form a separate tree while the topics treated in the other three sections form three branches of the same tree.

The basic difference lies in the place of human reasoning in determining *Halakhah*, conceived of traditionally as divinely revealed law. Human reasoning has a far greater role to play in jurisprudence than it has in other aspects of *Halakhah*. It is true that even in these other areas - those we might refer to as the dogmatic - human reasoning is applied to the revealed law. That this is so is obvious to every student of Talmud and *Halakhah*, as witnessed by some of the hermeneutical principles such as *kal vahomer; binyan av* and the Amoraic *sevara* and, indeed, in the whole idea of debate and discussion. But whereas in dogmatic *Halakhah* the basis is the revealed law, with human reasoning secondary to it and around it, in jurisprudence reasoning is normally the basis of the laws themselves. The details of what is included in a sale and what is not, of contractual obligations, of transfer of property, of mine and thine generally, as discussed in *Bava Kamma, Bava*

Metsia and *Bava Batra*, are, with few exceptions, based on human reasoning rather than on the exegesis of Scriptural verses.

It is noteworthy how different are the discussions in the three *Bavot* from, say, the discussions regarding forbidden food in tractate *Hullin*. In the latter, the main role of human reasoning is to discover how the Scriptural laws are to be understood and applied. The laws themselves are in Scripture. The same applies, to give another illustration, to the discussions on what constitutes forbidden work on the Sabbaths and Festivals in tractates *Shabbat* and *Betsah*. In connection with jurisprudence, on the other hand, the laws themselves are based on human reasoning, the Scriptural verses speaking not of the laws themselves but of broad principles such as the eighth commandment and the many injunctions to practise justice and pursue righteousness.

There is a great deal to be said for the solution provided by the famous Rosh Yeshivah, R. Simeon Skopf (*Sha'are Yosher*, Warsaw, 1927, Sha'ar V, chapter 1) to the old problem why a doubt regarding Biblical law is treated strictly (*safek deoraita lehumra*) and yet doubt in cases of ownership are treated leniently in favour of the one who has possession (*safek mamona lekula*). Why should the prohibition 'Thou shalt not steal' be treated more leniently than the prohibition of, say, forbidden food? Rabbi Skopf's reply is that in the case of forbidden food the prohibition comes first and the discussion of the procedural rules afterwards. The prohibition is there in Scripture. It is thus logically significant to discuss which procedure is to be adopted where there is a doubt whether the given law applies, e.g. where there is a piece of meat which may be either permitted meat or forbidden and it is not known which. Here the procedure is stated, that the stricter view is to be followed and the meat is forbidden. With regard to *dine mamonot*, on the other hand, the law follows on the procedural rules. The law here, as in other systems of jurisprudence, depends on the consensus of the authorities. It is logically meaningless to discuss what is to be done where there is doubt as to whether 'Thou shalt not steal' applies since what constitutes 'stealing' has first to be determined and determined, moreover, by the same authorities who lay down the procedural rules in cases of doubt. There cannot, in effect, be any doubt in the matter of 'Thou shalt not steal' since this prohibition cannot be invoked until the authorities have done their work. When the legal authorities have decided in each case then we have either a definite prohibition or no prohibition at all.

The matter is, however, rather more complicated in that the difference between what we have called dogmatic law and jurisprudence is not categorical but one of where the main emphasis lies. There are, after all,

Scriptural rules regarding *dine mamonot* too, such as the particular types of fine to be imposed, the disqualification of certain types of witnesses on theological grounds and the different penalties for the goring ox that is otherwise docile and for the goring of the *muad* ox. (That these also have had a history and that their development can be traced to some extent is not germane to our discussion of the laws as they appear in the Codes.) The ordination of judges (*semikhah)* belongs in the category of this dogmatic aspect of *dine mamonot*. No matter how learned in the law a judge may be, he cannot function as a judge unless he has been ordained as such and this rule is considered by the Rabbis to be Scriptural. Here the law of *semukhin* was not invented by the Rabbis (at least, not as it is discussed by the legal authorities rather than among the historians). The discussions of the talmudic Rabbis and their successors on *semikhah* is of the same order as their discussions concerning which food is permitted and which forbidden.

We can see, from the above, that the *Tur* in his preamble to *Hoshen Mishpat* considers both these aspects of *dine mamonot*. First, he observes the non-dogmatic basis of the majority of these laws. Justice, truth and peace are necessary if human society is to endure. No appeal to revelation is required. The appeal is to the innate good sense of human beings as human beings, not as Jews who believe in revelation. But he then considers the dogmatic aspect and how human reasoning has operated here to make the law viable. It is perhaps no accident that the *Tur* sees fit to provide this kind of preamble only to *Hoshen Mishpat*. All this is strictly relevant to the question that has been aired in issues of this journal, whether there exists such an entity as *Mishpat Ivri* as distinct from other branches of *Halakhah* and whether there is any point in examining *Mishpat Ivri* is isolation from *Halakhah* in general.

TUR HOSHEN MISHPAT I

'Rabban Simeon b. Gamaliel says: The world endures by virtue of three things: justice, peace and truth' (*Avot* 1:18). Rabbi Jonah (Gerondi, c.1200-1263) of blessed memory comments that this does not mean the world was created for the sake of these three things since, at the beginning of the chapter (*Avot* 1:2), it says, the world *stands* upon three things and they are not the three mentioned here.[1] Rather, first it is said, the world was created for the sake of three things: the Torah, service in the Temple and benevolence. For the sake of the Torah, as it is written: 'The Lord possessed me in the beginning of his way' (*Proverbs* 8: 22), the Torah declaring: I have been created before all creatures and they were brought into being for my sake. And so, too, for the sake of service in the Temple; the Holy One, blessed be He, choosing Israel of all the nations and choosing the Temple of all places wherein they should worship Him, from which it follows that for its sake the world was created. And so, too, with regard to benevolence, the attribute of love, which makes men acceptable to God, blessed be He. But here it says 'the world endures', meaning, after it has been created it endures because of these three.[2] The world endures because of the judges who adjudicate between man and his fellow, otherwise whoever is the more powerful would prevail. And so, too, with regard to truth, as the Rabbis say (*Shabbat* 104a): 'Falsehood has no legs', whereas truth is the foundation and the supreme coagulent for all things. And so too, with regard to peace, as the Rabbis say (*Avot* 3:2): 'Pray for the peace of the ruling power for where it not for the fear of the ruling power man would swallow up his neighbour alive'. This is the meaning of the rabbinic saying (*Shabbat* 10a): 'Whoever renders a just and true decision it is as if he had become a partner with God in the work of creation'. For the Holy One, blessed be He, created the world that it might endure and the wicked who rob and plunder destroy it by their deeds, as we find in connection with the generation of the deluge. Their fate was sealed only because of the robbery of which they were guilty, as it is written: 'for the earth is filled with violence through them' (*Genesis* 6:13), the verse concluding: 'and behold, I will destroy them with the earth'. It follows that the judge who shatters the high hand of the wicked, taking from them ill-gotten gains and returning these to their rightful owners, causes the world to endure, thus bringing to fruition the divine will for the world to endure. Thus the judge is a partner of the Holy One, blessed be He.

God only knew Abraham, calling him friend, because he walked in the way of justice and trained his children in that way, as it is written: 'For I know him, that he will command his children and his household after him, and they shall keep the way of the Lord, to do righteousness and justice' (*Genesis* 18:19). Moses our teacher, on whom be peace, master of all the prophets, took Jethro's advice regarding justice, to appoint judges to warn Israel and to command them concerning justice and the Lord concurred with his counsel. Joshua, after having made a covenant with Israel to serve the Lord, concluded his words with the idea of justice, as it is written: 'So Joshua made a covenant with the people that day, and set them a statute and judgement in Shechem' (*Joshua* 24:25), since justice is the foundation and the supreme principle in God's service. After him, every judge judged his people, turning them away from the evil way to the worship of God to walk in the way of Abraham by practising righteousness and justice. As a result they were saved from their enemies; until there arose Samuel, a prophet faithful to God. He judged Israel all the days of his life, travelling around year by year to Beth-El, Mitspah and Gilgal, judging Israel in all these places. The Sages remark (based on *Shabbat* 56a) that he did not journey by the same route each year so that he was able to turn the heart of all the people to the worship of God, to walk in the way of Abraham our father, on whom be peace. He anointed David as king of Israel. David, too, walked in God's way more than any leader before him, as it is written: 'And David executed judgement and justice to all his people' (*2 Samuel* 8:15) 'and Joab repaired the rest of the city' (*1 Chronicles* 11:8), upon which our Sages of blessed memory comment (based on *Sanhedrin* 49a): Joab repaired the rest of the city through the merit of David who practised judgement and justice. There arose in his stead his son, the beloved of the Lord, who loved to walk in the statutes of David and his father, asking of the Lord an understanding heart to judge his people that they might understand the difference between good and evil. It was pleasing to the Lord that he had made this request and He gave him so wise and understanding a heart that there was none like unto him before him and none that came after him. And Jehoshaphat, too, who walked in the ways of his fathers and whose heart was lifted up proudly in the ways of the Lord, strengthened himself in the idea of justice by appointing judges. 'And he said to the judges: Take heed what ye do; for ye judge not for man, but for the Lord, who is with you in the judgement' (*2 Chronicles* 19:6). And also of Josiah Scripture testifies: 'And like unto him there was no king before him, that turned unto the Lord with all his heart' (*2 Kings* 23:25), which the Rabbis understood to mean (*Shabbat* 56b) that in connection with every decision he had rendered before he had reached the age of 18 he returned the money to its owner out of his own pocket. And King Messiah, may he be revealed speedily in our day, is also praised by Scripture in connection with the idea of justice, as it is written: 'But with righteousness shall he judge the poor, and decide with equity for the meek of the land...' (*Isaiah* 11:5).

Corresponding to the great reward for the practice of justice is the punishment of one who sets it aside and perverts it, as we have learnt (*Avot* 5:8): 'The sword comes into the world because of the postponement of justice and the perversion of justice'. And David declared: 'I have done justice and righteousness; leave me not to mine oppressors' (*Psalm* 119:121), implying that one who refrains from practising justice will be delivered into the hands of his oppressors. And Jerusalem would not have been destroyed nor would Israel have been exiled were it not that they had set justice aside, as it is said: 'She that was full of justice, righteousness lodged in her, but now murderers' (*Isaiah* 1:21). And it is written: 'They judge not the fatherless, neither doth the cause of the widow come unto them' (*Isaiah* 1:23), followed by: 'Ah, I will ease Me of Mine adversaries, and avenge Me of Mine enemies' (*Isaiah* 1:24). And it is by virtue of justice that she will be redeemed in the future, as it is written: 'Zion shall be redeemed with justice, and they that return of her with righteousness' (*Isaiah* 1:27). And it is written: 'Seek justice, relieve the oppressed, judge the fatherless, plead for the widow' (*Isaiah* 1:17), after which it is written: 'Though your sins be as scarlet, they shall be as white as snow' (*Isaiah* 1:18). And justice brings near the redemption, as it is written: 'Keep ye judgment and do justice, for My salvation is near to come and My righteousness to be revealed' (*Isaiah* 56:1). And the Holy One, blessed be He, desires justice more than all the sacrifices, as it is written: 'To do righteousness and justice is more acceptable to the Lord than sacrifice' (*Proverbs* 21:3). It does not say more than a burnt-offering or a sin-offering but more than sacrifice (implying more than all the sacrifices).

In many passages we are warned by Moses our teacher to practise justice: 'Ye shall not respect persons in judgment; but ye shall hear the small as well as the great; ye shall not be afraid of the face of man; for the judgment is God's' (*Deuteronomy* 1:17). He furthermore warned us about it in the form of a positive commandment: 'In righteousness shalt thou judge thy neighbour' (*Leviticus* 18:15); 'And ye shall judge righteously' (*Deuteronomy* 1:16). And he commanded that judges be appointed in every place, as it is written: 'Judges and officers shalt thou make thee in all thy gates' (*Deuteronomy* 16:18): the term 'judges' denoting those appointed to judge and the term 'officers' those who stand in the presence of the judges ready with rod and staff to enforce their decisions.

R. Jeremiah said (*Sanhedrin* 7b): 'which thou shalt set before them' (*Exodus* 21:1). The verse should have said: 'which thou shalt teach them' but it refers to the insignia of the judges, the rod, the lash, the shoe (for the ceremony of drawing off the shoe, *Deuteronomy* 25:5-9) and the trumpet. Rav Hai (Gaon of Pumbedita 939-1038) writes that the Court must have ready in the place where the judges sit a rod wherewith to exercise dominion, a strap wherewith to flog offenders and a trumpet wherewith to proclaim the ban. A scroll of the Law must also be present in the Court, as we say (based on *Bava Kamma* 82a, but the reading in the current versions is different): It is an enactment of Ezra that the Courts sit on Mondays and Thursdays. And we ask: What is the reason? Because many people are present there (coming into the towns on these market days). If you want I can say: Because it would be too much trouble to take out a scroll of the Law (from the synagogue).

We have learnt in the first chapter of tractate *Makkot* (7a): 'The law regarding the setting up of a Sanhedrin applies both to the Holy Land and to outside the Holy Land'. The *Gemara* concludes that there is this difference between the Holy Land and outside it: in the Holy Land there is an obligation to have a Sanhedrin in every district and every city whereas outside the Holy Land there is only an obligation to set up a Sanhedrin in every district not in every city. This applies only at a time when there is ordination (*semikhah)* but nowadays, when there is no ordination, all the laws regarding the appointment of judges are set aside according to the (strict) laws of the Torah, as it is written 'set before *them* ' (*Exodus* 21:1), referring to the judges called *elohim* in this section, namely, those who are ordained, and we expound it thus (*Gittin* 88b) 'before *them*'' and not before laymen and we are laymen.[3] Consequently, according to the (strict) Torah law there are no judges but (nevertheless) we act as the agents (i.e. on behalf of) of the earlier (ordained) teachers (*Gittin* 88b). The conclusion is reached (*Bava Kamma* 84b) that we only act on their behalf in matters that occur frequently and which involve financial loss,[4] for example, cases of admission and loans, namely, where A claims money from B supported by the evidence of witnesses that B had admitted his debt in their presence or that B had borrowed from A in their presence. But no judgement is rendered in a case of infrequent occurrence even if financial loss is involved, for example, a case of physical assault. Similarly, no judgement is rendered in a case involving no financial loss, even if it is of frequent occurrence, such as putting a man to shame. The *Rambam* (Maimonides, 1135-1204, in *Yad, Sanhedrin* 5:10) writes that we do render judgement in cases involving doctor's fees (for recovery from a physical attack) and compensation for loss of work and so did the Geonim rule, stating that it is an everyday occurrence in Babylon to decide such cases. But it would appear from the words of my master and father the *Rosh* (Asher b. Jehiel, c.1250-1327), the memory of the righteous is for a blessing, that no judgement is rendered in such cases. So, too, the case of an ox injuring a human being is of infrequent occurrence and no judgement is rendered but the cases of a man injuring an ox and an ox another ox are frequent and decisions are consequently rendered in these cases. This only applies where the injuries were caused by *shen* ('tooth') or *regel* ('foot'), whether the ox did damage to another animal by rubbing against it (for pleasure, thus falling under the heading of 'tooth') or whether it ate fruit it was its habit to eat and all such cases or whether it did damage to food for which the payment is the full amount. But if it did damage by *keren* ('horn', i.e. malicious damage for which only half damages has to be paid, see *Exodus* 21:35-36) or its derivatives (e.g. kicking or biting) no judgement is rendered. For if the ox is docile (*tam*, i.e. it had not gored more than once before) the ruling is (*Bava Kamma* 15b) that the payment of half damages is in the nature of a fine (not compensation for loss) and no decisions are rendered in cases of fines. And if the ox is a *mu'ad* ('warned', i.e. it has gored three times so that the owner is not obliged to pay the full damages and this is not a fine) there is no law of *mu'ad* in Babylon (obviously not since the law of *tam* cannot be decided there). No decision is rendered even if the animal had been declared a *mu'ad* in the Land of Israel and was then brought to Babylon because such is of infrequent occurrence (*Bava Kamma* 84b).

The claim by a wife of her marriage settlement, the claim of an inheritance and the claim that a gift had been given are treated as similar to cases of debt and decisions are rendered concerning them in order to shut a door against the unscrupulous who would otherwise rely on the inability of the party to find experts (i.e., ordained judges) to try the case.[5] And so, too, decisions are rendered in cases of robbery. But no decisions are rendered in cases of fines. And so did the *Rambam* (*Yad, Sanhedrin* 5:9) write that there is no enforcement of payment for any of the fines imposed by the Sages on one who blows a trumpet to frighten his neighbour or one who smacks his neighbour's face (i.e. causing him no injury but embarrassing him) and so forth. And wherever the payment is that of only half the damage or more than the damage, payment cannot be enforced (since it is not compensation but a fine: *Bava Kamma* 15b) with the exception of the half damage to be paid in the case of *tserurot* ('pebbles', i.e. where pebbles sprang from under the feet of an animal and where the payment is half damage but *is* compensation, *Bava Kamma* 15b) which is in the nature of monetary compensation and not a fine. Outside the Holy Land we can enforce, in cases of robbery and theft, the actual amount stolen but not any addition due to increase in value. Not all cases of admission of guilt can be enforced outside the Holy Land. The law does recognise liability where there is an admission of guilt in cases of depreciation, shame and ransom (*kopher,* paid where a *mu'ad* killed a human being, see *Exodus* 21:30) e.g. where one says 'I have seduced the daughter of So-and-so' or 'My ox has killed So-and-so' but payment in these cases cannot be enforced by judges outside the Holy Land. Where payment is for indirect damage this is not treated as a fine (but as compensation) and can be enforced outside the Holy Land. And so, too, in the case of an informer, though no act was involved, payment of compensation can be enforced.

Now in all these cases where the Courts cannot enforce the law, if the injured party manages to seize property to the value of that which is due to him the property he has seized is not taken from him.[6] But *Rabbenu Tam* (Jacob b. Meir, c.1100-1171) writes (Tosafists to *Bava Kamma* 15b, end) that this only applies where the seizure was of that which caused the damage (i.e. the actual animal which gored) and only when the seizure was made at the time when the damage was done but not otherwise. For if seizure were to be effective in all instances where the seizure was made at a later date (lit. 'today or tomorrow') the victim will seize much more than his due and it will be impossible to reclaim the surplus since cases of fine are not adjudicated in Babylon. But my master and father, the *Rosh,* of blessed memory, writes that even if he seized some other property (i.e. not the animal itself) it is not taken from him and if he seized more than his due an assessment is made by the Court and the surplus taken from him. This does not come under the heading of fines (which cannot be enforced by the Court) since the payment for the damages has been made by the enactment of the Sages of blessed memory who have ruled (*Bava Kamma* 15b) that if he seized property it is not taken from him (thus the Court, when making the assessment, are not illegally deciding cases of fines). All the Court does is to sit in judgement for the return of the surplus (i.e. not for the original amount to be paid which is by the principle of seizure). From the language used by Rav Alfasi (the *Rif,* to *Bava Kamma,* chapter 8, beg.) it appears he holds, where the victim demands of the Court an on-the-spot assessment of the damage so that he may know the amount he is entitled to seize, the Court must pay heed to him. But my master and father writes that this is far from obvious. They must never, in fact, make any assessment for the purpose of collecting the amount due. It is only when the victim has already seized the property that an assessment is made, the Court saying to him: Return such-and-such an amount.

If the victim demands that the Court should accept the testimony of witnesses (to the damage) so that when, at a later date (lit. 'today or tomorrow'), he seizes property it will not be taken away from him, the Court is to pay no heed to him to accept the testimony of the witnesses in anticipation of a later seizure, for since no fines can be imposed in Babylon the Court must not accept the testimony, as we say: There is no *mu'ad* in Babylon (i.e., even though at the time no actual transfer of property is involved and there is a mere acceptance of the testimony). Consequently, the Court must not accept the testimony, even though at the time no money is extracted. But if the victim has already seized the property and then the perpetrator of the damage summons him to the Court for this, the Court instructs the victim to produce his witnesses (that the damage has been done). If the Court then discovers that the seizure has been lawful they say to the perpetrator: We cannot impose the fine but if you wish to redeem that which he has seized give him such-and-such an amount of money. And if he had seized more than the amount due to him he is instructed to return the surplus. If the victim is unable to produce witnesses, they instruct him to return that which he has seized.

R. Abraham b. David (of Posquières, c.1125-1198) of blessed memory writes that if the perpetrator of the damage admitted his liability and then witnesses came to testify to his liability we follow the opinion of Rav (*Bava Kamma* 74b) who holds that one who admits to liability in cases of fines is exempt from payment even if witnesses later came to the Court to testify to his liability. If the victim has seized the property and the perpetrator then admitted his liability we still take it away from him and we do not argue that seizure before admission of liability is treated as if witnesses had testified first (i.e., we do not argue that the seizure is accepted as a legal decision, akin to that rendered after witnesses had testified so that a later admission of liability is ignored). But the *Ramban* (Nahmanides, 1194-1270) finds this difficult since admission of liability is only acknowledged as such where it took place in a Court. Nowadays, since we no longer have Courts composed of experts (i.e., ordained scholars) it is as if the admission of liability took place outside the Court, an admission which does not exonerate from the payment of a fine, just as we say that there is no *mu'ad* in Babylon since for this purpose testimony before a Court is required and there are no Courts (in Babylon). Consequently, if he seized property it is not taken away from him whether he seized it before the admission of liability or after the admission of liability.

Rav Alfas writes (*Rif* to *Bava Kamma*, chapter eight, beg.), although fines are not enforced by the Courts, it is the practice of the two Yeshivot (of Sura and Pumbedita) to place the offender under the ban until he appeases his victim (i.e. by compensating him for the damage he has suffered).[7] But as soon as he gives him the amount due to him we remove the ban immediately irrespective of whether or not the victim is appeased. And so, too, writes R. Abraham b. David, adding that where the fine is a fixed amount, the 50 zuz to be paid in cases of rape and seduction (*Exodus* 22:15-16; *Deuteronomy* 22:28-29) for example, we place the offender under the ban until he pays that fixed amount, and so write some of the Geonim. But this is unacceptable to my master and father for there is no greater form of enforcement than this, to hold him by his testicles until he surrenders his cloak (an expression found in *Bava Metzia* 101b, i.e. since the Court is not empowered to inflict fines how can it compel, through the ban, the payment of these fines). And R. Sherira Gaon (of Pumbedita, c.906-1006) writes, we do not find in the Talmud that a ban is placed on him unless it be for the purpose of removing that which causes the damage (*Bava Kamma* 15b, i.e. the ban is only imposed where the animal is dangerous and its owner refuses to have it put down or placed under strict control). However the later (post-Talmudic) sages and the Heads of the Yeshivot relied on this (i.e. to extend the ban even where there is a refusal to pay as above) for they observed the great harm that is done as a result of the rule that fines cannot be imposed by the Courts. Consequently, they issued an enactment (i.e. although this was illegal in Talmudic times) that the one guilty of the assault be placed under the ban until he appeases his victim approximately. For there is no way to be more exact (i.e. to make a real, not an approximate, assessment) by saying: Such-and-such an amount have we fixed for you to pay and we have fixed it to receive this amount. To do that would be to decide in cases of fine. But the Court makes a private (lit. 'in their heart') approximate assessment which they do not reveal to others. They then place the offender under the ban until he appeases his victim and they see whether or not this approximates to the amount they have assessed. If it is approximately the same but the victim is unwilling to accept it they say to him: We have no power to keep him any longer under the ban and he is released from it forthwith. But if the amount he pays is far removed from the amount they had assessed approximately in private the ban is not removed until it does approximate to their assessment.

Also with regard to one who puts his neighbour to shame by insulting him verbally, although the law is that he does not have to pay him any compensation (*Bava Kamma* 91b), R. Sherira writes that he is placed under the ban until he appeases his victim in accordance with the latter's dignity (i.e. the compensation must depend on the dignity of the victim).[8] My master and father, of blessed memory, writes that this is very plausible since greater embarrassment is suffered by the victim of verbal insults than by the victim of a physical assault, for there is nothing worse than the evil talk and libel a man spreads about his neighbour.

The Jerusalem Talmud (*Bava Kamma* 8:6,6c) records: One who puts a scholar to shame must pay him full compensation. A certain man insulted R. Juda bar Hanina. The case came before Resh Lakish who imposed on him a fine amounting to a pound of gold.[9]

ANNOTATIONS

1 The earlier Mishnah in *Avot* is in the name of Simeon the Just but R. Jonah assumes that the two statements are complementary since the editor of the Mishnah recorded them both and since in the first the term *omed*, 'stands', is used whereas in the second the term used is *kayyam*, 'endures'. The commentary of R. Jonah is, in fact, on the first statement, of Simeon the Just, not on the second, but the *Tur* is, in any event, paraphrasing R. Jonah not quoting him verbatim. R. Jonah's Commentary to *Avot* is printed in the edition of *Avot* in the Romm, Vilna, edition of the Babylonian Talmud. Although R. Jonah's Commentary does not belong to the halakhic literature, it is used here by the *Tur* because the latter's formulation here is not really halakhic but a kind of homily on the importance of justice for society. A similar semi-homiletical preface is given by R. Mordecai Jaffe (c.1535-1612) to the section of his Code dealing with jurisprudence (*Levush Ir Shushan*, Venice, 1619, 1:1). For the *Tur* and the arrangement of his material see Chaim Tchernowitz, *Toledot haposekim* (New York, 1974, Vol.II, 199-220; and Menahem Elon *Hamishpat ha'Ivri*, second enlarged edition (Jerusalem: Magnes Press, 1978), 1058-1080.

2 Rabban Simeon b. Gamaliel, according to this interpretation, is not concerned with the metaphysical question, discussed by Simeon the Just, of the aim of creation but the more practical question of how society is to *endure* now that the world has been created. He offers a prescription for an ordered society. Justice, truth and peace are the essential ingredients of a viable society. There must be competent judges to administer the law and so prevent oppression of the weak by the strong; truth must be accepted as an abiding value; and society must so order its affairs that peace and harmony reign supreme. The Rabbinic saying that the judge is a partner of God means that the judges share in the divine creativity because without a stable society the world would collapse into chaos and God's purposes would be frustrated. The *Tur* proceeds to give a brief history of the administration of justice from Abraham through the just kings and leaders. Even in the Messianic age there is need for justice to be administered and the Messiah is praised for possessing the ability to see that this is done. Conversely, there are many instances of dire calamities befalling a state in which justice is perverted. The prophets teach that God desires justice more than all the sacrifices.

3 Having stressed the importance of justice and the judges who administer it, the *Tur* now turns to the great paradox that, according to the rabbinic understanding of the matter, only scholars who have been ordained (who have *semikhah*, the 'laying on of hands', believed to reach back to Moses, who 'ordained' Joshua) can act as judges and in the Diaspora in talmudic times and in the period of the *Tur* everywhere there are no judges with *semikhah*. The history of *semikhah* is fascinating but the details are obscure. (For the whole question and the attempts to revive *semikhah*, as a prelude to the advent of the Messiah, in 16th century Safed see the article SEMIKHAH in *Encyclopedia Judaica*, Vol.14, pp.1140-1147 and Elon, *supra* n.1, at 18-30). It appears from the talmudic sources quoted here by the *Tur* that the authorities in Palestine in talmudic times, zealous for the honour of the Holy Land, refused to ordain any of the scholars, no matter how eminent, who resided in Babylon. The Palestinian Amoraim have the title 'Rabbi', because they have *semikhah*, whereas the Babylonian Amoraim only have the lesser title 'Rav'. The paradoxical situation prevailed from the beginning of the third century that while Babylonian Jews possessed the full machinery of justice in the Exilarch and his Court, police officers and prisons, their judges had no standing in the eyes of the strict Torah law. In Palestine, on the other hand, the judges had the authority conferred upon them by *semikhah* but possessed little autonomy in the administration of justice. Obviously such a situation was impossible. To cope with it, the Babylonian teachers introduced the legal fiction that in certain cases the Babylonian courts were able to exercise their powers because they were authorised so to do by the Palestinian authorities, whose agents they became and on whose behalf they were authorised to act. (The main talmudic sources are: *Gittin* 88b; *Bava Kamma* 15b; 27b and 84a-b; *Sanhedrin* 2b-5a). The Jewish Courts in the middle ages followed the rule laid down for the Babylonian Courts but the details of how exactly the Courts composed of technical 'laymen' were to function is far from clear and the problem aggravated by the ruling (*Bava Kamma* 15b) that even where the Courts had no power, in cases of fines, for instance, the seizure of property by the offended party to the value of the compensation due to him (had there been 'expert' judges to decide the matter) was recognised. It is to these problems that the *Tur* now addresses himself. *Cf.* D.M. Shohet, *The Jewish Court in the Middle Ages* (New York: Herman Press, 1931), chapters VI and VII, pp.120-150; A Gulak, *Yesode Hamishpat ha'ivri* (Berlin: Dvir, 1922), iv. 24-38.

4 This is not too exact since the Court can compel a recalcitrant husband to divorce his wife where she has good grounds for her divorce petition (*Gittin* 85b) and proselytes are accepted even though a Court of three is required for this purpose (*Yevamot* 46b). Exceptions to the rule are made in these cases because the release of the wife from an intolerable burden and the bringing of a soul 'under the wings of the Shekhinah' are no less praiseworthy aims than the obtaining of financial compensation. See R. Moses Isserles, *Darkhe Mosheh*, ed. H.S. Rosenthal (Jerusalem: *Makhon Yerushalayim*, 1979),

la and R.Y.M. Epstein's '*Arukh hashulhan, Hoshen Mishpat* (Warsaw: M. Zederbaum, 1884), Chapter1.

5 The legal principle in this paragraph is that a Court of 'laymen' is not empowered to impose fines, even where the law demands it, because 'laymen' have no power to try the case. In ancient Jewish law a Court-enforced payment could be either for the purpose of compensating a victim (*mamon*) or as a fine to the perpetrator (*kenas*). In the latter case the purpose of the payment is not to compensate the victim but to punish the offender, except that since the punishment has to be inflicted the money is not paid into the Court, as, say, in English law, but to the victim. But, since the basic aim in these cases is not that of compensation, the Court of 'laymen' is not empowered to act on behalf of the 'experts'. The *Tur* here discusses whether or not certain border-line cases fall under the heading of 'fines', which cannot be administered in Babylon and hence everywhere else in the period of the *Tur*.

6 In this paragraph and the next the *Tur* discusses the extent to which the law recognises seizure of property in cases of fines, etc. The *locus classicus* is *Bava Kamma* 15b where the conclusion is reached that although the payment of half-damages for an ox that is a *tam* is in the nature of a fine, which cannot be imposed in Babylon, yet 'if he seized it, it is not taken away from him'. *Rabbenu Tam* finds it hard to accept that the Talmud allows seizure of property by a man whose case the Courts have no power to decide. Such a carte-blanche admission of seizure into the law can so easily lead to abuse. Consequently, *Rabbenu Tam* is compelled to interpret the Talmudic passage in a forced manner, namely, that the reference is only to seizure of the ox itself and only if the seizure is made at the time. The *Rosh* disagrees and allows seizure of any property to the value of the claim. But the *Rosh* is then faced with the problem of who is to decide whether the amount seized is accurate. The only way this can be determined is by the Court sitting in judgement on the case and this would involve trying cases of fines in 'Babylon'. The *Rosh's* neat solution is that since seizure is a legal right the amount seized to the value of the claim is not in dispute at all so that all the Court has to do is ascertain whether there is a surplus and, if there is, to assess its value. The decision here is not one of fines but of compensation, i.e. to the offender.

7 The powerful weapon of the ban was used by the Courts in the middle ages for the enforcement of the law (see Shohet, *supra* n.3, at 133-150). The *Tur* discusses here whether the use of the ban to enforce payments of fines is contrary to the rule that these cannot be enforced by Courts of 'laymen'. The eventual decision is that, though this is illegal according to talmudic law, the post-talmudic teachers are empowered to enact new legislation since otherwise justice will not be done. In all this the tension is clearly to be observed between the need for the Courts to have coercive powers and the opposite need to preserve the continuity of the law. The post-talmudic authorities never went so far as to abolish entirely the talmudic rules against enforcement of fines by a Court of

'laymen' but they did not scruple to endow these Courts with the terrible power of the ban.

8 In talmudic law there is no redress for slander or, 'insulting words' i.e. defamation of character. Here, too, the power of the ban is invoked. At a later stage the Courts, by special enactments, *takkanot*, intervened more directly, compelling the man guilty of character assassination to pay full compensation to his victim, see *Shulhan Arukh, Hoshen Mishpat* 420:38.

9 There is some evidence that scholars tended to abuse the scholar's privilege mentioned here, even encouraging others to insult them so as to lay claim to the 'pound of gold'. Thus while the *Shulhan Arukh, Yoreh De'ah* 243:7 records the rule that the Court is to impose a ban on anyone who insults a scholar, *Isserles* (ad loc.) states that 'nowadays there are no scholars' so that the law of the 'pound of gold' no longer applies.

---

* Rabbi, New London Synagogue.

MAHARAL'S CONCEPTION OF LAW - ANTITHESIS TO NATURAL LAW THEORY

by

RIVKA SCHATZ*

I

In the last few years there has been a growing interest in the thought of Rabbi Judah Loew ben Bezalel, known as the Maharal of Prague (1512-1609). Most researchers viewed him favourably because they perceived in him a humanist, historically-situated in the transition period between the middle ages and modernity. Ben Zion Bokser[1] saw the significance of the Maharal's thought in its emphasis on individual experience as opposed to universal theories and thus the Maharal symbolized for him the struggle for an individual faith in the face of abstract theology and metaphysics. Additionally the Maharal symbolized the direct relationship of man to nature. He states on pp. 79-80:

> Like the fate of any one organ which affects the life of the rest of the body, so does the fate of any individual affect the lives of all others who comprise the larger body of the human community. Their lives are pledged to our welfare, as our life is pledged to theirs. Our love of each other is in a certain sense a love for what is really part of ourselves; and one who hates others is really guilty of self-hatred.

André Néher,[2] who devoted much attention to the doctrines of the Maharal, also perceived this humanistic strain as his main contribution. Unlike Bokser, Néher focused on the universalistic dimension and the political predictions which he discovered in Maharal's philosophy. He based himself

* First published in Hebrew in *Da'at*, Bar-Ilan University, 1979.

** Edmonton Professor of Jewish Mysticism, Hebrew University of Jerusalem.

1 B.Z. Bokser, *From the World of Cabbalah, The Philosophy of Rabbi Judah of Prague* (New York: Philosophical Library, 1954).

2 A. Néher, *Le Puits de l'Exil, La théologie dialectique du Maharal de Prague* ; see as well his article in Hebrew, "The Maharal of Prague as Humanist", in his book *Uvekhol Zot* (Jerusalem: Rubin Mass, 1978).

on the assumption which M. Buber[3] defined as the transition from a theological to a sociological approach.

In my opinion these conceptions created an idealized interpretation of the Maharal's doctrines, while his actual philosophy and its roots remained outside the realm of discussion. The Maharal's political views are not the subject of this article, although there is no doubt that the issue to be dealt with in this article on the Maharal's philosophy of law have important social and political implications. Needless to say, these views will emerge in quite a different light than those already mentioned.

I would like to make clear at the outset that my position is the antithesis of those conceptions which seek to establish the Maharal as the representative of any humanist position - Jewish or general philosophic. In order fully to explicate my position I would like to present a central problem essential to the Maharal's thought and show that this problem emerges systematically as the underlying goal of his book *Tiferet Israel* (The Splendour of Israel), which is the most systematic of Maharal's works in this regard. The remainder of his writings cannot be properly understood without clarifying the goal of this theological tractate. Within the context of Jewish philosophy, the Maharal stands in opposition to the Maimonidean, rationalist stream and many of his polemical arguments resemble the southern French critiques of Maimonides.[4] Crudely-speaking, one can place the Maharal in the camp of the "defenders of the faith" as against the philosophic rationalists. The "defenders of the faith" feared the rationalists' attempt to subjugate the Torah (the Bible) to philosophy and the resulting lack of observance of the Divine commandments. They also feared the rationalist's understanding of immortality as a purely individualist category and his subjugation of reality to the necessary law of nature. Of course Maimonides was the chief antagonist of the "defenders of the faith". And indeed the Maharal wrote this philosophic treatise as a clearly apologetic work, that of someone taking part in a historical debate to which he devoted himself wholeheartedly. The total structure of his arguments rest on the philosophy of law. From a literary point of view the book is an interpretation of the festival of Shavuot, the holiday of the giving of the law. The central question that emerges from the book is the nature of Jewish law. I have therefore purposely chosen to carry

3 M. Buber, *Ben Am L'artso* (Jerusalem: Schocken, 1945). On the Maharal's approach to education, see A. Kleiberger's interesting book, *Hamahashavah hapedagogit shel haMaharal miPrague* (Jerusalem: Magnes Press, 1982).

4 See Julius Guttmann, *The Philosophies of Judaism* (New York, Garden City: Doubleday & Company, Inc.), 275.

on the discussion within the categories of legal philosophy, since it is clear that Jewish law is in fact identical to the Torah.

The sixteenth century abounds in philosophies of law and politics which were conceived to be rooted in the general principles of natural law (*ius Naturae*). A basic assumption of this theory is that law derives from the social nature of man and positive law assumes the existence of natural law. The general principles of law are therefore rooted in a general consensus. Furthermore, the Bible, or in the language of the West the "Old Testament", was perceived as the source of natural law - a fact not without significance for our discussion.

The Maharal could not have read the writings of Hugo Grotius since they were published after his death. Nevertheless one can find traces of Grotius' theory in the philosophy of Jean Bodin, a contemporary of the Maharal whose works on the philosophy of law and politics were published in the 70's and 80's before the advent of *"Tiferet Israel"*. The Maharal himself was interested in the theological writings of Gentile philosophers (indeed it is possible that Bodin himself returned to Jewish cultural conceptions towards the end of his life). What is of relevance to our discussion is that Bodin's highly favourable attitude towards Judaism emerged from his philosophy of natural law. In order to praise Judaism it was appropriate to point out that the Patriarch Abraham had accepted natural law. Since Abraham represents the first Jew, then natural law first emerged from Judaism. Judaism was thus worthy of praise for its universality and its message to humanity. This view of Judaism was held by philosemitic Christian philosophers. However, even those Christian thinkers who maintained natural law - while excluding Jews from participating in the rights it provided - conceived of Judaism before Jesus as possessing historical significance in the development of early natural law theory.[5] Of course, the goal of this paper is not an analysis of Jean Bodin but of the Maharal, and the issue of natural law did not commence in the sixteenth century. Nevertheless it is important to be aware that this topic was of fundamental philosophic concern in the Christian world, and its implications were essential to the Maharal's doctrines, as I shall demonstrate.

The formulation of natural law theory is rooted in the classical period, of Cicero and the Stoics. However for our purposes what is important is the definition and functioning of this theory in the Scholastic world, particularly in the thought of St. Thomas Aquinas. According to Marvin Fox, Aquinas'

---

5 See Jacob Guttmann's interesting ideas on this question concerning the personality of Jean Bodin in his article "Uber Jean Bodin in seinen Beziehungen zum Judentum", *MGWJ* XLI, 315-347, 459-489.

definition and indeed acceptance of natural law was not unrelated to the tradition of Christian-Jewish polemics. What is of relevance to our discussion is that this affected the interpretation of Maimonidean philosophy, an important element in the understanding of the Maharal. In his article,[6] Fox discusses this issue, which has a bearing on our topic, by stressing rather the difference between Maimonides and Aquinas on the conception of natural law. He argues that Maimonides rejected the strict formulation of natural law accepted by Thomas thought even though elements of this conception can be found in Maimonidean theory. Indeed Fox's general thesis is that Jewish philosophy did not accept the principle of natural law.

In 1944 Alexander Altmann published an article[7] in which he proved the existence of a natural law theory in the writings of Rav Sa'adia Gaon[8] under the influence of the Mutazila thought. I don't want to enter this debate nor can I. What is important for our discussion is that the Maharal interpreted Maimonidean thought as resulting from the definition of Jewish law in terms of "natural law".

What are the essential points of this conception of Maimonides? Let us review St. Thomas' definition of natural law as it appeared in the *"Summa Theologica"* and as presented in Fox's article.

1. Natural law theory is grounded in the conception of human nature.
2. Man is a rational creature, and as such he participates in the workings of the Eternal Intellect, and has a "natural" tendency to aspire to this rational end. This participation in the workings of the Eternal Intellect is called "natural law".
3. Natural law is the source of moral action., which is inherently rational. Morality is good because it is identical with reason. Reason naturally obligates man to act morally.
4. Natural law is universal, and law is law only insofar as it reflects "natural law". All other law is a perversion of natural law.

I would like to show in the rest of this article that Maharal built his legal theory on the basis of this definition of natural law and its internal logic. Maharal, however, radically altered the inner elements of the equation, to use a mathematical metaphor. This change of values completely reversed the

6 See Marvin Fox, "Maimonides and Aquinas on Natural Law", *Dine Israel* 3 (1972), v-xxxvi.

7 See "Saadya's Conception of the Law", *Bulletin of the John Rylands Library* XXVII (1944).

8 882-942, the father of medieval Jewish philosophy. He lived in Fayyum, Egypt.

original conception. If law is the expression of a world-view - and this claim emerges from the Maharal's writings - then his philosophy is a direct confrontation with the following basic principles of natural law philosophy.

1. A definition of human being as ultimately not tied to nature.
2. Man is divine, and he participates in the laws of the Divinity, the Eternal Intellect. This does not necessarily imply a connection with rationalism - rather it finds expression in action and not cognition. The Eternal Intellect is the underlying structure of reality and thus guarantees it being a universal truth. This truth is acquired by man through the Divine commandments and decrees.
3. The Divine Intellect determines the ideal of man's conduct. Ideal here is defined in terms appropriate to man's metaphysical nature and is not connected with ethics. Morality is not an expression of universal law and therefore is not related to the idea of the good. The good is identical to necessary law, being the first outcome of God's intellect.
4. There is only one objective law, the Divine law which contains within it the concept of truth. The good is equivalent to truth because it teaches man to preserve the harmony of all existence, which includes the natural and metaphysical order.

A delineation of these essential principles will aid us to comprehend the underlying basis of the development of the Maharal's system and to focus on his philosophical claims against Maimonides. Of course the above is an outline of his principles which will be more fully elaborated in the course of the discussion.

I would like to point out that wherever the term man (in Hebrew, *adam*) appears, Maharal means to refer to Jewish man. Similarly whenever the term law appears, it refers to the Torah (meaning Bible, Jewish law). Natural law, as hinted at in the Bible, in the seven commandments given to the children of Noah, applies to the Gentile world that did not accept the true universal law hidden in the Torah. The Rabbinic statement that God imposed the law on Israel against its will is interpreted by the Maharal to signify the philosophic and legal necessity of the Torah in which the Gentile world did not take part. The individual Jew is not defined in societal categories as such in the realm of legal concepts, but rather in terms of belonging to the Jewish people. All these features are important to attain the right perspective for the Maharal's humanism. I will proceed in two ways to clarify this claim of the Maharal.

1. Firstly I will examine his arguments against Maimonides, with emphasis on the differences in world-view which emerge from the legal system.
2. Secondly I will describe the philosophic position which is at the source of this alternative world-view, namely that the Maharal's underlying assumptions are derived from the fundamentals of Kabbalistic thought.

The Maharal pours his wrath on Maimonides for attempting to provide humanistic reasons for the Divine commandments. One can see an example of the larger issue at stake in the discussion of the "bird's nest". (The Biblical command states: "If a bird's nest chance to be before thee in the way in any tree ... thou shalt not take the mother bird with the young but thou shalt surely let the mother go and take the young to thee" - *Deuteronomy* 22:6). The Rabbis stated in the Mishnah tractate *Berachot* 33b with reference to this question that, "If one (while praying) says 'may thy mercies extend to a bird's nest' ... He is silenced." The Maharal said:

> Maimonides wrote in 'The Guide to the Perplexed' (Part III, chapter 8) that the reason for the Biblical injunction of the 'bird's nest' was that the eggs and chicks of the mother are not edible ... and therefore normally it would be reasonable to leave it. If the Bible had pity on the sufferings of animals and birds, how much more so on men.

The Maharal continued:

> Maimonides gave a reason for the commandments, namely that the suffering of the mother bird is greater than the utility that man can attain, thereby employing humanistic a fortiori reasoning as decisive in interpreting the Divine commandments and the ways of the Torah. (Chapter 6)

This led the Maharal to a series of proofs to attack the use of humanistic principles as a legitimate legal tool and he accused Maimonides of violating the talmudic injunction forbidding "calling God's decrees a sign of his mercy". Maimonides' interpretation of the Divine commandments is in principle faulty, says the Maharal, since if the Bible were merely a "book of morals" why does it permit the ritual slaughter of animals at all, instead of distinguishing among the various laws of ritual slaughter. The concept of mercy is not a primary principle determining the views of the Torah. The value of observing the Divine commandments is rooted in the commandments having the force of decree. As he states:

> *Mitsvot* were not given for utilitarian purposes because they were not given at the behest of those who observe the law. Thus the law must be a yoke on man. (Chapter 6)

Not to be cruel to a mother-bird has the force of a fiat on man, and is not tied to humane considerations . The Maharal strongly emphasized that Maimonides' dwelling on the definition of the *Mitsvot* in rational, human terms clearly displays the direction of his thought. Furthermore the Maharal criticized the theological conception of "since He is merciful so be you merciful" that emerges from Maimonides' moral interpretation of the Divine law. In his opinion it completely missed the point since it rooted the law in a theological fiction. Even the basic assumption that God created the world to establish the good is rejected by the Maharal. Indeed we shall see that the Maharal systematically, almost cruelly, rejects the good from any conception of natural law.

Maharal responded to Maimonides' attempt to provide criteria in Jewish law that are rational and self-evident, as well as establish limits where rational criteria are no longer relevant. He said about Maimonides, "Certainly this interpretation has no basis"; a criticism which had implications for his whole system.

> It is written concerning the entire Torah, "who is as this nation possessing laws and statutes that are just as this torah", and it is further written "ye shall *keep and perform* (these laws) since *they* are a sign of your wisdom and intelligence in the eyes of the nations .... therefore *everything* in the Torah whether general or specific are words of wisdom.[9] (Chapter 7)

Here Maharal is subtly criticizing Maimonides by claiming that "in the eyes of the nations" one has to fulfill the law through action and not assert its rationality. Israel's wisdom consists of her being worthy of the law and not in understanding it. In this Maharal commenced his frontal attack on the Maimonidean system of values.

"The Mitsvot were given to purify mankind" - which is absolutely removed from all ethical theories or moral training and only achieved through the acceptance of a discipline whose Order is provided by the Eternal Intellect. "And this is the purification of the soul when it is attached to the intellect." Man's purification is in accepting the decree of a divine system that obligates man in its totality. This legal totality possesses an underlying structure that

---

[9] Emphasis supplied.

is beyond the law, an autonomous wisdom that can only be expressed through the action of observing the commandments. This is the only way to attain this "wisdom" (and wisdom is not rationality). Man does not stand before a rational order accessible to his comprehension; the Maharal even rejects the possibility of understanding the laws of nature which are seemingly more apparent and comprehensible. He rejects the view that cause and effect are discerned from nature, as evident in the medical theories which define man as a material creature.

> Do not think as do some men, i.e. medical doctors, that limbs of man are natural like those of animals, because it is not so and they are quack doctors and do not know that man's form and his limbs are Divine and therefore limbs are man's perfection. (Chapter 4)

He adds:

> Men with scientific temperament that pursue intellectual questions independently, and these are called the philosophers, desire to outwit reality and its structure so that they think they have arrived at the truth. (Chapter 4)

Instead of employing reason as a criterion of understanding it is better to employ the objective structure of the "Universal" Intellect whose laws are the laws of man's existence reflecting his status above nature. What is "natural" to man is not nature (physis) but the super-natural order. There is therefore a clear correlation between man and the legal and metaphysical order. Observance of *mitsvot* spontaneously brings out man's natural being, not through intellectual effort or ethical consciousness but "as a tree emerges from the seed".

To return to his point, if the ground of natural law was man and his nature then the Maharal as well is interested in "natural law" except that he defines man as essentially a metaphysical being who belongs to The Order as he terms it - the Order that is trans-natural. The Jewish legal system - to use legal categories - or the Torah, is a type of *logos*. It is the first product of the first cause - to use philosophic language. This first cause necessarily contains within it the metaphysical order and its law, indeed it is The Order itself. In other words, the law is the most authentic representative of metaphysical law, and therefore upholding the law entails total attachment to the absolute order of existence. Existence here is a general term, and not referring to "natural" existence.

The "more dense" the legal system, i.e. the greater the number of commandments - in his words a system that is a "yoke on man" - the more man is involved in intensive activity, fulfilling his potential as man. This fulfilling of human potential is achieved when man removes himself from his physical, material essence. The great value of action is paradoxically that it guarantees true spiritual action. Spiritual activity, therefore, is rooted in action - i.e., performing the Divine commandments. As for the criterion of "the good" - so central to the system of natural law - the Maharal says:

> All the ways of the Torah are good in themselves". - Thus, the good cannot be found outside the religious act nor is it subject to intellectual criteria - rather, it is the act itself. "When man observes the *mitsvah* that God has given him, not to transgress prohibitions nor leave the limits of the law then shall he attain peace. And when man transgresses the law and enters into another domain not worthy of him, then there is no peace; peace is only attained when everyone remains in his proper domain. At any rate God did not command man to perform the *mitsvah* because it is good in itself nor to do the good, but rather the Divine commandments represent the purification of men, so that man should leave material nature. He should not say God wants the *mitsvah* in itself, for instance ritual slaughter. God doesn't desire ritual slaughtering in itself, rather ritual slaughtering is an action which is correlated to the order of man and not commanded per se. This is what we mean by purification of the soul. (Chapter 7)

The implication of this quotation is that the content of the commandment does not render it a purifying agent; it is the fact that the commandments are directed to the spiritual causes of man's existence and are in full accord with these that does so. In truth, his presentation of the commandments as a force operating within us, to bring out the hidden aspect of our existence, contains a significant amount of kabbalistic elements in the guise of philosophic interpretation. For our purposes it is important to see how the Maharal deepens in a fundamental manner the antagonism between Maimonides' conception and his own.

The *Mitsvot* viewed as a "Natural entity" are, in his words, the greatest nonsense that the human imagination has contrived. In fact it leads to the natural sciences which endanger the true perception of nature.

> In nature there is no impurity of the dead, nor does water purify. There is nothing natural about the Divine Law, it is just decree. One is forbidden to transgress this law and the reason is that the Divine Commands emerge from the Order which follows from the Wise Commands, and for this reason the dead cause ritual impurity, etc. All is Divine wisdom but for man it is a fiat and decree. (Chapter 8)

The Maharal is very extreme in this stand. He claims that the very attempt to question a transgression is totally to misconstrue the concept of law. This does not mean that a law forbidding a transgression is arbitrary. On the contrary, it is a necessary law within its own categories, but not within the framework of natural law.

It seems to me that we can conclude from the above discussion that the disagreement between Maharal and Maimonides is not merely semantic. To the best of my knowledge I know of no other instance where the discussion was carried to the fine points of the different world-views in the Maharal's effort to dethrone the all-powerful rationalism.

The Maharal not only attacks the individualistic starting-point of Maimonides but the ultimate goals of his concept of human perfection. He argued that these humanistic goals threatened the status of the Torah and encouraged the diminishing of its value. The advantages of a naturalistic interpretation of the Divine commandments are less than the disadvantages since

> human actions emerge superior to that of nature. Men would like to achieve success autonomously through the acquisition of reason, and they are not aware that man's real success is in his attachment to God since it was despicable in their eyes to attain success in divine matters through action. They did not fathom the Divine secret that man's actions are above nature. (Chapter 9)

His claim is that from a rationalistic perspective emerges a world-view that establishes the attaining of reason as the highest priority in the hierarchy of values. It is this which causes the *vita contemplativa* to be seen as higher than the *vita activa*. For the Maharal this error harms ideas - such as immortality - since "the intellectual achievements are not the essence of man". Man's essence comes to full expression in action, because action is the only contact with the spirit, as we saw, and according to Maimonides one can attain immortality without the Torah. In his opinion, Maimonides' doctrines were an attempt to find favour in the eyes of the scientists. After all, philosophy deals with "material objects" *(banimtsa'im)* which do not possess a criterion of truth and honesty. "The Torah, although dealing with material objects, does not speculate on them but on God's decrees and therefore it is truth." "Speculation on the essence of things", in his terms, is of no metaphysical consequence. Engaging in the legal discussions of "oxen and donkeys"[10] are not cognitive questions but means of engaging God's laws and therefore the way to attain perfection. Otherwise, it would be better to speculate on "spheres"[11] instead of legal matters. Maimonides' rationalist hierarchy, acquiring the "intelligences", drove him to rage and thus he

10 The above are classic examples of the legal discussion in the Talmud.
11 Heavenly matters.

attempted to sever the connection between the object of the speculation and its influence on the "Active Intellect" of Maimonidean thought. An object of the intellect that has a high classification in the hierarchy does not guarantee anything and has no essential meaning. The essence, or as he terms it the "'hidden meaning' of the conception", was not attained

> because knowledge pertaining to man himself is not considered much, and the knowledge of the laws of man is knowledge of God's decrees that have no relevance to man [this is completely anti-humanistic!]. Rather they have relevance to the Divine King who issues fiats which relate to His Divine kingship. (Chapter 11)

"The Torah is God's decree and is not dependent on anything", "it is wisdom and holiness". On what does the Torah not depend? On rationalism, humanism, and natural law? He continues and defines it well: law does not logically follow from its object. For example, the laws of oxen are not dependent on existent oxen whereas the concept of oxen follows from existent oxen. This is used to explain the fact that the law is in no way derived from its material objects, a claim that undermines the central thesis of natural law.

II

It is clear that when a man engages in such a sweeping attack on the philosophical camp, he possesses another truth. Here we leave the discussion of the Torah as a legal system, and move to the Kabbalistic basis of the doctrine of man and Torah in the conception of the Maharal. One cannot understand the full emotional impact of the Kabbalistic conception of the Maharal without reading Gershon Scholem's article on "The meaning of the Torah in Jewish Mysticism".[12] Scholem's article possesses a broad historical perspective as well as depth of intellectual insight, and most importantly one appreciates the great intimacy of this theme in Jewish consciousness. There is no important spiritual conception in Jewish history that was not adopted and translated into the language of the Torah. The Torah was called the Idea, the Intellechy, the organic fabric of the world, The Word or Logos of God, often changing according to the spiritual needs of the time.

The influence of Kabbalistic ideas on the Maharal's concept of the Torah is particularly interesting, since these ideas are contained within the rationalistic structure of the Aristotelean conception of nature. Even the utopian ideas of the Maharal's system are the result of his philosophy of

12 See, Gershom G. Scholem, *On the Kabbalah and its Symbolism* (New York: Schocken Press, 1969).

nature, if one may use this term. I would like to re-emphasize the Maharal's central point of criticism, as discussed in Part I of this article, of the view that Law is based on natural law which is essentially rationalistic. This does not mean that Maharal did not recognize the basic laws of Aristotelean natural philosophy or that he claimed that natural life is irrational. On the contrary, the Maharal argued in philosophic language that nature is completely enclosed in a system of laws, without exception, further that there is no breaking out of this system of law, nor are there miracles in the sphere of nature. Nature is seen as the perpetual motion of form and matter, of potentiality moving to actualization, and, as in all systems of law, its laws are inviolable. Indeed the Maharal is a great admirer of the law. The system of laws of nature attains perfection autonomously. The only creature which is part of nature, yet transcends it, is man. Man's structure is tied to the 613 Divine commandments of the Torah, which consists of two systems of 248 positive commandments and 365 transgressions which man should avoid. In the natural domain the system of 365 transgressions are parallel to the days of the solar year which symbolize nature; while the 248 positive commandments parallel the unique numerical construction of the super-natural sphere. The Intellechy, the spiritual entity which actualizes the potential soul of man, possesses a structure which corresponds to the soul. In this regard it is related to the concept of human perfection. Thus the concept of perfection which determines the ultimate form of man is not related to his being a natural creature, rather to his being transcendent. This function belongs to the Torah, which is, in the words of the Maharal, "the Form of all existence". The domain of nature contains, then, no utopian element but is complete in its own right. Man, however, is a *priori*-ly constructed as a creature destined for perfection who is above nature, and therefore one can say that man is by definition - in his ultimate perfection - a creature with utopian possibilities. His potentialities aspire to the spiritual plain in order to be released from the chains of nature. However, in his liberation from nature he is forbidden to harm his natural existence and certainly the Maharal does not want a struggle of spirit versus nature. Thus the commands forbidding transgressions symbolize this limitation, since transgressing the 365 laws entails leaving the natural world, which is also a necessary fabric of man's life insofar as he is a creature of nature. The positive commandments, however, carry man by positive action to the spiritual realm and remove him from nature. Thus man's perfection is attained through action, and not via contemplation. The guarantee, almost a naturalistic one, that man will indeed go out to the realm of spirit is built into the soul of man, which possesses an inner hierarchy between matter and spirit. The "image" *(Tselem)* is the means whereby man achieves the *mitsvot*, the laws of the soul, "in God's *image* was created". The "image" is a *"pneuma"* which is the form of the body, but is not purely spiritual as it is not material. Similarly the observance of the Divine positive commandments is not related to the material world. Man's actions seem material, but man is not a natural creature.

Another interesting criterion, according to the Maharal, is that from a naturalistic perspective all men are equal. There is an egalitarianism in nature, whereas the Divine aspect is not equal in all men. Here the Maharal's answer points to the difference between Israel and the Gentiles.

> But this world is a natural world and not the "other" world. Therefore the Divinity is not revealed to all equally, but only to some. (Chapter 5)

All nations are under the number seven, which points to the natural order. But Israel was given the number eight, as hinted in the religious symbol of the eighth-day circumcision, and this number completes the nature of the spirit. Laws of nature which do not immediately respond to the laws of human spiritual existence become perfected by the Torah.

> Therefore the Jewish people are referred to as particularly human because they possess the Divine dimension, not present in nature. Torah and the Divine commandments are above nature and all that is above nature and a perfection of nature is beyond the number seven. (Chapters 6 and 19)

The number eight is "beyond nature" - the medieval Hebrew term for metaphysics. This dimension was not created in the six days of creation. Man is the only creature who was created imperfectly, otherwise he would belong to nature, and "the Torah teaches that man is lacking and requires completion". From the total structure of his thought it is clear that the supernatural utopian element is realized in man when he lives in this duality. Man is not required to employ practical mysticism to negate the material itself. The mystic component emerges in the apprehension of reality as a system of laws operating in a reality which is not immanently comprehensible - neither the natural nor the metaphysical system. From a Jewish perspective, another key element emerges: these two systems of law were revealed in the corpus of the Torah. The latter components of his thought, i.e. his concept of Torah and man's soul, are taken from Kabbalistic thought.

The correlation between the Divine Mind and man's soul is a point which wasn't emphasized in Kabbalistic thought in the various interpretations of the essence of the Torah. Here the Aristotelean formulations, such as form and matter, and form actualizing the potentiality of matter, are decisive. Another point is that the goal of human perfection in this context is not determined solely by the inner logic of his utopian doctrine.

G. Scholem rightly emphasized the two elements which characterize the kabbalistic utopia,[13] firstly the theory of the change and grouping of letters, secondly the doctrine of "eras" or "jubilee years", i.e., either a different reading of the Torah or a different Torah in every historical jubilee. The problem of the Maharal emerges in a different form. There is no doubt that the issue grows out of historical kabbalistic thought as well as naturally arising from his philosophy.

The utopian element in the Torah, according to the Maharal, is reflected in its representing a trans-temporal system. This idea is contained in his concept of "holy time", a time not defined with reference to movement nor with reference to fulfilling potentiality. This state of being is trans-temporal and is hinted at in a hypothetical manner in the idea of the Sabbath. In nature there is no resting, no static situations, since these concepts contradict the idea of nature. The state of passivity on the Sabbath hints at a different system of law which is not possible within the framework of nature. In nature the acquisition of form (and for Maharal there is no being without acquiring form) is connected to motion and time. These hypothetical possibilities are expressed in the quality of "trans-temporalness"[14] as the Maharal defines them; the "trans-temporalness", as opposed to time, is not a coming to be - it is a type of "conceivable existence", on the basis of Aristotelean law.[15] Other orders are not subject to prophecy, and therefore the Maharal claimed that the world-to-come is not mentioned in the Torah. Even prophets could not prophesy in this realm and their prophecy thus relates to this world. This is of no consequence since the world-to-come is not a completion of this world, even where there are hints in this world of a different system of law, like the laws of the Sabbath in nature, circumcision

13 *Supra* n.12.

14 In Hebrew *'atah* or *'itah*.

15 The question of time and its relationship to movement was one of the problems which gave rise to the controversy against Aristotelean physics, particularly in Christian Scholasticism. It is possible that the Maharal was influenced by the writings of Levi ben Gershon with regards to this distinction, since the latter as well distinguished time and trans-temporalness. See Shlomo Pines in his article "Scholasticism after St. Thomas Aquinas and the Doctrines of Hisdai Crescas and his Predecessors" in *Ben Mahshevet Yisra'el lemahshevet ha'amim* (Jerusalem: Mosad Bialik, 1977), 185-188 . His treatment of the problem of prophecy is also reminiscent of the philosophical controversies influenced by Christian Scholasticism.

of man, and the system of numbers which possess an utopian quality. The important point is to accept the law as decree, "which is real obligatory Wisdom". The Torah is the totality of being that which has materialized and that which will be. In his words: "the Torah contains all." He saw many deep secrets in the hidden layers of the Palestinian Talmud's *midrashim* on the tablets (of the commandments) that wished to escape.[16] Moses and God each grabbed the tablets as in the *Mishnah* where "two take possession of a talith" (i.e., two gain equal mastery over the tablets).[17] Moses grabbed the laws *(Mishpatim)* that are self-evident to man; God took hold of those laws *(Hukim)* which are hidden to man; in the middle are the statutes *(Edut),* and these are the main ones that have not yet come into being.

The Maharal raises a question, internal to the issue of the doctrine of the Jubilee years, about the law that corresponds to the structure of being of the various degrees of form and matter. He confirms the statement of the Rabbis: "In the future to come, the Divine commandments will be annulled." He adds:

> but this does not entail a change in the Torah, in any respect. The reference to the commandments being annulled is for the period of the world-to-come, but does not mean that the Torah will be annulled, God Forbid; rather 'the Divine commandments are annulled' refers to the future, when they will assume a different form than now. Because the Torah represents the structure of this world ... But in the days of resurrection, that is the world-to-come, the structure will be different from that of this world, and therefore the *mitsvot* of the Torah are annulled ... At any rate this is not a negation of the Torah, because the Torah contains all the structure of existence. Even in the Torah one can find hints of the order of existence which is for the period of the resurrection to be ... But the Torah exists as in the beginning ... Therefore let it not be said that, God forbid, the Torah is annulled but rather the Torah said the commandments are for this period of time and no more, and thus are written in the Torah all the eternal orders of reality. Though we do not understand the words of the Torah, in the future we shall certainly achieve comprehension. We will understand that the commandments relate to man as he is in this world, with a body that he possesses in this world. In the time of resurrection they relate to the structure of the world of resurrection. Therefore even if we admit that in the time of the resurrection the *mitsvot* are annulled, as the literal reading of the Talmud indicates, this does not entail any change in the Torah. (Chapters 48-49)

However, there have been those who have viewed matters differently and interpreted Maharal in a revolutionary manner. I refer to Rav Shmuel

---

16 Chapter 48.
17 *B.M.* 1:1.

Alexandrov, who was related to the Maharal's family, and saw himself (at the beginning of this century) as a revolutionary advocate of a purely spiritual Judaism in the Renaissance period of the Jewish people. Thus Rav Alexandrov interpreted "the world of resurrection" of the Maharal in the light of the Russian revolution and, following in the footsteps of Sabbateanist theory on the passage just quoted, said:

> So what if he does not intend the Divine commandments in a true halakhic manner ... And more than that they said that a sin done intentionally is more than a positive deed done without intention.

But this same Maharal - whom Rav Alexandrov called "an advocate of his system - the spiritual giant the Maharal of Prague, my master, my ancestor, may he rest in heaven, may his glory be praised" - cannot be interpreted in the light of Sabbateanism. Alexandrov discussed this point with Rav Kook, since he hoped to find in him an associate, but this is not the place to enter into this problem.

The thinking of Maharal is without historical interest, he is an orthodox thinker of his time and not a revolutionary. He was interested in providing a philosophical basis for the status of Jewish law, in a historical context where Christianity was attacking it.[18] His answer to Christianity was that Jewish law did not become annulled with the emergence of Jesus, as Christianity claimed, but that it represents the general laws of existence and therefore will continue. The Jewish people are the sole observer of this law, whose truth lies in its being the law of the cosmos. Rather than coming to inform us of hypothetical, new worlds, he saw his function as strengthening the iron-law of his time.

In conclusion, my claim is that the Maharal defended Judaism using the framework of legal philosophy. His arguments are opposed to a conception of Jewish law as natural law. Though his claims are in direct opposition to the idea of natural law, they assume the inner logic of this theory. His argument essentially relates the definition of law to the definition of man. This correlation is achieved on a metaphysical basis common to both, which is neither moral, nor rationalist. His assumptions, both in terms of the definition of man and in the definition of law, emerge from Kabbalah. Finally "natural law" for him is metaphysical, intended for a people with a metaphysical potential. The Torah's laws reflect universalist principles - however they were not intended to be the foundation for a universalistic

18 See my article on the above-mentioned problem: "Existence and Eschatology in Maharal's Teaching", *Immanuel* 14 (1982), 86-97; 15 (1982-83), 62-72.

world-view in the humanistic sense of a law intended for all mankind. Even more his world-view explains the conflict of Israel and the nations of the world, explained in metaphysical terms. The whole structure of the Maharal's values do not correspond to humanistic thought both in its starting-point and in its goals. In this article I have focused on this one point, but it seems to me to be central.

ANOMALY AND THEORY IN THE ANALYTIC SCHOOL**

by

NORMAN SOLOMON*

I

The purpose of this article is to describe and exemplify a certain type of reasoning which characterizes the writings and teachings of Rabbi Hayyim Soloveitchik and his circle and which, through their influence, is common in present-day *yeshivot*.

In the 1960's I proposed the name 'Analytic' for the Soloveitchik method,[1] for it is incontrovertible that Soloveitchik and his circle engage far more than other traditional exponents of Jewish Law in the analysis of legal concepts. Any analogy with Analytical Positivism, however, as represented in the works of, say, Austin, Kelsen and Hart, must be regarded with caution. Positivists claim to regard law as a self-sufficient discipline independent of, say ethics or theology, and Soloveitchik and his followers indeed give the impression that *halakhah* is a self-contained, comprehensive system, and Heschel for this reason dubbed them 'Pan-halakhists'.[2] Heschel was, however, wrong. It is true that the Analysts, like other traditional Jews, regard *Torah* as a comprehensive, independent system; but (a) they do not regard *halakhah* as coextensive with *Torah*, (b) *halakhah* itself comprises

---

* The following logical symbols are used in this article:

(a)	for all values of 'a'
∃	there is
.	and
v	or
⊃	implies (if .... then ...)

A series of dots is used to indicate the number of a proposition, e.g ....(1) means 'proposition 1'.

** Director Designate, Centre for the Study of Judaism and Jewish/Christian Relations, Selly Oak Colleges, Birmingham; Recognised Lecturer, Department of Theology. University of Birmingham.

1 In a Ph.D. thesis *'The Analytic Movement in Rabbinic Jurisprudence'*, University of Manchester, 1966. See "Hilluq and Haqira", *Diné Israel* 4 (1973), lxix-cvi (Hebrew version in *Midor Dor* I (1979), 9-48); "Definition and Classification in the Works of the Lithuanian Halakhists", *Diné Israel* 6 (1975), lxxiii-ciii; "Concepts of *Zeh Neheneh* in the Analytic School", *The Jewish Law Annual* 3 (1980), 49-62.

2 Abraham Joshua Heschel, *God in Search of Man* (New York: Farrar, Strauss and Giroux 1955), 328.

many matters which no western lawyer, certainly no Positivist, would understand as 'law', and (c) I am now convinced that the Analysts do in fact have recourse to non-halakhic criteria both in application of the law and in the formulation of its leading concepts.

There are, in addition, several important differences between Analytical Positivism and *any* traditional school of Jewish Law. The question of the extent and comprehensiveness of the system is one, the identity of the law-giving 'sovereign' is another. Moreover, the teleological stance which underlies any religious system of law is firmly rejected by Positivists.

Despite these reservations I shall continue, for convenience, to refer to the Soloveitchik circle as 'the Analytic School'. I shall proceed to characterize on formal grounds what appears to be their most distinctive way of argument.

Paradigm and Anomaly

Thomas S. Kuhn has described 'normal science' as a process of puzzle-solving.[3] The scientist works on the basis of a 'paradigm', that is, an accepted example of actual scientific practice, including law, theory, application and instrumentation; examples would be Ptolemaic astronomy, Aristotelian dynamics, corpuscular optics, to name but a few now discarded paradigms. His discovery, observations, research, are fitted into that paradigm as the pieces of a jigsaw are fitted together.

Such a paradigm may well be challenged by some anomalous observation, and indeed in the course of 'normal science' the paradigms are constantly developed and reformulated.[4] Anomalies can become sufficiently numerous and serious to stimulate new discoveries, leading to new theories and to the 'scientific revolutions' which are characterized by the creation of new paradigms. Thus the discovery by Priestley, Lavoisier and others in the mid 1770's of gases which were clearly not air was such a serious anomaly to those working within the phlogiston 'paradigm' that further investigations were stimulated leading to a radical revision of the paradigm and the birth of modern chemical theory.[5]

It is necessary to clarify the formal structure of this process before showing its application in the Analytic School. My example is chosen because it is well-known and clear-cut; one should note, however, that the

3 Thomas S. Kuhn, *The Structure of Scientific Revolutions* (Chicago: University of Chicago Press, 2nd edition, 1970), 35-42.

4 See *supra* n.3, especially Chapter VII.

5 *Supra* n.3, at 53f. and references.

Analytic School does not provide instances of such radical paradigm-restatement, for it does not wish to challenge or revolutionize the general world-view of traditional Judaism.

According to Ptolemy, the motion of all heavenly bodies is reducible to circles or combinations of circles.[6]

Using conventional logical symbols,[7] let 'x' stand for 'any object', 'H' for the predicate 'is a heavenly body', and 'C' for the predicate 'moves in circles or a combination of circles.'

Then

$$(x) \quad H_x \supset C_x$$

(read - 'for all values of x, if x is a heavenly body, x moves in circles or a combination of circles).

The practice of astronomy which derived from Ptolemy's example and teaching, modified subtly in the course of the Middle Ages, is the 'paradigm' within which astronomers up to and arguably including Copernicus worked. Observation yielded innumerable anomalies, and astronomers struggled to accommodate these anomalies within the established paradigm. This meant the introduction of *ad hoc* hypotheses, that is, hypotheses with no justification other than their power to explain the particular anomaly they were designed to cover. The particular configuration of superimposed circles devised to account for the observed orbit of Jupiter, for instance, arose from no general principle of science and explained no other observed phenomenon. In this way the number of *rules* in astronomy increased, and their level of generality decreased. The formula

$$(x) \quad H_x \supset C_x$$

could only be made to work by the addition of specific additional rules in each case to which it was applied.

With Copernicus a period of confusion set in, with the proliferation of alternative paradigms, and not until the acceptance of Newtonian mechanics did a new paradigm emerge within which 'normal' science could proceed. The new paradigm, like the old, was linked to a theory of motion, viz, that

6 On the Ptolemaic system and its eventual rejection see, for instance, J.L.E. Dreyer, *A History of Astronomy from Thales to Kepler* (New York: Dover Publications, 1953), and for a more modern view T.S. Kuhn, *The Copernican Revolution* (Cambridge, Mass.: Harvard U.P., 1957).

7 A list of symbols precedes these notes.

every object travels at a constant velocity in a straight line unless acted upon by some force.

The gains from the new theory were three: (a) the elimination, at least for the time being, of troublesome anomalies; (b) the elimination of the need for *ad hoc* hypotheses to account for the observed motions of individual heavenly bodies; and (c) the increased generalisation which enabled the same small set of laws to account for both heavenly and terrestrial motion.

When we examine our examples of Analytic reasoning we will discover how the Analysts, by characteristically redifining or reclassifying concepts in Jewish Law, (a) remove apparent anomalies from the system; (b) eliminate the need for *ad hoc* hypotheses of the type common in traditional casuistry; and (c) provide ideas of more general application than those they replace.

How far can there be any justification for drawing such a close analogy between scientific and legal reasoning? 'Is' is not 'ought' (cf. Hume);[8] moreover, the actual procedure followed by the scientist in his laboratory is in many ways unlike that of the lawyer in his study or in the courts.

Nevertheless, it is reasonable to expect that there are *formal* resemblances in the interplay between any rational system of thought and the area of reality to which it relates, for these formal resemblances relate not to the *content* of the system but to its *structure*, and belong to the highly general science of logic, rather than, for example, to law and science in their own right. Neil MacCormick, for instance, spends a good deal of time in showing how deductive justification may be validly used in the legal process, in particular in making inferences from the general rule to the individual case.[9] The logical symbolism he uses, his warnings that unless the premisses are in fact correct the conclusion validly derived from them may be false, and all his other purely logical observations, would be equally pertinent if he were addressing himself to natural scientists rather than to lawyers. It is when he considers the *content*, rather than the *formal* structure, of law, that the limitations of purely deductive reasoning become apparent; it is useful only in 'clear' rather than 'hard' cases,[10] and even when valid inference from the general to the particular has been made, and when in addition we have established that it is the duty of the judge to act in accordance with such inference, a further step is required for the judge actually to apply the rule, and this is not entailed by any argument at all, for 'acts are not determined by

8 David Hume, *An Enquiry Concerning the Principles of Morals*, especially section 1.

9 D.N. MacCormick, *Legal Reasoning and Legal Theory* (Oxford: Clarendon Press, 1978), Chapters II-IV.

10 *Op. cit.*, Chapter VIII.

logic.'[11] Law - the same is of course true of the natural sciences - deals with the contingent, and therefore cannot be *reduced* to deduction, even though formal deductive procedures are essential to its correct practice.

II

Paradigm of the Analytic Argument

I shall now present the characteristic Analytic argument in its most general form, at the same time formally distinguishing it from the most characteristic procedure of traditional casuistry.

We commence with a statement of law, which may be expressed in the form 'for all values of p, if p then q':

$$(p) \quad p \supset q \qquad \text{....(1)}$$

This is contradicted by a particular instance:

$$\exists(p) \quad p.{-q} \qquad \text{....(2)}$$

(read: 'there is a value of p, such that both p and not -q)

How can one escape from the contradiction?

Traditional casuistry does so by accepting (2) and by modifying (1) to

$$\textit{most}\ (p) \quad p \supset q \qquad \text{....(3)}$$

(read: 'for most values of p, if p then q')

The *Analysts*, on the other hand, divide p into p' and p", and present two universal statements, one of which is:

$$(p') \quad p' \supset q \qquad \text{....(4)}$$

For the second, there is a choice, subject only to the condition that it is consistent with $\exists(p'')\ p''.{-q}$.

One possibility is:

$$(p'') \quad p'' \supset r \qquad \text{....(5)}$$

11 *Op. cit.*, 33.

where 'r' may or may not be a modified 'q'.
In the extreme case one might have:

$(p'') \quad p'' \supset -q$ ....(5a)

or even the combination:

$(p'') \quad p'' \supset r.-q$ ....(5b)

Several modifications of this basic plan are possible, but each of our three examples will be seen to conform to the basic outline. One obvious modification - this will be found in our first example - is where the first proposition is negative in form:

$-\exists(p) \quad p \supset q$

The second proposition will of course be:

$\exists(p) \quad p \supset q$ (*not* $\exists(p) \quad p.q$)

and the others will be modified accordingly.

Before turning to the actual examples, let us examine the philosophical implications of adopting propositions (4) and (5) rather than (2) and (3). (4) and (5) are *universal* propositions, whereas (2) and (3) are *particular*. (4) and (5) are thus general rules to the effect that if p, then *always* q, whereas (2) and (3) tell us no more than that if p, perhaps q, propositions from which we cannot, in specific instances, infer q even when p is known. This is the difference between a *rational* system of law, within which deductive inferences may be made from general rules to specific instances, and a mere collection of rules where one can never be sure of an inference from the general rule to the case in hand, but needs a special rule for each case. As MacCormick writes,[12] 'The ascription of rational purposes to the established rules is a necessary condition of asserting that the specific cases ... must be instances of a single general conception.' The Analysts, insisting on the generality of their rules, are making possible the ascription to the rules of rational purposes, whereas traditional casuistry undermines this by dividing one case ever more finely from another irrespective of general principle. This is analogous with Newton, who brought generality and thus reason into the

12 *Op.cit.*, 125.

description of the motions of bodies, as against the Ptolemaic astronomers, who constantly devised ad hoc hypotheses of limited application to the point where the whole system forfeited rationality.

Example 1

Naftali Trop - Bava Kamma Section 1[13]

Several intertwined questions are handled here by Trop, and a single solution proposed for all of them. I shall analyse only that part of his discussion relating to the two apparently contradictory rulings of Maimonides.

The first of these rulings concerns *shor mu'ad*. If an ox is *mu'ad* and then gores and kills a man not only must the ox be killed but its owner pay *kofer* (ransom) for the life of the victim. But how can such a case arise? Since the ox has to be killed even on the first occasion he kills a man, how can he ever become *mu'ad* with regard to men? Maimonides indicates several possibilities, and one of them is that if an ox has killed three other animals he becomes *mu'ad* in respect of killing, and the owner is thus liable to pay *kofer* if on the next occasion the victim is human.[14]

The second ruling is: 'If an ox is *mu'ad* for its species it is not (thereby) *mu'ad* for other species; if it is *mu'ad* for man it is not *mu'ad* for animals.'[15]

Several commentators point to the discrepancy between these rulings, and we will demonstrate it formally.

Let 'M' stand for *mu'ad*, 'a' for 'any ox', and the subscripts x, y.... for classes of victim.

Maimonides' second ruling becomes:

$$-\exists(M) \qquad M_{ax} \supset M_{ay} \qquad ....(1)$$

This may be read: 'there is no type of *ha'ada* (=*mu'ad*) such that if an ox is *mu'ad* for victims of class x it must also be *mu'ad* for victims of

13 Naftali Trop, *Hiddushe HaGaRNaT Nezikin* (the volume carries no details of publication, but is uniform with a volume on *Nashim* published in Jerusalem in 5715), 5-7. Naftali Trop (1871-1928) was born at Grodno, and studied under Shkop and J.L. Bloch at Telz. Most of his active career was spent as head of the Hafets Hayyim's yeshiva at Radin, near Warsaw.

14 Maimonides, *Mishneh Torah, Nizke Mamon* 10:3, on the basis of *B.K.* 41a.

15 Maimonides, *loc. cit.*, 6:8.

class y.' This is analogous to proposition (1) in the paradigm, being universal; though of course it is negative, not positive, in formulation.

The first ruling may be written:

$$\exists(M) \qquad M_{ax} \supset M_{ay} \qquad ....(2)$$

that is, 'there is a value of M for which it is true that if a is *mu'ad* for x it must be *mu'ad* for y' - thus contradicting (1).

How does traditional casuistry handle the problem? Karo states that the ruling in (1) applies only to cases of injury, not killing.[16] Expressed formally, he has now modified and *weakened* proposition (1) to:

$$\exists(M) \qquad -(M_{ax} \supset M_{ay}) \qquad ....(3)$$

Note that (3), unlike (1) which it replaces, is not a universal proposition; it tells us only that for *some* values of M, it is not true that M_{ax} implies M_{ay}. (2) and (3), the propositions retained by Karo, both lack generality, and cannot be expressed as universal propositions because he has failed to formulate any *principle* by which we can know when M_{ax} implies M_{ay} and when it does not. He has in effect reduced Maimonides' rulings to *ad hoc* rules for what happens in particular cases rather than general statements of legal principle. Such is the path of traditional casuistry.

Now let us examine what the Analyst does. Trop first makes a *'haqira'* as to whether the responsibility for payment when one's property has caused damage arises (a) from negligence, or (b) from the mere fact that one's property has caused damage, though if one had taken reasonable precautions one would be exempt from payment.[17] (The analogy with discussion by western jurists on the nature of tortious liability is obvious.)[18] His decision is that the basis of responsibility differs in cases of loss of life from in cases of mere damage to property *(nezikin* - he presumably does not intend this

16 J. Karo, *Kesef Mishneh* on *Nizke Mamon* 10:3.

17. On *hakira* as used by the Analysts, see Solomon, *supra* n.1.

18 Shimon Shkop (1860-1939), who taught Trop at Telz, alludes to a "consensus between the laws of the Torah and the laws of the peoples that whoever brings something new into the world is its owner with regard to rights......" and develops this into something like a theory of strict liability. (See his *Hiddushe Rabbi Shimon Yehuda Hacohen* to *Bava Kama* , New York, 1947, p.1.) Several of the Analysts make use of the distinction between strict liability and liability arising through negligence, but it is not clear to what extent they were influenced by western jurisprudence, and it is probable that such influence as there was was confused and indirect.

term to cover personal injury as well as damage to property). The payment of *kofer* for loss of life of one's fellow man arises from the breach of a duty of care which the Torah imposes on us towards other people; this duty applies towards *persons*, not things or animals, and therefore strict liability rather than negligence remains the basis for compensation for damage to property. (Trop does not elaborate on the reason why the Torah imposes a duty of care with regard to persons rather than things; presumably he sees this as an obvious consequence of the higher value attached by the Torah to human life than to animals or inanimate objects.) Now, so long as an ox is *tam* in every respect the special duty of care does not arise - one is not obliged to supervise a 'normal' ox constantly to make sure it does not attack anyone. However, as soon as the ox has left its state of being *tam*, even though it is not yet positively *mu'ad* with regard to people, the duty of care arises, and from it the liability to *kofer* should the ox gore a man.

That there are difficulties in harmonising these ideas with the whole of rabbinic teaching on *tam* and *mu'ad* need not be denied, and indeed Trop himself faces many of the problems. Our concern, however, is only to show the *logical form* of the argument, and that we shall now proceed to do.

Trop is in effect telling us that there are two aspects of *ha'ada*. The first (let us represent it by M') is *ha'ada* with regard to strict liability in tort; to this, the following proposition applies:

$$-\exists(M') \qquad M'_{ax} \supset M'_{ay}. \qquad ....(4)$$

The second aspect of *ha'ada* (we will represent it by M") is with respect to the special duty of care to humans, and the consequent liability to *kofer*. Using 'h' as the subscript to indicate 'human victim', we get:

$$(M'') \qquad M''_{ax} \supset M''_{ah} \qquad ....(5)$$

Both (4) and (5) are, in the strict logical sense, unlike (2) and (3), *universal*. They are not *ad hoc* statements of specific rules, but formulations of legal principle. They are, in addition, both amenable to a still higher level of generalization, which is apparently Trop's aim, He is telling us, firstly, that liability for damage to property is strict and, secondly, that liability for homicide (the situation with regard to personal injury is unclear) is subject to breach of a duty of care; he sees propositions (4) and (5) as instances of these generalisations.

Trop's achievement is thus that, like the scientist who rejects the *ad hoc* hypothesis but constructs a more general hypothesis to account for what previously appeared to be an anomaly, he has put forward a general theory of tortious liability which ought to accommodate without strain all the rules and instances with which he is concerned. Karo *narrowed* the application of the rules, increasing their *number;* Trop *widened* the application, *decreasing* the number. This increase in the *generality* of the statements of law is at the same time a declaration of belief in the *rationality* of the system as a whole.

Example 2

Hayyim Soloveitchik,[19] *Hiddushe Rabbenu Hayyim Halevi al Harambam, Edut,* 3:4.

Maimonides rules: 'According to the law of Torah evidence in both monetary and capital cases must be oral .... but the rabbis (ruled) that decisions in monetary cases might be made on the basis of written evidence.'[20]

Nahmanides objected that it would follow from this that documentary evidence in marriage and divorce, which have the status of capital issues, would be worthless; yet all authorities agree that, for instance, a woman may be permitted to remarry on the basis of a written bill of divorce provided only that, if necessary, the signatures are confirmed.[21] Indeed, as Soloveitchik points out, Maimonides himself rules this expressly,[22] thereby creating an apparent contradiction in his own words.

Let us formalise the contradiction.

Let 'K' stand or 'case', and the subscripts 'c' and 'o' for 'capital' and 'oral evidence required' respectively.

Then:

(K) $K_c \supset K_o$ ....(1)

---

19 Hayyim Soloveitchik (1853-1918), founder of the Analytic Movement, was born in Volozyn, and taught there for some years until the 1891 closure. He was rabbi of Brisk (Brest-Litovsk) from then until his death, and taught and inspired a large circle of disciples. His *Hiddushim al Harambam* was first published in 1936 at Brisk, though he had personally "combed and curled" the text.

20 *Mishneh Torah, Edut* 3:4.

21 Nahmanides, *Commentary on Maimonides' Sefer Hamitsvot, Shoresh* 2.

22 *Mishneh Torah, Gerushin* 1:16.

But, if marriage and divorce cases are capital cases and nevertheless do not require oral evidence, we have:

$\exists(K) \qquad K_c.\text{-}K_o \qquad$ ....(2)

which contradicts (1).

Traditional commentators[23] simply deny that the generalisation in (1) is applicable to marriage and divorce, and they thus modify and weaken (1) to:

$\text{most } (K) \qquad K_c \supset K_o \qquad$ ....(3)

whilst retaining (2).

In fairness, it must be conceded that there is some rationale for this. *Rashba*, for instance, argued that witnesses of *kiddushin* are exempt from the detailed *derishah vahakirah* examination to which witnesses in capital cases are subject since although *kiddushin* may have *consequences* of a capital nature the act of *kiddushin* is not itself in this category.[24] *Mahashevet Mosheh* argues likewise that Maimonides would hold that although the validity of a bill of divorce can have consequences in capital cases the signatories to the bill are not, at the time of signing, actually giving testimony in such a case. We could in this way retain (1) in its universal form, simply denying that marriage and divorce are instances of K_c. Nevertheless, this is essentially an *ad hoc* approach, devised to cover an apparent anomaly and doing no more than just that. It reduces the sphere of application of the original generalisation and adds a new rule, a new 'epicycle', rather than helping us to reduce the number of rules in the system.

Soloveitchik, at any rate, sidesteps this approach. We must distinguish, he says, between (a) *edut bikhtav*, evidence which has been committed to writing, and (b) *edut shebishtar*, a document which is itself evidence, the creation of a legal fact. (The distinction is like that in modern western law between a probative and a constitutive document.) Probative documents are not admissible in *any* capital cases, *including* marriage and divorce; only a special rabbinic concession for the facilitation of commercial life permits their use in monetary cases. Proposition (1) is thus fully upheld, and the law of evidence seen to be of universal application, subject only to the clearly stated exception which has no bearing on the basic legal principle.

23 For instance, Rabbi Moshe b. Gershon Mendel Kreisberg in his commentary *Mahashevet Mosheh* on Nahmanides, *loc. cit.*

24 *Rashba, Responsa* Vol.3 No. 111.

Proposition (2), however, is rejected, and in its place we can have an entirely new legal principle to the effect that constitutive documents are not subject to the laws of evidence. In terms of our paradigm we have not, this time, split (1) into two new universal propositions (4) and (5), but retained (1) and added a new universal proposition.

Whereas the traditional, casuistic approach to the problem threw light on only the one problematic case, Soloveitchik's solution, being on a much higher level of generality, illumines several long-standing issues in the laws of contract and evidence and sets a clear line of demarcation between the two fields.

Example 3

Isaac Zeev Soloveitchik[25] - 'Half a Woman'

This example has the great advantage that, the original being only six lines long, a full translation can be given. The translation will be literal, and will capture as far as possible the inelegance of the original which, we must assume, was committed to writing by some disciple of no literary skill.

> The Gaon Rabbi Isaac Zeev, long may he live, said that in "half a woman" what is lacking is not in the act, on the part of the man and the woman, who only want half of her, for the *kinyan* of *kiddushin* does not depend on his volition, like purchasing whichever part of a field they want, because with *kiddushin* it is only necessary that they should want *kiddushin*, but as to how much, it doesn't depend on what they want, because it is an act of giving and not a *kinyan*, and *kiddushin* is to all of her and the act is to all of her, but the law of half a woman is, because he actually says "half", the Torah makes it as if there were a *hallut* on half and the *kiddushin* does not take effect.

The reader may with justification feel confused; but such is the obscurity of the less carefully written Analytic texts, which are unintelligible unless one is in the position to draw on a substantial body of related material.

---

25 Isaac Zeev Soloveitchik (1886-1959), popularly known as 'Reb Velvele Brisker', a son of R. Hayyim, succeeded his father as rabbi of Brisk in 1918, and from 1940 until his death lived in Jerusalem with no formal position, but with a wide circle of students and admirers.

The present extract appears (actually in 7 lines) in a presumably unauthorized collection of *Hiddushe HaGRaH* published in Jerusalem in 1955. It appears again in a collection entitled *Hiddushe HaGRaH al Hashass* (Jerusalem, 1969), this time in 5 lines. The books are probably titled as they are because most of the contents are his father's *hiddushim* - where, that is, they can be distinguished.

We must at least cite Rava's statement, to which IZS alluded. Rava said[26] that if (in the course of an otherwise valid act of betrothal) a man says (to the woman he is betrothing) 'Half of you is betrothed to me' there is no effective *kiddushin* at all, 'for the Torah says: "(If a man take) a woman"[27] - (meaning, a whole) woman, not half a woman.'

Let us now attempt to formalise IZS' comments.

Let 'x' stand for 'any object which is physically divisible into parts x', x", x''' and so on.

Let 'Q' stand for 'It is legally possible to make a *kinyan* on (= to acquire)...'

Then:

$$(x) \qquad Q_x \supset (Q_{x'} \cdot Q_{x''} \cdot Q_{x'''} \ldots) \qquad \ldots(1)$$

that is, if it is legally possible to make a *kinyan* on an object 'x', it is legally possible to make *kinyanim* on its separate parts (i.e., as regards the basic law of conveyance - it is of course possible that there may be some incidental impediment to a particular partial *kinyan* - e.g. the vendor may be under some contractual obligation not to sell the object piecemeal).

Now *kiddushin* is commonly spoken of as an instance of *kinyan*, with a woman as its object, yet Rava states that it cannot be applied to part only of a woman. So there is at least one value of 'x', viz. where 'x' is a woman, where (1) will not apply, and we have instead:

$$\exists(x) \qquad Q_x . -Q_{x'} . -Q_{x''} . -Q_{x'''} . \ldots \qquad \ldots(2)$$

which contradicts (1).

One could, of course, just leave it at that, and state that *kiddushin* is an exception to the rule, weakening (1) to:

$$\text{most } (x) \qquad Q_x \supset (Q_{x'} \cdot Q_{x''} \cdot Q_{x'''} \ldots\ldots) \qquad \ldots(3)$$

Perhaps this is all that Rava does, pegging the exception to a convenient biblical quotation. But this is merely an *ad hoc* solution, inventing a special rule to account for a single case, and offering no rationale.

IZS, however, follows the Analytic paradigm. There are two different processes, he says, to which we attach the term '*kinyan*'. One is the

26 *Kidd.* 7a.
27 *Deut.* 22:13.

acquisition of a physical object, the other is the creation of a new personal status. Physical objects are divisible, personal status is not, and *kiddushin* effects not the acquisition of a woman as a physical object but the creation in her of a new status. Status applies not to the woman's *body*, which is divisible, but to her *personality*, which is not. (IZS might perhaps contrast this with being a slave. The case of the man who is half free and half slave is frequently discussed in the Talmud; but slavery, unlike marriage, has an element of bodily ownership.)

Let us complete the formalisation of the argument.

Q has been divided into:

Q' - the sort of *kinyan* applicable to physical objects

and Q'' - the creation of a new personal; status

We thus have:

$$(x) \qquad Q'_{x} \supset (Q'_{x'} . Q'_{x''} . Q'_{x'''} ....) \qquad ....(4)$$

and

$$-\exists(x) \qquad Q''_{x} . Q''_{x'} . Q''_{x''} . Q''_{x'''} .... \qquad ....(5)$$

Both (4) and (5) are universal statements, and both of significance far beyond the academic problem of betrothal of half a woman. (4) establishes the divisibility of ownership of physical objects as related to the actual physical divisibility of those objects. (5) establishes the indivisibility of persons *as* persons, and consequently the inapplicability of legal status to anything other than whole persons. Between them, the two propositions establish a clear line of demarcation between persons and things and emphatically place wives in the former category.

Once again, therefore, we find that where the traditional casuist accounted for an anomaly by an *ad hoc* rule, the Analyst, following the basic paradigm outlined above, has used the anomaly to create a more general theory, decreasing the number of individual independent rules.

The reader may wonder whether we are reading too much into the half dozen lines of IZS' *hiddush*. Can we be sure that he is really talking about creation of a status as opposed to acquisition of a physical object? To answer this I must summarize another passage, this time from a collection of IZS' comments on the weekly *Sidra*.[28] He poses the old question why, if the Patriarchs observed the commandments of the Torah before they were given at Sinai, did Abraham not circumcize before he was ordered to, and why did Jacob marry two sisters.[29] His reply to this throws much light on the Analytic concept of law, though many aspects of this cannot be treated here.

Circumcision and marriage, he explains (I am not following closely his own, or rather his redactor's language), are not, within the laws of Torah, a mere physical operation or change of social status respectively; if they were, then Abraham might effectively have circumcized before he was commanded to do so, and Jacob would have been bound by the social convention which was to receive divine authorization only at Sinai. Circumcision is, rather, the way in which one moves from a *status* of being uncircumcized to a *status* of being circumcized; marriage is the set way by which one changes from unmarried to married *status*. But until these statuses were actually *created* by the Torah (or, in Abraham's case, by express divine command), such a process was meaningless. Had Abraham performed the physical operation of circumcision before he was commanded to, he would not have attained the Torah *status* of being circumcized, for without divine command the status itself did not 'exist'. In Jacob's case, the prohibition of marrying two sisters was without meaning before the Torah was given, for it stems not from the Noachide type of *ishut* (husband/wife relationship) which alone 'existed' before Sinai, but from Israelite *ishut,* which was not 'created' in Jacob's time. As IZS puts it, the *'etsem heftsa shel ishut* (the actual *substance* of the husband/wife relationship) of Israel is different from that of Noachides.

Reading this comment of IZS in conjunction with his discussion of 'half a woman' we must conclude that not only is IZS demonstrating that the specific cases he deals with are instances of more general laws; but these general laws have rational purposes - rational, that is, within the terms of IZS' own theology - to wit, they embody the ideals of human relationships and justice 'created' by the Torah.

---

28 *Hiddushe HaGRIZ al Hatorah* (New York, 1973) section 5 on page 3. From the title page we learn that the contents of the book are *'mipi hashmu'a'* - things *heard* from IZS but, as usual, committed to writing by we know not whom.

29 *C.f. Yoma* 28b.

III

I should now like to state clearly what I claim to have shown in the preceeding analyses, and to comment briefly on its relevance to theories of law in general and Jewish law in particular.

The three examples are all quite ordinary instances of the sort of thing to be found in the published works of the Analysts or heard in the lecture halls of the *yeshivot* in which their methods have been adopted.

I do *not* claim that the same pattern of reasoning is never to be found in earlier rabbinic writing, but only that the paradigm as a whole, the *approach* in which this pattern is a frequent and instantly recognizable feature, is unique to the Analytic School, at least within Jewish jurisprudence. In Kuhn's vocabulary,[30] a 'paradigm' is a (scientific) achievement which possesses the characteristics that (a) it is 'sufficiently unprecedented to attract an enduring group of students away from competing modes of scientific activity', and (b) it is 'sufficiently open-ended to leave all sorts of problems for the redefined group of practitioners to resolve.' Kuhn instances Ptolemy's *Almagest*, Lavoisier's *Chemistry*, Lyell's *Geology*, and similar scientific achievements. In the more restricted field of Jewish law we might instance the development of *derashah* in the schools of Ishmael or Akiva, the '*havayot* ' of Abaye and Rava, the codification of Maimonides, as 'paradigms' of legal research and development; and certainly the Analytic School would be in this category. None of them - scientists or Torah scholars - invented a totally new approach, and historians will discover precedents amongst the forerunners of each. But all, through their 'paradigms', determined the form and direction of further research in their field for a period of time. My claim, then, is that the Analytic School constitutes just such a paradigm, characterized by the particular form of argument I have instanced. But it is, as Kuhn stresses in his own field,[31] the paradigm as a whole, rather than the specific method, which has priority.

It is clear that despite the move towards conceptualism and generality in the work of the Analysts, if we have regard to how they understand the system of Torah-Law as a whole, priority must be allocated not to the high-level generalisations which they extract from the earlier rabbinic material but to that material itself. That is to say, an Analyst is always prepared to revise his generalisation in the light of an earlier, authoritative rabbinic text; but although he might make use of the generalisation to modify his

30 Kuhn, *supra* n.3, at10.

31 *Ibid.*, Chapter V.

interpretation of the rabbinic text he would never utilise it to *reject* the text. He has, in Hart's terminology,[32] a 'rule of recognition', in accordance with which he recognises as valid law the formulation of principles and rules by certain earlier rabbis; formulations of principles and rules by later rabbis, including himself, are valid only in so far as they can be shown to be correctly inferred from the earlier ones. This feature is not unique to the Analytic School, but is common to all schools of Torah-law. There is, however, amongst the Analysts, a special tension which seems to me to be generated by their 'paradigm' of conceptual analysis, for the more general the statements of legal rules and principles the more they are likely to conflict with specific rule applications by earlier authorities; this is surely the reason that the Analysts tend to make a very sharp distinction between the authority they ascribe to the '*Rishonim*' (pre-sixteenth century rabbis) and the considerably lower esteem in which they hold the '*Aharonim*' (later rabbis), for this distinction frees them from the need to accommodate all the statements of the '*Aharonim*'' to their generalisations, thereby substantially relieving the tension.[33]

One might consider this question of priority as between positive law (viz., the law as expressed by those authorities accepted through the Torah 'rule of recognition') and principle (viz., the 'derived' principles of the Analysts) in terms of the Dworkin/MacCormick debate with regard to the relative priority of rules and principles of law. The Analysts, in common with all traditional exponents of Torah-law, take a positivist stance in so far as their criterion of the validity of any particular statement of law is that it be subject to a rule of recognition; this rule defines the *sources* of law, and certainly does not include the writings of the Analysts themselves. One is tempted to suggest, therefore, that the Analysts would regard their own formulations of legal principle as belonging to the law in a quite different sense from that in which the traditional rules belong to it, as against Dworkin, who seems to conceive of rules and principles as equally parts of the legal system, though calling for a different type of handling, - the rules, unlike the principles, being subject to a rule of recognition, and being in practice much easier to identify.

---

32 H.L.A. Hart, *The Concept of Law* (Oxford: The Clarendon Press, 1961), 97.

33 M.A. Amiel (1883-1945), himself a leading Analyst, reminiscing about Shkop's lectures at Telz in the 1890's, writes (in *Sefer Hayovel lerabbi Shimon Yehuda Hacohen Shkop*, Vilna, 1936, 42): '...the Telz approach encourages free criticism; not, of course, criticism of the *rishonim*, whose every word we regarded as holy of holies - but a "critique by pure reason" in those areas where we have no unchallengeable tradition.'

But is it at all correct to draw an analogy between, on the one hand, the 'rules' and 'principles' of the jurists and, on the other hand, the general concepts of the Analysts and the traditional formulations of Torah law? There are at least the following objections to this course:

(i) Traditional formulations of Torah law do not consist of rules only, but include express statement of what Dworkin and others call 'principles'. Dworkin, distinguishing principles in the generic sense from rules,[34] instances the court's statement in *Riggs* v. *Palmer* [35] that 'No one shall be permitted to profit by his own fraud.....' This 'principle' is explicit in Torah sources, i.e. what we may call the 'positive law' of Torah, as *'shelo yehe hote niskar'*.[36] The six principles Dworkin lists as emerging from *Hennessy* v. *Bloomfield Motors, Inc*.[37] can likewise be paralleled to some extent in the older sources of Torah law. W.S. Wurzburger,[38] in arguing that from a Jewish perspective the obligation to promote moral values rests upon a legal foundation, has given a useful account of several of the 'principles', such as that 'Thou shalt do what is good and right......'[39] which are incorporated within the *halakhah*, and in the light of which halakhic rules are applied. There is, indeed, a problem of the relationship between rule and principle within the system of *halakhah* as a whole, but it would be a mistake to identify this with the problem of the relationship between the Analytic concepts and the traditional sources, for the latter, the 'positive law', is not simply a body of 'rules'.

(ii) Conversely, it would be erroneous to regard the Analytic concepts as a body of 'principles, policies and other sorts of standards.'[40] Certainly, the three examples treated above are far more like general rules or definitions than like principles which teach us the standards (*sc.* moral or ethical or sociological standards) according to which we should apply the traditional rules.

Nevertheless it seems to me that there is a valuable analogy to be drawn between the way that MacCormick understands the relationship between principles and rules and the way Analysts see the relationship between their analyses and the traditional rule formulations. This is, moreover, an analogy

---

34 Ronald Dworkin, *Taking Rights Seriously* (London: Duckworth, 1977), 23f.

35 115 N.Y. 506, 22 N.E. 188 (1889).

36 Mishnah *Shevi'it* 9:9 is probably the earliest statement of the principle.

37 32 N.J. 358, 161 A.2d 69 (1960).

38 Walter S. Würzburger, "Law as the Basis of a Moral Society", in *Christian Jewish Relations* 14/1 (March, 1981), 6-18 (Institute of Jewish Affairs, London).

39 *Deuteronomy* 7:18; see *Sifri* 72, *ad loc.*

40 Dworkin, *supra* n. 34, at 22.

which cannot be drawn on the Dworkin model, for Dworkin regards principles as distinct in both form and content from rules.

MacCormick writes that 'the notion of formal justice requires that the justification of decisions in individual cases be always on the basis of universal propositions to which the judge is prepared to adhere as a basis for determining other like cases and deciding them in the like manner to the present one.'[41] He is saying, in effect, that principles are implied in the *logic* of rules, that the form of words in which a rule is expressed could not form a *basis for inference* without an implied principle which can function as the *ratio decidendi* of the case to which it is proposed to apply the rule. The principle is thus, *contra* Dworkin, not an additional statement of law with an independent place in the system, but part of the requirement of universalizability needed to enable the rule to be utilized in the justification of decisions. Principles possess an 'explanatory and justificatory function',[42] they establish the 'coherence' of rules,[43] and generally facilitate the development of the law.

It seems to me that the Analytic paradigm is distinguished from other Torah-law paradigms precisely in the manner in which it effectively asserts the *rationality* of the Torah-system. We have seen that the characteristic form of argument contrasts with the more traditional approach by providing solutions in terms of universal rather than particular propositions; this is closely analogous with the way MacCormick sees specific law-rules not merely as *illustrating* universalizable principles of law but as logically presupposing them.

Now, if we maintain that the distinguishing feature of the Analytic paradigm is its implicit assertion of the rationality of the system of Torah-law, how are we to understand the declarations by many of its leading protagonists of the inadequacy of human reason to plumb the depths of Torah? Epstein, for instance, bemoans this inadequacy at great length,[44] and Baruch Dov Leibovitz impresses on his disciples that 'The Torah cannot be understood by the logic of human reason, but by the ways and principles of

41 MacCormick, *supra* n.9, at 99.

42 *Ibid.* at 238.

43 *Ibid.* at 106 and Chapter VII.

44 Moshe Mordecai Epstein (1866-1933) came under Soloveitchik's influence in Vilna, and is particularly strongly associated with the Slobodka (Kovno) yeshiva, part of which he took with him to Hebron in 1923, and after the 1929 riots in which tens of his students were murdered by the Arabs, to Jerusalem, where he died. The reference is to his *Levush Mordecai* on *B.M.* (Jerusalem, 1929), Introduction.

the Torah; therefore one should adapt one's understanding to the Torah, not the Torah to one's understanding.'[45]

This question may be approached from both the theological and jurisprudential angles, and we will take the former first. The 'rational purpose' which MacCormick has in mind, in effect the *ratio decidendi* of the case - he instances Lord Atkin's famous 'neighbour principle'[46] - is certainly not what the Analysts would wish to deny; on the contrary, their whole effort to 'understanding the Torah' is directed precisely to this end, and they do not deny the power of the divinely assisted human brain to achieve it. What they are denying - this is an aspect of their reaction to the *Haskalah* movement - is the power of the human intellect to fathom the profound wisdom which, they believe, underlies the divine commandments. Epstein is indeed explicit on this point.[47] Rationalist ethics, in his view, is inadequate for the comprehension of even those commandments, such as helping the needy, which have in the past been categorized as 'rational commandments' - for, as he asks, surely such a commandment is an invitation to interfere with God's will, for if God did not wish that particular man to be needy does He not have an infinite number of ways in which to help him? The Analysts are convinced of the transcendent reason of Torah, and of the logical and purposeful nature of its detailed structure; in emphasising the shortcomings of human reason they are (a) rejecting the claims of philosophers to provide exhaustive, satisfying, rational explanations for the commandments, and (b) urging their disciples to learn constantly, for there is no end to learning, and one can always discover more of the divine wisdom which permeates Torah, though however much one discovers it is but 'a drop in the ocean'. The Analysts are not so much *rejecting* rationalist ethics as declaring its *inadequacy* to tell the glory of God. As Leibovitz puts it: 'The world and intelligence were both created by the word of Torah; for the fact that men despise theft and murder and so on is because a portion of the Torah has been placed within them.'[48]

We must now approach the question from the jurisprudential angle. Is the Analytic disparagement of human reason akin, for instance, to Dworkin's contention that only Hercules, 'a lawyer of superhuman skill, learning, patience and acumen', could in fact discover the correct answer, within a

45 Baruch Dov Leibovitz (1867-1939), a devoted disciple of Soloveitchik. The quotation is from his son-in-law, Rabbi Reuben Grossowsky's biographical introduction to Vol.2 of Leibovitz' *Birkat Shmuel* (New York, 1954), 6.

46 MacCormick, *supra* n.9, esp. at 157-160.

47 M.M. Epstein, *supra* n.44, at 15.

48 *Supra* n.45, at 4.

given system of law, to every 'hard' problem?[49] Would they share his contention that the discretion of judges is so limited that there is, in principle, only one 'correct' answer to each problem? We may readily grant that the Analysts would accept that only Hercules - better, a Samson - could actually demonstrate the correctness of all their principles and apply them infallibly to particular cases, and their disparagement of human reason certainly includes this notion, though it is equally certainly not exhausted by it. Do judges, or interpreters of Torah, according to the Analysts, have 'strong' or 'weak' discretion, and even if, as both Dworkin and MacCormick maintain, they have 'weak' discretion only, can we say whether their disagreements arising from the exercise of discretion are primarily speculative, thus in principle capable of right decision, or, as MacCormick holds, basically 'practical disagreements over what is best, all things considered, to do,' and *not* in principle subject to 'correct' decision?[50]

We must distinguish between the system of Torah-law as a whole, viewed through history, and the activities of the Analysts themselves. Within Torah-law as a whole there are several in-built discretionary processes, both of a clearly legislative nature, as in the enactment of rabbbinic legislation, and judicial, as in *hora'at sha'ah* , or the nunerous instances where the codes counsel decision *kefi re'ot eine hadayyan.*[51] However, it is none of my purposes here to discuss the role of discretion in Jewish law as a whole, or even the practice of the Analysts individually when acting in a judicial capacity. Within their characteristic sphere of activity, viz. theoretical exposition of Torah, it is clear that no discretionary procedure is envisaged, whether 'strong' or 'weak', but there is a constant sense of discovery, of revealing what is 'there' already; as was implicit in my earlier analogy with Kuhn's descriptions of the natural scientist at work, the Analysts proceed as if their task is one of observing and understanding an objective world, not, indeed, the objects of nature, but the 'facts' of the Torah as the objective creation of God. With regard to this work they frequently, if disingenuously, disclaim originality or novelty,[52] and thus by implication

49 Dworkin, *supra* n.34, at 105.

50 MacCormick, *supra* n.9, at 248.

51 *Cf.* the principle of *shuda dedayne* (e.g. *Ket.* 94a) - though it is possible that this type of procedure relates only to assessment of evidence, not to discretion in the interpretation of law.

52 Another Soloveitchik disciple, Elhanan Bunem Wasserman (1875-1941), quotes his master as saying: "It is not for us to make *hiddushim:* only the *rishonim* were able to do this. Our task is simply to understand what is written" (*Ohel Torah,* Baranovichi, 1924, Introduction).

any possibility of the conscious exercise of discretion in their interpretation of the earlier sources. Samson, like Hercules, would ultimately find *the* answer, in terms of the system, to any question put to him. But in one respect the Analysts would agree with MacCormick, who writes: 'Dworkin postulates a Hercules who can construct a best-possible theory of a given legal system. But Hercules can construct that only at the far end of an infinite regress of theories.'[53] MacCormick, like Aristotle, abhors an infinite series; but my hunch is that the Analysts and their Samsom would revel in the infinite regress of mutually modifying Torah theories. In the days since Aristotle mathematicians have learned to handle these situations; they should not exceed the capabilities of a Samson.

53 MacCormick, *supra* n.9, at 255.

LEGAL POSITIVISM AND CONTEMPORARY *HALAKHIC* DISCOURSE

by

ALAN J. YUTER*

I Positivism and Jewish Law

Unlike natural law theories, legal sociology, or history of law, legal positivism focuses upon the legal order, its constituent norms and the hierarchy of those norms. In Hans Kelsen's formulation of legal positivism,[1] this hierarchy is abstracted from specific legal content. Ethical, political, and ideological motives are irrelevant to the evaluation of legal orders.[2] There are, however, many scholars of Jewish law who are passionately committed to the relevance, efficacy, and religious worth of their subject and, as consequence, adopt a positivist posture in their *apologia* of *Halakhah*.[3] For these scholars, changing moral climates, historical relativism, and textual criticism are "modernist" ideological concerns that are equally out of place in legal positivism as they are in theological Orthodoxy.

For the academic scholar of Jewish law, legal positivism provides an analytic tool whereby Jewish law is studied without approval [as in the cases of Orthodoxy and, until recently, American Conservatism] or disapproval [as in the cases of Reform Reconstructionism, and Secularism]. Orthodox positivists who justify their approach by appealing to the unchanging will of an eternal Lawgiver assign to the Deity the role of author of the Torah, or first constitution of the Jewish people. According to Hans Kelsen's model, *Halakhah* may be considered to be a theological positivist order, but the role

---

* Rabbi, Congregation Ohr Yisrael, Spring Valley, New York; Adjunct Faculty, Rockland Community College.

1 Hans Kelsen, *Pure Theory of Law*, trld. M. Knight (Berkeley, Los Angeles, and London: University of California Press, 1967).

2 "Uncritically the science of law has been mixed with elements of psychology, sociology, ethics and political theory. This adulteration is understandable, because the latter disciplines deal with subject matters that are closely connected with law. The Pure Theory of Law undertakes to delimit the cognition of law against these disciplines, not because it ignores or denies the connection, but because it wishes to avoid the uncritical mixture of methodologically different disciplines." - Kelsen, *supra* n.1, at1.

3 See Appendix.

of the Godhead in *Halakhah* would be formal, not theological. God merely serves as the ground, or first principle, that justifies compliance with the constitution, *without* any metaphysical assumption regarding either the personality of God or the content of His constitution.[4] Still, most halakhists fail to appreciate the difficulty in theological positivism:

> A theological ethics that regards God as the highest norm-creating authority cannot state that somebody else has ordered to obey the commands of God - because this would have to be an authority higher than God. And if the norm: "One ought to obey the commands od God" were presumed to be posited by God, it could not be the reason for the validity of God-created norms, because it would itself be a God-created norm.[5]

The unanswered question for the halakhist is "why one should obey the commands of God?" In his outstanding study of the Biblical concept of *berit*, or covenant, Professor José Faur demonstrates how Jewish law must be understood in a non-theological positivist model.[6] Significantly, no metaphysical or mystical axiom appears in Faur's halakhic positivism. Faur first shows that monotheism, as a doctrine, is independent of revelation.[7]

He then argues *against* the doctrine of natural right - "that there are certain rights that do not depend on legislation and authority, but are necessitated by the very order of the universe," and *for* the doctrine of positive right "that every right is the result of legislation, and thus depends on promulgation and authority. Fundamentally, it [legal positivism] rejects the notion of an objective criterion of right and wrong."[8] Faur's reading of the Covenant doctrine coincides with Kelsen's legal positivism, but differs with conventional Orthodox positivists. By rejecting the natural right theory that assumes an "objectively" correct morality, Faur endorses only one functional dogma: "the individual has the duty to obey the decrees of authority or society."[9] By distinguishing between law and theology, Faur finds that:

---

4 Kelsen, *supra* n.1, at 194-195.
5 Kelsen. *supra* n.1, at 203.
6 "Understanding the Covenant", *Tradition* 9 (1968), 33-55.
7 *Ibid.*, at 34.
8 *Ibid.*, at 37.
9 *Ibid.*, at 39.

> Although essentially Judaism means obedience to God's law, God's law is not identical to the revealed will of God. Revelation, though proceeding from God and recorded in the Bible, is not as such authoritative ... The basis of Judaism is not conformity to the revealed will of God, but conformity to the Sinaitic law.[10]

Faur's view of halakhic positivism focuses solely upon the legal norms of Jewish law. Since both man and God possess free will, any law is conditioned upon a *berit,* a covenant or pact, that would be mutually binding: only after the *berit* was ratified by Israel, during which God himself is absent, is the covenant in force. This pact is not unilateral, for Israel, at God's behest, authorized God to give the law:

> The authority of the Mosaic law does not rest on the fiat of God's will, but upon the fact that it was accepted as such by the entire people of Israel. As thus conceived, divine authority is not the effect of an Absolute Power, who dictates His will to his inferiors, but of negotiation between two parties who are equally free to assent and dissent.[11]

Faur's critique of natural law also parallels Kelsen's because both Kelsen and Faur recognize the dogmatic quality of assertions that a particular morality may be "objectively" correct or that values may be derived from nature. For Kelsen the secularist as well as Faur the religionist, positive law has no theological content and both argue that only legislated, or positive law is the content of any legal order.

II The Basic Norm in the thought of Hans Kelsen

Central to Kelsen's legal positivism is the doctrine of the basic norm. This norm is not a legal norm because (a) it is not derived from any higher norm and (b) it does not carry a sanction. This *Grundnorm,* or "ground norm", stands outside the legal order, but serves as its justification. Like Faur's dogma "that one has a duty to obey authority," Kelsen's basic norm only posits that "one ought to behave according to this specific constitution."[12] Since this basic norm is the same for any legal order, its content is derived from its function, rather than dogma. Like Faur in his treatment of the Sinaitic covenant, Kelsen argues that "the presupposition of the basic norm does approve any value transcending positive law."[13] The

10 *Ibid.,* at 41.
11 See Appendix.
12 Kelsen, *supra* n.1, at 201.
13 *Ibid.*

basic norm only authorizes the specific and general norms of the legal order; it is not itself a legal norm. It is

> the reason for the validity of all norms belonging to the same legal order, the basic norm constitutes the unity of the multiplicity of these norms. This unity is expressed also by the fact that a legal order may be described in rules of law that do not contradict each other.[14]

The theological implications that many halakhists read into the basic norm of Jewish law is consistent with the legal positivism of Kelsen's Pure Theory.

It has been argued that Kelsen's basic norm is a flawed doctrine, and cannot be used as a litmus test for legal positivism in general or halakhic positivism in particular. Actually, Kelsen's basic norm formulation not only stands the attack of its critics, it is an appropriate model for halakhic positivism as well. In his *Concept of Law*, Professor H.L.A. Hart espouses a doctrine concerning a "rule of recognition",[15] which is an alternative to Kelsen's basic norm. This rule of recognition operates in conformity with the way the legal order is viewed and accepted by the society under its rule. Hart also believes that law must have a moral minimum.[16] His insistence upon communal assent is of importance to Kelsen only insofar as legal orders, to be valid, must enjoy a modicum of compliance, and Kelsen as well as Faur reject the natural law doctrine that there exists an identifiable moral minimum in every legal order. Hart himself is unable to explain why Kelsen's basic norm has no substantive content other than that the constitution must be obeyed.[17] What troubles Hart is the "purity" of Kelsen's pure theory; Kelsen's positivism makes no assumptions concerning non-legal issues, and the basic norm, insofar as it is a non-legal norm, has no meaning whatsoever once it is separated from the legal order it serves.

Like Hart, Graham Hughes looks in vain for a specific extra-legal content in Kelsen's basic norm:

> all [that] the rules and rulings [of a legal order] have in common is common descent from the same basic set of procedures of rule making, and that this feature of legitimate descent from procedures appears to be the reason why the rules are *accepted as binding*. If the external observer now wishes to give a systematic account of the order he has observed he might well characterize it as resting on the

14 *Ibid.*, at 205.
15 H.L.A. Hart, *The Concept of Law* (Oxford: The Clarendon Press, 1961), 97.
16 *Ibid.*, at 189.
17 *Ibid.*, at 245 note 3.

> presupposition of the validity of the basic norm, by which he would mean nothing more than certain basic procedures are actually accepted in that society as authoritative rules.[18]

But for Kelsen's basic norm, itself the centerpiece of his pure theory, communal approval is irrelevant. If the legal order is effective, then the consistent normative hierarchy is valid. By appealing to a "psychological or sociological analysis of the motivations underlying acceptance", Hughes' view approaches Hart's doctrine of the rule of recognition.[19]

Professor Julius Stone is also unable to determine whether Kelsen's basic norm is intrasystemic or extrasystemic:

> The adjective "basic" is indeed itself inapt for a norm which Kelsenite theory places at the top of the pyramid of hierarchy of norms. "Apex" norm would be far more appropriate especially ... because it would still leave Kelsen's ambiguous term a residue of meaning to which that term is less sytematically incongruous.[20]

Stone focuses upon the logical connection between the basic norm and the legal order it authorizes. Kelsen's basic norm could be regarded either as intrasystemic, within the legal order, or, since it is not a legal norm, extrasystemic and, as such, the highest norm in a hierarchy of legal norms, thus an "apex" norm.

For Kelsen, the norm allows for the objective behavior of people to be assigned a normative value, and, as such, it provides the condition for the legal evaluation of behavior. This confusing metaphor is borrowed from the theory of knowledge of Immanuel Kant:

> According to Kant's epistemology, the science of law as cognition of the law, like any cognition, has constitutive character - it "creates" its object insofar as it comprehends the object as a meaningful whole. Just as the chaos of sensual perceptions become a cosmos, that is, "nature" as a unified system, through the cognition of natural science, so the multitude of general and individual legal norms .... becomes a unitary system, a legal "order", through the science of law. But this "creation" has a purely epistemological character. It is fundamentally different from

18 Graham Hughes, "Validity and the Basic Norm", *California Law Review* 29 (1971), 699, emphasis supplied.

19 *Ibid.*, at 703.

20 Julius Stone, "Mystery and Mystique in the Basic Norm", *Modern Law Review* 26 (1963), 44.

> the creation of objects by human labor or the creation of law by the legal authority.[21]

The norm is the condition for legal discourse in the same sense that, for Kant, space and time are conditions for human knowledge. Just as the sensibilities of space and time are contributed to knowledge as the *a priori* conditions of the knowing subject,[22] the basic norm is the "transcendent logical condition" of legal discourse.[23] Significantly, Kant denies that this transcendent, or non-empirical knowledge is metaphysical, even though it transcends empirical experience.[24] Just as space and time are *a priori* concepts that have no empirical content, the basic norm of a legal order contains no content because it transcends the legal order. The sensibilities of space and time apply to all knowledge in the same way that the basic norm: "obey the historically first constitution" applies to every valid legal order.

III The Basic Norm in Jewish Law: A Case Study

The recent debate between Professors Menahem Elon and Izhak Englard concerning the nature of modern halakhic research reflects two different understandings of Jewish law. Englard claims that Jewish law is a religious positivist order and assigns to the [Orthodox] rabbinate the sole authority to interpret the law. Any prescriptive judgment on the part of an academic scholar invalidates the intellectual detachment of the judgment. For Elon, objective philological and historical research into Jewish law often reveals trends, ideas, and policies that are unnoticed by contemporary [Orthodox] rabbis, and he prescriptively argues that Jewish law be integrated into Israeli

21 Kelsen, *supra* n.1, at 72. In this study, references are taken from Kelsen's *Pure Theory* rather than his *General Theory* (1945) because it is in the former that this aspect of his theory is more fully developed.

22 Immanuel Kant, *Critique of Pure Reason* (London, Macmillan, 1964), 204. See also Kelsen, *supra* n.1, at 202.

23 Kelsen, *supra* n.1, at 223.

24 For Kant, there can be no knowledge of the noumenous object, because it is not conditioned by experience. See his antinomies of pure reason, *supra* n.22, at 384f., in which the logical deduction of pure [non-experiential] reason leads to unavoidable contradictions.

law.[25] Englard, in turn, rejects Elon's "historicism" as an unscientific heresy similar to Conservative Judaism,[26] as well as his prescriptive hope that the study of Jewish law would "prepare" for its reception into the law of Israel.[27] Both Englard and Elon defend their positions with reasoned arguments, but their divergent views stem from radically different uses of positivist thought and rhetoric. Kelsen's pure theory is an appropriate analytic tool in this discussion because it alone

> describes the law and attempts to eliminate from the object of this description everything that is not strictly law: Its aim is to free the science of law from alien elements.[28]

The merits of Elon's and Englard's positions can be evaluated by examining how they treat Jewish law as a normative order, and how their descriptions of what Jewish law *is* coheres with their prescriptions of what Jewish law *ought to be.*

In his *Ha-Mishpat Ha-Ivri,* Elon devotes a chapter to a discussion of the sources of law and their application to Jewish law.[29] Although Kelsen, unlike Elon, does not consider literary and historical "sources" to be sources of law in the pure sense,[30] they focus their attention upon the specific acts of legislation which create the norms of the legal order. In Elon's scheme, historical scholarship provides the description necessary for accurate prescription; the meanings of texts must be clarified so that the norms contained therein may be understood correctly.

Although Elon acknowledges Kelsen's pure theory and its search for an ultimate principle from which other legal principles are derived,[31] he retreats into theology in his discussion of the basic norm. According to Elon, the basic norm of Jewish law is:

---

25 Menahem Elon, *Ha-Mishpat Ha-Ivri* (Jerusalem: Magnes Press, 1973) I, chapter II shows the flexibility of Jewish law to respond to changing situations, and Elon associates the lack of flexibility with the loss of national autonomy (at 70). He argues for the integration of Jewish law in the legal order of the State at I, 117-118, and "More About Research into Jewish Law", *Modern Research in Jewish Law,* ed. Bernard S. Jackson (Leiden: Brill, 1980), 85.

26 Izhak Englard, "Research in Jewish Law - Its Nature and Function", in Jackson, *supra* n.25, at 52-53.

27 *Ibid.,* at 56.

28 Kelsen, *supra* n.1, at 1.

29 Elon, *supra* n.1, at 1.

30 Kelsen, *supra* n.1, at 232.

31 Elon, *supra* n. 25, at 213f.

> that all that appears in the Pentateuch renders the legal order of Jewish law binding... [it is] the eternal legislation of Jewish law that is not given to change, addition, or diminution.[32]

The source of this "basic norm" is the word of God:

> To answer this question [concerning the source of the Torah's authority] we leave the realm of Jewish legal concepts and enter the realm of faith: it is a fundamental assumption of Judaism that the source of the authority of Torah lies in the Giver of the Torah.[33]

Unlike Faur, who recognizes that the basic norm must be an unconditioned ultimate principle, Elon's formulation of the basic norm centers upon the revealed text of the Written Torah, which is conditioned by yet another basic norm, God's will. He does not explain how God is authorized, as does Faur, to legislate. Elon's emphasis upon the written Torah, as the historically first constitution, is no less problematic. As a text, the Pentateuch is a *literary* source of law: *deoraita,* or Torah law, derives from the Divine will, and not because it is found in the Pentateuchal text. Dogmas concerning the *nature* of revelation are irrelevant to any legal discussion. In spite of Elon's imposition of a theological content upon his version of Jewish law's basic norm, Elon never allows his theology to effect his program, for "the law is not in heaven."[34] In this regard, Elon's basic norm is functional and formal, not theological. Elon's citation that the sciatic nerve rule derives from Sinai is significant because, according to the Mishnah[35] and Maimonides,[36] the

---

32 *Ibid.*, at 215-216.

33 *Ibid.*, at 216. This "Giver of the Torah" doctrine need not reflect a theological dogma. According to Kelsen, "the concept of God presents itself as a personification of the world order .... The state is also essentially conceived as a person, and as such is merely the personification of an order." See his "God and the State", in *Essays in Legal and Moral Philosophy* (Boston: Reidel, 1973), 70. For Kelsen, the doctrine of causality, originally assumed to be grounded in God, is a reflex of the doctrine of retribution. See "The Principle of Causality in Modern Science", in *Society and Nature* (New York: Arno, 1974), 262. These doctrines may or may not be "real", but they exist in and are created by human beings insofar as human beings try to understand their universe. Thus, the "Giver of the Torah" may be the Lord who revealed Himself at Sinai, or the personification of the Jewish world order.

34 *Deuteronomy* 30:12.

35 *Mishnah Hullin* 7:6.

36 *Commentary to the Mishnah, ad loc.* See Elon's discussion, *supra* n.25, at 216-217.

rule *is not* derived from the Pentateuch's account of Jacob's dream, but is preserved in the Oral Torah. Its normative status stems from its origins in *Torah*, or God's will, and not because it is recorded in the Pentateuch. The modern halakhic scholar examines the norms of Jewish law as a given , while the bible critic studies a literary source of law. Since the basic norm of Jewish law is that "Israelities ought to obey the words of God contained in the [Oral as well as Written] Torah," any judgment concerning the nature of God or the literary transmission of the Torah document is *legally* meaningless.

While Elon does not develop his views on the nature of revelation, he often demonstrates how halakhic norms authorize his program of the integration of Jewish law into the legal structure of an autonomous Jewish state. In his discussion of annulment of marriages where a *get*, or writ of divorce that must be initiated by the husband, is unobtainable, Elon argues that *hafkaah* [annulment] is talmudically authorized and that although the procedure has not been implemented in recent halakhic history, it is still a legitimate practice that is appropriate in an autonomous Jewish society.[37] He also prefers responsa literature and *Halakhot*, or rulings accompanied by analysis and summary, so that the current expression of Jewish legal opinion not be disconnected from its legitimating sources. In his summary of the criticism of Maimonides' *Yad*,[38] as well as subsequent efforts of codification,[39] Elon finds that Codes are treated too authoritatively. By employing the *genres* of *Halakhot* and responsa, Elon believes that the historical processes of halakhic development will be artificially inhibited by a popular acceptance of particular codes. Elon hereby implies that the rabbinate ought to exercise the authority they need to possess, and that the conservatism that developed in the Jewish Diaspora is unjustified in a modern Jewish state. While Elon does not presume to issue *pesakim*, or decisions, like the Orthodox rabbi, the program he advocates is clearly ideological, but within the historical parameters of halakhic norms.

Whereas Elon's program is defended in terms understandable to a legal positivist, Izhak Englard's rhetoric is positivist in nature, but his methodology is not. For Englard, *Halakhah* is described as a rabbinic oligarchy, not as a normative order. In place of a discussion of the relative values assigned to the norms of Jewish law, Englard emphasizes the theological basis for the law over and above the legal content:

---

37 Elon, *supra* n.25 at 711-712.

38 *Ibid.*, at 997.

39 See Appendix.

> The emphasis ... on substance of the legal solution is likely to blur the distinctive features of a legal system .. By open rejection of the formal basis of the normative order, a person places himself outside the original system. Thus, a judge, by declaring the American Constitution to be normatively irrelevant, would step outside the traditional American system; his declaration would signify the creation of a new normative system.[40]

For Kelsen, the term "normative order" is a system of norms that regulates human behavior.[41] Englard uses the term to signify the normative judgments of the rabbinic oligarchy. By emphasizing that the "formal basis" of Jewish law is grounded in theological-political dogma, Englard leaves the discipline of law and enters the realm of theology:

> The religious elements [of Jewish law] go to the essence of the normative order. Its validity lies ultimately in its supra-human authority; its ends are of a transcendent nature.[42]

Although Englard employs Kelsenite terms like "normative order" and "validity", his imposition of theological-political content upon the basic norm is inconsistent with Kelsen's doctrine that regards the basic norm as the *formal* assumption authorizing obedience to the historically first constitution, and to which no ideological content or approval is implied.

While Englard explicitly defines the theological content of the basic norm or the hierarchy of his so-called "normative order", he defines *Halakhah* as "the set of norms considered binding by orthodox Judaism."[43] Thus, the divinely ordained rules that are not given to change or ideological manipulation are alive and well in the sociological practice of the Orthodox community. While this observation may be empirically valid, its *legal* validity is not justified by legal norms.

In his critique of Elon's "historical" method, which he identifies with Conservative Judaism, Englard finds Elon guilty of a scientific error as well as a theological heresy:

> The assertion that Conservative Judaism is more scientific than Orthodox Judaism is as completely unfounded as the argument that the legal solution elaborated by the modern scholar is more scientific than that suggested by the Orthodox rabbi.[44]

---

40 Englard, *supra* n.26, at 25.
41 Kelsen, *supra* n.1, at 14.
42 Englard, *supra* n.26, at 23.
43 *Ibid.*
44 *Ibid.*, at 53.

For Englard, the scholar only engages in description, but the Orthodox rabbi is authorised to engage in prescription as well as description. Elon's adoption of historical methodology, for Englard, makes ideological assumptions that are scientifically questionable and theologically incorrect. But this normative judgment on Englard's part is justified only if *Halakhah* is viewed as a rabbinic oligarchy rather than as a Kelsenite normative order:

> If Jewish law constitutes the object of study, one has to accept it in its integral entirety. It is *totally unacceptable* that the modern scholar should reach a legal solution different from that of the [orthodox] Rabbi.[45]

Englard's term "totally unacceptable" is unacceptably ambiguous because it is not at all clear whether the "scholarly solution" referred to above is unacceptable because scholars ought not to engage in prescriptive judgments, in which case Englard bears the onus of demonstrating that halakhically committed individuals who are engaged in the study of *Halakhah* are not authorized to make normative judgments, or because Englard finds the prescription to be theologically and politically improper, in which case Englard's judgment is "normative" rather than "objective".

Englard's view that Jewish law is a rabbinic oligarchy rather than a normative order is underscored in his rejection of Justice Silberg's interpretation of the Ochnai oven legend.[46] In contrast to Silberg, who believes that the legend teaches that Judaism embodies a Rule of Law,[47] Englard argues that the Talmudic account teaches a religious rather than legal doctrine. According to the legend,[48] Rabbi Eliezer b. Hyrcanus protests to his colleagues that their ruling, reinstating a state of ritual impurity upon a defiled earthenware oven after it is shattered, is incorrect. After hearing and rejecting R. Eliezer's arguments by majority vote, the Talmud reports R. Eliezer's three miracles, none of which are accepted by the court as sources of law. Appeals to nature suggest that value, or "ought" statements, can be derived from "is" statements, or facts of nature. Convinced that his view represents an old authentic *Halakhah*, R. Eliezer summons a *bat kol*, or

45 *Ibid.*, at 52, emphasis supplied.

46 See Englard's "*Tanur shel Ochnai - Perushah shel Aggadah* ", *Shenaton Ha-Mishpat Ha-Ivri* 1 (1974), 45-46.

47 Moshe Silberg, *Kakh Darkah shel Talmud* (Jerusalem: *Mifal ha-Schichpul,* 1962), 68f.

48 *Bava Metsia* 59b.

oracle,[49] that reveals the will of God, the Giver of the historically first constitution. The sages reply that God's will is legally irrelevant because the normative order makes no provision for a "transcendent" or "supra-human authority" to intervene in legal debate. Even if one knows what God actually desires, the only *legal* criteria is the majority vote of the Talmudic court, the authorized organ of norm creation.[50]

The message of the Ochnai oven legend lies in the affirmation that *Halakhah* is foremost a normative order, and not a theological or political oligarchy. This doctrine is described most aptly by Elon:

> And even the oracle - the revelation from heaven - is not authorized to intervene in the establishment of the law because the Torah - once given - is "no longer in Heaven", and the law in that [Ochnai oven] case is established on the basis of what is written in the Torah - "the law follows the majority." .... God Himself, the Giver and Source of the law, who, as it were, by means of an oracle, made it known that R. Eliezer's view was the correct Torah truth, is forced to admit that his children [= the authorized sages] - who think differently, and who are the majority - have defeated Him [= have ruled against God legitimately].[51]

In Kelsen's terms, the doctrine *"Torah min hashamayim"*, or revelation, is a statement that the basic norm of Jewish law, like any law, transcends experience and authorizes the legal order of norms to assign legal value to human behavior. The doctrine "*Lo bashamayim Hi*," the law is not [now] in Heaven, indicates that *Halakhah* is indeed a normative order initiated by God to be developed by and for human beings, and *any* ruling consistent with those norms is valid, but any appeal to metaphysical truth is not.

Since legal positivism, insofar as it is a scientific tool, makes no evaluation about the worth or binding quality of the legal orders it describes, positivist rhetoric cannot be mustered to defend the "unchanging" quality of Jewish law. Legal positivism can only determine whether specific decisions or norms are valid, or consistent with the principles of the legal order. If the Orthodox rabbinic oligarchy is indeed the only authorized organ of legislation, then that authorization must be demonstrated. I am *not* arguing

---

49 For the definition of *bat kol* as oracle, see Saul Lieberman, *Hellenism in Jewish Palestine* (New York: Jewish Theological Seminary, 1962), 194-199. The *sugya's* continuation, "My sons have bested me", indicates that the voice or echo was a Divine oracle in this context. Significantly, neither the oracle nor the fact that the old *Halakhah* was in accordance with R. Eliezer's view, as witnessed by the rule of *M. Kelim* 5:10, are of the same legal weight as a majority opinion of the court.

50 Elon, *supra* n.25, at 228.

51 See Appendix.

that Englard is wrong in his assertion that only the Orthodox rabbi can prescribe Jewish law; that assertion, however intriguing, is not within the scope of this essay. For Englard to make his case as a legal positivist, he would have to examine the authority of a State endorsed rabbinate, the authority of which is not accepted as universal, even within Orthodoxy. He also would be required to demonstrate that a halakhic argument, based on dogmatic assumptions, offered by a learned lay professional electrician, a professor of *mishpat ivri*, or a young gentleman in a *kollel* without any "official" position whatsoever, do not have halakhic validity. It is still unclear how post-talmudic rabbinates, charismatic sages, or *rashei yeshivah* (heads of Talmudic academies) are legally authorized norm creating organs in the absence of a Great Sanhedrin.

Appeals to theology, politics, history or sociology are ideological in nature, and inappropriate to a positivist study of law. This too is a condition of Kelsen's positivism:

> If we do not understand by "ideology" everything that is not natural reality or its description, but nonobjective presentation of the subject influenced by subjective value judgments and glorifying or disfiguring the subject of cognition; and if we designate as "reality" not only the natural reality as the subject of natural science, but every subject of cognition including the subject of the science of law, namely positive law, as legal reality; then a presentation of positive law must keep itself free from ideology.[52]

APPENDIX

Note 3:

> For Rabbi J. David Bleich, *Contemporary Halakhic Problems* (New York: Ktav, 1977), xiii-xiv, "Judaism is fundamentally a religion of law, a law which governs every facet of the human condition. The Torah contains not merely a set of laws but also canons of interpretation as well as principles according to which possible conflicts may be resolved. He continues, at xvi, by affirming that "the methodology by which some opinions are accepted and others excluded from application to practice constitutes a highly complex aspect of Halakhah ... Decision making is also bound by rules of procedure." Perhaps the most articulate and concise formulation of Orthodox positivism is R. Moses Tendler's: "The literal interpretation of the theological doctrine of divine revelation differentiates Torah (= Orthodox) Judaism from the organized faith communities that have arisen as deviants from the traditional form ... The Pentateuch and the oral tradition are of

52 Kelsen, *supra* n.1, at 105.

equal authority, are equally obligatory on all Jews as the direct instructions of God himself to his nation, Israel ... Empathy, charity, kindness (sic) are the results of observance of the Torah commandments governing our mutual responsibilities. They are not the motivations of these observances. I feed the poor because the Torah so ordains." See *The Condition of Jewish Belief* (New York: American Jewish Committee, 1966), 236-242. According to these views, Jewish law is a divinely ordained normative order in which ethics are part of, and not transcendent to, the law.

Note 11:

Ibid., at 44. A significant distinction can be drawn between the positivist rhetoric in Bleich's thought and Faur's. Bleich never discusses any relativist, or tentative element of the covenant. *All* of Torah is binding because all the Torah is a reflection of the Divine will. For Bleich (*supra* n.3) the orthodox rabbinic intellect can understand the Torah's esoteric secrets: "To the (orthodox) scholar, a novel .... insight affords a more convincing demonstration of the Divine Presence than a multitude of philosophical arguments. It is a form of divine confrontation that must be experienced in order to be understood. Yet it is a relationship which every Jew may experience .... in miniature form, through Torah study." This experience allows the scholar to perceive "God speaking to him through the leaves of the Gemara, from the paragraphs of the Schulhan Aruch, and the words of the verses of the Bible. The Sages long ago taught 'Kudsha berich hu ve-oraita had', God and Torah are one." The Sages to whom Bleich refers is Moses De-Leon, the author of the Zohar! (See Zohar 73a, cited in Elliot M. Dorff, *Conservative Judaism: Our Anscestors to our Descendants* [New York: United Synagogue, 1979], 234). According to Bleich, the Torah content and the Divine will cannot be distinguished, and this unity, described in terms borrowed from a non-legal tradition in Judaism, merges in the mystical experience of Torah Study. While Bleich believes that the Torah scholar's correct views follow from a mystical experience, he also makes the positivist claim that Jewish law is a canon of rules, interpretation, and principles for resolving contradictions (Bleich, p. xii-xv). Faur, unlike Bleich, does not believe that man can know God from the content of the Torah or from any mundane source (Faur, at 38-39), and he cannot accept the doctrine that all that God wills is Divine law: "God's law is not identical to the revealed will of God. Revelation, though proceeding from God and recorded in the Bible, is not as such authoritative" (at 41). Bleich's "positivism" is merely authoritarian rhetoric, whereas Faur's positivism is a thoughtful examination of Jewish law as a normative order of legislation and he, like Kelsen, takes pains to distinguish the legal from the non-legal elements in Judaism.

Note 39:

For Elon, any code that presumes to be final "is not desirable, not only because the meaning of the solution and ruling may be given to dispute, but rather because this type of code is not appropriate in the world of *Halakhah*, it even endangers the capabilities and health (of *Halakhah*)" - *supra* n.25 at 1121. Elon's attitude towards codes is consistent with his treatment of the principle that "the law follows the latter day authorities (*halakhah ke-vatra'e*). In his citation of the Asheri (*Piske ha-Rosh, Sanhedrin* 4:6) and R. Joseph Kolon (*Teshuvot ha-Maharik* 84), Elon finds that the entire tradition is mediated by latter day authorities (at 235). While Elon treats this doctrine consistently, he fails to distinguish between Maimonides' Code, which claims to be a systematization of Toraitic and Rabbinic norms that are binding upon Israel, and subsequent efforts of Codification. Maimonides' Code is only a *compilation* of talmudic law, and not a *revision*, or authoritative Code. Any deflection from talmudic law that is unjustified by talmudic methodology would, for Maimonides, be unjustified, while the *Asheri* would regard just such deflections to be legitimate if the post-talmudic sages approved. By failing to distinguish between Maimonides' effort at compiling talmudic law and subsequent codifications, Elon ignores the possibility that subsequent practice may indeed be invalid according to a Halakhah that is understood as normative order. For example, current Orthodox practice ignores the prohibition against dancing on Simhat Torah because of "custom". See *Shulhan Arukh Orah Hayyim* 330:3, *Isserles, gloss ad loc.* and Kagan, *Mishneh Berurah, ad loc.*

Note 51:

After R. Eliezer offers "all the proofs in the world", which nevertheless fail to convince his colleagues, he exhausts his recourse to *legally* valid juridic activity. By appealing to Nature's miraculous intervention, which is manifest in a Carob tree uprooting itself, a creek changing its course, and the tottering of the Academy's walls, R. Eliezer claims that his opinion is confirmed by Nature's will. R. Joshua scolds the walls for tottering because Nature cannot be consulted in legal debate, for Nature's self-suspension has no legal meaning. Appeals to subjective reason or to miracles are ultimately grounded on a claim that God makes continuous legal revelations to his chosen; when a *bat kol*, or oracle, comes forth from heaven to endorse R. Eliezer's ruling, R. Joshua excommunicates R. Eliezer for persisting in a line of argument that challenges the authority of the court, the Divinely ordained norm-creating organ. This pericope rejects the claim of individuals who, in a religious society, claim religious political or legal power because *they* know God's will. The God who promulgated the Law authorized exclusive norm-creating jurisdiction to the human court, thereby disenfranchising those who arrogate to themselves the right to read God's mind. By admitting that His intrusion into legal discussion is inadmissible (*nitshu li vanai*), God actually reaffirms the authority of the court to reject all arguments, even His own, no matter how compelling and regardless of their source, when they are not grounded in legally recognized sources of law..

IS THERE ALWAYS ONE UNIQUELY CORRECT ANSWER TO A LEGAL QUESTION IN THE TALMUD? *

by

HANINA BEN MENAHEM **

The judicial process has been studied both in general terms and with regard to particular legal systems and a vast amount of literature has been written on the subject.[1] However, notwithstanding a few partial historical descriptions,[2] very little attempt has ben made thus far to analyse the judicial process within the context of Talmudic Law.

In this paper I propose to consider a jurisprudential dilemma related to the judicial process with special reference to talmudic Law. The dilemma is this: Is there always one and only one correct answer to any legal question? Does the bulk of binding legal material, i.e. rules, principles precedents etc., dictate always one uniquely correct answer to any legal question? Is a litigant in a trial always entitled to a specific ruling? This is a recurrent issue in contemporary legal philosophy and the subject of an ongoing debate. I shall begin by presenting here at the outset a very crude outline of this

---

* A paper presented to the first international Conference of the Jewish Law Association, held on Mount Scopus, Jerusalem, August 1980.

** Lecturer, Faculty of Law, Hebrew University of Jerusalem.

1 The literature is too vast to be listed. Apart from general works dealing with the subject there are many studies specifically devoted to the judicial process, amongst which the following can be singled out: B.N. Cardozo, *The Nature of the Judicial Process* (New Haven: Yale University Press, 1921); J. Stone, *Legal Systems and Lawyers' Reasoning*..(London: Stevens & Sons Ltd., 1964); E.H. Levi, *An Introduction to Legal Reasoning* (Chicago: University of Chicago Press, 1949); R.A. Wasserstrom, *The Judicial Decision* (Stanford: Stanford University Press, 1961); N. MacCormick, *Legal Reasoning and Legal Theory* (Oxford: Clarendon Press, 1978).

2 H.P. Chajes, "Les Juges Juifs en Palestine de l'an 70 à' l'an 500", *Revue des Etudes Juives* 39 (1899), 39-52; A. Kaminka, "Hamase betor makor lehalakha", *Mehkarim betalmud* (Tel Aviv: Dvir,1951), 1-41; E.Z. Melamed, "Hamase bamishnah kemakor lahalakhah",*Sinai* 46 (1959-60), 152-166; B. De Vries, "Huveda kegorem lehidush hahalakhah", *Festschrift zu L. Jung* (New York: Shulsinger Brothers, 1962), 143-148; A. Weiss, *Studies in the Literature of the Amoraim* (Hebrew) (New York: Yeshiva University, 1962), 313-334; S. Zuri, "Hamassim bebet dino shel R. Ami", *Sinai* 6 (1940), 26-35, 193-201; J. Neusner, *A History of the Jews in Babylonia,* (Leiden: E.J. Brill, 1965-1970); Lamm & Kirschenbaum, 'Freedom and Constraint in the Jewish Judicial Process", *Cardozo Law Review* 1(1979), 99-133.

jurisprudential controversy. I shall then proceed to show that Talmudic Law sometimes grants judges full autonomy to make a choice between conflicting and incompatible norms and that consequently in those instances no one uniquely correct answer exists. I shall conclude by arguing that a certain controversial post-talmudic institution can be explained in terms of this talmudic conception.

Let us call those who adhere to the view that there is always one uniquely correct answer proponents of a monistic view, and let us call their opponents proponents of a pluralistic view. Now it is clear that there are legal questions with regard to which there is no dispute: proponents of the pluralistic view concede that there are legal questions which yield only one correct answer. Three conditions have to be satisfied simultaneously: (a) there must be a clear, unequivocal norm; (b) the legal principles and precedents which are applicable to the case at issue must be clear, unequivocal and consistent with each other; (c) the case at issue must be clearly and unequivocally within the limits of (a) and (b). Proponents of the pluralistic view concede that there are cases, indeed the great majority of cases, which satisfy these three necessary conditions. However, at the same time they claim that it is inevitable that at least in some cases, one or more of these conditions will not be met. When this is so it does not mean that anything goes. Norms, principles and precedents from other fields of the law preclude various otherwise-possible solutions and serve as constraints that must be taken into account in the process of reaching a decision. However, in this case there is no one uniquely correct answer which a litigant has a right to demand. As against this position stand adherents of a monistic view. They too have to make concessions to their opponents. They do not claim that every judicial decision is the correct one. Obviously this is not the case. Moreover, they concede that in some cases, what have been termed 'hard cases', we might not be able to demonstrate the correct answer at all. But, they claim, the fact that one cannot demonstrate the correct answer does not mean that it does not exist. Much of the attack levelled against the monistic position concentrated around this last point, which seems very much like a metaphysical belief. In any case the monists hold that a litigant is always entitled to a specific ruling and that it is the task of the judge to discover if possible this uniquely correct ruling.

Basically, the pluralistic position has two lines of reasoning. First, the argument from the open texture of the law and the unavoidable vagueness in which the law is sometimes expressed. These two features which all legal systems share preclude the possibility of having always one uniquely correct answer. This argument which has received an admirable formulation by

H.L.A. Hart in his *The Concept of Law* [3] demonstrates the main avenue in which the dilemma has been approached. The debate has been concluded mainly in terms of general jurisprudence without any specific reference to a particular legal system.

The other line of reasoning derives the alleged pluralistic nature of the law from its content. Here attention is drawn to specific norms which a particular legal system happens to contain and which, so it is claimed, amount to granting full autonomy to the agent to choose any of a number of alternating modes of behaviour. The difference between these two lines of reasoning is that the former seeks to establish pluralism as a necessary feature of the law whereas the latter claims only that pluralism is a possible feature of the law. I side with proponents of the pluralistic position. I believe that the second more restrictive line of reasoning, though it has been relatively little discussed, is the more powerful one and the less vulnerable to objections from its opponents. It is the peculiarities of particular legal systems which drive home the limits of abstract analysis and which force us to modify the rather dogmatic conception depicted by general jurisprudence.

In what follows I propose to show that talmudic Law does contain norms which support the pluralistic position. My contention is not, nor need it be, that talmudic Law contains such norms as a general matter. Rather, I attempt to show that these norms figure in the system in exceptional cases.

But first, a word of caution. We must guard ourselves against a very common, indeed tempting fallacy. Everyone who is familiar with talmudic Law is well aware of the great variability and differentiation of legal opinions recorded in the Talmud with regard to almost every legal issue. Our sources record and discuss a multitude of diverse legal opinions and this is considered as a characteristic feature of the Talmud. Is this very fact not sufficient to establish the pluralistic nature of talmudic Law? To show the fallacy of this argument we must look briefly into the attitudes in the Talmud itself towards this celebrated phenomenon of dissension.

On the one hand, one finds talmudic expressions and dicta which imply very clearly a negative attitude towards dissension; statements which consider dissension as the outcome of a morally and socially deteriorated situation, and which express the belief that it will be eliminated in the future. Thus we read "When the haughty of heart multiplied dissension increased in Israel; when the disciples of Shammai and Hillel multiplied who had not served their masters sufficiently, dissension increased in Israel and the Torah became

3 H.L.A. Hart, *The Concept of Law* (Oxford: The Clarendon Press, 1961).

like two Torot."[4] This, compared with the ideal situation described in the *Tosefta*: "At the beginning there was no dissension in Israel ..."[5], shows that dissension is considered as a negative phenomenon. The belief in the future elimination of the dissension is expressed in a tannaitic dictum in *Eduyot:* "R. Simeon says: Elijah will not come but to conciliate disputations",[6] and this theme is repeated in the *Yerushalmi* : "And the dissension will not be eliminated until the son of David comes."[7] An alleged dictum of the Prophet Mohammad runs as follows: "Difference of opinion within my community is a sign of the bounty of Allah." It is clear that the above citations do not endorse this Mohammedan conception. It is equally clear that these citations rule out the possibility of inferring a pluralistic position from the great variability of legal opinions recorded in the Talmud. The widespread divergence in legal matters is an unfortunate but temporary phenomenon which has to be endured until better days come when it will be abolished.

On the other hand, one finds talmudic passages which prima facie imply a more positive attitude towards dissension, and which have been exploited in an attempt to show a pluralistic conception in the Talmud. One finds statements scattered throughout the Talmud to the effect that the various dissenting opinions were all "given by one and the same shepherd"[8] or that "one leader uttered them all."[9] And there is of course the famous saying that "these and these are the words of the living God,"[10] referring to the controversy between Bet Shammai and Bet Hillel. On the basis of this last citation, B. Jackson claims that Jewish Law denies that there is always one uniquely correct answer - ascribing this view not to the deficiencies of the human intellect but the superiority of the Divine who can transcend the law of contradiction.[11] However, a careful examination of these citations reveals that they do not justify the dissension nor indeed do they deal with the jurisprudential status of dissenting opinions but are concerned with a different problem altogether. The problem is this. Given the dissension one might be puzzled by a theological difficulty: how do we know that a particular

4 *Sot.* 47b.
5 *T. Hag.* 2:9 and parallels. See also B. De Vires, *Mehkarim besifrut hatalmud* (Jerusalem: Mosad Harav Kook,1968), 172-178.
6 *Eduy.* 8:7.
7 *Y. Hag.* 2:2 (77,4).
8 *Bamidbar Rabba, Parasha* 15 (22).
9 *Hag.* 3b.
10 *Erub.* 13a.
11 *Supra*, 6, 33f. and literature there cited.

opinion chosen from amongst many others as the legally binding one actually represents the will of God? The answer given is that all legal opinions by virtue of being sincere attempts to discover the true will of God are qualified candidates to be a model for the *Halakhah*. In other words, the will of God will be accomplished by following any of them. On the theological level the content of the binding law is immaterial; what is important is the form and manner in which the law is determined. One might even say that these citations support the claim that "Halakhic truth is not and need not necessarily be identical with absolute or divine truth."[12] But from this it does not follow that "it is possible to have more than one valid solution to a legal problem."[13] On the legal level, that is, the level of the binding (valid) law, there is according to these citations one uniquely correct answer. The saying concerning the controversy between Bet Shammai and Bet Hillel concludes after all: "But the law follows the opinion of Beth Hillel."[14]

Likewise, the pluralistic position cannot be established merely by showing that different norms within the system prescribe contradictory behaviour. When this occurs - and no doubt it does - it is in most cases due to an oversight of the legislator and represents an anomalous situation which is accounted for by a canon of interpretation such as *lex posterior derogat priori*. Proponents of the monistic position can claim that the contradiction is merely an illusion. Prima facie it exists but on reflection it fades away.

However, the matter is altogether different if one and the same piece of legislation contains two incompatible norms, making both of them parallelly binding in such a way that the reconciliative devices often available are ruled out. There is no hierarchical order between the two norms: the legislator does not say 'follow A; if you cannot follow B', nor does he say 'follow A and B' which would amount to a logical contradiction, but rather 'follow either A or B'. Practically speaking this would mean that the addressee of that piece of legislation is given full autonomy to follow either of the two conflicting modes of behaviour. In this case there is a clear indication that the problematic situation is not a result of an oversight of the legislator but was deliberately created. No doubt, such legislative behaviour is rare. One might even argue that it is undesirable. But if we could show that talmudic

12 Lamm and Kirschenbaum, *supra* n.2, at 102.

13 *Ibid.* Lamm & Kirschenbaum regard these two different theses as one and the same. The difference between them, however, is borne out by the very story that they cite to support their view - the oven of Akhnai. Here the "uniquely correct answer" in the legal level is evidently not identical with divine truth.

14 *Erub.* 13a.

Law does occasionally resort to this technique, we have, I believe, succeeded in showing that at least in these cases there is no uniquely correct answer which those affected by this piece of legislation have a right to demand.

Now, to show that talmudic Law does in fact employ this technique I propose to examine the way in which talmudic legislation meets the challenge of legal doubt. In the present context a legal doubt is defined as an inability to decide on the merits of the case between two equally persuasive but mutually exclusive opinions, or two equally authoritative but opposing masters or two equally reliable but conflicting traditions. A legal doubt thus defined may occur at three different levels - the legislative, the judicial and the individuals. By the legislative level I mean any talmudic determination of an halakhic controversy made in general terms either by a named authority or anonymously whether or not this determination is accepted as halakhically binding. This is, admittedly, not what is commonly understood by an act of legislation. However, it has this resemblance to an act of legislation, that there is here an attempt to create a general norm. The judicial level is the level at which an actual controversy between two parties is pending for a decision; the individual level is the level at which an individual may find himself when he is confronting a legal doubt in the above sense about his own behaviour. We shall limit the present examination to the legislative level. We may distinguish among three types of solutions, employed by the Talmud whenever a legal doubt as defined above occurs, which, I submit, reflect different approaches to our jurisprudential dilemma. These solutions instruct the judge how to decide in an unsettled issue pertaining to monetary matters.

First, what might be termed 'either-or'. Here the Talmud adopts the two conflicting opinions, transforming both into valid legal norms.[15] It is this solution which provides the example we are seeking. Second, an intermediate solution - 'Let it be divided'. The controversial sum of money is split between the two parties; thus a compromise is achieved between the opposing views.[16] Third, 'the burden of proof lies on the plaintiff'. Here neither view is adopted nor is there any attempt to compromise. The instruction is to invoke the principle that he who claims money must make his case.[17] It is hard to detect any regularity in the employment of these solutions. It has to be conceded however that the 'either-or' solution is not

15 Examples are cited below.

16 See *Tosafot* on *B.B.* 62b.

17 See *ibid.*

the most frequent one. But frequency is not at issue. What is important is its very occurrence. Here are a few examples.

The general rule is that a creditor who seeks his money back from the heirs of his debtor cannot recover the loan unless he takes an oath that the debt is still outstanding.[18] Now if the creditor dies before taking this oath there is one opinion, endorsed by Rab and Samuel, which holds his heirs do not inherit this debt because they are unable to take an oath that the debt is still outstanding. In its legal formulation this rule appears thus "A man cannot bequeath an oath to his children,"[19] that is to say, a man cannot leave to his heirs any money whose recovery from those who hold it is conditional upon his taking an oath. The legal effect of this opinion is that the heirs of a debtor in such a case are under no legal obligation to pay back their father's debt. Against this view there is another opinion, endorsed by R. Eleazar, to the effect that the heirs of the creditor - in the circumstances described above - can take a similar oath, that their father did not give them any instruction that the debt had been paid, and then they are entitled to exact the money from the heirs of the debtor.[20] After various unsuccessful attempts to decide which of the two opinions should prevail thc Talmud concludes:

> R. Hama said: Now since the law has not been stated either in accordance with the view of Rab and Samuel or in accordance with the view of R. Eleazar, if a judge decides as Rab and Samuel it is legal; if he decides as R. Eleazar it is legal.[21]

The inability to decide on the merits of the case is solved by adopting both opinions. Consequently, on the judicial level there is no doubt. Both opinions are correct and the judge is called upon to choose one of them. A very concrete manifestation of the pluralism which results from this solution is found in R. Papa's comment thereon that there is no way to predict what would be the legal outcome of a case in which a document is being presented to the heirs of the debtor by the heirs of the creditor and that its fate depends on the judge before whom the document is presented. No doubt, this sounds an extremely realistic evaluation of the law. The heirs of the creditor come before the court to seek justice but they cannot claim that they have a right to a specific ruling. But, unlike the American realists, R. Papa does not deny the concept of normativity. Rather he calls attention to the consequence

18 *Ket.* 87a.
19 *Shev.* 48a.
20 *Ibid.*
21 *Shev.* 48b.

of having two conflicting, equally binding, norms incorporated into the system.

Let us see another example pertaining to the laws of inheritance. Biblical law provides that a firstborn son is entitled to a double portion of his father's estate vis-à-vis his brothers.[22] The Talmud reports a tannaitic controversy regarding the scope of this right.[23] Does this right extend to profits that were not due at the time when the father died but were incurred after his death? The Sages hold that a firstborn son is not entitled to a double portion in this case whereas Rabbi is of the opinion that the right of the firstborn son covers this case as well. For reasons that need not occupy us here, the Talmud cannot determine which opinion should prevail. One suggestion is that of R. Hiyya : "He who acts in accordance with the opinion of Rabbi is acting correctly; he who acts in accordance with the view of the Sages is acting correctly."[24]

It was not only in halakhic disputations regarding monetary matters that this technique was employed. It was likewise used in ritual controversies such as the appropriate manner of reciting the *Shema*,[25] the appropriate time of reciting the afternoon prayer[26] and the appropriate order of putting on one's shoes.[27]

So far we have seen a few examples of particular halakhic controversies that ended in the adopting of both opinions. But the technique has a much wider application. The Talmud in *Eruvin* proposes a legal rule according to which in any halakhic disputation that was not settled the subject of the disputed norm may follow either opinion provided he remains consistent in his choice:

> Whenever you come across two Tannaim or two Amoraim who differ from one another in the manner of the dispute between Bet Shammai and Bet Hillel a man should not act either in accordance with the lenient ruling of one master and the lenient ruling of the other master, nor in accordance with the restriction of the one and the restriction of the other, but either in accordance with the lenient and restrictive ruling of the one or in accordance with the lenient and restrictive ruling of the other.[28]

22 *Deuteronomy* 21:17.
23 *B.B* 124a.
24 *Ibid.* 124a-b.
25 *Ber.* 11a.
26 *Ber.* 27a.
27 *Shab.* 61a.
28 *Erub.* 7a.

This last rule shows that at least here the Talmud does not demand consistency in the halakhic system as such but only insists that the agent himself should be consistent.

The 'either-or' solution is based on the implicit assumption that it need not be the case that every legal question has one uniquely correct answer, whereas the other two solutions mentioned above are clearly in accordance with the monistic position.

One might object to the above analysis on the ground that the pluralism which results from the 'either-or' technique is analogous to that which results from any law that grants judges discretion. Now, the reader may have noted that I used the term 'autonomy' rather than the more common legal term 'judicial discretion'. The reason is that I believe a distinction has to be made between the 'either-or' examples and the more common laws of discretion. Consider the law which prescribes a certain course of behaviour that can be accomplished in more than one way, e.g. the law may prescribe that everyone has to give 10% of his income to charity without any further specification. Now, the giving can be accomplished in more than one way: I can give charity to A, B, C, etc. Does this example support the pluralistic position? I believe that there is an important difference between the charity example and the case where two conflicting norms are prescribed. A typical legal rule is composed of the following:[29] a norm act (give charity); a deontic operator (ought, permitted, forbidden); the subject of the norm (the addressee, the agent); the object of the norm (A, B, C) ; conditions of application (having an income). The norm act plus the deontic operator constitute the norm. We have to distinguish between the case where one and the same norm covers an equivalence class of objects or conditions of application and the case where two incompatible norms are deemed by the legislator to be legally equivalent. I reserve the term 'discretion' to any case where one and the same norm is being considered. I employ the term autonomy where a choice is to be made between two conflicting norms. In the charity example, A B C etc. constitute an equivalence class of objects of one and the same norm. Giving charity to any member of the equivalence class is deemed as an act of complying with the norm. The 'either-or' examples are of a different character. Here two conflicting norms are prescribed. Complying with one norm is *ipso facto* the violation of the other. The uniqueness of the 'either-or' examples can be further demonstrated if we consider another common type

---

29 This terminology is derived from G.H. von Wright, *Norm and Action* (London: Routledge & Kegan Paul, 1963) quoted in S. Munzer, "Validity and Legal Conflicts", *Yale Law Journal* 82 (1973), 1141.

of judicial discretion. Consider the law which provides a sentence of from one to ten years imprisonment for those convicted of a certain crime. Whenever the legislator grants judges discretion as in this example the judge is called upon to transfer the indefinite language of the legislator into practical, concrete and definite terms. The role and function of the judge is that of an authoritative interpreter. The legislator, as it were, postponed legislation, leaving the completion of this task to the court. In the 'either-or' example the judge has a different function. His role is not to complete the task of the legislator but to carry out his fully articulated will. The court has, however, an autonomy to choose between two courses of action. I conclude, then that the 'either-or' solution constitutes a concrete example of a law which leads to more than one 'uniquely' correct answer and cannot be reduced to the more common laws of discretion.[30]

In the remainder of this paper I wish to relate the foregoing discussion to a certain legal institution which came into existence in the 15th century. From the 15th century onwards (but earlier, as it is sometimes claimed)[31] one finds in the Responsa literature a novel legal institution which later attracted sharp criticism from both rabbinic and academic circles. According to this institution the defendant in a civil case could avail himself of the fact that there was a divergence of legal opinion to claim that the opinion favouring his position was the correct one notwithstanding any view to the contrary.[32] The result of such a plea was that the court was estopped from giving judgment against the defendant even though the court held that the opinion on which the plaintiff relied was the correct one. The history of the institution, which is known as the *Kim Li* argument, constitutes a very important chapter in the history of Jewish Law. Its origin goes back to Germany of the 15th century, a period in which reverence, dread and respect for earlier generations - all to an unprecedented extreme - dominated the halakhic world. However, amongst later Jewish authorities there were those who showed great reservation towards this institution and who were reluctant to apply it.[33] Consequently many restrictions were imposed on the doctrine and its applicability was limited. However, it has survived and still occurs -

30 The 'either-or' example provides an excellent example for a possible contribution of particular jurisprudence to general jurisprudence. S. Munzer argues that it is possible for a legal system to contain conflicting yet valid rules. His theoretical discussion is followed by an hypothetical example (*supra* n.29, at 140). The 'either-or' solution provides a real example and reinforces his general argument.

31 See M. Elon, *The Principles of Jewish Law* (Jerusalem: Keter, 1975), 134.

32 See *Pahad Yitshak* by Isaac Lampronti, s.v. *Kim Li*.

33 See *Arukh hashulhan* by Jehiel Epstein, *Hoshen Mishpat* 25:13.

though in a much more technical form - in the decisions of the Rabbinic Courts in Israel. In general it can be said that one's attitude towards the *Kim Li* argument reflects one's self-image. Those who restrict the applicability of the argument or exclude it altogether are those who tend to believe in legal innovation, legal freedom and legal independence. Those who readily allow the use of this devise are those who tend to lean heavily on their predecessors and who dare not depart from them in legal matters. For the present purpose I shall content myself with the above general exposition of the argument and shall save the reader the technicalities with which the argument has been surrounded. But I give here one concrete example.

Most rabbinic authorities hold that a legal obligation can be created for an unspecified undertaking, for example covering all expenses of curing a sick person.[34] Maimonides, however, is of the opinion that unless the obligation is fixed and known exactly at the time of its undertaking, no legal obligation can be created.[35] Now suppose A undertakes to pay all expenses of curing B's sick child and suppose that later A wants to withdraw from his undertaking. According to the doctrine of *Kim Li* A could avail himself of Maimonides' view and plead that this is the correct ruling - therefore he is not bound by his undertaking - thereby inhibiting the court from giving judgment against him, even though the court holds that such an undertaking is legally valid. The inhibition of the court to give judgment against the defendant in spite of its conviction to the contrary is the main feature which distinguishes the doctrine of *Kim Li* from the talmudic principle "the burden of proof lies on the plaintiff." The talmudic principle operates only when the court itself is in doubt and hence cannot reach a conclusion. The principle is invoked by the court itself on its own initiative. The doctrine of *Kim Li,* on the other hand, is invoked primarily by the defendant and operates even though the court has no doubt whatsoever.

There are at least two ways to account for the inability of the court to give judgment against the defendant when the latter raises the *Kim Li* argument. The prevailing view is that the very existence of conflicting halakhic opinions creates an objective legal doubt. The individual conviction of the judge that the law actually follows one opinion rather than the other cannot suppress or overcome the objective doubt. Hence, the principle that no money can be recovered unless the plaintiff can show that the legal basis for his claim is correct, is applied. The underlying assumption of this is that every legal question yields one uniquely correct answer. The existing

---

34 See *Tur, Hoshen Mishpat,* 60 sec.9.
35 *Maimonides, M.T., Mekhirah* 11:16.

halakhic disputation casts doubt on the correctness of the proposed ruling of the court and hence the court lacks the power to exact money from the defendant. Under this account, the objection voiced against the doctrines of *Kim Li* is well understood. The court is deprived of the main functions habitually assigned to courts, viz. to give an authoritative interpretation of the law.

I suggest that the *Kim Li* argument can be explained in terms of a pluralistic conception of the law. The very existence of halakhic controversy manifests the fact that the system contains more than one arrangement that might govern the case at issue. Hence if the defendant successfully shows that his position is backed by law the plaintiff's claim has to be dismissed. The proposed ruling of the court does represent the law, but the law also provides that there is a parallel arrangement equally valid that governs the case at issue. The connection between the present discussion and the earlier part of this paper must be clear by now. My suggestion to account for the *Kim Li* argument in terms of a pluralistic conception is based on the Talmudic 'either-or' solution described above. But there is this difference: as we have seen, the either-or solution grants judges full autonomy to make a choice between conflicting norms. The doctrine of *Kim Li* does not grant judges any similar autonomy. Once the argument is invoked by the defendant, the judge is bound to apply it and to dismiss the claim. However, if we ask why the argument has this effect, if we are unwilling to regard it as a magical formula, then the answer according to the present account is that the system contains more than one arrangement. The doctrine of *Kim Li* is then less radical than the 'either-or' solution but is conceptually-speaking based on it.

PART TWO

CHRONICLE

CURRENT RESPONSA, DECISIONS OF BATE DIN AND RABBINICAL LITERATURE

1. JUDGES UNDER THREAT

In a contribution to the Tevet 5740 issue of *Hama'ayan* , Dr. Abraham S. Abraham discusses a number of questions pertaining to interpersonal obligations in face of danger. Perhaps the most intriguing of these is the obligation of a judge to hear a case and to render a just verdict despite a threat directed against him.

The biblical passage "You shall not be afraid of the face of any man" (*Deuteronomy* 1:17) is understood as an admonition directed to judges. This exhortation is amplified in the *Sifre* , *ad loc* ., with the comment, "Lest you say 'I am afraid of so-and-so lest he kill my son or lest he kindle my stack [of corn].'" R. Yonatan Eibeschutz (*Urim vetumim* 12:2) states that this exhortation applies only in the case of a judge who has already begun trying a case. However, prior to accepting a case for adjudication, a judge who has reason to be afraid of one of the litigants may justifiably decline to involve himself. Indeed, the *Gemara* (*Sanhedrin* 6b), cites this verse in stating that a judge who has already heard the litigants' arguments and knows in which direction "the verdict inclines" is forbidden to withdraw because of fear.

The problem which must be addressed is why this prohibition differs from others. The general principle is that all prohibitions are set aside in face of danger to life. If so, it should follow that a judge who feels threatened should be permitted to withdraw in order to prevent danger to himself or to others. *Teshuvot Shevut Ya'akov*, 1, no.143, states that in cases of genuine danger this is indeed the rule with regard to the prohibition "You shall not be afraid of any man" as well. Nevertheless, declares *Shevut Ya'akov* , *halakhah* provides that a mere threat directed against a judge must be disregarded on the grounds that, in general, no Jew is to be suspected of actually contemplating a murderous reprisal against a judge because of an unfavourable verdict. However, when a real danger does exist, concludes *Shevut Ya'akov* , the judge may withdraw even after hearing arguments.

R. Moshe Schick, *Maharam Schick al Taryag Mitsvot* no.416, also declares that a judge may withdraw at any time because of a threat to life. *Maharam Schick* asserts that the ruling recorded in *Sifre* follows the position that one must suffer martyrdom rather than misappropriate the property of another. Since normative *halakhah* is not in accordance with that view, a judge may likewise withdraw from a case in face of danger.

In the following issue of *Hama'ayan*, Nisan 5740, the editor, R. Yonah Emanuel, draws attention to a statement of Rabenu Yonah (*Shaare Teshuvah* 3:188) that apparently is at variance with the position of *Shevut Ya'akov*. Rabenu Yonah states "A person must deliver himself to danger ... one who sits in judgment should not fear that he may die (at the hands of) any man, as it is said, 'You shall not be afraid of the face of any man.'"

Rabbi Emanuel also cites an anecdote recorded in *Sanhedrin* 19a. A slave of King Yanai committed an act of homicide. Thereupon Shimon ben Shetah summoned Yanai to appear before the *Bet Din*. Upon Yanai's demurrer, the colleagues of Shimon ben Shetah refused to support the demand that the trial of the king proceed. They were obviously afraid of incurring the wrath of Yanai. Shimon ben Shetah called on God to punish his colleagues. The *Gemara* concludes the narrative by stating that the angel Gabriel cast them to the ground and they died.

A similar event is recorded by Josephus (*Antiquities* 14:9). Herod was summoned before the *Sanhedrin* because he had unjustly put people to death. When he appeared, attired in his royal robes and attended by armed warriors, the members of the *Sanhedrin* fell silent. Shammai then chastized the judges of the *Sanhedrin* and predicted that they would fall by the sword.

The question thus far is whether or not the judge may withdraw from a case because of fear. A further question which presents itself is whether, even according to the position of *Shevut Ya'akov* (who maintains that in the face of genuine danger the judge may recuse himself) and the judge who finds it impossible to withdraw may render an unjust verdict in favor of one of the litigants who has threatened him with death? The discussion in *Hama'ayan* presents two opposing viewpoints in response to this question.

Rabbi Eliezer Waldenberg, Jerusalem scholar and member of the Supreme Rabbinical Court of Appeals, is quoted (*Hama'ayan* , Nisan 5740) as stating that in the face of a real threat to life even subversion of justice is warranted. He bases himself on the *Gemara (Ketubot* 19a), which permits false testimony in the face of danger. Rabbi Waldenberg states that the same principle applies as well to rendering an unjust verdict. This is also the opinion of R. Moshe Schick, *Teshuvot Maharam Schick, Orah Hayyim,* no.303, and *Maharam Schick al Taryag Mitsvot* no.416.

Dr. Abraham (*Hama'ayan*, Tevet 5740) quotes Rabbi Emanuel as expressing the view that it is not reasonable to assume that miscarriage of justice is permissible even in face of danger. Dr. Abraham responds with the observation that the transgression involved is no different from other transgressions, which are suspended in the presence of danger.

It seems to this writer that the prohibition involved in rendering a false juridical decision is indeed qualitatively different from other transgressions. *Baba Kamma* 38a reports that the Romans sent two officials to the sages in the Land of Israel to study *Torah.* The officials expressed satisfaction with what they learned with the exception of one aspect of tort liability in which Jewish law seems to manifest prejudice against non-Jews (the Jewish owner of an ox which gores the ox belonging to a non-Jew is not liable for damages, while the non-Jewish owner of an ox which gores an ox belonging to a Jew must make restitution). Despite their discomfiture with this legal provision, the officials promised that they would not divulge this aspect of Jewish law to the governmental authorities in Rome. R. Shlomoh Luria, *Yam shel Shlomoh, Baba Kamma* 4:9, raises an obvious question. Imparting this information to the Roman officials could easily have had catastrophic consequences for the entire Jewish people. There was, after all, no guarantee that the officials would be kindly disposed and would not deliver a full report to the government in Rome. Why, then, did the sages not misrepresent the law by telling the Roman emissaries either that, in the case in question, both a Jew and a non-Jew could be culpable for damages, or that neither would be culpable? *Yam shel Shlomoh* responds by declaring that *Torah* may not be falsified even in the face of danger; falsification of even a single detail is tantamount to renunciation of the *Torah* in its entirety.[1]

It seems to this writer that *Yam shel Shlomoh's* position is reflected in the well-known narrative related by the *Gemara, Gittin* 56a. Bar Kamza determined to betray the Jewish people to the Roman Emperor:

> He went and said to the Emperor, the Jews are rebelling against you. He said, How can I tell? He said to him: Send them an offering and see whether they will offer it [on the altar]. So he sent with him a fine calf. While on the way he made a blemish on its upper lip, or as some say on the white of its eye, in a place where we [Jews] count it a blemish but they do not. The Rabbis were inclined to offer it in order not to offend the Government.. Said R. Zechariah b. Abkulas to them: People will say that blemished animals are offered on the altar. They then proposed to kill Bar Kamza so that he should not go and inform against them, but R. Zechariah b. Abkulas said to them: People will say one who makes a blemish on consecrated animals is to be put to death. R. Johanan thereupon remarked: Through the forbearance [*anvatnuto*] of R. Zechariah b. Abkulas our House has been destroyed, our Temple burnt and we ourselves exiled from our land.[2]

1 See, however, R. Elijah ben Samuel of Lublin, *Teshuvot Yad Eliyahu* no.48, who disagrees with this position.

2 Soncino translation, with revisions.

It is popularly assumed that the *Gemara*, in describing *anvatnuto* of R. Zechariah ben Abkulas, is censuring him for misplaced humility and lack of initiative. This understanding is reflected in a note in the Soncino translation (page 255, note 2), which renders this term as "humility". Yet *Rashi* translates the term *anvatnuto* as "his forbearance" or "his patience". Forbearance is a matter quite different from humility and does not seem to warrant censure.[3] The *Gemara's* categorization of R. Zechariah's action is thus a statement of fact and is not a criticism.

The reaction of the sages was quite predictable. The prohibition against offering an animal with a blemish may certainly be ignored in order to preserve life. Bar Kamza, who instigated the Roman Emperor, was certainly in the category of a *rodef*, an aggressor who caused the death of innocent victims through his actions. Causing the death of the messenger who had made a blemish in the animal would certainly have been permitted as an act of self-defense. But R. Zechariah ben Abkulas did not respond in the obvious, intuitive manner of his colleagues. His concern was not with any single infraction of Jewish law. He was concerned lest "people will say that blemished animals may be offered on the altar" and lest "people say that one who makes a blemish on consecrated animals is to be put to death." The overriding concern was that the act might not be perceived as an *ad hoc* emergency measure designed to prevent loss of innocent lives, but that it might be misinterpreted as normative *halakhah*. Falsification of *halakhah*, opined R. Zechariah b. Abkulas, is not permissible even in face of the threat of death, destruction of the Temple, and exile of the Jewish people. Perversion of the *mesorah* (tradition), even with regard to a single *halakhah*, is tantamount to denial of the Sinaitic revelation.

Of interest in this regard are the comments of R. Ya'akov Emden, *Migdal Oz, Even Bohen* 1:35. R. Ya'akov Emden cites *Teshuvot Radbaz* to the effect that one must suffer martyrdom rather than deny the veracity of the Law of Moses and adds that the same applies with regard to denial of the Oral Law and the words of the sages.

It would thus seem quite logical that a false judgment may not be issued even in face of a threat to life. A false judgment is tantamount to a perversion of the law and falsification of the *halakhah*. Rabenu Yonah, who apparently maintains that a judge may not decline to sit in judgment despite a threat to his life, may also have been prompted by the consideration that failure to render judgment may also lead to distortion of the law. It may be

---

3 See, however, R. Elijah Vilna, *Divre Eliyahu, Parshat Mishpatim*, s.v. *lo tiheyeh ahare rabim.*

noted that *Rambam, Hilkhot Sanhedrin* 22:1, followed by *Shulhan Arukh, Hoshen Mishpat* 12:1, distinguishes between a *mumheh lerabim* (*i.e.* a publicly appointed judge) and others who are qualified to serve as judges but who hold no official position. The latter may decline to hear a case for fear "lest he kill my son or lest he kindle my stack [of corn]" but a *mumheh lerabim* dare not decline even under such conditions. This distinction may perhaps be explained if it is understood that the formally established *Bet Din* is obligated to guarantee transmission of the law. No person may falsify the *mesorah*, but members of the publicly appointed *Bet Din* incur the additional obligation of actively guaranteeing its preservation. Hence, under no circumstances may they allow the *halakhah* to fall into disuse and thus into oblivion by declining to sit in judgment.

2. TEACHER'S UNIONS

A decision of the Rabbinical Administrative Board of Torah Umesorah, The National Association of Yeshivot and Day Schools, prohibiting teachers from joining national labor unions, has been disseminated widely. The statement, which is entirely declarative in nature and contains neither an analysis of halakhic issues nor citation of precedents, has evoked much comment. This pronouncement, dated 2 Kislev 5741, is particularly noteworthy since the late R. Moses Feinstein, then honorary chairman of the Rabbinical Administrative Board, in his *Igerot Mosheh, Hoshen Mishpat*, no.59, had sanctioned strike action by Yeshivah and Day School teachers, at least under certain limited circumstances.

It is a well-established principle of Jewish law that the residents of any town may promulgate rules and regulations for the common benefit of the townspeople. *Rosh, Baba Bathra* 1:33, states that members of a particular profession or craft may establish regulations which are binding upon all such professionals or artisans. The members of such professions or crafts are deemed to be "townspeople" entitled to exercise coercive power upon members of their own "society" for the common benefit. This principle is recorded by *Rambam, Hilkhot Mekhirah* 14:10 and *Shulhan Arukh, Hoshen Mishpat* 231:28. Hence, persons engaged in a common trade or profession are entitled to unionize and to impose organizational discipline upon one another. Moreover, when acting in a representative manner on behalf of all persons engaged in a given occupation, not only is a union entitled to engage in strike action but it may also legitimately forbid both its own members and outsiders from acting as strikebreakers.

Persons earning a livelihood from the teaching of *Torah* , argues Rabbi Feinstein, are in a somewhat different position. The compensation of such persons is not in the form of a fee for services rendered but payment in lieu of not engaging in some other remunerative activity (*sekhar batalah*). Teachers who are underpaid might well seek other employment, but in the event of their not being otherwise gainfully occupied, the obligation of teaching *Torah* falls upon their shoulders even during a strike period. Since teachers must teach even when on strike, the net result, according to Rabbi Feinstein, is to nullify the very concept of a strike. Although it is clear that when not engaged in earning a livelihood every person is obligated both to study and to teach *Torah* , Rabbi Feinstein does not address the question of whether teachers might not "strike" and spend the time as volunteers teaching *Torah* in other institutions or in faculty seminars teaching one another. Nor does he raise the question of whether striking teachers might not be permitted to offer to conduct classes in their own homes since it is not clear that the obligation to teach *Torah* obliges the teacher to spend either the time or the carfare required for him to travel to his students.

Rabbi Feinstein does advance one further significant consideration. Society has an obligation to provide for the *Torah* education of children. Although, intrinsically, the teacher has no greater obligation in this regard than does any other member of the community, nevertheless, in accepting employment, he has accepted delegation of this responsibility. Therefore, opines Rabbi Feinstein, the teacher may not withdraw, even for purposes of earning a livelihood in some other fashion, unless he provides a suitable replacement.

Despite these considerations, Rabbi Feinstein maintains that strike action is warranted under certain conditions, namely, when the level of compensation is so low that the teachers are not able to fulfill their responsibilities properly. Under such circumstances, if a strike will succeed in producing the necessary remedy, teachers are justified in suspending instruction temporarily in order that ultimately *Torah* study be maximized and enhanced. Such a determination, Rabbi Feinstein cautions, can be made only upon careful assessment of all factors and should be considered only as a last resort.

The propriety of strike action by Yeshivah teachers is also discussed in the course of a wide-ranging decision of a Tel-Aviv Rabbinical Court, *Piske Din Bate hadin harabaniyim,* VIII, 160-161. In its decision, the *Bet Din* cites the above mentioned responsum of Rabbi Feinstein, but places even heavier emphasis upon the consideration that work stoppage on the part of

Yeshivah teachers must inevitably lead to *bitul Torah* , i.e., disruption of *Torah* study, which, in and of itself, is a serious transgression.

When strike action is warranted, Rabbi Feinstein rules that teachers are entitled to payment for the period during which they performed no teaching services. Although he does not explicitly state the basis for such a claim on the part of striking teachers, it must be remembered that, essentially, they are paid, not for teaching, but for refraining from pursuing other means of earning a livelihood. Teachers who strike solely in order to make it possible for them to be able to discharge their duties adequately are indeed fulfilling their duty and, it may be argued, if not otherwise gainfully employed during the strike period, are entitled to compensation. Rabbi Feinstein further advises that striking teachers be paid for time missed even when the strike cannot be justified in accordance with *halakhah.* It may be presumed, says Rabbi Feinstein, that teachers who strike are driven to such action by "pain and poverty". Since their intentions are unexceptionable, it is only equitable that they not be penalized financially.

In light of this published responsum it is clear that the Torah Umesorah proclamation is not directed against unionization *per se* but against membership in national unions whose actions and policies are not governed by halakhic considerations and constraints. Indeed, the text of the document bans affiliation solely with "secular" labor unions. Moreover, the same document calls for the formation of an "Irgun Hamorim" (Teachers' Organization) under the aegis of Torah Umesorah for the purpose of "advancing the status of Yeshivah teachers materially and professionally". Such a body would undoubtedly enjoy the prerogatives which Jewish law conveys upon craft guilds and, to all intents and purposes, would function as a union without affiliation with any secular group.*

J. David Bleich**

* This material has appeared in a somewhat different form in *Tradition.*

** Professor of Talmud, Yeshiva University; Professor of Law, Benjamin N. Cardozo School of Law.

JEWISH LAW IN THE STATE OF ISRAEL

1. *UNDUE INFLUENCE AND CONFLICT OF INTERESTS*

The issues before the Court in *Ephraim Muberman v. Minna Segal* [1] were undue influence on a party to an agreement, and the question of conflicting interests in the case of an executor purchasing part of the estate from a beneficiary under the will.

The appellant was the executor of his father's will, and the respondent an elderly and infirm lady who had lived with the appellant's father for a number of years prior to his death. The respondent's legacy consisted of an apartment and the right to receive the rents from the other apartments in the building of which the appellant's father was co-owner. As a result of her declining health, the respondent decided to leave her apartment and move into an institution for infirm and elderly people. The respondent then signed an agreement with the appellant, under which she transferred her legacy to him, in exchange for a fixed and unlinked monthly stipend, which was to cover her fees at the institution. The institution closed down, and the respondent moved to another, only to find that her stipend was insufficient to meet her new monthly fees. The appellant refused to increase her allowance, whereupon the respondent sued him in the District Court, claiming that as executor of the estate he had acted improperly in acquiring her legacy and had employed deceit and undue influence in persuading her to sign the agreement. Her alternative plea was that the Court declare the appellant liable to maintain her at the new institution.

The District Court rejected the first claim, on the grounds that the agreement had been initiated by the respondent and was to her own advantage, but it upheld the second claim. The son appealed the decision, on the grounds that his liability ought not to exceed the sum specified in the written agreement.

The Supreme Court dismissed the appeal, and invalidated the agreement on the grounds that it had been signed while the respondent was under the undue influence of the appellant, and that in his capacity as executor of the estate the appellant was not entitled to enter into such an agreement with the respondent without the prior authorization of the Court.

Elon J. pointed out that the respondent did not understand Hebrew, and had relied upon an English translation of the terms of the agreement provided by the appellant's lawyer. Moreover, the respondent relied implicitly on the

1 C.A. 604/77, *P.D.* 32(3), 86.

appellant in all financial matters, and regarded him as her guardian, appointed by his late father. The appellant's actions, when taken as a whole, constituted the exercise of undue influence and excessive pressure upon the respondent, besides running contrary to the spirit of the will and the intentions of the testator. On these grounds, the agreement was invalid.

On the question of the executor's right to acquire part of the estate without the Court's permission, Elon J. held that even if such a right existed, which he doubted, it would still be subject to judicial review, and any transactions found to be unfair or unreasonable could be declared invalid. Although no such principle is articulated in the *Succession Law, 5725-1965*, it is enunciated in the contexts of agency law[2] and guardianship,[3] and by virtue of its rationale, i.e. the prevention of a conflict of interests, it ought also to apply to an executor.

The principle of invalidation on the grounds of conflict of interests is operative in various areas of Jewish Law,[4] including the rights of an executor. In view of the facts that s.150 of the *Succession Law, 5725-1965*, expressly excludes the application of *art.46 of the Palestine Order in Council, 1922*, from this law,[5] and that the intention of the legislators is to apply Jewish succession law in the State of Israel,[6] it is only fitting that the principle be applied in the form in which it is articulated in the Jewish legal system.

According to R. Abraham b. David Posquières (*Rabad*), a twelfth century Provençal scholar:

> An executor[7] may take money from the estate for purposes of commerce in the same way that he may give estate funds to a trustee for that purpose. He is also entitled to the commission he would have paid the trustee. The court, however, must be informed of all his actions.[8]

---

2 *Agency Law, 5725-1965*, s.8(3).

3 *Capacity and Guardianship Law, 5722-1962*, s.48.

4 A depositee may not buy a perishable deposit himself, but he must sell it to others, "in order to avoid suspicion" (*Shulhan Arukh, Hoshen Mishpat* 292:19). An agent is similarly restricted, even though he is prepared to pay the price stipulated by the principal (*Shulhan Arukh, Hoshen Mishpat* 185:2 and commentaries to *Tur, ad loc.*).

5 Article 46 has since been repealed: see Sinclair, *The Jewish Law Annual* III (1980), 165-169.

6 Preamble to the Succession Bill, Ministry of Justice, July 1952, pp.6-7.

7 The term used is *epitropos*, which is the general term for custodian or guardian in Jewish legal sources.

8 *Tur, Hoshen Mishpat* 290:16, citing *Rabad*.

R. Jacob b. Asher (*Baal Haturim)* disagreed with *Rabad's* view and maintained that an executor may not sell to himself under any circumstances.[9] Most authorities, however, accepted *Rabad's* view.[10] R. Joseph Caro supported it in his *Bet Yosef*[11] and R. Moses Isserles incorporated it into the authoritative *Shulhan Arukh.* In the words of the latter:

> In the same way that the executor may give estate money to others, he may take it himself, provided that he does so in court in order to avoid suspicion.[12]

Clearly the discussion centres on the circumstances in which the executor's conflict of interests might be avoided. There is no doubt that in the first instance, such a conflict is presumed, and prima facie will be instrumental in invalidating any transaction carried out by the executor involving the estate. Only the permission of the court serves to remove this prima facie invalidation.

Elon J. proceeded to survey the principles of English Law in this area and arrived at a similar conclusion.

Judgment was given in favour of the respondent, and the appeal was dismissed.

2. *THE AGNOSTIC WITNESS AND THE OATH*

The petitioner in *Moshe Becker* v *Justice Haim Eilat*[13] was a road-safety expert, who had been summoned as a witness for the defence in a homicide case. On entering the witness stand, he was asked to take an oath, as provided by the *Criminal Procedure Law, 5725-1965*, s.154, which states:

> Before taking his testimony, the court shall caution the witness that he must testify truthfully or be liable to the penalty prescribed by the law. The witness shall take an oath to testify truthfully: Provided that if he states that he is prompted by reason of religion or conscience he may refrain from taking an oath and may make a solemn affirmation unless the court is satisfied that those reasons are not invoked in good faith.

---

9 *Tur, Hoshen Mishpat* 290:16.

10 *Ritba, B.B.* 144b, *s.v. Rav Safra; Nimuke Yosef* on the *Rif, ad loc.*

11 *Tur, Hoshen Mishpat* 290:16.

12 *Shulhan Arukh, Hoshen Mishpat* 290:8.

13 H.C. 172/78, *P.D.* 32(3), 372. See C.P. Shelach, "The Agnostic Witness and the Oath", *Mishpatim* 9 (1979), 508.

The petitioner refused to take the oath on the grounds that he was an agnostic, and requested to be allowed to make a solemn affirmation. The magistrate refused, saying that agnosticism did not constitute grounds for refraining from taking an oath under s.154; nor did he believe that the petitioner's reasons for not taking the oath were invoked in good faith.

The High Court of Justice addressed itself to two issues: (1) Is an agnostic witness permitted, by reasons of conscience, to make a solemn affirmation rather than an oath?; (2) What are the criteria, if any, for determining whether a witness's reasons are given in good faith or not?

In granting the petition, the Court held that an agnostic witness may make a solemn declaration on grounds of conscience, and is not required to take an oath. This finding was reached on the basis of the interpretation of s. 156 according to the principles of Jewish Law, and not, as argued by the petitioner, on the position under the *Criminal Procedure (Evidence) Ordinance*, which preceded the *Criminal Procedure Law* of 1965.

Elon J. observed that in Jewish Law, a witness is not required to take an oath in order to verify his testimony,[14] since the obligation to tell the truth was already imposed on him by the ninth Commandment,[15] and if he is prepared to breach this Commandment, then there is no reason to expect him to be more observant of the third,[16] and to refrain from taking the Divine Name in vain.[17]

Witnesses were charged to tell the truth before the trial commenced and were reminded of the penalties for perjury. The contents of the charge varied according to the severity of the case. In monetary matters a brief warning was given,[18] but in capital cases, the witnesses were subjected to a lengthy discourse, the opening section of which is as follows:

> Perhaps what you are about to say is mere conjecture or hearsay, based on secondhand information, on what you heard from a trustworthy person ... Perhaps

---

14 See M. Elon, *Hamishpat Ha'ivri* (Jerusalem: Magnes Press, 1973), 504. The *shevu'at ha'edut* (oath arising from testimony) mentioned in the *Talmud* is a different institution, i.e. an oath imposed upon a witness, who when called to testify, denies all knowledge of the event.

15 "You shall not bear false witness against your neighbour" (*Ex.* 20:13; *Deut.* 5:17).

16 "You shall not take the name of the Lord your God in vain" (*Ex.* 20:7; *Deut.* 5:11).

17 See *Tosafot Kidd.* 43b, *s.v. vehashta; Resp. Hatam Sofer, Hoshen Mishpat,* 162; *Resp. Mishpete Uziel,* 3, *Hoshen Mishpat,* 13.

18 *Sanh.* 29a.

> you are unaware that we will in the course of the trial subject you to intensive interrogation.
>
> Know that capital cases are unlike monetary cases. In a monetary case one may make restitution and his offence is expiated, but in a capital case the witness is accountable for the blood of the man (unjustly executed) and the blood of his posterity until the end of time...[19]

From the beginning of the fifteenth century, a change occurred in the basic position outlined above, and the custom arose for witnesses to take an oath prior to giving testimony. In 1405, R. Isaac b. Sheshet Barfat (*Ribash*), then residing in Algiers, was asked if testimony which had not been given under oath was acceptable. He replied that it was acceptable, since there is no requirement for the witness to swear to tell the truth in order for his testimony to be admissible:

> In certain places, however, it is customary to make the witnesses take an oath in order to charge them, but this is not required by law.
>
> In our community, we are accustomed to make witnesses take an oath before giving testimony in a case in which the defendant is suspected of sinful conduct. This is to ensure that they do not suppress the truth in order to ingratiate themselves with him and to provide them with an excuse, namely, that the taking of the oath left them no option but to tell the truth.[20]

R. Simon b. Tsemakh Duran, a younger contemporary of *Ribash,* also dealt with this new development, and in a responsum addressed to a R. Amram of Spain, R. Duran states as follows:

> Regarding the practice in Christian countries to make witnesses swear prior to their testimony, although there is no basis for this in strict law, it was adopted by many great authorities, and in this community, it was followed by R. Issac B. Sheshet.
>
> In any case it does not constitute a violation of the prohibition on taking the Divine Name in vain, since oaths may be taken on an optional basis.
>
> Moreover, the court may impose such an oath if perjury is rampant, since there are those who believe that breaking an oath is more severe than perjury and will not perjure themselves under oath ...
>
> It is not, however, my practice to make witnesses swear unless they refuse to give testimony, even though in Christian countries the oath is administered after the custom of the gentile courts, i.e. in all cases even where the witnesses are prepared to give their testimony. This does not mean that it is permitted to adopt gentile ways, for it is only done because the Jewish witnesses have assimilated

19 *Maimonides, Hilkhot Sanhedrin* 12:3.

20 *Resp. Ribash* 170.

> gentile attitudes (and without the oath, they would not feel bound to tell the truth).[21]

The change attested to in the responsa was brought about by moral, social and psychological forces, and the resulting law is formulated in the following ruling of R. Moses Isserles *(Rema)* in his *addenda* to the *Shulhan Arukh:*

> Where the court sees fit to make the witnesses swear to tell the truth - they are allowed to impose an oath.[22]

This view was incorporated into the draft bills[23] which preceded the *Criminal Procedure Law, 5725-1965*, and provides the key to understanding the present section. The oath in s.154 serves merely as a means of impressing the witness with his obligation to tell the truth: it does not serve "to exclude any competent witness, but merely to add a stimulus to truthfulness wherever such stimulus is feasible."[24]

The petitioner therefore was entitled to refuse to take an oath on grounds of conscience, and could make a solemn declaration instead.

Regarding the criteria for determining whether a witness's reasons for refusing the oath were given in good faith, Elon J. concluded that there must be firm grounds for reaching a negative conclusion, and the standard to be applied is less than beyond all reasonable doubt, but more than mere suspicion. In the final analysis, everything depends upon the circumstances of the case.

The problem is likely to occur less frequently in future, since the general requirement that a witness should (subject to the proviso) take an oath has now been removed by the *Evidence Law Amendment (Warning of Witnesses and Removal of Oath) Law 1980*. Instead, s.2 of the Law provides that a witness shall be warned that he must tell the whole truth, and of the consequences of committing perjury. The judge retains under s.5 a *discretion* to administer an oath if he feels that this will help in discovering the truth, but the witness may still decline to take it on grounds of religion or

---

21 *Resp. Tashbetz* 3:16.

22 *Hoshen Mishpat*, 28:2. See M. Elon, *supra* n.14, at I.107-110, and Z. Warhaftig, "*Shevu'at Ha'edim Bevate Hamishpat Beyisra'el*", *Yavneh* 3 (1949), 147-151. In general, Jewish Law frowns upon oath-taking (see *Shulhan Arukh, Orakh Hayyim*, 156).

23 *Evidence Bill* 5713-1952, ss.19-20; *Amendment of Evidence Ordinance Bill*, 5716-1955.

24 Citing J.H. Wigmore, *Evidence in Trials at Common Law*, revd. ed. J.H. Chadbourn (Boston & Toronto: Little, Brown & Co., 1976), VI. 414.

conscience, and opt to affirm instead, unless the court believes that he is acting in bad faith.

3. *REFUND OF ESTATE DUTY*

The case of Bank Leumi of Israel Trust Co. v. *Director of Estate Duty* [25] turned on the interpretation of the *Estate Duty Law, 5709-1949,* s.28, as amended *(Estate Duty (Amendment no.3) Law, 5724-1964,* s.29), which provides as follows:

> Where the Director is satisfied that the duty has been overcollected, and an application for the refund thereof is made to him within ten years from the date of receipt of the notice of assessment, he shall refund any amount overcollected.

The petitioners had paid estate duty on property purchased by an overseas resident, notwithstanding that such property is exempt from duty under s.55 of the *Encouragement of Capital Investments Law,* 5719-1955. Two years later, they discovered their error and applied to the Director of Estate Duty for a refund. Upon refusal of their request, they petitioned the High Court for an order nisi directing the Director of Estate Duty to appear before the District Court and show cause why a refund was not due to the petitioners under s.28 of the *Estate Duty Law 5709-1949.*

The respondent argued that the true import of s.28 of the *Estate Duty Law 5709-1949* was that refunds could be made on the basis of claims arising at the time of the assessment.[26] The respondents claimed that no refunds could be given on claims made after this time, since the legislator would hardly have intended that at any time within ten years, a fresh claim could upset the assessment. The result of such an interpretation would be chaos and pandemonium in the Director's office. The petitioners claimed that the section was to be interpreted literally, and as such the section applied to all claims, irrespective of when they were made, provided that they were still within the ten year limit.[27]

Elon J. held that the section ought to be construed in accordance with its literal meaning, notwithstanding the fact that the legislator may have intended otherwise. The source for this rule of interpretation lies in the

25 H.C. 333/78, *P.D.* 32(3), 202.

26 Some support for this argument is to be found in *Hava Michaeli* v. *Director of Estate Duty,* H.C. 61/64, *P.D.* 18(2), 492, 494.

27 *Frumin and Sons* v. *Director of Customs and Excise* , C.A. 33/72, *P.D.* 28(2), 459, 466.

principles of Jewish Law, which includes a rich and complex body of tax law based in the main on medieval communal enactments.[28]

The rule is articulated in the responsa of the thirteenth century Spanish scholar, R. Solomon ibn Abret (*Rashba*). According to *Rashba*, double taxation is illegal, so that A, living in community X, and owning property in community Y, was only liable to pay property tax once, namely, in Y. In order to avoid the loss of revenue entailed in adhering to this principle, a particular community passed an enactment under which A was required to include property in Y in his tax declaration to community X. He was, however, entitled to a refund of the amount paid to community Y. Now, in the present case, the amount deducted by Y was far in excess of the property tax which would normally have been due to X, and the latter did not wish to deduct this sum from A's taxes, claiming that the enactment was never intended to apply in such a case. A argued that the enactment was clear and unambiguous, and the mere fact that on this occasion he stood to gain by it ought not to work to his disadvantage.

Rashba decided in favour of A, on the grounds that the terms of the enactment were both clear and unambiguous.

On the fundamental issue of the language of the law versus the intention of the legislator, *Rashba* ruled that "where there is both heart and mind (i.e. the wording is unambiguous), and the issue is whether to interpret according to an unarticulated condition, we follow the plain meaning of the enactment and disregard the unarticulated condition."[29]

Elon J. also pointed out that estate administration was of necessity an uncertain business, since the relevant facts are not always readily available. Jewish Law gives expression to this consideration in the dictum "we claim on behalf of the heirs",[30] i.e. the court will claim property rights on their behalf which, by virtue of their ignorance of the testator's affairs, they themselves are unable to claim.

28 See M. Elon, *The Principles of Jewish Law* (Jerusalem: Keter, 1975), 662-701.

29 *Resp. Rashba* 5:282.

30 *Gitt.* 58b, *B.B.* 23a and see *Shulhan Arukh, Hoshen Mishpat* 107, 108.

4. *RAPE OF A WIFE*

Moshe Cohen v. *State of Israel*
C.A. 91/80 (unpublished)

In this case, the issue before the Supreme Court was whether the term "unlawful" in the definition of the crime of rape under s.345 of the *Penal Law, 1977,* [31] applied to intercourse between a husband and wife or not. According to the Common Law, no such intercourse could be unlawful, since it constituted one of the basic conditions of the marriage agreement freely entered into by both parties.[32] Israeli courts have, however, rejected this doctrine, and interpreted the term "unlawful" in a wider sense.[33] In the present case, the Supreme Court upheld the decision of the District Court that coercive sexual relations between husband and wife constituted "unlawful intercourse" for the purpose of the definition of rape in Israeli Criminal law.

In rejecting the husband's appeal, Bekhor J. supported the District Court's interpretation of the term "unlawful" in s.345 in terms of the personal law of the parties, which in this case was Jewish law. In formulating the halakhic position on this issue, Bekhor J. relied upon a recent opinion by the Advisor on Jewish law to the Ministry of Justice,[34] from which he extracted the following principles:

1. Although the wife's right to sexual intercourse is Biblically mandated,[35] this is not the case in relation to the husband. He may therefore agree to relinquish any such right (accruing to him by virtue of the marriage contract) whereas his wife may make no such stipulation.[36]

---

31 "A person who has unlawful sexual intercourse with a female against her will by the use of force or threats of death or severe bodily harm, or when she is in a state of unconsciousness or otherwise incapable of resisting, is liable to inprisonment for fourteen years."

32 M. Hale, *The History of the Pleas of the Crown*, ed. S. Emlyn (1788), 629: "The husband cannot be guilty of rape committed by himself upon his lawful wife, for by their mutual matrimonial consent, the wife hath given up herself in this kind unto her husband, which she cannot retract." See also P. English, "The husband who rapes his wife", *The New Law Journal* 126 (1976), 1223, and Note, "The Marital Rape Exemption", *New York University Law Review* 52 (1977), 306.

33 Cr.A. 352/62 and Cr.A. 354/64, 20(2) *P.D.* 136.

34 N. Rakover, "Coercive Relations between Husband and Wife in Jewish Law" (Jerusalem: Ministry of Justice, 1980, *Sidrat Mehkarim Usekirot bamishpat ha'ivri* no. 55).

35 *Ex.* 21:10.

36 *B.M.* 94a.

2. "A woman is not a captive who may be compelled to have intercourse with one who is hateful to her." This statement of *Maimonides* [37] in relation to a *moredet*, i.e. a woman who refuses to have intercourse with a husband she finds repulsive, is accepted in spirit even by those who disagree with him over the specific circumstances in which such a woman may be divorced.
3. According to the *Talmud* and many *Poskim*, the *halakhah* prohibits a husband from forcing his wife to have intercourse against her will. [38] In this context Bekhor J. cited with approval the following extract from a recent work on the halakhic attitude to women:

> The fiction of the Judeo-Christian sex ethic has even convinced many Jews that Judaism shares Christianity's negative attitude towards sex in general and toward female fulfilment in particular. Nothing could be more mistaken.[39]

In rejecting counsel's argument that Jewish law does not dispute the husband's right to his wife's intercourse, but only the use of force in implementing it, Bekhor J. observed that this was not the conclusion arrived at by the Advisor on Jewish Law to the Ministry of Justice. Moreover, the husband possesses other rights in relation to his wife which he may enforce against her will, e.g. running the common home, etc. Bekhor J. rejected the argument that since the prohibition mentioned in (3) above did not carry any penal sanction in the *halakhah*, it ought to constitute a basis for the crime of rape in Israeli law.

The sole purpose in referring to this prohibition was to interpret the phrase "unlawful intercourse", and in that context, the fact that it carries no penal sanction in the *halakhah* is irrelevant.

In conclusion, Bekhor J. pointed out that this was an instance in which the approach of Jewish law was more progressive and liberal than that of the Common Law.[40]

---

37 *Hilkhot Ishut* 14:8.

38 *Erub.* 100b; *Maimonides, Hilkot Ishut* 15:17; *Shulhan Arukh, Even Ha'ezer* 25:2. In general, see Rakover, *supra* n.34.

39 M. Meiselman, *Jewish Woman in Jewish Law* (N.Y.: Ktav and Yeshiva University Press, 1978), 116.

40 On the phenomenon of Common Law rules derived from Christian interpretations of Scripture, e.g. the doctrine of the unity of man and wife based on *Gen.* 2:24, and the extent of their acceptability in Israeli law, see *per* Landau J. in C.A. 257/57, 12 *P.D.* 577, and *per* Cohn J. in C.A. 479/60, 15 *P.D.* 699.

5. *GOOD FAITH IN FULFILLING CONTRACTUAL OBLIGATIONS*

Saul Roth et al. v. *Yeshufeh Building Co. Ltd.*
C.A. 148/77, 33(1) *P.D.* 617

The appellants in this case were appealing against a decision of the District Court, dismissing their action for breach of contract against the respondent. According to the appellants, the apartment they had purchased from the respondent was only made available to them some six months after the delivery date specified in the contract of sale. Moreover, the apartment was handed over to them in an unfinished condition, since it did not comply with all the specifications provided in the building plan attached to the contract. In dismissing the action, the District Court relied upon s.10 of the contract of sale between the parties, which provided that the act of taking possession of the apartment by the purchaser "shall constitute absolute and conclusive proof of the vendor having fulfilled all his obligations under ... the contract." In another section (s.9), the contract provided that where the purchaser received notice of the availability of the apartment but did not take possession within ten days, this would also constitute absolute and conclusive proof of the vendor having fulfilled all his obligations under the contract. Since the appellants had, in fact, taken possession of the apartment, they were no longer able to sue the respondent for breach of contract. At the same time, the District Court rejected the appellant's claim that s.10 of the contract was void on the grounds of its restrictive nature,[41] or because it was "contrary to public policy" under s.30 of the *Contracts (General Part) Law*, 1973.[42]

The Supreme Court, however, allowed the appeal and returned the case to the District Court, although the justices differed in their reasoning.

---

41 Restrictive contractual terms are defined in s.15 of the *Standard Contracts Law*, 1964, and the District Court held in accordance with the generally accepted view, that this definition constitutes a *numerus clausus* of restrictive terms. Since this definition did not cover s.10 of the contract, it could not be voided on grounds of restrictiveness. In his judgment in the Supreme Court, Shamgar J. related to this point, and held that if a contractual term breached the spirit, but not necessarily the letter of s.15 of the *Standard Contracts Law*, it would still be void. In any case, it had not yet been established whether the contract of sale in this case was a standard one or not (at 622).

42 The District Court held that in the light of the case-law, the rubric of "public policy" under s.30 of the *Contracts (General Part) Law*, 1973, covers cases such as conditions in fine print which escaped the attention of one of the parties. In this case, however, the appellants both read and understood the whole of the contract, and signed accordingly.

According to Shamgar J., the category of public policy under s.30 of the *Contracts (General Part) Law* did extend to the present case and the District Court was wrong in ruling otherwise. Contracts for the sale of apartments ought to be treated differently from regular contracts of sale. This is because of the grave housing shortage in the country, the very high prices and the tremendous pressures upon those seeking to purchase apartments. The courts have an obligation to exercise *judicial* control of such contracts, above and beyond that exercised by the legislature. The control of contracts for the sale and purchase of apartments is therefore a matter of vital public interest, and since s.10 of the contract in question effectively placed the purchaser at the complete mercy of the vendor, it is void on grounds of public policy. The rest of the contract, however, could stand without s.10, and was therefore valid.[43]

According to Elon J., however, the category of public policy did not apply to this case; instead, s.10 of the contract of sale was void on the grounds that it was in contravention of s.39 of the *Contracts (General Part) Law*, according to which:

> an obligation ... arising out of a contract shall be fulfilled ... in good faith.

Under this section it is the conduct of the parties in relation to their rights arising out of the contract, rather than the terms of the contract itself, which is relevant. Elon J. rejected the "public policy" approach, since the public interest in the performance of contractual obligations is itself a vital one, and may only be displaced in very exceptional circumstances.[44] Consequently, Elon J. preferred to allow the appeal on the grounds of lack of good faith on the part of the respondent, rather than on the basis of the contract offending against public policy.

In defining the concept of "good faith", Elon J. turned to the canons of "the upright and the good" (*yashar vetov*) in Jewish law, and argued that in the interpretation of general concepts of this nature, the ancient legal heritage of Israel ought to play a significant role.

There are two aspects to the concepts of "the upright and the good" in Jewish law. The first is a general, moral directive, and bereft of any legal

43 This is in accordance with s.19 of the *Contracts (General Part) Law*, 1973, which provides that: "Where a contract is severable and the ground for rescission relates only to one part therof, such part alone shall be capable of rescission."

44 For a lengthy exposition on this point, see Elon J.'s decision in *Dicker* v. *Moch*, 32(2) *P.D.* 141, surveyed in *The Jewish Law Annual* III (1980), 157.

sanction.[45] The second is of a legally binding character, and is incorporated in the Talmud and Codes, e.g. the right of pre-emption *(dina debar matsra)*.[46]

According to various authorities, however, the general, moral directive also constitutes the source for the residuary capacity of the Rabbis to complement the uprightness and goodness of the laws of the Torah in accordance with "changes in the conduct of human affairs according to both time and place."[47] In the words of *R. Asher b. Jehi'el* (late thirteenth and early fourteenth century Germany and Spain):

> From all this (i.e. provisions such as the right of pre-emption) we may assume that whoever attempts to evade the enactments of the Sages, may be prevented from carrying out his evil design ... For the Talmud could not foresee every situation that would arise, and therefore we have to resort to analogy (in order to arrive at the correct decision).[48]

In the light of all this, Elon J. concluded that in accordance with the notion of "the upright and the good" in Jewish law, s.39 of the *Contracts (General Part) Law* empowers the judge to take action in order to ensure that no person obtains an unfair advantage over another by manipulating the law in "bad faith". The court must achieve a balance between the exercise of this residuary capacity and censoring purely "immoral" behaviour which falls short of "bad faith". The line between the two is indeed a very delicate one and must be drawn with great care and on a case by case basis.

Asher J. concurred with Elon J. in dismissing the appeal on the grounds of s.39.

---

45 E.g. "Beyond the letter of the law" *(lifnim mishurat hadin)* and "the ways of the pious" *(midat hasidut)*. For the various levels of normativity of these and related concepts (n. 46 below), see A. Lichtenstein, "Does Jewish Tradition Recognize an Ethic Independent of *Halakhah* ?", in *Contemporary Jewish Ethics* , ed. M.M. Kellner (N.Y.: Sanhedrin Press, 1978), 102.

46 "This rule (i.e. right of pre-emption) obtains because it is said, "And you shall do what is upright and good" (*Deut.* 4:18), and the Sages have held that since the sale is the same, it is good and right that this place should be bought by the owner of the adjacent field rather than by an outsider" (*Maimonides, Hilkhot Shekhenim* 12:5, following *B.M.* 108a).

47 *Magid Mishneh, Hilkhot Shekhenim* 14:5. Also, see M. Silberg, *Kakh Darko Shel Talmud* (Jerusalem: Faculty of Law of the Hebrew University of Jerusalem, 1964), 97; M. Elon, *Hamishpat Ha'ivri* (Jerusalem: Magnes Press, 1973), I.171, 179, and II.512.

48 *Resp. Rosh* 78:3. See Elon, *supra* n.47, at 346.

6 *ILLEGAL CONTRACTS*

Howard v. *Miarah*
C.A. 311/82, 35(2) *P.D.* 505

The appellant in this case sold a plot of land to the respondents for the sum of 150,000 *lirot*, and received a down-payment of 95,000 *lirot*. In the contract of sale, the area of the plot was specified as 600 sq. meters. In fact, 30 sq. meters had already been transferred to the local municipality, and a further 180 sq. meters requisitioned under the *Roads and Railways (Preservation and Development) Ordinance, 1943*. Upon their discovery of the discrepancy between the area specified in the contract and the area which they were actually entitled to receive, the respondents wrote to the appellant requesting a reduction in the purchase price in accordance with s.28 of the *Sale Law, 5728-1968*. The appellant rejected their offer, and instead sued them for breach of contract, demanding the payment of the penalty specified in the contract.

The District Court held in favour of the respondents, finding that they had been unaware of the above-mentioned discrepancy at the time of signing the contract. The respondents, therefore, were fully entitled to request a reduction in the purchase price under s.28, and their doing so did not constitute a breach of contract. On the contrary, it was the appellant and not the respondents who was in breach in this case.

Now, in the course of the action in the District Court, it became apparent that the actual purchase price was in fact 205,000 *lirot*, the additional 55,000 *lirot* constituting payment for various building materials stored on the land. The Court, however, found that the actual value of the materials was no more than 16,500 *lirot*. On this basis, the appellant advanced an alternative argument, namely, that the contract was illegal under sec.30 of the *Contracts (General Part) Law, 5733-1973*, since it contained a hidden agreement, the purpose of which was to conceal taxable income from the taxation authorities. This fact being known to both parties, they were in *pari delicto*, and hence the 95,000 *lirot* already transferred to the appellant as a down-payment ought to remain in his possession. The District Court rejected this argument on the grounds that there was no evidence of any actual concealment of taxable income having taken place. The contract, therefore, was not in fact tainted by illegality.

The Supreme Court unanimously upheld the decision of the District Court, two out of the three justices holding that the mere presence of a hidden agreement is not sufficient to make a contract illegal. In this case, there was no evidence of actual concealment of taxable income, nor had it been sufficiently proven that the respondents were aware that they were perpetrating an illegal act. According to Shamgar J., the same rigorous standard of proof with respect to evidence of illegality[49] which applied before the *Contracts (General Part) Law 5733-1973* also applies under it, irrespective of the discretionary nature of s.31.

In his judgment, Elon J., who concurred with Shamgar J. in dismissing the argument of illegality, addressed himself to ss.30-31 of the *Contracts (General Part) Law, 5733-1973*, with a view to establishing their basis within the principles of Jewish law. The two sections provide as follows:

> 30. A contract the making, contents or subject of which is or are illegal, immoral or contrary to public policy is void.
>
> 31. ..... in the case of avoidance under section 30 the Court may, if it deems it just so to do and on such conditions as it sees fit, relieve a party of the whole or part of the duty under section 21 and, in so far as one party has fulfilled his obligation under the contract, require the other party to fulfil the whole or part of the corresponding obligation.

According to one learned author, the provision in s.31 directing the court to use its discretion is "in accordance with neither English nor Civil law ... but is an original solution derived from sources other than those normally employed by the Israeli legislature."[50] In Elon J.'s view, the second part of this opinion is inaccurate, since it ignores Jewish law, which is both a primary source of Israeli legislation as a whole and of the *Contracts (General Part) Law 5733-1973* in particular. The fact that both the preamble and the commentary to the draft bill of this Law refer to Jewish law is sufficient indication that the sections in question are indeed based upon that legal system and do not constitute an "original construction of the Israeli legislature."[51]

The general position in Jewish law with regard to illegal contracts is to separate as far as possible "the religious and the legal sides of the act, and to refrain from nullifying the rights of acquisition and legal action arising from it because of the prohibition involved."[52] This trend, stated by the late

---

49 *Cahane* v. *Levi* C.A. 874/75, 31(2) *P.D.* 334.

50 D. Friedman, "On the Interpretation of Modern Israeli Legislation", *Tel Aviv University Law Review* 5 (1976-77), 618.

51 *Ibid.*

52 *Jacobs* v. *Cartoz* C.A. 110/53, 9(2) *P.D.* 1401, 1413.

Silberg J. in both his classical decision in *Jacobs* v. *Cartoz*[53] and his seminal work, *Talmudic Law and the Modern State*,[54] is in direct contrast with the Common Law attitude, i.e. that the Court refuses to entertain any action under such a contract for fear of soiling its hands in the process.[55] In criticising the latter approach, Silberg J. made the following point:

> The result of this moral indignation is that, while penalizing the offending claimant, it also awards a prize to the offending defendant (i.e. in a case in which both parties are in *pari delicto*). The only difference is that it does not directly award this prize, but leaves it in the hands of the one who took it by himself.[56]

In Jewish law, there is no such causal connection between the commission of an offence and the voiding of a civil contract, or any other legal transaction which occurred incidentally to a violation of the law. Naturally, where the contractual element itself "activates the offence", e.g. enforcing the payment of usury on a loan, it is not actionable in Jewish law.[57] In the case of a Biblical injunction, too, such a separation will not be made.[58] In general, however, it is the position in Jewish law that "the violation of the law or of morality is one thing, and the validity of the contract is another."[59]

According to Elon J., it is this principle of separation which constitutes the basis for s.31 of the above-mentioned Law. In his view, this principle is in fact a manifestation of the general capacity of Jewish law to distinguish

53 *Ibid.*

54 *Talmudic Law and the Modern State*, trans. B. Bokser (New York: Burning Bush Press, 1973), 70-83.

55 See *Holman* v. *Johnson* (1775) E.R. 1120, per Lord Mansfield: "No Court will lend its aid to a man who founds his cause of action upon an ... illegal act. If ... the cause of action appears to arise *ex turpi causa* or the transgression of a positive law of this country, there the Court says he has no right to be assisted."

56 Silberg, *supra* n.54, at 75.

57 *B.K.* 30b; Maimonides, *Hilkhot Malveh Veloveh* 4:6; *Shulhan Arukh, Yoreh De'ah* 161:11.

58 *Tem.* 4b. See E. Shochetman, *Ma'aseh Haba Ba'averah* (Jerusalem: Mosad Harav Kook, 1981), 22-48. Shochetman's exhaustive analysis covers most of the aspects of the question of illegality in Jewish law and is a valuable contribution to this field. In the opening section he shows, *inter alia*, how the talmudic dispute in *Tem.* 4b is confined to Biblical injunctions. Hence, the resulting decision against separation does not apply to rabbinic prohibitions.

59 Silberg, *supra* n. 58 at 82.

between the "legal" and the "religious" aspects of the *halakhah.* [60] The court may, however, exercise its discretion in a case where the enforcement of the legal obligation would, in the prevailing social conditions, amount to an encouragement of criminal conduct, e.g. the court will not order the refund of money paid for the procurement of false testimony if the witness should fail to testify falsely.[61] According to Elon J. the element of discretion in s.31 is, therefore, not "an original construction of the Israeli legislature" but is derived from the principles of Jewish law.

In relation to s.30, however, it is clear that its basis lies in English law, since it declares a contract which is found to be illegal, immoral or contrary to public policy, void, i.e. the principle of separation is not applied. Elon J., however, links the two sections, and by redefining "void" as "dormant" seeks to establish that the contract is not void under s.30 in the same way that such a contract is "void" in English law, but is merely "dormant", i.e. still awaiting its fate, which is determined only after the court has exercised its discretion in accordance with s.31. Under this section the contract may either be revived, in whole or in part, or condemned to eternal slumber. In the interim period, therefore, it is in a state of "dormancy".

Elon J. also observed that in the light of both the general principle that contracts ought to be honoured rather than nullified, and the principle of separation in Jewish law, sections 30 and 31 of the *Contracts (General Part) Law, 5733-1973* ought to be applied restrictively, and with a view to preserving as much of the agreement between the parties as possible. He did not, therefore, regard the hidden agreement in this case as sufficiently illegal to bring the contract within these sections, and concurred with Shamgar J. in dismissing the appeal.

Two points in this judgment merit further consideration. First, the question of illegal contracts as such does not appear in any of the literary sources of Jewish law. (In fact, it is debatable whether or not the concept of

60 Elon, *supra* n. 28, at 253: "This approach of Jewish law to the question of a contract involving a transgression illustrates its capacity to distinguish between the "legal" and the "religious" aspects of the *halakhah,* notwithstanding their common source and it is precisely because of the material link between law and morals that Jewish law deprives the transgressor of those additional benefits which result from the invalidation of the civil aspects of the contract." The point concerning the "material link between law and morals", in the context of this issue, was also made by Silberg *(supra* n.54, at 82-3), and ought to be complemented by the proposition that where the court feels that justice will best be served by not enforcing the contract, it is free to act accordingly (see Shochetman, *supra* n.58, at 240ff; 256ff).

61 *Responsa Shevut Ya'akov* 1:145; see also *Pithe Teshuvah, Hoshen Mishpat* 32:2, no.1.

contract law in the commonly accepted sense of the terms exists in Jewish law.)[62] Moreover, the one talmudic *sugya* dealing with the question from an analytical perspective, i.e. the dispute between Abaye and Raba in *Temurah* 4b-5a, ought to lead to the conclusion that in Jewish law, any act contrary to Divine law is invalid, due to the rule that in a dispute of this nature between these two *amoraim*, the *halakhah* is decided according to Raba.[63] In the light of other talmudic statements, however, it would appear that the scope of this *sugya* is a limited one, and is confined to Biblical prohibitions and to "essential illegality: which can be rectified by invalidating the act in question."[64] In all other cases, Jewish law does distinguish between the "legal" and the "religious" elements of an act, although at the same time, it preserves a certain discretion to invalidate the "legal" element either in whole or in part, according to the demands of equity and justice. The separation of the elements is indeed an all-pervading characteristic of Jewish law, and is not confined to this issue alone.[65]

Secondly, Elon J.'s theory of "dormancy", although initially attractive, is somewhat forced. If the court does not use its discretion under s.31, but merely declares the contract void, can it be held to have put the "dormant" contract to sleep? Surely the court in such a case treats the contract as void *ab initio*, and no further act is required on the court's part to make this voidness absolute. In any case, according to Jewish law, the legal act in an "illegal" agreement is always valid. The court may order the parties not to insist upon their rights under the agreement: however, nothing it says can affect the legal validity of the agreement itself.

7. *"BEYOND THE LETTER OF THE LAW"*

Kitan v. *Weiss*
C.A. 350/77, 33(2) *P.D.* 785

In this case, the appeal was against the decision of the District Court awarding the respondent damages for the loss of her husband, who was shot to death by a watchman employed in the appellant's textile factory. At the time of the shooting, the watchman was in a state of mental depression, and was drinking heavily as a result of the loss of his son in an automobile accident. The respondent's husband, a lawyer, had represented the watchman

---

62 See S. Albeck, *Dine Hamamonot Batalmud* (Tel Aviv: Dvir, 1966), 22ff.
63 See *B.M.* 22b.
64 See Shochetman, *supra* n.58, at 48.
65 Shochetman, *supra* n.58, at 256ff.

in a civil suit against the driver responsible for the accident. The driver had been acquitted of the criminal charges, and the compensation paid by his insurance company fell well below the amount expected by the watchman. Owing to his heavy drinking, the watchman's economic situation had deteriorated, and he imagined that the blame lay with the respondent's husband who had failed to obtain sufficient compensation from the insurance company. Taking the gun provided by the appellant in his capacity as watchman, he shot the respondent's husband and killed him.

The District Court found that the appellant ought to have foreseen the potential danger in the watchman's depressed mental state and heavy drinking, and to have taken steps to relieve him of his weapon. Having failed to do so, the appellant was liable to pay compensation to the respondent and her family for the loss of her husband. It was, however, established that the watchman's license to act in this capacity and to carry a gun was entirely in order at the time of the shooting.

All three justices of the Supreme Court concurred in allowing the appeal, and the decision of the District Court was reversed on the grounds that there was insufficient evidence to establish the existence of the necessary chain of causation between the appellant's responsibility for its watchman, and the watchman's shooting of the respondent's husband.[66] Since the watchman's license was in order at the time of the shooting, the appellants had fulfilled their legal obligations concerning the safety of their watchman, and were therefore not liable to pay the respondent any compensation whatsoever.

Elon J., commenting on the appellant's offer to pay a further voluntary amount in compensation to the respondent and her family, beyond the sum already paid, observed that this type of offer corresponds to the institution of "beyond the letter of the law" in Jewish law.[67] This institution is particularly relevant in the area of tort law, where the *Talmud* itself introduces the concept of "Heavenly law" in order to bridge the gap between the legal and the moral aspects of responsibility for damage to both one's

---

66 On the issue of the chain of causation in Israeli tort law, the court. approved the following decisions: *Dagani* v. *Solel Boneh* C.A. 358/56, 11(2) *P.D.* 871; *Cornfeld* v. *Shmuelov* C.A. 451/66, 21(1) *P.D.* 310; and *Ringer* v. *Leon* C.A. 390/62, 17(3) *P.D.* 1662. Also see I. Englard, "On the Scope of Responsibility and the Chain of Causation in Tort Law" (Heb.), *Legal Studies in Memory of Abraham Rosenthal* (Jerusalem: Magnes Press, 1964), 55.

67 On this concept, i.e. "*lifnim mishurat hadin*", see Nahmanides, *Commentary to the Torah, Sefer Devarim* 6:18 and *B.K.* 99b; *B.M.* 24b and 30b. Also see M. Elon, *Encyclopaedia Judaica* XII.113, and Silberg, *supra* n.54, at 104ff.

fellow man and his property.[68] The rule that a person occasioning damage to another is "exempt from human law but liable according to the law of Heaven" applies to cases such as breaking down a fence in front of a neighbour's animal, and hiring false witnesses to testify against him.[69] In both these cases, and in other instances of "Heavenly law" cited in the *Talmud*, the common factor is the absence of any direct causal connection between the act done and the resulting damage.[70] According to Elon J., the rule requiring the person responsible to provide compensation for indirect damage of this type is a manifestation of the more general obligation to go "beyond the letter of the law" which, on occasion, may be translated by the Sages into positive law.[71]

In the context of the Israeli legal system, Elon J. suggested that the judge ought to take an active part in persuading the litigants to follow their moral obligations and to go "beyond the letter of the law". Such a step would be in accordance with the spirit of Jewish law, whereby:

> there is a special reciprocal tie between law and morality ... which finds its expression in the fact that from time to time Jewish law, functioning as a legal system, itself impels recourse to a moral imperative for which there is no court sanction, and in doing so sometimes prepares the way for conversion of the moral imperative into a fully sanctioned norm.[72]

Thus, the judge is required to act as the arbiter of both the legal and the moral obligations of the parties to the case.

This approach was severely criticized by Shamgar J., who gave the leading judgment for the Court. In addition to factors such as the lengthy period of time normally elapsing between the incident in question and the court hearing, the systematic blurring of the border between law and morality in a system of a positive law such as Israeli law is totally unacceptable, the results of such an approach being only inequality and unfairness.

In his reply to this criticism, Elon J. observed that he did not have in mind any systematic introduction of moral obligations into the judicial process, but only that in special circumstances, the judge ought to use his discretion in order to request of the parties to act in accordance with moral

---

68 See A. Gulak, *Yesode Hamishpat Ha'ivri* (Berlin: Dvir, 1922), 2,18.

69 *Tos. B.K.* 6:4; *B.K.* 55b-56a; Maimonides, *Hilkhot Hovel Umazik* 2:7.

70 See *Encyclopaedia Talmudit* VII.383-6.

71 See *Bayit Hadash, Tur Hoshen Mishpat* 12:4; Elon, *Hamishpat Haivri, supra* n.14, at I.176ff. For a different analysis of the relationship between these categories, see Silberg, *supra* n.54, at 94ff.

72 Elon, *Enc. Jud.* XII.113; I.173ff; II.619-20.

principles, in the same way that he uses his discretion with respect to concepts such as "public interest" and "good faith" in the *Contracts (General Part) Law, 5733-1973.*[73] Here, too, the judge weighs up "moral", rather than strictly "legal" principles, and nobody suggests that he is being discriminatory and unfair.

There is nevertheless a clear distinction between advising parties to a case as to their moral obligations in general, and interpreting a concept such as "public interest" and "good faith" in the context of an official piece of legislation, such as the *Contracts Law.* It is still open to question, therefore, whether the blurring of the border between morality and law, even in the informal manner suggested by Elon J., is really suitable for a positive system such as modern Israeli law. The general trend in this type of system is to restrict the exercise of judicial discretion, and in cases where this is unavoidable, to provide some basis for it - usually in the form of a standard concept - in the body of the law. The application of judicial discretion with respect to well-tried concepts explicitly incorporated into the law is, it is submitted, very different, and in positivist terms, far more acceptable, than the exercise of the general moral discretion suggested by Elon J.

8. *NECESSITY*

Afangar v. *State of Israel*
Cr.A. 89/78, 33(3) *P.D.* 141

The appellant in this case was a guest in a house under police surveillance. In the middle of the night, two plainclothes policemen attempted to enter the house, and were attacked by the appellant. Although the policemen had a valid search warrant, they did not produce it when confronted by the appellant at the door of the house. In the Magistrates' Court, the appellant was convicted of both assault and obstructing a policeman in the course of his duty. The District Court quashed the conviction for obstruction, but upheld the one for assault.

On appeal to the Supreme Court, the appellant argued that his actions constituted an act of necessity, within the terms of s.18 of the *Criminal Code Ordinance, 1936* (now s.22 of the *Penal Law, 5737-1977),* according to which:

---

[73] See *Roth* v. *Yeshufeh* C.A. 148/77, 33(1) *P.D.* 617 *(supra,* no.5) and *Howard* v. *Miarah* C. A. 311/78, 35(2) *P.D.* 505 (*supra,* no.6).

> An act or omission which would otherwise be an offence may be excused if the person accused can show that it was done or omitted to be done only in order to avoid consequences which could not otherwise be avoided, and which, if they had followed, would have inflicted grievous harm or injury to his person or honour or to his property or to the person or honour of others whom he was bound to protect or to property placed in his charge: Provided that in so acting he did no more than was reasonably necessary for that purpose, and that the harm inflicted by the act or omission was not disproportionate to the harm avoided.

The main issue before the Court was whether or not the appellant's actions in this case were performed in the course of protecting persons or property "placed in his charge".

The District Court had rejected the appellant's argument on the grounds that the "property" referred to in s.18, i.e. the apartment, did not belong to him. The Supreme Court, on the other hand, allowed the appeal.

According to Elon J., the language of s.18 ought to be interpreted widely, i.e. as a general obligation to save any person or his property from danger, even if there is no special relationship between the person or property threatened and the rescuer. Citing Jewish law,[74] Elon J. referred to the concept of the *rodef* which is defined by Maimonides in the following terms:

> ...if one person is pursuing *(rodef)* another with the intention of killing him, even if the pursuer is a minor, it is the duty of every Israelite to save the pursued, even at the cost of the pursuer's life... If it is possible to rescue the pursued at the cost of one of the pursuer's limbs .... this should be done. If, however, it is impossible to judge exactly and the pursued can be rescued only if the pursuer is killed, he may be killed, even though he has not yet killed anyone, for Scripture says, "You shall have no pity" (*Deut.* 25:12).[75]

Although the classical sources of Jewish law confine the law of the *rodef* to cases involving a threat of serious physical harm, later authorities extend it to any form of assault. According to the *Rosh:*

> If anyone sees an Israelite smiting his fellow, he is allowed to strike the assailant in order to prevent him from sinning, *even if the blows are not of a mortal nature.* [76]

The proportionality principle, i.e. that the rescuer's actions must be in proportion to the nature of the threat, is also articulated in the sources of

74 *Sanh.* 73a, 74a.

75 Maimonides, *Hilkhot Rotseah Ushmirat Hanefesh* 1:6-7.

76 *Piske Harosh, B.K.* 3:13. Also see *Yam Shel Shlomoh, B.K.* 3:9.

Jewish law.[77] In reply to a question involving the plea of self-defence, R. Israel Isserlein, a fifteenth century Ashkenazic scholar, held that chopping off an assailant's hand was an excessive act in the circumstances of the case, and left the proportionality principle unsatisfied:

> Who allowed him to chop off the assailant's hand? He should have found a less extreme method with which to defend himself ... only in a case in which there is a threat of serious physical harm is it permitted to resort to physical violence ... in this case, however, the attack was not a vicious one ... and granted that the defender did not intend it (i.e. his intention was not to chop off his assailant's hand, but as a result of his recklessness this is in fact what happened), nevertheless a man is always held responsible for his actions and the defender must be punished accordingly.[78]

The *poskim* also distinguish between cases in which the blow is administered in self-defence during the attack, and where it is struck after the attack, in which case it is an act of retaliation rather than of self-defence.[79]

Elon J. summed up the position on self-defence and necessity in Jewish law as follows:

> 1. Every person is obliged to save another person from being mortally wounded by a *rodef.* In the case of a lesser assault, there is no such obligation although it is a virtuous act to do so.
>
> 2. There is no need for any special relationship to exist between the victim and the rescuer before the law of *rodef* can apply.
>
> 3. Acts of self-defense are confined to the time during which the assault takes place, and not afterwards.
>
> 4. The principle of proportionality requires that all acts of self-defense be proportional to the attack, and must not be excessive.

Elon J. argued that this wide approach to the defense of necessity was shared by English and American jurists,[80] and recommended that it be

---

77 See *Rosh, ibid.*, and *Hagahot HaMordekhai, B.K.* 38.

78 *Pesakim Ukhtavim* , 208.

79 *Hagahot HaMordekhai, B.K.* 196. Also see *Shulhan Arukh, Hoshen Mishpat* 421:13

80 *R.* v. *Duffy* (1966) 1 All E.R. 62; *People* v. *Williams* (1965) 56 Ill. App. 21. 159; 205 N.E. 2d. 749.

adopted as such by the Israeli legislature, in accordance with other basic concepts, the roots of which lie in moral and social values.[81]

In the circumstances of the present case, both the midnight hour and the failure of the police to produce their warrants, were sufficient to justify the appellant's act as one of necessity within s.18 of the Ordinance.

Sussman J. concurred with Elon J.'s conclusion, although he objected to the use of Jewish Criminal law in the context of a modern legal system. According to Sussman J., the police had no right to enter the house without producing their search-warrant or explaining their intentions to the appellant. As such, they were acting beyond their legal capacity as police officers, and the appellant was perfectly entitled to act in the way he did.

Asher J. dissented, holding both that the facts indicated that the appellant was fully aware of the identity of the midnight visitors, and intended to obstruct them in performing their duty, and that s.18 of the Ordinance did not possess the wide meaning given to it by Elon J.

With respect to the application of the law of *rodef*, it is necessary to point out that the religious imperative, "not to stand by your brother's blood" (*Lev.* 19:16) and its ramifications are not paralleled in any secular legal system.[82] In terms of the actual decision, it is a matter of debate whether the correct balance between the citizen's right to defend his property and the duty of the police to investigate crime was achieved in this case.[83]

D.B. Sinclair*

81 Cf. *Roth* v. *Yeshufeh* C.A. 148/77, 33(1) *P.D.* 617, *supra* no.6.
82 See *Sanh.* 73a; Maimonides, *Hilkhot Rotseah Ushmirat Hanefesh* 1:4.
83 See S.Z. Feller, "A Strange Decision", *Mishpatim* 10 (1980), 339.

* Post-doctoral Fellow, Centre for Criminology and the Social and Philosophical Study of Law, Faculty of Law, University of Edinburgh

NON-FINANCIAL PRESSURES ON A HUSBAND TO GRANT A "GET"

Most reported cases dealing with the problem of a husband who refuses his wife a *get* have concerned the court's power directly to order that the *get* be given or to specifically enforce an agreement to *get*.[1] Another approach has been to bring pressure arising from other aspects of the marital relationship. The civil courts have occasionally been prepared to lend their support to such an indirect method of enforcing a *get*. Thus, in *Brett* v. *Brett* [2] the English Court of Appeal awarded a wife a large lump sum payment as maintenance, with a significantly reduced award should her husband grant her a *get* within three months.[3]

A different, and perhaps even stronger, form of pressure has now been utilised by Treyvaud J. in the Family Court of Australia, by making the extent of a father's access (or visitation rights) to children conditional on his granting a *get*. [4]

In the case of *Frey* v. *Frey* [5] the husband was seeking increased access to the two children of the marriage, return of his passport which had been impounded by the Court in earlier proceedings, and the setting aside of various financial orders made in earlier proceedings. These proceedings were an episode in protracted Family Court litigation stretching over nearly three years, in which time the husband had taken the children to Israel contrary to court orders; they had been returned to the mother only after she had obtained an order in an Israeli court. The question of access had been litigated on a number of occasions, mainly over issues of Jewish Holy Days. Treyvaud J. recognized, however, that the underlying issue in the present proceedings was

---

1 See the cases in note 14 *infra*.

2 [1969] 1 All E.R. 1007, [1969] 1 W.L.R. 478, noted at (1969) 43 *Australian Law Journal* 280, and M.J. Schecter, "Civil Enforcement of the Jewish Marriage Contract", *Journal of Family Law* 9 (1970), 425-429 at 429.

3 Followed in *Steinmetz* (1980) 6 Family L.R. 554 (Family Court of Australia, Full Court). See *Rubin* v. *Rubin* 75 Misc. 2d. 776, 348 N.Y.S. 2d. 61 (New York Family Court, 1973) where a wife's entitlement to maintenance was made conditional on her fulfilling her agreement to accept a *get* ; and *Waxstein* v. *Waxstein* 395 N.Y.S. 2d. 877 (New York Supreme Court, 1976) where at first instance the court withheld disposition of marital property until the husband cooperated in obtaining the *get*. See also the French courts' use of *astreinte*, a civil pecuniary penalty, for failure to give a *get*. H.P. Glenn, "Where Heavens Meet: The Compelling of Religious Divorces", *American Journal of Comparative Law* 28 (1980), 1-38 at 25-29.

4 *Cf. Pal* v. *Pal* 45 A.D. 2d. 738, 356 N.Y.S. 2d. 672 (New York Supreme Court, Appellate Division, 1974) discussed in the text *infra*.

5 Unreported; Family Court of Australia, Treyvaud J.; 22nd February, 1984.

the husband's failure to give the *get*, with the wife seeking to make additional access conditional upon his doing so.

As found by Treyvaud J., the facts fell within the classical "withholding of the *get*" pattern. He said that the husband wanted to use the *get* "as a weapon to bludgeon the wife to agree to a result which meets his own wishes", and observed that the husband's "actions and attitudes belie the impression that he desires to give of the genuine nature of his religious beliefs and principles. I think it proper to say that he is using his stronger position in relation to the wife and in relation to the dissolution of their marriage, according to Jewish law, to force her into a situation of compromising all disputes between them upon his terms." It might therefore be said that here was a case where it was appropriate for counter pressure to be employed to resolve this contentious issue.

The wife's argument for linking increased access to the giving of the *get* rested upon the prediction that improvement could be expected in the relationship between the parents once the *get* issue was resolved. With the grant of the *get* the main source of tension between the parties would disappear. The parents' relationship would improve, which would be reflected in the way in which both handled the children and lead to an improvement in the children's welfare. Section 64(1)(a) of the *Family Law Act* 1975 requires that the "welfare of the child" be regarded as the "paramount consideration" in custody and access proceedings.

This argument was accepted by Treyvaud J. He reasoned that since there are cases in which tension between the parents so affects children that it is in the children's paramount interest that all access by one parent be denied, then the court must be free to make access conditional upon other bases which would *reduce* such parental tension. In this case, granting of the *get* would probably reduce the tension and conflict and improve the parents' relationship and so was a proper basis upon which to allow any increase in access. "... There are cases in which tension between parents so affects children that access should be denied - there are many such authorities - likewise, if the court, in considering the welfare of the children as the paramount consideration can take a step which must inevitably of itself reduce the tensions between the parents, the conflict between them, and thus improve their relationship with their children and with each other, then it is proper in those circumstances to require access to be given or restricted upon the basis or condition that the *get* is given and obtained." The additional access sought by the husband was accordingly ordered, but only if the husband granted the *get*.

Treyvaud J. also briefly considered whether he had the power directly to order the husband to grant a *get* , but declined to rule on such a "significant" matter without the opportunity to consider it at greater length.[6]

The significance of this case may be seen by comparing it with the only other reported decision of which the writer is aware, which links a *get* with access to children. In the American case of *Pal* v. *Pal* [7] the husband sought to have the wife held in contempt for denying him his visitation or access rights, as agreed and incorporated into judgment in the civil divorce. Relief was denied because the husband had not performed his part of the agreement by cooperating in giving a *get.* This decision may be criticized on the ground that an excessively "contractual" approach is adopted to the question of the visitation rights. The question of the welfare or "best interests" of the children should properly take priority over the proprietorial or contractual interests of the parents,[8] even in the face of any "clean hands" argument which might be directed against the husband.

On the same basis, the decision in *Frey*, if viewed narrowly, might be criticized. It is hard to see that access and the grant of the *get* were sufficiently linked so as to make one dependent on the other. Would access itself be significantly improved once the *get* was given?[9] By contrast, in *Brett* [10] the failure to grant a *get* bore directly on the wife's ability to remarry and thereby obtain other financial support, and so was directly relevant to the size of a maintenance award.[11]

Despite such reservations, the decisions in both *Pal* and *Frey* are to be welcomed because a broader view is adopted which attempts to disentangle all the aspects of the parties' failed marriage, including particularly an aspect

---

6 See *Gwiazda* v. *Gwiazda* (unreported; Family Court of Australia, Emery S.J.; 23rd February 1983).

7 *Supra,* note 4.

8 M.D.A. Freeman, "Jews and the Law of Divorce in England", *Jewish law Annual* 4 (1983), 276-288 at 283; *Agar* v. *Agar* 32 App. Div. 2d. 198 (New York, 1969), where an agreement to apply Jewish law as to custody was held relevant but not so as to override considerations of the child's welfare.

9 On the facts it might also be doubted whether the giving of the *get* would really reduce the tension significantly, in the context of protracted and bitter litigation over both children and property, over a period of years. There had been many applications, in addition to the principal application for dissolution of the marriage.

10 *Supra* note 2.

11 [1969] 1 All E.R. 1007 at 1013 and 1015, [1969] W.L.R. 487 at 494 and 496; *Steinmetz, supra* note 3, at 556 ("the husband has it within his power to prevent the wife from remarrying and gaining the benefit of additional financial support which might come to her from marriage").

which might too easily be seen as outside the jurisdiction of the court. There is now an additional, recognized counter-pressure which can be brought to bear on a recalcitrant husband. It is submitted, however, that *Frey* is a much stronger decision than *Pal* because of the basis on which it rests. Treyvaud J.'s reasoning sets the giving of the *get* firmly within the overall family situation, but more particularly is rooted firmly in the context of a legitimate central concern of traditional family law - the "best" or "paramount" interests of the children of the marriage, who may be properly portrayed as innocent victims of their parents' conflict. The attaching of the *get* condition to access is done precisely because of the needs of the children. This approach, therefore, allows considerable pressure to be exerted on the husband, fully consistent with the other responsibilities of the court. Indeed, if approached from this perspective, stronger measures might have been appropriate in this case. Making the *get* a precondition to the husband obtaining *any* access at all would surely heighten the pressure on him, increasing the chances of achieving the desired result of obtaining the *get*, while still being acceptable as advancing the children's welfare in the overall framework of reducing tension between the former spouses.[12]

Treyvaud J.'s approach may be capable of extension in the making of orders arising out of other aspects of the marital relationship. For example, it is becoming increasingly common for separating parents to seek joint custody or guardianship of their children. Such an arrangement obviously requires a considerable degree of co-operation and harmony between the parents if it is to succeed. So it would be proper for a court to make such an order conditional upon the granting of a *get*, on the basis of the "absence of tension" argument used by Treyvaud J. in *Frey*. It may be that the incentive of maintaining contact with his children will be a more powerful influence on a reluctant husband than the kind of financial pressure utilised in *Brett*.

Recognizing the connection between giving a *get* and other aspects of the relationship between separating spouses might sometimes also have more subtle consequences. For example the refusal to grant a *get* might be a relevant factor in contested custody proceedings. A court might well take into account, in assessing a father's ability to cater for the well-being of his children, the way in which he has come to terms with the break-up of the marriage and his ability to co-operate with the other parent. This consideration might influence an otherwise reluctant husband to demonstrate cooperation by granting a *get*.[13]

---

12 The point was not argued by the wife in *Frey*.

13 Or a wife to accept a *get*.

Finally, it is submitted that the reasoning supporting the decision in *Frey* may be seen as significant in terms of the situations in which it permits such pressure to be exercised. It is clearly equally applicable to orders for access and custody in contested proceedings, even where there was no prior agreement between the parties. Being based on the interests of the children it might be appropriate for application even in the absence of a petitioner's fully "clean hands", where the overall equity of the situation made that desirable. It may be used to ground a positive order, and not merely, as in *Pal*, to deny relief.

Most importantly, the *Frey* reasoning may avoid the problem which has led many courts to deny relief to *get* -seeking wives on the basis that such relief would involve enforcing a purely religious obligation or breach the separation of Church and State.[14] In *Pal* itself the appeal court refused on this ground to uphold the lower court's order effectively to convene a *Bet Din*. *Frey* shifts the focus from rights to the more acceptable basis of the family's needs, and so may lessen the impact of arguments based on infringement of rights. Finally, the reasoning may justify a strong form of order. If the basis of the conditional order is the prospect of reducing tension and improving the parents' relationship, it would seem to follow that the condition to be attached to the relief should be that the *get* actually be given. To order submission to the *Bet Din's* jurisdiction but still allow a husband, for example, to argue against the *get* before the *Bet Din* would hardly reduce the tension and would therefore defeat the reasoning behind linking the *get* to the other relief sought. It is interesting to note that in *Brett* the condition attached was that the *get* actually be given.

14 *Morris* v. *Morris* (1974) 14 R.L.F. 163 (Manitoba Court of Appeal); *Wener* v. *Wener* 59 Misc. 2d. 957, 301 N.Y.S. 2d. 237 (1970); *Pal* v. *Pal*, *supra*; *B. v. B.* 57 R.G.Z. 250 (German Supreme Court, 1904); *Price* v. *Price* (1932) 16 D & C 290 (Pennsylvania Supreme Court); *Contra*, *Margulies* v. *Margulies* 42 App. Div. 2d. 517, 344 N.Y.S. 2d. 482 (1973) somewhat ambiguously; *Waxstein* v. *Waxstein* 90 Misc. 2d. 784, 395 N.Y.S. 2d. 877 (1976), affirmed 57 App. Div. 2d. 863, 394 N.Y.S. 2d. 253 (1977); *Stern* v. *Stern* (1979) 5 Family Law Reports (B.N.A.) 2810; *Koeppel* v. *Koeppel* 138 N.Y.S. 2d. 366 (1954); *Turner* v. *Turner* 192 So. 2d. 787 (Florida District Court of Appeal, 1967); *Shulsinger* 1977 Family Law Cases 90-207 (Family Court of Australia, Full Court).

In summary, the decision and reasoning in *Frey* adds a new, if subtle dimension to the resolution of the difficult *get* problem, which may be possible of extension both in the type of pressure which might be exercised and in the extent of that pressure.

Victor New*

* Lecturer, Department of Accounting and Business Law, University of Melbourne.

TOWARDS A NEW REGULATION OF THE RELATIONS BETWEEN THE STATE AND ITALIAN JEWRY

According to Article 1 of a decree dating back to 1930 (no.1731), the Italian Israelite Communities have legal personality and provide for the religious needs of the "Israelites" according to Jewish Law and traditions. Power is granted to the Communities as such to tax each member in proportion to his general income (Article 4).

The decree adds that one who changes his religion, or declares himself no longer willing to be considered an "Israelite" according to the above law, ceases to belong to the Community. As a result, he loses the right to avail himself of the Jewish institutions, and in particular their ritual services, including that of burial in the Jewish cemeteries.

The Constitutional Court was recently required to pronounce on the legality of the decree, in a case brought by a member (of Libyan origin) of the Rome Community, who challenged his obligation to pay tax.

Article 4 seemed to the Court to conflict with Article 3 of the Constitution, which asserts the principle of equality of all citizens before the law, without distinction, *inter alia*, of "race" and religion.

The "Israelites", who may be automatically enrolled in the registers of the Communities under this description, seemed clearly to suffer in this respect, in comparison with other citizens.

The Court recognized that this article conflicted with Articles 2 and 18 of the Constitution. According to the former, certain inviolable rights are guaranteed and recognized to citizens, either as individuals or as "social formations." According to Article 18, citizens have the right to associate freely, without authorisation, for any ends not forbidden to individuals by the criminal law.

The Court confirmed the principle that this article of the Constitution must be interpreted as including the freedom *not* to associate, - a principle completely opposed to that supported in the period when the rules concerning the Jewish Communities were issued, viz. that associations should be organised within the ambit of public structures under the control of the State.

This constitutional freedom, according to an earlier decision of the same Court (no.69, 1962), must be considered as broken if, by compelling those belonging to a group or category to associate, a right or a freedom or a principle constitutionally guaranteed is violated (in particular, Article 3 of the Constitution).

For this reason, the Court declared Article 4 of the 1930 decree to be unconstitutional (Sentence no. 239, July 13th, 1984).

Jewish reactions to this decision have differed. For many years, the 1930 decree had been considered a valid instrument for the unification of the Jewish "Communities" (*universitates*) - which had been separately regulated in the various Italian states before unification. The 1930 law had been regarded as a sort of "civil constitution" of a religious denomination made by the State legislator, perhaps the only example of a statute of a religious denomination formed and issued by a State.

Accordingly, some people did not hesitate to see the court's decision as a violent blow delivered to the Jews and Judaism,[1] almost an act of antisemitism, overlooking the fact that the Court preferred not to lay stress on the argument of the appellant that the 1930 decree was totally illegitimate, as being the result of an authoritative act of the State, rather than an agreement in conformity with the prescriptions of the Constitution (Article 8).

On the contrary, it has rightly been asserted that the Jewish world must, as a result of this decision, become conscious of the fact that it must participate in the radical change which occurs when one passes from the concept of "belonging by right" to that of "the right to belong". The Italian Jewish world, conscious of its own sovereignty (so it is argued), must be able to provide itself with a statute of its own; from which must derive those powers of representation which will be used to negotiate agreements with the State.[2]

The concept of sovereignty, however, does not seem to be suitable as a representation of the situation of the Italian Jewish world.

The modifications of February 18th 1984, made by mutual consent to the Lateran Concordat, introduced the principle of the freedom to accept or not to accept the teaching of the Roman Catholic religion in the schools, and it was decided that, though representing the freedom of conscience and the educational responsibility of parents, they and the students themselves exercised this right at the time of enrolment in their schools; their choice, however, must not cause any discrimination.

At least in this matter, therefore, the positions of the Church and of the other religious denominations seemed to be assimilated to a remarkable

1 *Cf.* V. Colorni, "Il diritto alle proprie radici", in *Il Giornale Nuovo,* August 3, 1984.

2 G. Fubini, in a commentary to the decision of the Court issued by the Turin bi-monthly *Ha-Keilla* (Oct.1984.); by the same author, *cf.* "L'autonomia statutaria nel quadro della Costituzione Italiana e lo statuto come legge sostanziale degli ebrei d'Italia" (report at the convention held in Turin on May 9, 1982) in *Diritto ecclesiastico* I (1982), 60-66.

degree. Article 1 of the Concordat, however, remains: it accords to the Roman Catholic Church a character of independence and sovereignty.

According to an authoritative advice accepted by the Constitutional Court in Sentence no.59 of 1958, a new organisation showing the characteristics of stability, the presence of a certain number of believers, and its own rules, must be considered a religious denomination.[3]

The Italian Jewish world can identify itself as belonging to this classification, owing chiefly to many centuries of recognition, and the presence of believers. The constitutional concepts of "social formation" (Article 2) or of "association" (Article 18) seem, on the contrary, restrictive.

Article 8 of the Constitution recognizes that religious denominations other than the Roman Catholic have the right to organise according to their own Statutes, provided that the latter do not conflict with the Italian legal system. The same article foresees that the relationship with the State will be regulated by the law on the basis of agreements between representatives of both sides.

Therefore it seems only right to affirm that the Italian Jewish world must be able to provide itself with its own Statute, which will not be the result. of any recognition of autonomy,[4] but of the power of self-determination[5] which the Constitution itself accords it.

Once it has expressed its identity through such a Statute, and appointed its representatives, the Italian Jewish world will be able to work towards such agreements with a renewed consciousness of the reality it represents.

Daniela Piattelli*

3 *Cf.* P. Gismondi, "Culti acattolici", *Enciclopedia del diritto* XI (1962), 440-446.

4 *Cf.* G. Sacerdoti, "Ebraismo e Costituzione: prospettive d'intesa tra Comunità israelitiche e Stato", in *Le Intese tra Stato e Confessioni religiose,* ed. C. Mirabelli (Milano: Giuffrè, 1978), 111 n. 44.

5 *Cf.* P. Gismondi, *supra* note 3, at 444.

* Professore Associato.

GERMAN LEGISLATION AGAINST DENYING THE HOLOCAUST

The criminal sanctions for denying that the Holocaust ever took place were reformed in West Germany after long and controversial discussion by the 21st Criminal Law Amendment Act of 13th June 1985,[1] which came into force on 1st August 1985.[2]

In the past few years a loophole has become apparent in German criminal law with regard to the prosecution of right-wing extremist and neo-nazi activities; this deficiency was felt to be particularly embarrassing politically. For about ten years neo-nazi propaganda had largely refrained from overt antisemitism, incitement to racial hatred and violence against segments of the population or the public instigation of crimes against Jews.[3] It adopted another course by denying or making light of the atrocities of the Nazi government. Cloaked in pseudoscientific jargon, it was and still is claimed above all that there was no genocide of the Jewish population of Europe under the Nazi regime and that the historical facts of the Holocaust and the death camps of the "Third Reich" were a lie, hence the popular catchword, "Auschwitzluege".

As the German Criminal Code (StGB) lacked a special statutory offence, the judiciary got out of the difficulty by other means. In its judgment of 18th September 1979 the Federal Court of Justice (BGH) held:

> Persons of Jewish descent have, on the strength of their right to personal integrity in West Germany, an entitlement to recognition of the persecution of the Jews under National Socialism. Anyone who denies the murder of Jews in the "Third Reich" insults every one of them. Even persons, who were not born until after

---

1 Bundesgesetzblatt 1985, part I, page 965.

2 Documents: Government Bill: Bundesratsdrucksache 382/82; 158/83 = Bundestagsdrucksache 10/1286; draft bill of the Social Democratic Party (SPD): Bundestagsdrucksache 10/891; draft bill of the Greens: Bundestagsdrucksache 10/3260; Report and Recommendation of the Legal Committee of the Bundestag (lower house of parliament) Bundestagsdrucksache 10/3242; Amendment of the Greens: Bundestags-drucksache 10/3255; Amendment of the S.D.P.: Bundestagsdrucksache 10/3256; Resolution by the Bundstag: Bundesratsdrucksache 193/85; Approval of the Act of Bundersrat (Federal Council - the upper house of parliament): Bundesratsdrucksache 193/85 (resolution).

3 These acts are, of course, punishable under the German Criminal Code (StGB), cf. §§ 130, 131 StGB.

> 1945 are affected by such utterances, if they would have been persecuted as "full-blooded Jews" or "half-breeds" in the "Third Reich".[4]

The judiciary has thereby classified the denial of the Holocaust as simple collective defamation of all Jews under §185 StGB.

That had several procedural consequences. Whereas most offences in Germany are so-called "Offizialdelikte", i.e. criminal offences rendering the accused liable to public prosecution, many crimes, including defamation, are prosecuted only upon application by the victim (so-called "Antragsdelikte"). If the injured party does not make an application, it is not possible for the Public Prosecutor and courts to conduct a criminal prosecution. Since only Jews and half-breeds are entitled to make applications, the applicant must begin by proving that he is a Jew or half-breed.

In addition to these procedural inadequacies was a deficiency in legal classification. Defamation is a relatively petty offence in German criminal law and typical crime against the honour of an individual. In the case of denial of the Holocaust on the other hand, it was fundamentally a matter of an assault on public order and social harmony, an attack against the Jewish community as a whole.

All parties agreed that denying or trivialising the Holocaust should be a statutory offence and that it should in future be prosecuted ex officio without a private application for prosecution. There was however dissent concerning systematic classification and the extent of the protection of the criminal law.

The Federal Government's Draft Bill[5] provided a new specific rule. Under §140 II StGB a person would be liable to criminal prosecution, if he.approved, denied or made light of the acts of genocide perpetrated under National Socialist rule. The act should be prosecuted ex officio. This solution was also favoured by the Christian churches in Germany and the Central Council of Jews in Germany, and was ultimately supported by the Knesset in its letter of 20th March 1985 to the German Bundestag.

On the other hand, the regulation met with criticism, in the course of which two arguments based on principle, legal policy and dogma were in the foreground. One objection was that the new rule created a special law for the protection of Jews and thereby encouraged a new isolation and ghetto formation. In addition another point was emphasized: it would be a novelty in German law and a unique phenomenon in criminal law, if the historical

---

4 Ref. number: VI ZR 140/78, Entscheidungen des Bundesgerichtshofes in Zivilsachen (BGHZ), vol. 75, pp. 160 et seq. = Juristenzeitung 1979, 811.

5 It was the last draft bill of the Social Democratic/Liberal coalition under Helmut Schmidt.

truth were protected by the sanctions of the criminal law. There have never been criminal sanctions in respect of other historical lies. The proponents of the Government's Draft Bill, on the other hand, argued that the creation of a special provision was justified by the historically exceptional and unique character of nazi genocide.

After long discussion the Legal Committee of the Bundestag reached a compromise, which became law after controversial debate in the Bundestag.[6]

The legislature has refrained from creating a special "Auschwitz" rule, and instead it has decided in favour of a procedural solution within the framework of the offence of defamation. §194 StGB was amended to the effect that defamation and defiling the memory of the dead in connection with the victim's persecution by the National socialist or another despotic and arbitrary regime can also be prosecuted ex officio without a private application for prosecution. The essence of the revised version of §194 StGB is contained in sub-section 1 sentence 2 of the paragraph. This provides that an application for prosecution is not required, if the act has been committed by circulating a piece of writing or making it available to the public, or at a meeting or on the radio, and if the injured party was persecuted as a member of a group under the National Socialist or another despotic and arbitrary regime, and if this group is part of the population and the defamation is connected with this persecution.

By these means other serious acts of violence have been equated with the Holocaust. The legislature in this instance was thinking primarily of the expulsion of Germans from the former German Eastern territories at the end of the war. This equation of victims of the Nazi regime with the expelled Germans has been sharply criticised by many as a manifestation of a set-off mentality, because the unique quality of the Holocaust is thereby obscured. The injured party must belong to a group (e.g. the Jews or the Silesians) and must himself have been persecuted precisely because of his membership of this group.

Under the new §194 sub-section 2 sentence 2 StGB an application for prosecution can also be dispensed with on the same conditions in cases of defiling the memory of the dead.

If the injured party is not interested in criminal proceedings he can oppose an ex officio criminal prosecution. Such opposition results in the creation of an impediment to an action in respect of the injured party who

---

6 Record of the discussion in: Verhandlungen des Deutschen Bundestages, 10. Wahlperiode, 135. Sitzung vom 25. April 1985, pp. 10075 et seq.

lodges an objection himself, not however with regard to others who are injured by the same act.

The 21st Criminal Law Amendment Act has closed two further small loopholes in the law in connection with neo-nazi propaganda.

Firstly, it was formerly the case that writings - here we are concerned predominantly with nazi publications - could no longer be confiscated and destroyed, if the criminal offence of producing them had become statute-barred after a short limitation period of 3-6 months. Under §76a sub-section 2 no. 1 StGB seizure is now possible even after the limitation period expired.

Secondly, it was formerly only the distribution of emblems of unconstitutional organisations, e.g. swastikas, which could be prosecuted. Under the new law a person also renders himself liable to criminal prosecution, if he imports, produces or stores such objects in order to distribute them (§86a sub-section 1 no.2 StGB).

A matter which causes no problems whatsoever for the British or American lawyer is a practically insoluble problem in German law. In Germany criminal and civil proceedings are strictly separated. §§403 et seq. Code of Criminal Procedure (StPO) are of no practical consequence. As a result, the victim cannot obtain any compensation for material or non-material damages in a criminal trial, but must bring a separate civil action in respect of these claims, a course of action which involves costs and risks. In Germany it would be impossible for there to be a trial like that of *Mel Mermelstein* v. *Ditlieb Felderer* before the Superior Court of Los Angeles in which the jury awarded $5.25 million ($500,000 in compensatory damages and $4.75 million in punitive damages) to the plaintiff, who claimed he was emotionally tortured by the taunts of the defendant who kept telling him that the Holocaust never happened.[7]

Eberhard Klingenberg*

[7] Cf. U.P.I., "Victim of Nazis Awarded $5.2 Million From Taunter", *Los Angeles Times*, Jan. 17th 1986 and D. Townsend, "$5.25 Million Awarded by Jury to Survivor of Hitler's Death Camps", *Los Angeles Times*, Jan. 18th 1986.

* Dr. Jur., Professor of Law, University of Tübingen, West Germany.

PART THREE

SURVEY OF RECENT LITERATURE

SURVEY OF RECENT LITERATURE

The present Survey covers literature appearing principally in 1981 and 1982, with some retrospect.

Contributors: P.S. Alexander (Manchester), J. Day (Oxford), M. Fishbane (Brandeis), B.S. Jackson (Kent), Y.S. Kaplan (Jerusalem), T. D. Mettinger (Lund), K. Nielsen (Aarhus), D. Piattelli (Rome), S.N. Rosenbaum (Pennsylvania), B.J. Schwartz (Jerusalem), G.J. Wenham (Cheltenham), K.W. Whitelam (Stirling).

Abbreviations:

BM	Beth Mikra
CBQ	Catholic Biblical Quarterly
HTR	Harvard Theological Review
JAAR	Journal of the American Academy for Religion
JBL	Journal of Biblical Literature
JJS	Journal of Jewish Studies
JLA	Jewish Law Annual
JNES	Journal for Near Eastern Languages
JQR	Jewish Quarterly Review
JSJ	Journal for the Study of Judaism in the Persian, Hellenistic and Roman Period
JSOT	Journal for the Study of the Old Testament
JTS	Journal of Theological Studies
OS	Oudtestamentische Studien
Proceedings VIII	Proceedings of the Eighth World Congress of Jewish Studies, Jerusalem 1982
RB	Revue Biblique
RQ	Revue de Qumran
Shenaton	Shenaton Hamishpat Ha'ivri
Shenaton Lamikra	Shenaton Lamikra ulcheker mamizrah hakadum
Sivan	A. Even-Shoshan et al., eds., *The Book of Sivan - a Collection of Studies ... in Memory of ... Shalom Sivan,* Jerusalem, Kiryat Sepher, 1979
VT	Vetus Testamentum
ZAW	Zeitschrift für alttestamentliche Wissenschaft

ADMINISTRATION OF JUSTICE

830. J. Friend, "Do not testify according to the majority", *BM* 26 (1981), 129-136 (Heb.). - After surveying the gamut of Jewish exegesis of *Ex.* 23:2, the author suggests that the consonants *rb* be vocalised *rob* ("majority") and that the pause be shifted to the next word. The three parallel sections of the verse would then form a progression: "Do

not go after the numerous to do evil, do not incline to testify according to the majority, and do not decide according to the numerous.". The warning to preserve justice and truth is thus issued to (potential) wrongdoers, witnesses and judges, in accord with the context of general admonition in which the precept is found. B.S.J.

831. M. Lahav, "Jehoshaphat's Judicial Reform", in *Yaacov Gil Jubilee volume*, ed. Y. Hocherman *et al* (Jerusalem: Rubin Mass, 1979), 141-148. - The author discusses the judicial reforms instituted by Jehoshaphat as described in *2 Chron.* 19:4-11: the appointment of local judges, the establishment of a centralized court system with a High Court and the demand for absolute justice. Analysis of biblical material and an Egyptian parallel leads to the conclusion that this reform is the first of its type in ancient Israel which may be deemed historically factual. Accounts of earlier judicial measures taken by David and Moses are not historically trustworthy; they are rather literary reflections of the idea of the king as a wise judge. B.S.J.

832. E. T. Mullen, "The 'Minor Judges': Some Literary and Historical Considerations", *CBQ* 44 (1982), 185-201. - For the deuteronomistic writers of *Judges*, the *Shofet* was designated by Yahweh to deliver his people. The title "Judge" was chosen on theological grounds to act as an indictment of Israel's unfaithfulness to the deuteronomic law and as testimony to Yahweh's mercy. The different literary presentation of the "major" and "minor" judges (*Judg.* 10:1-5; 12:7-15) indicates a difference in literary purpose rather than office. There is no evidence to indicate any judicial activity on the part of these figures, with the possible exception of Deborah (*Judg.* 4:4). The story of Jephthah indicates that the offices of "deliverer" and "judge" were identical. K.W.W.

See also 926, 953, 975

ADOPTION

833. S. M. Paul, "Adoption Formulae: A Study of Cuneiform and Biblical Legal Clauses", *Maarav* 2/2 (1979-80), 173-185. - Family metaphors are used in the Ancient Near East to express political ties, such as the royal grant, or promissory covenant, prominent in suzerain-vassal relations. The formula of adoption, similarly, is found in the Bible in relation to the Davidic succession *(2 Sam. 7)* and more generally to express the bond between God and Israel. The author gathers examples of adoption formulae found in the Ancient Near East, and compares them with biblical terminology. B.S.J.

See also 864, 901.

AGENCY

834. S. Shilo, "Basic Issues in the Law of Agency - a Comparison of Jewish and Israeli law" (Heb.), *Diné Israel* 9 (1978-1980), 113-126. - A basic difference between Jewish and Israeli law is that the former defines an act done through an agent, even if its

legal significance is unknown, as agency. The tendency in Jewish law to endow material acts with legal significance, leads to a broader definition of agency in Jewish law than in Israeli law, or in other legal systems. Another aspect of Jewish agency law which makes it *sui generis* is the concept of an agent for an omission, which does not exist in other legal systems. Y.S.K.

See also 1023.

ARBITRATION

See 859.

BAILMENT

See 878, 1028.

BAN

835. A. Y. Collins, "The Function of 'Excommunication' in Paul", *HTR* 73 (1980), 251-263. - In *1 Cor.* 5 Paul condemns a Corinthian Christian to be expelled from the church and delivered to Satan for 'the destruction of the flesh' because of incest. This parallels the concerns of the Qumran community who also excommunicated members for sexual sins with a view to their destruction by Belial on the day of judgment (CD 7:21 - 8:3; 20:1-8). G.J.W.

836. R. Goldstein-Kestenberg, "*Herem Hayishuv* in a New Context" (Heb.), *Proceedings of the Seventh World Congress of Jewish Studies* (1981), 17-22. - According to this writer the origins of the *Herem Hayishuv* (Ban on settlement by outsiders) lie not in the *Talmud*, but in the social realities of the Jewish Medieval community. In this context, it is profitable to compare it with the *Jus Mercatorium* (Law Merchant), and to note the similarities between the two legal institutions. It is also noteworthy that a concept similar to the *Herem Hayishuv* appears in the 45th clause of the Salic Law. The writer also demonstrates certain similarities between various aspects of the *Herem Hayishuv* and Medieval Customary law. Y.S.K.

See also 862, 981, 1078.

BIBLICAL LAW

837. S. Amsler, "Amos et les droits de l'homme", in *De la Tôrah au Messie* (H. Cazelles Festschrift), ed. M. Carrez, J. Doré and P. Grelot (Paris, 1981), 181-187. - This study of Amos' oracles against the foreign nations (Amos 1-2) attempts to discover the theological basis on which the prophet can condemn the nations in the name of the God of Israel. He discusses various possibilities which he does not find entirely satisfactory: that the victims of the injustices condemned were all Israelites, that the nations concerned had an indirect association with the kingdom of Yahweh by virtue of having

been part of the Davidic empire, that the oracles presupposed the Noachic covenant with mankind, or that they presupposed the notion shared by all the ancient orient according to which the gods were guarantors of the cosmic order. Amsler prefers the view that the law revealed to Israel was regarded as having universal scope. He points out that although the oracles concern the nations, they were in fact addressed to Israel. J.D.

838. A. Bartal, "Otherwise... When My Lord Shall Sleep with his Fathers I and my Son Solomon Shall be Counted Offenders (1 Kings 1:21)", *BM* 23 (1978), 433-435, 523-524 (Heb.). - Bathsheba's use of *hata'im*, "sinners", in reference to her own and Solomon's presumed status should Adonijah reign is here understood as "legally culpable" and thus deserving of execution. This, however, is not, as most moderns suppose, because they are members of a rival faction and thus - in accord with ancient royal practice - to be done away with, but rather, as perceived by Abrabanel, because they will be considered guilty of particular offences: Bathsheba of adultery and Solomon, as her son, as unfit to rule. Thus, Bathsheba's plea to the dying David is that Solomon may reign, so that her sin - and David's - may remain undisclosed. B.J.S.

839. C. M. Carmichael, "Forbidden Mixtures", *VT* 32 (1982), 394-415. - C. examines the problematic laws prohibiting certain mixtures (*Deut.* 22:9-11). These are original to the Deuteronomist and constructed akin to the composition of proverbs. They represent clever, allusive, proverbial-type commentary upon certain happenings in the patriarchal narratives. They are not to be taken literally, unlike *Lev.* 19:19, by which time the Levitical legislator no longer understands their real meaning. Their inspiration comes from Jacob's cryptic comments upon his sons' activities (*Gen.* 49), and are judgments in condemnation of Judah, aimed at prohibiting Canaanite and Israelite marriages. The prohibition against planting two seeds in the vineyard is a cryptic judgment on Judah's dilemma over the perpetuation of his line (*Gen.* 30-38; *cf. Gen.* 49:8-12). The mixed seed, Er and Oran, and the seed that was sought through their union with Tamar came to nothing. The prohibition against ploughing with an ox and an ass is open to the use of figurative language, using animal and sexual imagery, to condemn the influx of Hivite women into Jacob's group (*Gen.* 34:29; 35:1-4) and Jacob's marriage between an Israelite and Canaanite. The prohibition against putting on a *shatnez* is a synecdoche referring to a luxurious garment which comes to represent a prostitute (Tamar). This is a negative comment upon Judah's (wool) involvement with the harlot Tamar (linen) in *Gen.* 38. Such negative judgments against a revered ancestor had to be expressed indirectly. K.W.W.

840. D. J. A. Clines, "Nehemiah 10 as an Example of Early Jewish Biblical Exegesis", *JSOT* 21 (1981), 111-117. - *Neh.* 10 is a fine example of the post-exilic interpretation of earlier Israelite law. It consists of a set of *halakhot*, probably devised by priestly or levitical lawyers and assented to by the people. Every *halakhah* has a certain novelty, while remaining an exegesis of earlier Pentateuchal law. C. assumes that *Neh.* 10 is preceded by Ezra's judicial appointments (*Ezra* 7:25), and the setting up of a *bet midrash* (*Neh.* 8:13-15) and Nehemiah's second governorship (*Neh.* 13). He traces five different types of legal development: (i) the establishment of machinery for carrying out a prescription (*e.g.* 10:35 allows the performance of *Lev.* 6:1-6); (ii) the machinery for carrying out a prescription (*e.g.* 10:39 allows the Levites to collect tithes,

cf. Deut. 14:23-26, *Mal.* 3:10); (iii) the creation of a new prescription for a Pentateuchal precedent (*e.g. Ex.* 30:11-16, *cf.* 10:33), (iv) the redefinition of categories for greater comprehensiveness (*e.g.* 10:36, *cf. Deut.* 26:2); (v) the integration of distinct and therefore potentially competing prescriptions (*e.g.* 10:36-40 - specifies that all Pentateuchal taxes are cumulative). C. identifies some of the exegetical principles guiding these developments. Every *halakhah* has some connection with a Pentateuchal law but a reapplication may bypass the letter of the law to preserve its spirit. Ancillary law is necessary for Pentateuchal law to be effectual. Since these laws are regarded as essentially harmonising, any apparent tensions have to be resolved by additions rather than mediation or compromise. This is not a systematic commentary on Pentateuchal law but rather designed to meet contemporary problems. C. concludes with an examination of *Neh.* 10 and earlier law on sabbath and intermarriage. K.W.W.

841. Peter C. Craigie, *Ugarit and the Old Testament,* Grand Rapids, Michigan: William B. Eerdmans Publishing Company, 1983, Pp. vii, 100, ISBN 0-8028-1928-1, Price: $5.95. - This is an introduction for the general reader to the discovery of Ugarit and its relevance to the study of the Old Testament. It includes an account of the proposed Ugaritic parallel to *Deut* 14:21 (seething a kid in its mother's milk), at 74-76, 108 (but omitting Haran, *JJS* 30 (1979), 23-35: see Survey no. 310, *JLA* 111). B.S.J.

842. M. Fishbane, "Revelation and Tradition: Aspect of Inner Biblical Exegesis", *JBL* 99 (1980), 343-361. - A study of inner-biblical exegesis used to reapply or reinterpret divinely revealed authoritative traditions with particular reference to law, homily and prophecy. The first part examines the reapplication or reinterpretation of legal provisions to fit new situations or unseen contingencies (e.g. *Num.* 27: 1-11; 36: 1-14; 9:6-14; 27: 8-11; 2 *Chr.* 29, 30). The author also deals with the way in which legal traditions, developed to add operative force to earlier laws, were also represented as of divine origin while their human origins are obscured (2 *Chron.* 30, *cf. Num.* 9; 2 *Chr.* 35:6). The rubric *Vehen ta'ase* is often used to introduce later legal explications (*Ex.* 23:4, *cf. Deut.* 22:1-3; *Ex.* 23:10-11, *cf. Lev.* 25:3-7). Fishbane also deals with the addition of protective restrictions (e.g. *Jer.* 17:19-27) and the subsequent recombination of earlier and disparate texts to create a new divine law (e.g. *Ex.* 22:30 and *Ex.* 23:19 combined in *Deut.* 14: 21). He sees this, along with the study of homily and prophecy, as reflecting an incipient canonical consciousness whereby the authority of revelation predominates over tradition. K.W.W.

843. B. Halpern, "The Centralization Formula in Deuteronomy", *VT* 31 (1981), 20-38. - The writer concentrates on the two basic formulae for cult centralization in *Deuteronomy* which are distinguished by the interchange of the verbs *swm* and *škn* (14:23; 16:2,6,11; 26:2; *cf.* 12:21; 24:24) is the only instance of the centralizing formula in Deuteronomy that qualifies "the place that Yhwh chooses" without attaching to it the placing of the name. He distinguishes two strata in the centralizing laws: 12:2-12 is secondary to 12:13-19. The early strand begins with the unique formula in 12:14 and contains no verb of motion. A distributive interpretation of 12:14 is a distinct possibility. He claims that this theory has far- reaching implications: *Deuteronomy* represents a conservative balwork against cultic innovation rather than a reform programme, it protects the Levites against rival claims to priesthood (*esp. Deut.* 18:6-8),

and it is not designed to disenfranchise existing priesthoods or close existing shrines but to recognise and ratify their claims. This code thus enforces a Levite priestly monopoly as the cultic *status quo*. K.W.W.

844. M. Haran, "Behind the scenes of History: Determining the Date of the Priestly Source", *JBL* 100 (1981), 321-333. - H. argues that P. is pre-exilic and preceded D. He sees P. as earlier than the law code of *Ezek.* 40-48, which looks merely as an epigonic outgrowth of the priestly source. P.'s early composition and later publication explains the fact that although it is pre-exilic it remains undetectable until the post-exilic period and Ezra. Ezra promulgated and canonised this source, which was already quite ancient, as part of the complete Pentateuch. The utopian idealism and idealistic laws of P. were not designed to be put into practice. P. was unlike D., which was moralising and designed to move its readers to reform. He detects strong sectarian features emanating from a semi-esoteric circle of the Jerusalemite priesthood and dating to the time of the reforms of Ahaz and Hezekiah. K.W.W.

845. M. Haran, "Behind the Stage of History - On the Dating of the Pentateuchal Priestly Source" (Heb.), *Zion* 45 (1980), i, 1-20. - Hebrew version of 844.

846. C. Houtman, "Ezra and the Law. Observations on the supposed relation between Ezra and the Pentateuch", *OS* 21 (1981), 91-115. - This essay consists of two parts. In the first Houtman gives a historical survey of opinions on the view that Ezra was responsible for a re-edition of the Pentateuch *(cf. IV Ezra* xiv 18ff.). In the second part he discusses the question of the identity of Ezra's law-book, or better, the identity of the law-book which the books of Ezra and Nehemiah presuppose. He concludes that this was neither the P Code, nor the Pentateuch as a whole, but rather a law- book which contained some laws agreeing with those in the Pentateuch but also some laws not known in the Pentateuch. In support of the possibility of such a document existing he cites the example of the Temple Scroll from Qumran. J.D.

847. Niels Peter Lemche, *Det gamle Israel. Det israelitiske samfund fra sammenbruddet af bronzealderkulturen til hellenistisk tid,* Aarhus: Forlaget Anis, 1984, ISBN 87-7457-028-5, Pp.240, Price: Dkr.130,00. - The author tries to present the history of Israel in ancient times as a social process. His study is based on a supposed general late date of the historical traditions in the OT, which were hardly written down before the middle of the 1st mill. B.C.E. Thus the OT view of the history of Israel is only the expression of a late reconstruction, and very little of this is of any use, especially as a witness to the pre-monarchical history of Israel. The O.T. law material, as it is transmitted by the O.T., is mostly to be found in very late sources, and in its present shape it reflects the customs of the post-exilic Jewish community. The O.T. picture of the religious history of Israel is based on the concept of God in the Torah, and this picture is retrospectively used as a kind of "filter" through which we now see the pre exilic Israelite religion. This religion was as a matter of fact a "Canaanite" religion, and only the experiences of the Babylonian exile transformed it into the Jewish law religion.
K.N.

848. P. Maon, "Responsabilité", in *Supplément au Dictionnaire de la Bible* (fascicule 55), ed. H. Cazelles and A. Feuillet (Paris, 1981), 357-356. - A comprehensive survey, including sections on semantic analysis, responsibility in law, and conclusion, together with useful bibliographical citations. J.D.

849. A.D.H. Mayes, "King and Covenant: a Study of 2 Kings chs. 22-23", *Hermatheia* 125 (1978), 34-47. - The author claims that "the widespread view that the original Deuteronomy, subsequently edited until its present form, was a law book found in the temple in the time of Josiah and made the basis of a reform by Josiah, is not tenable. Since, moreover, there is no evidence of the existence of Deuteronomy earlier than this one can only point to the period between Josiah's reform and 598 B.C., when the deuteronomistic historical work containing Deuteronomy was compiled, as its probable time of origin The Book may to a certain extent have been the deposit of that reform, in that Josiah's reform measures, insofar as they may be deduced from *2 Kings* 23 4-20, are reflected in Deuteronomy; but it was really only as a result of the redactional work of the deuteronomist that the connection between Deuteronomy and the reform of Josiah became firmly established. - As far as Josiah's covenant is concerned, this too must be seen as deriving from deuteronomistic theological interests. Josiah instituted a reform; but that any covenant was involved in this, whether a covenant between king and people or between king and people on the one hand and Yahweh on the other, is not to be established from 2 Kings 22f." J.D.

850. J.G. McConville, *Law and Theology in Deuteronomy*, Sheffield: J.S.O.T. Press, 1985, I.S.B.N. 0 905774 78 7 (pbk.79 5), Pp x, 240, Price: £18.50 or $28.50, £8.95 or $13.50 (pbk.) (Journal for the Study of the Old Testament Supplement Series 33). - The author describes his purpose as to "explore how the distinctive theology of Deuteronomy is reflected in its laws, in particular laws dealing with cultic matters (the sanctuary, sacrifices, festivals, etc.)." In so doing, he relates the laws to the narrative structure of the book, as speeches delivered on the eve of entry into the promised land. In the course of his analysis, McConville throws doubt upon traditional literary-historical analyses of Deuteronomy, and sees the laws as a product of the theological tendencies of the book, rather than as earlier, discrete sources which have been edited into a later, theological framework. It would be interesting to see how the author would relate the non-cultic laws to this thesis; in any event, his work is a stimulating and important contribution to the study of one of the major sources of biblical law. B.S.J.

851. E. Nielsen, "Moses and the Law", *VT* 32 (1982), 87-98. - N. examines the notion of and critical stances towards Moses as law-giver in the Pentateuchal traditions. He argues that the Law of Holiness (Lev. 17-26) is a Judaean parallel to the Deuteronomic legislation which suggests that circles in Judah did *not* associate Yahweh's laws and commandments with any special activity on the part of Moses. He believes that the promulgation of laws (sacred, moral and religious) originally belonged to the cult but that through Deuteronomy and P. it became historically and eventually exclusively associated with Moses. This recognition of Moses as the law-giver coincided with the first phase of the Deuteronomic movement after 722 B.C. It became an accepted factor in Jerusalem after 587 B.C., and thereafter completely dominated the law traditions of the Old Testament. The author concludes that it is beyond doubt that

the notion of Moses as law-giver was established through the Deuteronomic traditions. K.W.W.

852. W. Gunther Plaut and Bernard J. Bamberger, *The Torah: A Modern Commentary*, New York: Union of American Hebrew Congregations, 1981, ISBN 0-8074-0055-6, Pp. xxxvi, 1787, Price $25.00. - This is a lavishly produced Pentateuch, designed for use in American Reform congregations. The Hebrew text is accompanied by the Jewish Publication society translation; the *Haftarot* are also included, in Hebrew and English. In addition to the commentary, written by Plaut and (for Leviticus) Bamberger, a substantial series of introductory essays to the books is contributed by Professor W.W. Hallo, of Yale University. An advisory Board, consisting of many of the leading scholars of the American Progressive movement, both from Hebrew Union College and beyond, has contributed criticism and suggestions. As a result, the general public has a commentary which reflects modern scholarly discussion, and indeed cites modern literature, though not to the exclusion of reference to the traditional commentaries. Sources to which reference is made in the commentary or essays range from Ancient Near Eastern Literature to Abraham Lincoln. This edition should find a wide use, well beyond its denominational origins. It will assist students and discussion groups, and provide a useful starting point for researchers on many topics in Biblical law. B.S.J.

853. G.A. Yee, "A Form-Critical Study of Isaiah 5:1-7 as a Song and a Juridical Parable", *CBQ* 43 (1981), 30-40. - The writer argues that *Is.* 5:1-7 is composed of two different literary forms: a song and a juridical parable. He compares *Deut.* 32 as an example of a major Old Testament song which contains a lawsuit and then discusses the formal aspects of what Simon terms juridical parables *(2 Sam* .12:1-14; 14:1-20; *1 Kings*. 20:35-43). There are formal and functional similarities between the song and the juridical parable. In *Is.* 5:1-7 the juridical parable is used in the overall framework of the song to lead the southern kingdom to condemn itself. K.W.W.

See also 872, 873, 902, 941, 942, 945, 969, 992, 998. 1055.

BIBLIOGRAPHY

854. J.D. Wilkenfield, *A Bibliography of Israel Law in English and Other European Languages 1972-1979*, Jerusalem: The Harry Sacher Institute for Legislative Research and Comparative Law, 1979, Pp. 82, Price:$5.00. - The present bibliography is designed as a supplement to that of Judith Wegner, published by the same Institute in 1972. As the title indicates, it is a bibliography of Israel law, not specifically Jewish law, although there is a brief section (16 items) on Jewish law, most but not all of them dealing with Jewish law in the context of modern Israeli law. The present editor looks forward to regular updating and further improvement in the future, in what is undoubtedly a useful tool for comparative lawyers abroad. Since many of the latter will use the bibliography to order photocopies of individual items, librarians would doubtless be assisted by abandonment of the purely legal convention of restricting the pagination cited to the page number of the beginning of the article. B.S.J.

CAPACITY

See 856.

CLASSIFICATION

855. D. Altshuler, "On the Classification of Judaic Laws in the *Antiquities* of Josephus and the Temple scroll of Qumran", *AJSreview* 7-8 (1982-83), 1-14. - The author contests a comparison and suggested historical link made by Yadin between the Temple Scroll and the *Antiquities* of Josephus, based upon the presence in both of them of topical classification of laws. The classification of Josephus is apologetically motivated, and suggests that God's laws have temporal, not spatial implications; for the Qumran community, by contrast, the presentation of the law emphasises spatial referents of god's presence, implying the eternity of the cult and restoration of the state.
B.S.J.

See also 860.

COLLECTION OF ESSAYS

856. J. David Bleich, *Contemporary Halakhic Problems*, New York: Ktav Publishing House Inc. and Yeshiva University Press, 1983, ISBN 0-87068-451-5, Pp. xvii, 423, Price: $20.00 (The Library of Jewish Law and Ethics, X). - This volume is a sequel to that noted in *Survey* no. 162 (*JLA* II). Part I reviews various issues which have been debated in contemporary halakhic literature; it includes chapters on Medical Questions; Marriage, Divorce and Personal Status; Business and Commerce. Part II carries lengthier analyses of specific issues, including Settlement in Judea and Samaria, the Entebbe rescue, Mental Incompetence, Capital Punishment in the Noachide Code, and *Hetter Iska*. The author's approach will be familiar to readers of the *Jewish Law Annual*.
B.S.J.

857. D. Daube, *Ancient Jewish Law. Three Inaugural Lectures*, Leiden: E.J. Brill, 1981, ISBN 90 04 06531 8, Pp. xii 129, Price: Gld. 48. - The three extended lectures which comprise this book were delivered to inaugurate the Norman and Sadie Lee Program in Jewish and Western Civilisation at the University of Judaism at Los Angeles. They comprise:

(1) "Conversion to Judaism and Christianity." In the pre-exilic period, conversion to Judaism was far more easy for a woman than for a man. For a woman, a marriage in itself brought her within the community of her husband. Conversely, through divorce she reverted to her original community. The cases of Ruth and Orphah provide examples. With the exile, baptism was introduced, first for women only, and then also for men. A difference developed between Judaism and Christianity as to the need for circumcision; the position of Joshua ben Hanani is highlighted. The connection of baptism with the idea of re-birth is explored in relation to both talmudic

and New Testament sources. The last section of this essay traces the complicated history of the rule regarding the status of the child of a Jewess and a Gentile. The early sources assume such a child to be a Gentile. The first movement towards the later rule (that the child is Jewish) is found in the view of Simeon of Teman, in the second century A.D., for whom the child was Jewish, though a *mamzer*. Acceptance of such a child as a full Jew is not earlier than the 4th century. An Excursus considers the relationship of the Book of Ruth to the Book of Esther.

(2) "Error and Ignorance as Excuses in Crime." Comparison is made between biblical and other ancient sources on the effect of a mistake in criminal contexts. Whereas *Mal.* 14 and Sophocles, Antigone (448f.) imply exemption, biblical sources such as *Judges* 14 (Samson's *beenu* marriage), *Gen.* 20 and *I Sam.* 14 suggest a more severe attitude. In some sources, a distinction is found between inadequacy of information and inadequacy of understanding.

(3) "The Form is the Message." The author here considers aspects of the history of legislative forms, from the biblical apodictic to the participial form of tannaitic literature (in which even a decree of the High Priest John Hyrcanus is transmitted in the Talmud). The forms reflect different views of the role of revelation: the bible presents such legislation as direct commands of god; for the Rabbis, their sudsidiary legislation fulfils an already revealed divine will. It is in this context that the forms of the Sermon on the Mount are to be considered: the "antitheses of the sermon ... stand in between, representing a fresh impulse on the one hand, a faithful acceptance of the traditional framework on the other." The essays also considers the "diagnosis" form and the talmudic "*le'olam*" ("the Stoic Ever").

These studies build upon both published and unpublished earlier work of the author, which he lists in the Preface. D.P.

858. M. Humbert, ed., *Mélanges à la mémoire de Marcel-Henri Prévost*, Paris: Presses Universitaires de France, 1982, ISBN 2 13 037872 2, Pp. viii, 329, Price: F.130 (Publications de l'Université de Lille - Droit et Santé). - This memorial volume to a distinguished French scholar is sub-titled *Droit biblique - Interpretation rabbinique - Communautés et Société*", and is divided into three sections on these themes. The first part carries articles by Prévost, Cazelles, J.-Ph. Levy, Jackson, Cardascia, and Rabello; the second, by Piattelli, Dupuy, Yaron, M. Cohen, Kirschenbaum, Falk, B. Lifshitz, Englard, Passamaneck; the third, by Nikiprowetsky, R. Delmaire, Platelle, Humbert, and D. and J.-M. Delmaire. Many of the articles are noted individually in this *Survey*.
B.S.J.

859. Nahum Rakover, ed., *Jewish Law and Current Legal Problems*, Jerusalem: The Library of Jewish Law, 1984, Pp. 253, Price: $25.00. - This volume carries the Proceedings of the First International Seminar on The Sources of Contemporary Law: The Bible and Talmud and Their Contribution to Modern Legal Systems, held in Jerusalem in August, 1983. Both the conference and the publication programme of which this volume forms part reflects the impetus given to the study of Jewish Law in the wake of the Foundations of Law Act, 1980 (see Rakover, *JLA* V (1985), 80-84). The contents are: Haim H. Cohn, "The Lesson of Jewish Law for Legal Change" (15-28); Meyer S. Feldblum, "The Emergence of the Halakhic Legal System" (29-36); Norman Solomon, "Extensive and Restrictive Interpretation" (37-54); Yedidya Cohen,

"The Kibbutz as a Legal Entity" (55-65); Reuben Ahroni, "The Levirate and Human Rights" (67-76); Haim Shine, "Compromise" (77-84); Emanuel Rackman, "The Church Fathers and Hebrew Political Thought" (85-95); John Wade, "The Influence of Religion upon Law" (97-107); Bernard Meislin, "The Ten Commandments in American Law" (109-120); Ya'akov Bazak, "Maimonides' Views on Crime and Punishment" (121-126); Yehuda Gershuni, "Extradition" (127-136); Nahum Rakover, "Coercion in Conjugal Relations" (137-159); Isaac Braz, "The Privilege against Self-Incrimination in Anglo-American Law, the Influence of Jewish Law" (161-168); Arnold Enker, "Self-Incrimination" (169-175); Malvina Halberstam, "The Rationale for excluding Incriminating Statements, U.S. Law Compared to Ancient Jewish Law" (177-190); Stanley Levin, "Due Process in Rabbinical and Israeli Law, Abuse and Subversion" (191-194); David A. Frenkel, "Transplants" (195-201); Moshe Drori, "Artificial Insemination, Is It Adultery?" (203-216); Hershel Schachter, "Medical Malpractice" (217-223); Yitzchak Shapira, "Euthanasia" (225-231); Netanel Roberg, "Therapeutic Abortion" (223-241). An appendix carries the full conference programme. B.S.J.

860. Isadore Twersky, *Studies in Jewish Law and Philosophy*, New York: Ktav Publishing House, Inc., 1982, ISBN 0-87068-335-7, Pp. xvi, 226 + 75, Price: $29.50. - This volume provides a photomechanical reproduction, thus without updating, of 19 articles and book reviews, seven of them in Hebrew. A major part of them concern Maimonides' *Mishneh Torah*. Of particular interest are "The Mishneh Torah of Maimonides" (*Proceedings of the Israel Academy of Sciences and Humanities* V/10 (1976), 265-296) and (in Hebrew) "The Structure of Mishneh Torah: Juridical and Philosophical Guidelines" (See *Survey* no.445, *JLA* IV); as the author notes, he has since treated some of the themes of these articles more fully in his *Introduction to the Code of Maimonides* (Survey no. 458, *JLA* IV). There are also essays on the *Shulhan Arukh* and a review essay of Urbach's *Ba'ale Hatosafot*. A common theme is the complex dialectic between what the author calls "halakic Creativity and meta-halakhic concerns (e.g. philosophy, mysticism, pietism, or at a later period, hasidism, mussar)". B.S.J.

COLLECTIVE RESPONSIBILITY

861. A Phillips, "Double for all her sins", *ZAW* 94 (1982), 130-132. - P. interprets the phrase "Double for all her sins" (*Is.* 40:2) literally. Jerusalem has received double its punishment, i.e. twice the length of time it deserved. This means that a second innocent generation, with no responsibility for previous events, have also been punished. However, it is their vicarious suffering which is necessary for the glorious future promised by the prophet. K.W.W.

COMMERCIAL LAW

862. Edward Zipperstein, *Business Ethics in Jewish law*, New York: Ktav Publishing House Inc., 1983, ISBN 0-88125-005-8 (Hard), 022-8 (pbk.), Pp. xvi, 180, Price: $15.00 (hard), $8.95 (pbk.). - This study, which relies heavily on secondary sources, is

written by a Los Angeles public accountant, who brings to bear a combination of economic, legal and Hebraic training. He provides a sketch of Jewish economic history, and then deals, in a series of short chapters, with some well-known topics, such as methods of property acquisition, *ona'ah*, usury, *dina demalkhuta*, slavery and the position of the worker. The ethical outlook towards wealth and business practices is surveyed, through the Prophets, Proverbs and Rabbinic writings. There are also chapters on *Herem Hayyishub*, and some decisions from the *responsa* of Maharshal, and the book concludes with Appendices on the economic element in anti-semitism, and on the theory underlying it (Werner Sombart, and others). There is much of interest here for the lay reader. B.S.J.

COMPARATIVE STUDIES

863. M.J. Selman, "Comparative Customs and the Patriarchal Age", in *Essays on the Patriarchal Narratives*, ed. A.R. Millard and D.J. Wiseman (Leicester: Inter-Varsity Press, 1980), 93-138. - Van Seters and Thompson have demonstrated the weakness of many comparisons between the patriarchal narratives and the legal texts from Nuzi. However there still remain many valid parallels between social customs attested in Genesis and the customary law of the ancient Near East. But extrabiblical legal texts need more careful handling so that it is clear whether they are typical or exceptional. The biblical chronology of the patriarchs makes it likely that the closest parallels should be found in early second-millennium texts from cultures nearest to that of ancient Israel. Rarely though can a parallel custom be used to date a biblical text, because social practice usually changed very slowly. S. concludes by listing thirteen social customs mentioned in Genesis that are illuminated by extrabiblical legal texts, including the granting of birthright, the status of the eldest son, laws of inheritance, provision of dowry, prohibitions on taking second wives, and other aspects of marriage. G.J.W.

864. E. Volterra, *Diritto Romano e Diritti Orientali*, Naples: Jovene,1983, Pp. xii, 308, Price: IL 30,000 (Collana "Antiqua", 22). - In the last year of his life, the late Professor Volterra had the satisfaction of seeing this classic study, first published in 1937, made generally available once again. In a Note which precedes this photographic reprint, he tells us that some months after the original publication he was deprived of his teaching position, and all mention of his name in scientific writings was forbidden. During the war, the remaining copies of the book were destroyed. Despite the late author's desire to replace it with a more systematic and up-to-date treatment, the scholarly community will be grateful that the original is now once more available. The three substantial chapters are devoted to a survey of scholarship on the influence of oriental laws on Roman law, from the 16th century to date; the originality of the oldest Roman law and its relationship to other systems of Mediterranean law; and the influence of oriental law on post-classical Roman law. For the early period of Roman law, Volterra strongly affirms the juristic independence, both historically and conceptually, of the Roman institutions, despite the parallels which have been suggested by various scholars. As for the later period, he stressed the importance of study of the imperial constitutions, and of relating them to the laws of the provinces to which they were directed. In the course of his discussion, the author compared many of the institutions

of Roman private law with their Greek as well as Oriental equivalents: notably on such matters as *patria potestas*, adoption, succession, dowry, property, manumission. Although research has necessarily advanced since 1937, Volterra's work still retains its value, perhaps more for its comparison of juristic forms than for its historical conclusions. B.S.J.

865. Judith R. Wegner, "Islamic and Talmudic Jurisprudence: The Four Roots of Islamic Law and Their Talmudic Counterparts", *American Journal of Legal History* XXVI (1982), 25-71. - The author takes the Islamic doctrine of the "roots of jurisprudence", and proposes that each of the four corresponds, both linguistically and conceptually, with a basic source of Talmudic law. Specifically, *Qur'an* corresponds to *miqra*, *Sunna* to *mishnah*, *ijma* to *hakol* (juristic consensus as found in the Gemara), and *qiyas* to *heqqesh*. The article concludes with a comparison of Shafi'i's theory of the roots of the law with the juristic bases of talmudic law. In the light of the comparison, the question of influence upon Shafi'i is considered. B.S.J.

See also 831, 833, 834, 836,875, 893, 902, 905, 910, 917, 921, 928, 943, 980, 996, 1046, 1068.

CONFLICT OF LAWS

866. B. Lifshitz, "The rules governing conflict of laws between a Jew and a Gentile according to Maimonides", *Mélanges ... Prévost* (*supra* no. 858), 179-189. - Noting that Jewish law leaves relatively little scope for (internal) conflict of law rules, the author considers contracts between parties whose customs differed, claims made by one party that the law of the state, rather than Jewish Law, should apply (as a result of *dina demalkhuta dina)*, and litigation in Jewish courts between a Jew and a Gentile. The latter is studied with particular reference to the rulings of Maimonides. B.S.J.

See also 862, 967, 1051, 1067, 1070.

CONTRACT

867. I. Francus, "Commentaries and Explanations on the Law of *Ona'ah* (Overreaching)" (Heb.), *Sinai* 89 (5741), 134-144. - A study of the problems of overreaching and underpayment in Jewish law as reflected in various sources both in the *Talmud* and the *Tosefta*. Y.S.K.

See also 878, 916, 935, 1021, 1027.

CONVERSION

868. J. Milgrom, "Religious Conversion and the Revolt Model for the Formation of Israel", *JBL* 101 (1982), 169-176. - The author challenges the view, implicit in the

Mendenhall-Gottwald revolt model for the formation of Israel, that religious conversion is either attested or possible before the Second Temple period. He denies the new consensus that the use of *ger* in P indicates proselyte and, hence, a full Israelite. He follows Ibn Ezra (on *Lev.* 18:26) and Weinfeld that the *ger* and Israelite are not equated because the *ger* is only obliged to obey the laws that affect the purity of the congregation or the land. The distinction in P does not exist in civil law *(jus)*, which holds they are of equal status, but in religious law *(fas)*. There is a precise legal distinction in P between the *ger* and the Israelite. The *ger* may have worshipped Israel's God and was required to offer purification offerings to the sanctuary, but there was no obligation to follow all the religious prescriptions incumbent upon Israelites. He was neither an *ezrah* nor part of the *kahal* but a *ger*. D.'s law of *herem* and its law on intermarriage (*Deut.* 7:3; *cf. Exod.* 34:10; *Josh.* 23:12) presumes that Canaanites qua Canaanites were present at least in the eighth century. D.'s law of the *kahal* is a northern Israelite polemic against Judah, particularly against the Davidids. Thus the assumption of the revolt model that Israel was formed by mass conversion is unwarranted. Conversion of individuals is not attested until the post-exilic age, and the phenomenon of mass conversion not until the Hasmoneans and the advent of Christianity. K.W.W.

869. J. Nolland, "Uncircumcised Proselytes?", *JSJ* 12 (1981), 173-194. - N. examines the claim of McEleney that there was a significant strand of Jewish thought in the first century, prior to Pharisaic dominance, especially in the Hellenistic world, which allowed for the possibility of a convert to Judaism being accepted without the need for circumcision. He finds no evidence within first century Jewish writings (particularly, *Philo*: *Epictetus* II, ix, 20f; *Pes.* 92a) to support such a claim. K.W.W

870. J. Schatzmiller, "Converts and Judaizers in the Early Fourteenth Century", *HTR* 74 (1971), 63-77. - Inquisitors claimed that Jews who temporarily converted to Christianity were readmitted to Judaism by an immersion rite *(tebila)* designed to undo their baptism. But Rabbi Ibn Idreth denied this was necessary. A document from Toulon about 1320 confirms the existence of this rite. It contains the confessions of the Jew Salves Barbe before the inquisitor Bertrand de Cigoterio and describes how he was first immersed in the sea and later in hot water. Ibn Idreth's remarks should therefore be viewed not as denying the existence of the practice, but its necessity. To affirm the necessity of a Jewish immersion would be to admit the efficacy of baptism. G.J.W.

See also 1006, 1066.

COURTS

871. Lawrence H. Schiffman, *Sectarian Law in the Dead Sea Scrolls: Courts, Testimony and the Penal Code*, Chico Ca.: Scholars Press, 1983, ISBN 0-89130-568-8 (569-6 pbk.), Pp. xv, 278, Price: $15.95, $10.95 (pkb.) (Brown Judaic Studies 33). - An introductory chapter describes the principal sources of Qumran Law, their interrelationship, and the nature of Qumran Biblical exegesis which the author argues represents the origins of the Qumran lists of rules (the result, he suggests, of regular

study sessions which were part of the life of the sect). Individual chapters are then devoted to detailed study of the rules concerning judges and their qualifications of witnesses, the law of testimony, reproof as a requisite for punishment, the restoration of lost or stolen property, the use of the divine names, the sectarian penal code, and the communal meal. A concluding chapter summarises various aspects of the law for the light it throws on the sect's self-perception, and the nature of its society. This is a stimulating and scholarly study, the interest of which for the early history of Jewish law is enhanced by the frequent comparisons made by the author with early rabbinic sources.

B.S.J.

See also 982, 1045, 1059.

COVENANT-*BERIT*

872. E. Kutsch, "Bund" and G. Wanke, "Bundesbuch", in *Theologische Realenzyklopädie* 7 (Lieferung 3, Berlin and New York, 1980), 397-410 and 412-415. - The article on "Bund" by Kutsch deals with three main areas. (I) Old Testament, which has sections on *berit* between human partners, *berit* in the theological realm, and comments on usage in the Targums and Septuagint. Kutsch's well-known but controversial opinion that *berit* in the theological realm (and sometimes between human partners) does not mean "covenant" but "obligation" is here summarized. There is also a massive bibliography. (2) Early Judaism, which has sections on Ben Sira, the rest of the Apocrypha and Pseudepigrapha, from "obligation" to "covenant", Qumran, Philo and Josephus, and the Rabbis. (3) New Testament and the early Church, which has sections on the texts, individual references, the Epistle to the Hebrews, the words at the Last Supper, Paul, and the Apostolic Fathers.

The article by G. Wanke on "Bundesbuch" gives a useful, up-to-date survey of the Book of the Covenant. It includes sections on the name and extent of the work, its contents and structure, its origin and function, and its place in the Pentateuch. There is also a valuable bibliography. J.D.

873. D.J. McCarthy, "Covenant and Law in Chronicles - Nehemiah", *CBQ* 44 (1982), 25-44. - The author examines the specific meaning of covenant and its relationship to law in *Chronicles-Nehemiah. Chronicles,* despite its borrowings from traditional language, develops not just a structure for covenant-renewal, but also its own precise vocabulary *(darash, kana azab, ma'al).* Covenant renewal is to revalidate the cult, to purify it to allow God to be present. the focus changes in *Ezra-Nehemiah,* although the same factors, kings, prophets, cult functionaries and fidelity are involved, except with different emphasis. The distinctive vocabulary of *Chronicles* is not characteristic of *Ezra-Nehemiah.* Although there is continuity, *Ezra-Nehemiah* places a great emphasis on the written law to strengthen the temple community and preserve its identity in the face of foreign dominance. He notes a functional identity between the Mesopotamian *adu* ("loyalty oath") and covenant renewals in *Chronicles-Nehemiah;* the unity of the community on the basis of total fidelity to the community's central figure. The picture of covenant-renewal indicates that law in *Chronicles-Nehemiah* is not seen as pre-existant but as a means to relate to God through fidelity and humility. It can be

seen that *Chronicles-Nehemiah* has preserved an ancient form and not imported a new one of more or less exilic date. K.W.W.

874 E.W. Nicholson, "The Covenant Ritual in Exodus XXIV 3-8", VT 32 (1982), 74-86. - N. rejects the separation of the sacrificial offerings in *Ex.* 24:4-6 from the covenantal application of the blood in v.8. Nor does he accept such a ritual as a deuteronomic idea. He also rejects Kutsch's explanation of the rite as one of self-imprecation as analogous to the ritual described in Aeschylus's *The Seven against Thebes* 11.42ff. There is no evidence for such a use of blood in ancient Israel or for the use of blood as a description of kinship term. The blood rite is best understood as the use and significance of blood as holy, belonging solely to God, and conveying holiness to people or objects *(Ex.* 29:20f., *Lev.* 8:22ff.) In *Ex.* 24:3-8 Israel is consecrated as God's holy people. *Ex.* 19:6a is an interpretation of the ritual in 24:3ff., as constituting Israel as God's "kingdom of priests and a holy nation". K.W.W.

875. D.C.T. Sherriffs, "The Phrases *ina IGI* and *lipeney Yhwh* in Treaty and Covenant Contexts", *Journal of Northwest Semitic Languages* 7 (1979), 55-68. - The expressions *ina IGI DN* "before a divinity" in Late Assyrian (and Hittite) treaties and *lipne Yhwh* "before Yahweh" associated with covenant making in the Old Testament do not necessarily imply that the treaty or covenant was made in a sanctuary. Nor do they mean that the deity was present at the making of the treaty or covenant. Rather they indicate that the deity was a witness and judge, who would punish breaches of the treaty or covenant, and in some cases of Old Testament covenant making the expression also denotes the deity as covenant partner. J.D.

876. M.S. Smith, "*Berît 'am/berit 'ôlam:* a new proposal for the crux of Isa. 42:6", *JBL* 100 (1981), 241-248. - S. examines the sense and uniqueness of *Is.* 42:6 - *berit am,* "covenant of the people(s)." He finds previous explanations inadequate since they isolate the phrase from its immediate context or from its relationship to the rest of Second Isaiah. He suggests that the prophet plays upon and transforms the old royal theology of *berit olam (cf. Is.* 55:1-5 and *2 Sam.* 23:1-7). A comparison of *2 Sam.* 22 and *Is.* 42:5-9 illustrates this relationship. Drawing upon the dynastic promise to and mediatorial role of the Davidic king, the prophet envisages Israel in an image of a new kingship mediating blessings to the peoples. The slogan of the old dynasty was *berit olam* while that of the new dynasty is *berit am.* Smith points to the phonetic resemblance between the two phrases, the theological support from the context and also its historical plausibility. K.W.W.

See also 849, 1064.

CRIMINAL LAW

877. E. Ben Zimra, "The Use of Force in the Prevention of Crime" (Heb.), *Diné Israel* 9 (1978-1980), 85-112. - In this article.the use of force by one person in order to prevent the performance of a crime by another individual is discussed. According to one group of scholars, the use of force is legitimate only when the potential criminal is

under the direct control of the person contemplating the use of force. Another group believes that the use of force is only legitimate in order to prevent crimes of a special nature, and a third group maintains that force is always allowed when the aim is the prevention of crime. In general, however, all authorities were in agreement that any force used in these circumstances must be carefully controlled, and strict limitations were imposed in order to ensure such control. The writer also observes that there is no justification for the use of force against non-observant Jews in the present era, and only peaceful means may be used for purposes of restoring them to the correct path. Y.S.K.

See also 848, 871, 885, 1004, 1027.

DEBT

878. B.Z. Eliash, "The Basis of the Loan Concept in Jewish Law" (Heb.), *Sinai* 90 (5742), 44-67. - On the basis of various halakhic sources, the author attempts to define the basic elements of a loan in Jewish law, and to distinguish it from various transactions. According to Eliash, a loan is a transfer of money or assets in exchange for an obligation to return money or assets in the future. In this way, a loan is distinguished from both a deposit and a sale. Y.S.K.

879. M. Givati, "Remission of Debts: Theory and Practice", *BM* 25 (1980), 172-180 (Heb.). - The persuasive, hortatory formulation of *Deut.* 15:1-6 indicates that the sabbatical remission of debts was enacted to protect the destitute peasant from exploitation by the wealthy landowner while still ensuring the former the privilege of obtaining a loan. To what extent the prescriptions were followed in biblical times is unsure; by tannaitic times they had become ineffective despite their severe language. It was for this reason - to encourage loans to the needy - that the *prozbol* was instituted, and not, as sometimes thought, to enable the well-off to secure commercial loans. Parties to commercial loans would be likely to make use of previous enactments authorising them to transfer the loans to the court *(M. Shebi.* 10:1, 3, 5), while the peasant class would be insufficiently familiar with such technicalities. B.S.J.

880. M. Goodman, "The First Jewish Revolt: Social Conflict and the Problem of Debt", *JJS* 33:1-2 (1982: Yadin Festschrift), 417-427. - The First Revolt was brought on largely by an extremely unequal distribution of wealth that occurred during the preceding *pax Romana*. Jewish nationalism enabled the wealthier classes to direct the anger of landless peasants and unemployed urban proletarians (the Temple had just been completed) against Israel's foreign occupiers thus averting the class warfare one might have expected. S.N.R.

See also 1007, 1070.

DECALOGUE

881. B. Lang "'Du sollst nicht nach der Frau eines anderen verlangen', Eine neune Deutung des 9. und 10. Gebots," *ZAW* 93 (1981), 216-24. - Lang argues that *Ex.* 20:17/*Deut.* 5:21 seek to protect the marriage and possessions of those Israelites who have been absent for a long time. *Ex.* 34:24 is to be understood in the same way. Parallel laws are to be found in CH 27-31, 133-6, MAL 36, 45, and in the Roman *postiliminium.* J.D.

See also 859, 1004.

DOCUMENTS

882. M.A. Friedman, *Jewish Marriage in Palestine, A Cairo Geniza Study,* Tel-Aviv and New York: Tel-Aviv University and The Jewish Theological Seminary of America, 1980-81, 2 vols., Pp. xxiv, 492, xiii, 517 + 30 plates. - It is a pleasure to welcome the appearance of these two volumes, which originated in Professor Friedman's doctoral thesis. Volume II alone, an edition of sixty-seven manuscripts and fragments under the title *The Ketubba Texts,* greatly enriches the primary source material available to historians of Jewish law. Each document is described, transcribed, translated and annotated, with frequent reference not only to talmudic parallels, but also to modern scholarly literature commenting thereon. Photographs of many of the texts are also provided. The volume has a lavish apparatus: a word index, manuscript index, source index, and name and subject index (marred only, in my copy, by the binding of four pages of this last upside-down). Additionally, Professor Friedman has provided, in volume I *(The Ketubba Traditions of Eretz Israel),* an invaluable study of the documents, dealing with historical, linguistic, social and legal aspects. The legal topics considered include clauses affirming the volition of the parties (especially the groom) to enter into the contract (a clause absent from Babylonian formularies), the obligations of husband and wife, the time of writing the marriage contract, mohar and dowry, provisions for divorce, ransom and succession, and the concluding formulae and signatures of the document. Many points of detail receive elaborate treatment. While each of them is of independent interest to legal historians, they add up to a distinct Palestinian tradition of the marriage contract, in which, as Professor Friedman remarks, the position of women "appears to be more advanced in some respects than one would have imagined." These volumes went to press before the appearance of volume III of Professor Goitein's *A Mediterranean Society* ("The Family"), but the two are complementary (Goitein supervised Friedman's research). The current generation is privileged to have access to this new material, and fortunate in the service that has been rendered by its editors.

B.S.J.

883. J.-Ph. Lévy, "Sur trois textes bibliques concernant des actes écrits", *Mélanges ... Prévost (supra* no. 858), 23-48. - This article discusses three biblical texts which concern written legal acts. The author provides a substantial study of Jeremiah 32, considering the writing material, the role of Jeremiah in writing it, the sealing, and the relationship of the procedure to the form of *Doppelurkunde,* the

witnesses, and the deposit of the document. More briefly, he considers the written documemts to which reference is made in the Book of Tobit, and the parable of the steward in *Luke* 16: 1-8. B.S.J.

884. Gershon Weiss, "A Testimony from the Cairo Geniza Documents: *Son-in-law - Mother-in-law Relations*", *JQR* 68.2 (1977), 99-103. - From one fragment, T-S C 2, f.17, Gerson Weiss indicates that the year 875 marks the year when *shetarot* were issued. From another piece, from the15th cent., T-S Box G I, f.52, a deposition for litigation, with Judeo-Spanish phrases, Weiss draws an analogy which may explain the introduction of Judea-Arabic into Jewish legal practice (i.e., that the issues could be most unambiguously stated in the vernacular). M.F.

See also 888, 1070.

DURESS

885. E. Ben-Zimra, "The Principles of *Ones* (Coercion) Occasioned by another Person in Jewish Law" (Heb.), *Sinai* (5740), 238-270. - The situations discussed in this article are those generally dealt with under the rubric of necessity and duress in modern legal terms. The writer deals with the effect of a claim of duress or necessity upon legal acts, or omissions of legal significance, and upon the course of human or Divine punishment. The analysis is carried out in terms of the nature of the coercive or threatening act; the type of danger to which the victim was subjected; the mental and physical state of the victim, and the evidentiary requirements for each one of these elements. Y.S.K.

EVIDENCE

886. H.H. Cohn, "The Proof in Biblical and Talmudical Law", in *La Preuve en Droit*, ed. C. Perelman and P. Foriers (Bruxelles: E. Bruylant, 1981), 77-98. - This article surveys the biblical modes of proof, rabbinic rules of cross-examination and of the qualifications required of witnesses, and presumptions and other devices mitigating the heavy burden of proof (two eye-witnesses). B.S.J.

887. H. Hefetz, "The Role of Evidence in the Halakhah" (Heb.), *Diné Israel* 9 (1978-1980), 51-85. - The article pinpoints the unique role played by the evidence of witnesses in Jewish law. According to Hefetz, the role of witnesses is purely evidentiary and entirely independent of the question of establishing the truth. The witness functions as an aid to the judge in arriving at his decision when the standard forms of proof are insufficient to tip the scale in favour of one or other of the litigants. In the same way that the judge must possess various qualifications in order to fulfill his role, the witness must answer to certain requirements before entering the special proof-category of testimony in Jewish law. Y.S.K.

See also 859, 871, 885, 991.

GUARDIANSHIP

888. J. Greenfield and S. Applebaum, "Israel Museum Exhibit Reveals Wife and Mother from Bar Kochba Period", *Biblical Archaeology Review* 7:4 (1981), 12. - This note contains the first English translation of a complete document from the Babata Archive. The document, in Greek and Aramaic, deals with thrice-married Babata's attempts to change the court-appointed guardian of her "orphan son" or assume the guardianship herself. S.N.R.

HISTORY OF JEWISH LAW

889. Joseph Baumgarten, "The Pharisaic-Sadducean Controversies about Purity and the Qumran Texts", *JJS* 31.2 (1980), 157-70. - In a thoughtful analysis, Baumgarten attempts to determine the position of the sect on halakhic aspects of purity which also involved Pharisaic-Sadducean controversies. He takes up the issue of *Tebul Yom*, of Bones of Animals, of *Nissoq*, and of the immersion of the Menorah. Baumgarten suggests that in the first three cases Qumran materials suggest that the sect was rigorous in its construction of the rule, like the Sadducees and in contrast to the Pharisaic position. In the fourth case the Temple Scroll appears strict, while the Sadducees appear lenient. Baumgarten outlines the issues regarding the immersion of the Menorah but does not draw a final conclusion. He does, however, doubt that the Sadducees reflected in the preceding sources are not the historical sadducees, but some other heterodox group from the period (to whom the name Sadducees were attributed, as sometimes happens).
M. F.

890. Shean Freyne, *Galilee from Alexander the Great to Hadrian 323 BCE to 135 CE*, Wilmington, Delaware: Michael Glazier, Inc. and University of Notre Dame Press, 1980, ISBN: 0-98453-099-2 and 0-268-01002-1, Pp. xviii, 491, Price: $27.50. - This is an important and ambitious exercise in the integration of social, religious and economic history, focused upon Galilee because of its importance for Christian history, but recognising the importance of much wider historical perspectives. Professor Freyne, inspired by the example of and encouragement from Professor Hengel, uses a well-balanced array of sources, especially Josephus, New Testament, and early Rabbinic texts. For the general legal history of the period, his chapters on the cities, and on economic realities (land ownership, commerce, wealth distribution, taxation) are of great interest. For the student of Jewish law, chapter 8, "Galilee and the Halakhah" is particularly important. Before the destruction of the Temple, the *halakhah* had little attraction for the country people; the author explains this as understandable, on the grounds that Pharisaism as a way of life was more suited to the middle class townspeople. The country people appear to have found the figure of the holy man (the *hasid)* more attractive. After 70, Pharisaism had a limited success in Galilee, but its penetration was gradual, and there was no radical and immediate break with the traditions of the earlier period. Freyne's review of the evidence includes consideration of the problem of the *am ha'arets*, on which he broadly endorses the views of Oppenheimer *(Survey* no. 190, *JLA* II). B.S.J.

891. M. Heltzer, "The Story of Susanna and the Self-Government of the Jewish Community in Achaemenid Babylonia", *Annali dell'Istituto Orientale di Napoli* 41 (1981), 35-39. - The author concludes: "According to the *realia* of the story, "Susanna" received its present literary form in Achaemenid Babylonia in the V-IV cent. B.C.E. The evidence for this is (a) the personal name Susanna itself, given after the town of Susa, and (b) the institutions of ethnic self-government which, according to the scarce data we possess, did not differ from the self-government of other ethnic groups at this time." J.D.

See also 859, 931, 970, 1065.

HOMICIDE

892. J. de Vaulx, "Refuge (droit d'asile et villes de refuge dans l'Ancien Testament)", in *Supplément au dictionnaire de la Bible* vol.9 (Paris, 1979), 1480-1510. - This article is a very thorough treatment of the right of asylum of cities of refuge in the Old Testament and also contain useful bibliographical information. After an introduction dealing with the Hebrew vocabulary concerning refuge, the article contains three main sections, (1) the right of asylum in antiquity outside the Bible, (2) asylum and refuge in Israel, and (3) conclusions and synthesis. An appendix deals with the right of asylum in the post-biblical period up to the present day. J. D.

893. V. Kubác, "Blut in Gurtel und in Sandalen", *VT* 31 (1981), 225-226. - The force of David's deathbed sentence on Joab ordering Solomon to execute him for the murders of Abner and Amasa by which act in peacetime he had brought innocent bloodshed in war "Upon the girdle of his loins and the sandals of his feet" *(I Kings*. 2:5; *cf. 2 Sam*. 2:30; 20:9f) must be understood in the context of the ancient belief in the magical power of blood. Anat's bloodbath described in the Ugaritic Epic V AB/B (CTA 3 ii) illustrates this power of blood to revive and empower. Joab's similarly offensive magical act was punished accordingly. K.W.W.

894. J. Milgrom, "The Paradox of the Red Cow *(Num*. XIX)", *VT* 31 (1981), 62-72. - The writer claims that the key to the paradox of the Red Cow is that it is a *hatat* sacrifice or "purification offering" to remove contamination. The lustral ashes of the Red Cow are the only vestige of a pre-Israelite rite of exorcism for the corpse-contaminated. The demonic impurity of the corpse has been devitalized and the procedure for preparing the ashes has been restructured to conform to the *hatat* requirements and integrated into Israel's sacrificial system. The present form of ritual of the Red Cow *(Num*. 19) is later than the rituals for severe impurities of *Lev*. 12-15 which betray more primitive traces. K.W.W.

HUMAN RIGHTS

895. Haim H. Cohn, *Human Rights in Jewish Law,* New York: Ktav Publishing House, Inc. for The Institute of Jewish Affairs, London, 1984, ISBN 0-88125-036-8, Pp. viii, 266, Price: $20.00. - In this stimulating book, Justice Cohn, recently retired as Deputy President of the Israel Supreme Court and the author of numerous scholarly works, assesses the stance of the Jewish tradition on human rights issues. He finds much relevant, and mainly positive material on 25 of the human rights enumerated in the Universal Declaration of Human Rights. There are chapters on the Rights to Life, Liberty, and Security, Privacy, Reputation, Asylum, Marriage and Family, Property, Work and Renumeration, Leisure, and Education and Participation in Culture, on the Freedoms of Movement and Residence, Thought, Speech and Conscience, and Information, on Slavery, and on Rights of Equality, involving prohibitions of discrimination on account of race, religion, nationality, sex, birth or property. A further major section of the book deals with rights relevant to the administration of justice: equality before the law, judicial standards, procedural safeguards, freedom from torture and cruel punishments, retrospective legislation, etc. An introductory chapter deals thoughtfully with the relationship between rights and duties in the context of religious and secular systems of law, conceding that "human rights" as a concept is unknown to the Jewish tradition, which uses the more concrete duties as a means of implementing such values. Justice Cohn has collected and compressed an immense array of sources into a thought-provoking study, which will attract deserved attention from both laymen and jurists. B.S.J.

See also 837.

HUSBAND AND WIFE

896. J. David Bleich, "Jewish Divorce: Judicial Misconceptions and Possible Means of Civil Enforcement", *Connecticut Law Review* 16/2 (1984), 201-289. - The author argues that civil enforcement of a *get* in American courts ought not to fall foul of first amendment problems, since the *get* is a non-religious act of the parties (comparable to a contract under Jewish law), and not a decree of a rabbinic court. He notes a growing judicial recognition of the true character of the *get* in American courts, and urges "a policy of non-intervention expressed in the withholding of a decree of divorce in the absence of a *get* " as a permissible form of pressure. B.S.J.

897. M. Donaldson, "Kinship Theory in the Patriarchal Narratives: The Case of the Barren Wife", *JAAR* 79:1 (1981), 77-87. - The kinship theories of Lévi-Strauss conduce to reading the patriarchal narratives synchronically. This shifts the emphasis from fathers-and-sons and instead asks "who is the legitimate wife?" Lying between incest (Abram-Sarah) and exogamy (Esau), the answer is that the legitimate wife is a matrilateral cross cousin. S.N.R.

898. Ze'ev Falk, "Concerning Marriage in Hosea and Malachi" (Heb), in *Studies in the Bible and the Hebrew Language offered to Meir Wallenstein, on the Occasion of his*

Seventy-fifth Birthday, edited by C. Rabin, D. Patterson, B.-Z. Luria, Y. Avishur (Jerusalem: Kiryat Sepher, 1979), 188-195. - Falk deals first with *Hos*. 2-3, and makes a series of observations on the legal phraseology or topoi, with frequent references to rabbinic literature. For example, he states that the children's names *(lo' 'ammi,* etc.) imply a temporary annulment of their paternal relationship; that the marriage term *ishi* reflects a shift from a patriarchal notion of marriage to a more egalitarian one. Falk then digresses on old biblical family law, and suggests that *Zech*. 13:3, where the parents must kill their son for a false prophecy, is related to notions in *Deut*. 13:7-12, and reflects a reversion to older family laws, where relations executed punishment (vs. the pre-exilic development reflected in *Deut*. 21:19). Regarding Malachi, Falk interprets the fact that intermarriage desecrates the *Kodesh YHWH* (2:11) in light of the "holy seed" of Israel concept in *Ezra* 9:2 *(cf. Lev*. 21:15), or possibly as related to the idea of a holy covenant *(cf. Dan*. 11:28,30). Falk stresses that for Malachi marriage was a permanent affair; and draws an *a fortiori* comparison between the fact that God can annul his divorce with Israel and the teaching to Israel that their human love must overlook iniquities in marriage. M.F.

899. I. Francus, "The Approaches of the Babylonian and Jerusalem *Talmuds* to the Widow's Right to Claim her *Ketubah* from Movable Property" (Heb.), *Sinai* 86 (5740), 136-148. - The Gaonim changed the Talmudic law that a widow could only collect her *Ketubah* from immovable property and allowed her to collect it from chattels too. The article deals with two passages in the *Talmud* dealing with this law, with a view to clarifying the law in the Talmudic period. Y.S.K.

900. S. Friedman, "The Case of the Woman with two Husbands in Talmudic and Ancient Near eastern Law", *Israel Law Review* 15 (1980), 530-558. - The author considers *Yeb*. 10:1,3: the case of a woman who marries another man during the absence of her husband. Unlike the ancient Near East sources (Laws of Eshnunna 29, 30, LH 133-136, Assyrian Laws 45) rabbinic jurisprudence allows the deserted woman to marry another man only on the testimony that he had died. According to the mishnaic sources, if she re-marries without authorisation of the Beth Din, her second marriage is considered not valid and, on his return, she is allowed to return to her first husband. On the other hand, if she re-marries with such authorisation, her second marriage is considered valid; in this case, she is compelled to leave both men. This decision results from the fact that the Sages regarded as unlawful the co-existence of two valid marriages: no idea of a penal function is involved in this decision. D.P.

901. T. Frymer-Kensky, "Patriarchal Family Relationships and Near Eastern Law", *The Biblical Archaeologist* 14 (1981), 209-214. - The author sees the patriarchal material as authentically reflecting a general cuneiform tradition of the ancient Near East. A common pattern of the extended family is sketched which is seen as being patrilocal in residence, patripotestal in power and patrilineal in descent. The well rehearsed problems of childlessness, the barren wife, adoption and inheritance, particularly in *Gen*. 15 and 16, are examined in the light of cuneiform material. The consistent biblical motif of choosing the younger son over the older is seen to reflect the Near Eastern use of the terms "first-born", as well as "son", "father", "brother" and "sister", as the

description of a judicial relationship which is a matter of choice and can be entered into by contract as well as by birth. K.W.W.

902. Irwin H. Haut, *Divorce in Jewish Law and Life*, New York: Sepher-Hermon Press, 1983, ISBN 0-87203-110-1, Pp. xiii, 146, Price: $12.50 (Studies in Jewish Jurisprudence, V). - Prompted by the increasing problem encountered in the civil courts of dealing with failure to deliver or accept a *get*, this book seeks to provide the courts, the legal profession and the general public with an understanding of the principles of the Jewish law of marriage and divorce, with particular attention to the problem of *get*. He deals with the formalities of marriage, marital obligations, the *ketubah* (providing an English text), rabbinic *takanot*, the *get* and its formal requirements, the wife's right to sue for divorce, the *get* procedure (according to the *Shulhan Arukh)* and the legal consequences of divorce. Turning to modern problems, he deals with the relations between civil and religious divorce, the Conservative *ketubah*, and the response of American courts to the *get* problem, particularly in the state of New York. The response of Israeli courts is also briefly treated. In surveying rabbinic proposals to solve the *get* problem, he advocates a *takanah* which would empower the rabbinate to annul marriages as a last resort. The Opinions of Wachtler, J., and Jones, J. (dissenting) in *Avitzur* v. *Avitzur* are extracted in an Appendix. This book will add nothing new for the specialist, but may certainly assist the lay public in grasping the general character of the problem.
B.S.J.

903. *The Jewish Law Annual*, ed. B.S. Jackson, Leiden: E.J.Brill, Vol.IV, 1981, ISBN 90 04 06504 0, Pp. vii, 332, Price: Gld.108. - Part One consists in a major symposium on "The Wife's Right to Divorce", with articles which deal with the ancient Near East (Lipinski), Biblical law (Zakovitch), The New Testament (Lövestam), the intertestamental and early rabbinic period (Piattelli), the Roman Empire (Rabello), the Cairo Geniza documents (Friedman), and the period of the *Rishonim* (Shilo, on the particular problem of impotence as a ground for divorce). The modern problem of the wife denied a *get* by her husband is dealt with in articles by Washofski, Bleich, Novak and Chigier, and the relationship between civil and religious laws are considered by Meislin (for North America) and Freeman (England). An extract is published from the judgment of Judge Held in *Stern* v. *Stern*. Comparative perspectives on the problem are provided by Pearl (for Muslim law) and Derrett (Hindu law). The Editor in his Introduction argues for reversal of the normal rule of priority, which requires the parties to obtain a civil divorce before approaching the religious authorities. B.S.J.

904. Tryggve Kronholm, "Polygami och monogami i Galma testamentet. Med et utblick över den antika judendomen och Nya testamentet", *Svensk exegetisk Arsbok* 47 (1982), 48-92. - In his article on polygamy and monogamy the author gives a survey of Old Testament evidence of the existence of both polygamy and monogamy from the very beginning of Israel's history. It seems that for social and economic reasons polygamy was mainly practised by the more prominent men of the Israelite tribes and by the kings, while ordinary people practised monogamy or bigamy. The author emphasizes the underlying monogamous ethos in the creation accounts and in prophetic and wisdom literature. In a concluding survey of the attitude in post-biblical Judaism it is shown how NT, the Essenes, possibly also the Sadducees, the Samaritans etc. opposed

polygamy, while the Pharisees claimed that polygamy is accepted by the Torah. The controversy between the Rabbis and the Church Fathers on this point is seen as a continuation of inner-Jewish contradictory positions. The article ends with an English summary. K.N

905. H. Klein, "Natur und recht: Israels Umgang mit dem Hochzeitsbrauchtum seiner Umwelt", *Theologische Zeitschrift* 37 (1981), 3-18. - Various biblical episodes give an insight into marriage customs, probably of Canaanite origin, which though recorded were not officially sanctioned by the biblical writers. *Judg*. 21:19-23; *Gen*. 38:12-26; *Gen*. 34 reflect Canaanite methods of finding a marriage partner. *Hos*. 4:13 reflects the custom of ritualized adultery after the wedding. *Gen*. 2-3 and *Song*. 3:6-11 allude to ceremonies associated with the wedding itself. Probably Israelite men were allowed more liberty in following these foreign customs than their womenfolk. G.J.W.

906. J.R. Mueller, "The Temple Scroll and the Gospel Divorce Texts", *RQ* vol 10, no 38 (1980), 247-56. - Mueller seeks to draw some implications from the Temple Scroll on marriage, and also to try to solve some cruces in the gospels. He notes that *11Q Temple* LVII:17-19 is opposed to polygamy and divorce for the king, and suggests that it applies to the people as well. He further suggests that *11Q Temple* LXVI:11-17, which combines various biblical laws against incest, is an attempt to redefine this issue (also of concern to *Dam Doc*. V:7-11). He claims that *Dam Doc*. IV:20-21 is clarified by the Temple scroll and must be understood as opposed to polygamy and divorce. Further, with respect to Gospel passages, Mueller suggest that *11Q Temple* LVII, which is against polygamy and incest, and associates unchastity with incestuous marriage, may have influenced *Mark* 10:2, where the question is raised - without further qualification - whether divorce is permitted; and it may have influenced the phrase "except for unchastity" in *Mt*. 19:9, and indicate that the Greek *porneia* may refer to illicit marriage (not adultery). M.F.

907. J. Murphy-O'Conner, "The Divorced women in 1 Cor.7:10-11", *JBL* 100 (1981), 601-606. - The author argues that since *choristhenai* (*1 Cor*. 7:10) is an aorist passive infinitive, it should be translated "the wife should not *be separated* from her husband." Paul sometimes uses the passive with the connotation "to allow to be" (*1 Cor*. 6:7; *Rom*. 12:2). He thus translates 7:10a as "the wife should not allow herself to be separated from her husband", which is the reverse of "the husband should not divorce his wife" (7:11c). If it is wrong for the husband to issue a writ of divorce, it is equally wrong for the wife to accept it since this is disobedience to God. 7:1-9 is a reaction to a specific situation in Corinth, where ascetics were advocating married couples should abstain from sexual intercourse. It is this situation which might lead to divorce if the partners do not agree. Paul refuses divorce in 7:10-11 because the grounds were insufficient, but permits it in 7:15 where the reason is convincing. He concludes that Paul considered Jesus's prohibition of divorce, not as a binding precept, but a directive whose relevance to a specific situation had to be evaluated by the pastor. K.W.W.

908. Reinhard Neudecker, *Frührabbinisches Ehescheidungsrecht: Der Tosefta-Traktat Gittin*, Rome: Biblical Institute Press, 1982, ISBN pbk, Pp. XVII, 133, Price: $30.00 (Biblica et Orientalia 39) - This German version of Tosefta Gittin is based on the Erfurt

ms (now Ms.or.fol.1220 of the Staatsbibliothek, Berlin), photographs of which are supplied at the end of the volume. Variants from the Vienna ms, the Venice 1521 *editio princeps* of Alfasi, the Paris Genizah fragment of Gittin, and the Vatican codex, Hebr. 169, are regularly discussed. The commentary is devoted largely to elucidating, in rather "atomistic" fashion, basic problems of translation and meaning. Broader issues, such as the relationship between the various text-witnesses, the structure of the tractate, and the relationship of Mishnah to Tosefta, should have received more attention. Neusner's Tosefta translation and his *History of the Mishnaic Law of Women* came too late for Neudecker to use systematically, but he gives his reactions to Neusner's work on pp. XIII-XVI of his *Vorwort*. This is a useful and generally competent contribution to the study of early Rabbinic literature. P.S.A.

909. W.E. Phipps, "Is Paul's Attitude towards Sexual Relations Contained in *1 Cor.* 7:1?", *New Testament Studies* 28 (1982), 125-131. - No. In *1 Cor.* 7:1 Paul is quoting a slogan of the Corinthian Christians which he rejected. Paul approved of sexual intercourse within marriage. G.J.W.

910. T. Prewitt, "Kinship Structures and the Genesis Genealogies", *JNES* 40 (1981), 87-98. - Abram is the oldest of Terah's sons. This means, according to "some ideal political relationships common to anthropologically known contemporary systems", that Abram will be the chief "wife-taker" in the Hierarchized group Abram-Nahor-Haran. The article also notes a persistent south-south-westerly movement of the "Terah connubium". S.N.R.

911. W. Rudolph, "Zu Mal 2 10-16", *ZAW* 93 (1981), 85-90. - Rudolph rejects the view of S. Schreiner, who in *ZAW* 91 (1979), 207ff., had argued on the basis of *Ma.* 2:10-16 that Malachi tolerated divorce in the manner of Deuteronomy, but regarded the second marriage as inferior. Rudolph also notes other recent literature on Ma. 2:10-16. J.D.

912. A. Tosato, *Il matrimonio Israelitico*, Rome: Biblical Institute Press, 1982, Pp. xvi, 274, Price $19.00 (Analecta Biblica 100). - This book, part of the author's doctoral thesis, is in fact his second book on this theme; see also *Il matrimonio nel Giudaismo antico e nel Nuovo Testamento*, Rome: Città Nouva, 1976. The present work is richly documented and broadly conceived, more broadly than its title might suggest. For the author includes an account of non-matrimonial modes of "taking" a woman - as prisoner, slave or prostitute. His object in this is not merely historical; he seeks to combat modern attacks upon marriage, viewing them as equivalent to enslavement or prostitution. He is at pains to point out the superior rights enjoyed by the wife as compared with the slave or prostitute. He points out, on the basis of linguistic analysis, that there was a transformation of the status of the husband as well as the wife; that the wife was not a passive object in a commercial transaction; that the function of marriage was to assure the legitimacy of the offspring, in the interests of both parties; and that the resultant status of the wife was to be reserved exclusively and unilaterally to the man who became her husband - a reservation not equivalent to a property relationship, but rather a relationship of personal consecration. The availability of polygamy to the man but not the woman is seen as an advantage to the wife, protecting her from divorce; but

rights of divorce were enjoyed by both parties. Nevertheless, the woman was still in a position of relative inferiority, to be improved as the institution of marriage developed in the Jewish and Christian world. The author does well not to seek to conceal his conservative orientation; nevertheless, his intelligent and detailed marshalling of the sources, primary and secondary, make this a significant contribution to a difficult topic.

B.S.J.

913. R. Yaron, "The Missing Husband in Jewish Law", *Mélanges ... Prévost (supra* no. 858), 133-140. - The author considers the obligations of an absent husband to maintain his wife, and the problem of the missing husband, whose whereabouts and fate are unknown. In the latter case, the practice grew up of handing the wife a conditional *get*. The author discusses various complications which may arise therefrom, as provided for in the early rabbinic sources. B.S.J

914. Y. Yudlov, "A Judgment of the Venetian Rabbis of 1609" (Heb.), *Sinai* 84 (5739), 166-172. - This judgment, which is also referred to in the general *Responsa* literature, involved a *marrano* who for some fifteen years had enjoyed the status of *Kohen* and now wished to marry a divorcee. His argument was that there was insufficient evidence of his priestly status and, therefore, the marriage ought to be allowed since he was not, in fact, a *Kohen*. The case quickly became a *cause célêbre*, and the Rabbis of Venice, who rejected the *marrano's* argument, felt the need for a speedy response and published their decision in a separate volume which is presented in the present article. This type of *responsum* presenting various judgments on a particular issue, is a special, albeit rarely-found branch of the *responsa* literature in general.

Y.S.K.

See also, 856, 863, 864, 881, 895, 916, 921, 930, 995, 1006, 1021, 1022, 1033, 1064, 1070.

ILLEGALITY

915. E. Shochetman, "The Assistance of Sinners in Jewish Law" (Heb.), *Hamayan* 30 (5740), 31-35. - In this article, the author discusses, *inter alia*, the validity of a contractual obligation to pay wages for the performance of a sinful deed. In principle, such an obligation is valid: the court, however, will use its discretion not to enforce if it feels that such a step is unjustified in the circumstances of the case. An employer who hires a worker to commit a sinful act is nevertheless required to pay his wages, although the court may penalise a labourer and prevent him receiving them. Y.S.K.

916. E. Shochetman, *Ma'aseh Haba Ba'averah*, Jerusalem, Mosad Harav Kook, 1981, Pp.351. - Dr. Shochetman's book is a detailed and comprehensive study of the Talmudic and Rabbinic sources dealing with the validity of an act tainted by the commission of a transgression against the law. The approach taken is defined as a dogmatic one, i.e. free from all reference to historical development or literary context. Reference to manuscripts, however, would seem to be acceptable even at the cost of contradicting a large number of apparently "dogmatic" views within the *halakhah*. In fact, one of the

major theses in the book is that by rejecting the printed version of a particular *psak* and accepting the manuscript form, it is possible to discover the correct legal principle involved in the case in question.

The first chapter deals with the one Talmudic *sugya* in which the issue of illegality is treated in principle, i.e. the dispute between Abaye and Raba in *Temurah* 4b. On the basis of an extensive analysis of the Commentaries, Dr. Shochetam concludes that the dispute is confined to the effect of transgressions against Biblical injunctions essential to the act in question, and which cannot be rectified by annulling it. Consequently, although the *halakhah* is decided in accordance with the view of Raba, i.e. that "any act which the Divine law forbids has no legal effect at all", the scope of this ruling is extremely limited. In this light, it is possible to understand the many cases throughout the *Talmud* in which Raba's ruling would appear to be ignored. All such cases involve either the transgression of a Rabbinic injunction, or non-essential illegality, or a transgression which cannot be rectified by annulling the act. Since the majority of cases fall within this category, it is clear that in general, any legal act done, contrary to the *halakhah*, will nevertheless be valid. In the second chapter, the question of essential illegality is discussed, and the distinction between Biblical and Rabbinic injunctions is explained in terms of the conceptual difference between the two categories. It is also pointed out that where a Rabbinic enactment specifically provides that any act done contrary to it will be legally invalid, then such an act will indeed be null and void, irrespective of the above-mentioned distinction between Biblical and Rabbinic injunction.

The third chapter deals with non-essential illegality, e.g. the drawing up of a contract of sale on the Sabbath, or selling contrary to a binding oath, and in it, Dr. Schochetman provides numerous illustrations of his thesis that in each act falling within the terms of the dispute between Abaye and Raba, the rule is that illegal acts are both valid and enforceable. The one serious exception to this rule would appear to be a decision of R. Isaac b. Perez cited in the *Hagahot HaMordekhai* to *Shebuot* (3:784). According to Dr. Shochetman, however, the printed text of the *Hagahot HaMordekhai* is erroneous, and an examination of the manuscript (Oxford, Bodleian 6721 Cambridge, Or.71.1) reveals that R. Isaac b. Perez is not in fact challenging the general rule regarding illegal contracts, and his decision is based on entirely different grounds. All reservations on the part of later *poskim* as to the correctness of the general rule based on the decision ought, therefore, to be disregarded.

In the fourth chapter, the question of fulfilling *mitsvot* involving the commission of transgressions is considered, and a distinction drawn between essential and non-essential illegality.

The final chapter deals with the issue of illegal contracts, and after a brief reference to the problem of whether or not there is a law of contract in the accepted sense in Jewish law, Dr. Shochetman employs the fundamental distinction between monetary and religious obligations in Jewish law in order to conclude that all contracts, whether real or merely obligatory, will be valid in spite of the commission of an illegal act. The court, however, has a wide discretion not to enforce such a contract, and will not hesitate to use it in the interests of justice and morality.

In his conclusion, Dr. Shochetman mentions the observation made by M. Silberg (*Talmudic Law and the Modern State* (N.Y., Burning Bush Press, 1973), 75) with respect to the morality of Jewish law in this area. According to Silberg, the absence of any causal connection in Jewish law between the commission of an offence and the voiding of a civil contract results, on occasion, in a morally superior result to that obtained in the Common Law, according to which no court will soil its hands by dealing with any contract tainted by illegality. Whilst the moral indignation of the Common Law penalizes the offending claimant, it also awards a prize to the offending defendant - at least in a case where both parties are *in pari delicto* - by leaving the sum of goods already transferred, in his hands. In Jewish law, this situation is avoided by leaving the contractual obligation intact, and separating the agreement between the parties from the transgression involved in its performance. This is not the whole picture, however, and, as Dr. Shochetman points out, the discretion of the court to refuse to enforce a contractual obligation for reasons of justice and morality is also an important factor in the morality of Jewish law in this area. The separation of the contractual from the religious elements of an agreement must be complemented by the discretion of the court to refuse enforcement.

In his concluding remarks, Dr. Shochetman also mentions ss.30-31 of the Contracts (General Part) Law, 1973, which grants the court discretion to order the parties to a void contract to fulfil their obligations "if it deems it just to do so." Dr. Shochetman expresses satisfaction at this partial reception of Jewish law by the Israeli legislator (see Elon J.'s remarks in *Howard* v. *Miarah* C.A. 311/78, 35(2) P.D. 505), but regrets that it was not complete, i.e. that a contract, "the making, contents or object of which is or are illegal, immoral or contrary to public policy is (still) void."

It is clear, however, that the "other side of the coin" in Jewish law, i.e. the court's discretion to act freely in order to satisfy the claims of justice and morality, is not so readily available to the Israeli bench (see *Kitan* v. *Weiss* C.A. 350/77, 33(2) P.D. 785). In this respect, therefore, attention must be paid to the divergent institutional frameworks of Jewish and Israeli law respectively, and great care taken before the solutions of one system are recommended to the other.

The book concludes with five appendices on points of special interest raised in the body of the text, including the question of marriage and divorce against the *herem* of R. Gershom, and Maimonides' position on the dispute between Abaye and Raba. D.B.S.

INFLUENCE OF JEWISH LAW

See 865.

INSURANCE

917. S.M. Passamaneck, "His Majesty's spurious prize of war", *Mélanges ... Prévost (supra* no. 858), 207-225. - This is an illuminating analysis of a fascinating 18th century responsum, emanating from the Amsterdam Yeshivah *Etz Hayyim*, written by David Franco Mendes. It is set against the background of the Seven Years' War, and the author reviews the relevant historical and international law background. A claim was made under a contract of marine insurance between two Jews, for the loss of the value of cargo which had been impounded in a neutral (Dutch) vessel during the war. The "prize" was, however, "spurious", in that the vessel had escaped custody while on the high seas, and the loss had been occasioned when the assured's agents were obliged by the Gentile

courts to pay what they had received for the merchandise, which they had sold on reaching port. The respondent rules in favour of the insurer, on the basis of the custom of merchants and international law. Passamaneck considers why the case appears ultimately to have come to a Jewish forum. This is a valuable contribution to the history of comparative commercial law and international law, as well as Jewish law.

B.S.J.

INTENTION

See 992.

INTERNATIONAL LAW

See 917, 929.

JEWISH LAW IN ISRAEL

918. Per Bilde & Peter Steensgaard, eds., *Zionismen og Israel: religion, ideologi, stat: belyst ved det moderne Israel som eksempel.* Aros, Aarhus, 1983, ISBN 87-7003-421-4, Pp. 167, Price: 122 Dkr. - The main theme of this book is the relation between religion (Judaism) and ideology (Zionism). The book consists of 6 papers on the background of Zionism, its beginning, its history, and its development after the foundation of the State of Israel. One of the papers, written by the counsellor of the Israeli Embassy in Copenhagen, Ralph Walden (M.A., Oxon.), treats the relation between Jewish Religion and legislation in the State of Israel. Walden discusses the theoretical possibility of accepting Judaism as State religion and the practical (problematic) consequences of having *halakhah* as basic law in a modern democracy. Walden ends up by describing the extent to which *halakhah* has influenced the actual legislation in Israel. K.N.

919. Y. Danzier, "A Symbolic Gesture which is more Harmful than Advantageous" (Heb.), *Hapraklit* 33 (1981), 619-623. - In this short note, the writer criticizes the *Foundations of Law Act* 5740-1980, in the light of what he believes to be its purely symbolic nature. According to the writer, reference to the principles of "freedom, justice, equity and peace of the heritage of Israel" can only be symbolic, since not even the modern scholars of Jewish law are capable of reaching any sort of agreement on the definition of this type of general principle in Jewish law, *a fortiori* the judges of the Israeli courts. The law imposes upon the judge a task for which he is entirely unsuited and, as such, is a bad law. Y.S.K.

920. M. Keshet, "*Foundations of Law Act,* 1980" (Heb.), *Hapraklit* 33 (1981), 611-618. - This law, which requires the judge to turn to the "principles of freedom, justice, equity and peace of the heritage of Israel" when he is in doubt as to the relevant law for a particular case, is, in fact, a compromise between conflicting views. In this article, the constitutional aspects of the new law are analysed, and the conclusion reached that it is an attempt to encourage Israeli judges to indulge in "judicial legislation" in doubtful

cases. The author also believes that whereas it will have little significance in matters of Civil law, the *Foundations of Law Act*, 5740-1980, will have a considerable effect in the area of Constitutional and Administrative law. Y.S.K.

921. Aharon Layish, *Marriage, Divorce and Succession in the Druze Family*, Leiden: E.J.Brill, 1982, ISBN 90 04 06412 5, Pp. xxv, 474, Price: Gld.156 (Social, Economic and Political Studies of the Middle East, XXXI). - Israeli legislation has established Druze Religious Courts with exclusive jurisdiction in marriage and divorce, and concurrent jurisdiction in succession, both for the Druze resident in Israel, and, since 1970, also for those resident on the Golan Heights. This current substantial study is, as the sub-title indicates, "based on decisions of Druze arbitrators and religious courts in Israel and the Golan Heights." The author assesses these decisions in both legal and sociological terms: the former, in the light of traditional religious law, customary practice and modern legislation (especially that of Lebanon and Syria), the latter with an eye to the actual effect upon the status of woman. It reflects the author's intimate involvement with the Druze community and its institutions, and makes substantial use of interviews and other empirical data, as well as legal sources. Apart from its intrinsic interest, the book provides a wealth of material for comparison with the content and operation of Jewish religious law on these matters. B.S.J.

See also 916, 967, 979, 1033.

JURISDICTION

See 968, 985, 1070.

KINGSHIP

922. S. Abramsky, "The Leadership of Abimelech", *Sivan*, 163-176 (Heb.). - The authentic core of the Abimelech narrative is identified by the author as *Judg*. 9:1-7, 21-51. The tale as so delimited perceives of Abimelech's reign as a legitimate rule by virtue of dynastic succession, as traditional usage in the area of Shechem would require. Parallels to the use of various terms to refer to the ruler are adduced from the El Amarna letters and the Ugaritic and Alalakh tables. Archaeological finds in the area of Shechem are adduced to argue in favour of a date *circa* 1100 B.C.E. for the episode, at which time the town's fortifications, which had not been destroyed in the Israelite conquest, were finally toppled in the unhappy events of Abimelech's demise. B.S.J.

923. D. Daube, *Sons and Strangers*, Boston, Institute of Jewish Law, Boston University School of Law, 1984. - This is the Presidential Address delivered at the Second International Conference of the Jewish Law Association, New York, December 1982. The theme is the transition from non-hereditary Mosaic to hereditary Davidic rule. In his characteristically stimulating fashion, Daube considers this problem in relation to Moses, Gideon, Eli, Samuel, Saul, and David; there is an excursus on adoption. B.S.J

924. M. Garsiel, "The Controversy Between Samuel and the People On Establishing a King in Israel", *BM* 26 (1981), 325-343 (Heb.). - Rejecting the conclusions reached by recent studies which seek to present Samuel's denunciation of kingship as an essentially neutral or even favourable description of customary royal practice, Garsiel insists that Samuel's speech is an ironic warning of the excesses of monarchs. Samuel's words are informed with his historical knowledge of the despotic rulers of Nineveh and are not in accord with the ideology of Canaanite kingship. B.S.J.

925. F.E. Greenspahn, "An Egyptian Parallel to Judg 17:6 and 21:25", *JBL* 101 (1982), 129-130. - The author argues that *Judg.* 17:6 and 21:25 implies a negative assessment of the anarchy characteristic of Israel before the monarchy. This is illustrated by an almost identical assertion in Egyptian literature concerned with a near contemporary period. The *Harris Papyrus* no.1 states that "the land of Egypt had been overthrown with every man being his own standard of right *(s nb m 'k3f)* since they had no leader *(r hry)* for many years in the times of others." The Egyptian term translated "right" *('k.3)* means literally "straightness", precisely the denotation of the biblical *yasar*. Both passages portray monarchy as a beneficial institution which brought an end to the preceding period of anarchy. K.W.W.

926. C.R. Mabee, "The Problem of the Setting in Hebrew Royal Judicial Narratives", *Dissertation Abstracts International* 38 (1977), 844-A. - The construction and shaping of Old Testament narratives on the adjudication of legal disputes by secondary intentions makes it impossible to understand how the Israelite judiciary worked. This form-critical study considers the dual problems of the setting of the narrator (generative) as well as that reflected in the narrative itself (depicted). It is a detailed study of the stories depicting the king as judicial authority, adjudicating cases of criminal law based on established community norms and regulations *(1 Sam.* 22; *2 Sam.* 1, 4, 12, 14; *1 Kings*. 3, 20; *2 Kings* . 6). It draws upon comparative and legal anthropological material. M. concludes that royal judicial narratives represent a literary device whereby the narrator chooses to communicate something about the king. The stories reflect primarily what the narrator has to say about the king rather than the judicial process *per se*. They are only reliable for discovering the actual operation of the ancient Israelite judiciary in a general way. K.W.W.

927. S. Talmon, "The Biblical Idea of Statehood", *The Bible World,* eds. G. Rendsburg et al, New York: KTAV, 1980, 239-248 (C.H. Gordon Festschrift) - The Bible's position on statehood is not, as most commentators hold, a panegyric upon some non-monarchic and theocratic ideal. Rather, T. says, "Israel's political ideology ... is identical with the system of the monarchy." As such it reflects changes in the monarchy that accompany Israel's evolution toward empire. Withal, succeeding generations expected actualization of the Divine promise made to the patriarchs, hence actual kings were uniquely vulnerable to removal from office through popular pressure. S.N.R.

928. M. Weinfeld, "The royal guard according to the Temple Scroll", *RB* 87 (1980), 394-6. - In the law of the king in the Temple scroll the guards of the king are responsible for his moral and spiritual supervision as well as guarding him physically.

Weinfeld notes a parallel to this in the description of the Egyptian royal guard in Diodorus Siculus (Book I, 70), who drew upon Hecataeus of Abdera. In addition, he points to four other parallels between the two accounts. The two sources reflect royal ideologies prevalent in Judah and Egypt in the Hellenistic period. J.D.

See also 849, 876, 972, 1046, 1051, 1070.

LABOUR LAW

See 862, 895.

LAW OF WAR

929. J. Muffs, "Abraham the Noble Warrior: Patriarchal politics and Laws of War in Ancient Israel", *JJS* 33:1-2 (1982: Yadin Festschrift), 81-107. - Each element in *Gen.* 14 has its exact counterpart in the laws of war and the etiquette of booty restoration found in the international treaties of Boghazkoi and Ugarit. While this discovery enhances the authenticity of the text, it does not prove that the text itself comes to us directly from its second millenium forbears. S.N.R.

LEGAL ARGUMENT

930. E. Bashan, "Its Ways are Ways of Pleasantness" (Heb.), *De'ot* (1980), 171-176. - The verse "Her ways are ways of pleasantness *(Prov.* 3:17)" was used by the Rabbis of the Talmudic period and their successors to reject any juridical interpretation which might result in either suffering or injustice. Bashan observes that the Rabbis used their power under this principle to override the *halakhah* on the basis of ethical considerations alone. Various Rabbinic sources in which the principle provided a basis for halakhic decision are cited mainly from N. Africa and other Oriental countries. The areas in which the principle was used in these sources extend to torts, public law, *takanot*, Family law, and Succession. Y.S.

931. H. Ben-Menachem, "The Respective Attitude of the Babylonian and Jerusalem *Talmuds* to Judicial Deviation from the Law" (Heb.), *Shenaton* 8 (1981), 113-134. - In this article, the author deals with various instances of deliberate judicial deviation from the *halakhah* in the two *Talmuds,* and attempts to show how the Babylonian and Jerusalem *Talmudim* reflect conflicting approaches to the jurisprudential question of judicial discretion. According to Ben-Menachem, the stricter approach of the Jerusalem *Talmud* may be a reflection of the historical background, i.e. the struggle against sectarian Judaism and early Christianity. As a result of this struggle, the Rabbis of the Jerusalem *Talmud* tended to emphasise the superiority and exclusiveness of the *halakhah.* In Babylon, however, this threat did not exist, and consequently the Babylonian *Talmud* reflects a more liberal attitude to judicial deviation from the *halakhah.* Y.S.K.

932. I. Englard, "Mysticisme et droit. Réflexions sur les "Liqute Halakhot" de l'école de Rabbi Nahman de Bratslav", *Mélanges ... Prévost (supra* no. 858), 191-205. - The author notes the Jewish view that halakhic texts may simultaneously have quite different levels of meaning, including allegorical and mystical levels which are not in opposition to the legal or normative level. He gives examples of mystical interpretation of civil law texts. Nevertheless, one does find in the sources some indications of a more intimate relationship between the levels, such that a practical command finds its raison d'être at the symbolic level, or at the performance of the practical norm can have an influence in the mystical universe. The only systematic attempt to put civil law rules on a mystical basis was made in the school of Rabbi Nahman of Bratslav. The author examines the *Likute Halakhot* in this context. B.S.J.

933. Benjamin J. Gelles, *Peshat and Derash in the Exegesis of Rashi*, Leiden: E.J. Brill, 1981, ISBN 90 04 06259 9, Pp. x, 171, Price: Gld. 64 (Etudes sur le Judaïsme Mediéval, IX). - This is an interesting doctoral dissertation, in which the author reviews critically the places of *peshat* and *derash* in the work of *Rashi*. While advocating in some passages the use of *peshat*, Rashi in fact frequently uses both methods. Dr. Gelles concludes that *peshat* and *derash* "emerge not so much as conflicting forces but rather as the two ends of an exegetical spectrum, separated by intermediate shades of perception, including, no doubt, an area of methodological indeterminacy." The first part of chapter 4 deals specifically with halakhic texts B.S.J.

934. R.M. Grant, "Dietary Laws among Pythagoreans, Jews, and Christians", *HTR* 73 (1980), 299-310. - Dietary regulations were common among religious groups in antiquity. Explanations, either hygienic or allegorical, were offered by Pythagoreans, Jews and Christians. Plutarch compared Jewish food laws to Pythagorean and Egyptian ones. Aristeas, Philo and 4 Maccabees find an educational purpose in the laws: they inculcate virtue and control of the passions. The church while rejecting OT regulations introduced new food laws of its own *(Acts* 15), and used allegorization to explain their purpose. G.W.J.

935. Louis Jacobs, *The Talmudic Argument*, Cambridge: Cambridge University Press, 1984, ISBN 0 521 26370 0, Pp. xvi, 220, Price: £25.00 - After introductory chapters on the nature of talmudic argument and the literary form of the Babylonian Talmud, the author analyses 19 *sugyot* expounding the flow of the argument, and showing its relation to the literary structure of the *sugya* as a whole. He concludes that the article is such that the Talmud must be regarded as essentially the creation of its final editors, the Saboraim. Many of the *sugyot* analysed deal with problems of civil law, such as lost property, conveyance of a thing not yet in existence, the mental state of contracting parties, the basis of *kinyan hatzer*, and problems of wrongs punishable only in the divine forum *(B.K.* 55b-56a, *dine shamayim)*. This is a most rewarding book for anyone prepared to grapple with the details of the interaction of legal and literary concerns, which together represent the character of the Talmud. B.S.J.

936. Louis Jacobs, *Teyku, The Unsolved Problem in the Babylonian Talmud*, London and New York: Cornwall Books, 1981, ISBN, 0-8453-4501-X, Pp. 312, Price: $20.00. - This is a literary investigation of the 319 passages in the Babylonian Talmud

where a debate on a disputed point of law is ended with the term *teyku* (sometimes: *tibbai)* - a phenomenon missing from the Palestinian Talmud. Rabbi Dr. Jacobs argues that *teyku* ("Let it (the problem) stand" - there is no solution) is in logic the proper conclusion for every *baya*, the latter being constructed as a definitional problem so evenly balanced that there is no correct answer. Where the Talmud does provide such an answer, it is on the basis of authority only, not logic. While the practice of setting such problems may have been common amongst the talmudic rabbis (though particularly associated with some of them - the author provides statistics), the precise literary form of the *baya*, together with the attribution of the conclusion *teyku*, is argued to form part of the literary framework constructed by the editors of the talmud. The problem of *teyku* thus forms part of the more general problem of the redaction of the Babylonian Talmud. Rabbi Dr. Jacobs has compressed an enormous work of scholarship into concise but readable form, and has here made a major contribution to talmudic studies. For good measure, he adds Appendices on the interpretation of *teyku* by post-talmudic halakhists, and in the mystical literature. B.S.J.

See also 859, 865, 937, 1054, 1068, 1070.

LEGAL FICTIONS

937. S. Shilo. "Circumvention of the Law in Talmudic Literature" (Heb.), *Shenaton* 8 (1981), 309-355. - There is a basic distinction between the legal circumvention i.e. the *ha'armah* of Jewish law, and the legal fiction of secular law. The former uses existing categories in order to achieve a different result to that which would normally be achieved. The latter creates artificial categories in a fictitious manner. The author distinguishes between two types of circumvention. The first is aimed at preventing the operation of a particular law, and the second aims at changing the subjective element, i.e. the intention, attached to it. In general, it would appear that where the purpose of the circumvention is of a positive nature then the Rabbis are prepared to support it. On the other hand, where the purpose is viewed in a negative light, then the Rabbis would disapprove of such a circumvention. Shilo suggests that the main characteristic of the circumvention is that it appears to be within the law, and to the "officious bystander" at any rate, nothing of an illegal nature is taking place. Y.S.K.

LEGISLATION

See 920.

LEVIRATE

938. E.W. Davies, "Inheritance Rights and the Hebrew Levirate Marriage. Part I", *VT* 31 (1981), 133-144. - Although the primary purpose of levirate marriage in *Gen.* 38, *Deut.* 25:5-10 and *Ruth* was to provide an heir for the deceased husband, this was not its sole purpose. It is clear that a man's "name" *(Deut.* 25:6) was closely connected with

his property *(Num.* 27:1-11; *2 Sam.* 14:4ff; *Ruth* 4:10). The levirate marriage was not simply to ensure the continuity of the family but also to prevent the alienation of the ancestral estate. Furthermore, the widow by marrying the brother-in-law or nearest kinsman would have ensured her protection and support even if she remained childless.

K.W.W.

939. E.W. Davies, "Inheritance Rights and the Hebrew Levirate Marriage. Part 2", *VT* 31 (1981), 257-268. - The main purpose of Levirate marriage was to provide a male heir for the deceased husband's estate and to ensure protection for the widow. However, this may have been limited by the kinsman's attempts to evade responsibility for a variety of reasons. The levirate obligation may have been contrary to his own interests since if there was no male heir the inheritance would normally pass to the dead man's brother *(Num.* 27:8-11), or it may have diminished and divided his own estate *(cf. Ruth* 4:6) and that of his children. The Deuteronomic provision (25:5-10) was no longer binding *(cf. Gen.* 38) and also provided a ceremony by which the obligation would be renounced. It placed further restriction on the application of the law since it was now confined to brothers living together on the undivided family estate. The book of Ruth probably represents an attempt to extend this restrictive practice to include more distant relatives where the immediate family was unable or unwilling to oblige. K.W.W.

See also 859.

LITERARY FORM

940. Baruch Bokser, "Talmudic form Criticism", *JJS* 31.1 (1980), 46-60. - A succinct and valuable analysis of Form Criticism and its assumptions and tasks and possible achievements as this pertains to rabbinic Literature. Bokser distinguishes various techniques, formulae and investigative procedures. The examples are mostly drawn from the master Samuel's teachings, on which Bokser has contributed a monograph *(Samuel's Commentary on the Mishnah)*, and other studies; see *AJSRev* 4 (1979). Among various observations, particularly of note is Bokser's observation that the received dispute form in rabbinic literature is not necessarily original, and may result from juxtaposed traditions, themselves subsequently reworked. M.F.

941. P.E. Dion, "'Tu feras disparaître le Mal du Milieu de toi'", *RB* 87 (1980), 321-349. - In 1963 J. L'Hour examined the laws which end with the formula *ubi'arta hara miqqirbeka* "so you shall purge the evil from the midst of you" *(Biblica* 44 (1963), 1-28), *cf. Deut.* 13:2-6, 17:2-7, etc. He concluded that these laws contained casuistic legislation which was authentically Yahwistic and of great age. Dion modifies L'Hour's conclusions. He provides a new examination of these formulations, including Phoenician *(KAI* 26) and Akkadian parallels (Gilgamesh, Prologue to Hammurabi's law code). He calls attention to the "formula of dissuasion" which sometimes accompanies the *bi'arta* formula *(Deut.* 17:12-13, 19:19-20, 21:12). The two formulas reflect different attitudes: the *bi'arta* aims to extirpate the evil, for the preservation of the community; the dissuasion intends to prevent the repetition of the wrongdoing. J.D.

942. B.S. Jackson, "Legal Drafting in the Ancient Near East in the Light of Modern Theories of Cognitive Development", *Mélanges ... Prévost (supra* no. 858), 49-66. - The history of legal drafting is here considered in the light of theories of language acquisition, and particularly the cognitive development theory of Piaget. Examples are given of development in drafting from the treatment in a single clause of only one variable to the combination of multiple variables, the development of motive clauses, the phenomenon of "completomania", the development of consistency in the use of drafting forms, the growth of integration, as shown in paragraphing devices, the development of abstraction (Daube's examples of the "action noun" and the "diagnosis form"). A pilot comparison is attempted of the cognitive characteristics of different biblical law documents, and the approaches applied to the history of the homicide sources in the Bible. In the course of discussing many of the examples, comparison is made with the form-critical approach. A related article, with greater emphasis on the theoretical base of this approach ("Historical Aspects of Legal Drafting in the Light of Modern Theories of Cognitive Development"), is published in *International Journal of Law and Psychiatry* 3 (1980), 349-369. B.S.J.

943. Bent Mogensen, *Israelitiske leveregler og deres begrundelse* , Gad, København, 1983, ISBN 87-12-07111-0, Pp. 286, Price: 146 Dkr. - This book on Israelite Behaviour Maxims and their justifications in the Old Testament was accepted as a licentiate dissertation in Aarhus. It discusses examples of behaviour maxims from OT, Egyptian wisdom - and a wellknown Danish book (by Emma Gad) on good manners. The author analyses the form and content of the OT maxims and divides into two groups: 1. Proverbs, Ecclesiastes; 2. the Decalogue, the Book of the Covenant, the Holiness Code, Deuteronomy - each of which having its own characteristics. The book ends up with a stimulating survey of the history of research of the field. K.N.

944. Jacob Neusner, "Redaction, Formulation, and Form: The Case of Mishnah", *JQR* 70.3 (1980), 131-47. - Neusner stresses that our estimation of the plan and program of the formation of the Mishnah must be derived from internal evidence, and also start with the end-product, working backward from there to the earliest units, his 'cognitive units'. In his essay Neusner seeks to clarify the procedures whereby he obtained the results noted in his *Redaction and Formulation of the Order of Purities in Mishnah and Tosefta* (Leiden, 1977). Neusner discusses the thematic nature of Mishnah's organisation, and the logical exposition from primary to secondary and tertiary refinements. He also notes the relationship of this to stylistics. The principles of organisation of Tosefta are different, and the question must always be asked just how it is *related* to Mishnah. Comments by Richard Sarason appear on pp. 147-52. M.F.

945. Rifat Sonsino, *Motive Clauses in Hebrew Law, Biblical Forms and Near Eastern Parallels,* Chico Ca.: Scholars Press, 1980, Pp. xix, 336, ISBN 0-89130-0 (318-9 pkb.) (Society of Biblical Literature, Dissertation Series 45). - This book seeks to provide a comprehensive, form-critical account of the incidence of the motive clause in Biblical law. A preliminary chapter assesses modern discussions of the forms of Biblical and ancient Near Eastern laws in general, concluding that the background is usually too blurred to reconstruct an original *Sitz im Leben.* The author then turns to the motive clause in Biblical law. He distinguishes it from both "explicative notes" and

"legal parenesis"; his definition nevertheless includes both justification of the content of the law, and motives for its obedience. He finds a wide variety of formal characteristics within motive clauses. In order to assess the distribution of motive clauses in the different legal collections of the Bible, he provides guidelines to the identification of the "individual legal prescription" (80-85). He accepts that some subjective evaluation is inevitably involved in the adoption of these criteria. One may add that the identification of the motive clauses themselves is subject to the same difficulty. The net result is that the statistics on the distribution of motive clauses should be treated with extreme care. Nevertheless, the author has raised many questions which call for more detailed study. His general conclusions, regarding the particular incidence of motive clauses in "moral" and "political" laws, as opposed to "cultic" and "civil" rules, is used to explain the greater incidence of the motive clause in the Bible than in the ancient Near Eastern collections. These latter, and their comparison with the Biblical laws, are the subjects of separate chapters. The author also draws conclusions for the literary-historical study of Biblical legal texts: motive clauses are not restricted to late sources, and should not be regarded as editorial additions merely because they are motive clauses. For an interesting review article on this book, see B. Schwartz, *JSS* 28 (1983), 161-163. B.S.J.

946. Zipora Talshir, "The Detailing Formula 'Vezeh (Ha) davar ... '", *Tarbiz* 41 (1982), iv, 23-36 (Heb.). - The author examines a formula used to introduce detailed specification in both legal and non-legal passages. She elaborates on its significance in a number of texts. B.J.S.

See also 935, 936, 1065.

MEDICO-LEGAL PROBLEMS

947. B. Freedman, "Leviticus and DNA: A Very Old Look at a Very New Problem", *Journal of Religious Ethics* 8 (1980), 105-113. - Recombinant DNA research, which has the potential to produce new hybrid organisms, is discussed in the light of halakhic interpretations of *Lev.* 19:19, which forbids mixed breeding. This is often seen as a prohibition based on natural law, and on some views this would rule out manipulation of DNA. However Halevy's *(Book of Instruction* Commandment 62) interpretation of the commands could permit DNA research aimed at healing, e.g. manufacture of insulin, but would still rule out research aimed at improving the species, or research for reasons of pure curiosity. G.J.W.

See also 856, 859, 1057, 1066.

NEW TESTAMENT

948. F.F. Bruce, "The Trial of Jesus in the Fourth Gospel", in *Gospel Perspectives* I, ed. R.T. France and D. Wenham (Sheffield: JSOT Press, 1980), 7-20. - B. endorses the arguments of A.N. Sherwin-White against P. Winter that John's gospel gives an essentially reliable account of the trial of Jesus. The arrest, charges, court procedures,

and punishments fit Roman practice and are at various points corroborated by Mark's gospel and archaeological discovery. John certainly interprets the trial of Jesus from a theological perspective, but this does not distort the actual record of events. G.J.W.

949. T. Callan, "Pauline Midrash: The Exegetical Background of Gal. 3:19b", *JBL* 99 (1980), 549-567. - Callan discusses the Pauline theme that Gentile Christians have no need to keep the Jewish Law and the two occasions when the giving of the law is used as part of the argument. *2 Cor.* 3:7-18 uses Moses' veiling of his face *(Ex.* 34:29-35) as an argument against the law, thus giving a typically negative twist to something which originally exalted Moses and the law. *Gal.* 3:19b-20 is more obscure. He argues that Paul presupposes a midrashic interpretation of the giving of the law typical of contemporary exegetical traditions which he has again used negatively. The negative assessment seems to presuppose that meditation is inferior to direct dealing and that it was necessitated by the weakness of the people. Paul views the giving of the law in the light of the golden calf incident; Moses' first breaking of the tablets indicates that the effect of the law is to make the human situation worse by making sin a violation of the law. K.W.W.

950. G. Dautzenberg, "Ist das Schwurverbot Mt. 5:33-37; Jak. 5:12 ein Beispiel für die Torakritik Jesu?", *Biblishe Zeitschrift* 25 (1981), 47-66. -*Mt.* 5:33-37 and *Jas.* 5:12 both prohibit the use of oaths. The paraenetic form of the saying in James is more primitive than the antithetic Matthaean formulation. Though the *Mt* saying mostly ante-dates the evangelist, it is unlikely to go back to Jesus himself because both Jesus and Paul use solemn asseverations which are virtual oaths. Sayings introduced by 'Amen' are generally acknowledged to be dominical, yet they are often followed by an implicit oath formula (e.g. *Mk.*14:25). Similarly Paul calls God to witness the truth of his statements (e.g. *Rom.* 1:9). Comparison of *Mt.* 5:33-37 with *Jas.* 5:12 and early Jewish criticism of oaths (Philo, Josephus, DSS) suggests that the rejection of oaths was a development within early Jewish Christianity concerned to prevent the desecration of God's name. It was not part of Jesus' critique of the law. G.J.W

951. W.D. Davies, "Paul and the Law: Reflections on Pitfalls in Interpretation", *Hastings Law Journal* 29 (1978), 1459-1504. - For Paul 'the law' means all the Old Testament. It includes at least four elements, commandments, history, wisdom, the whole revealed will of God, i.e. it is a culture, not just individual rules. Commentators by focussing on only one aspect of law have misunderstood Paul. Four pitfalls are discussed. First. law is not just commandments, so it is false to suppose that Paul was opposed to law as such, only certain elements within Judaism. He saw Christianity as the fulfilment of the old covenant. Second, Paul's belief that Jesus was the messiah did modify his view that the law was eternal and immutable. Third, Paul's remarks about the law vary with the situation he is addressing in the different churches: his teaching is not a monolithic unity. Fourth, Paul's moral imperatives have often been overlooked in evaluating his attitude to the law. He believed Jesus had become the torah, the revealed will of god. Morality involves being 'in Christ', imitating him, and obeying his specific instructions. In making Christ the centre of the law Paul simplified it. G.W.J.

952. J. Duncan M. Derrett, *Studies in the New Testament*, vol. III: *Midrash, Haggadah, and the Character of the Community*, Leiden: E.J. Brill, 1982, ISBN 90 04 069596 2, Pp. xii, 261, Price: Gld. 110. - The first two volumes in this series were noted at *Survey* no. 228 *(JLA* II). Twelve articles are reprinted with further annotations. Two more are here printed for the first time: "History and the Two Swords" (on the quotation of *Is*. 53:12 in *Lk*. 22:36-38) and "The Two Malefactors *(Lk*. xxiii 33, 39-43)". There are also Addenda to vols. I and II. As the sub-title indicates, the author is concerned in this volume to interpret New Testament passages in the light of Jewish aggadic methods and texts. B.S.J.

953. J.W. Fuller, "Of Elders and Triads in 1 *Tim*. 5:19-25", *New Testament Studies* 29 (1983), 258-263. - The argument in *1 Tim*. 5:19-25 is based on *Deut*. 19:15-20, and shows that *1 Tim*. 5 is dealing with the trial of a church elder. *Deut*. 19:17 insists that witnesses must prove their accusations before God, the priests and the judges. *1 Tim*. 5:21 reminds the judge Timothy that his verdict will be assessed by "God, Christ Jesus and the elect angles." G.J.W.

954. M. Hengel, *The Charismatic Leader and His Followers*, trld. J.C.G. Greig, Edinburgh: T. & T. Clark, 1981, ISBN 0 567 03001 6, Pp. xiii,111, Price: £8.95 - This is a translation of Hengel's classic study of 1968, in which he argues that the relationship between Jesus and his disciples differs from the rabbinic model, and has more (though not everything) in common with charismatic-prophetic leaders of the Maccabean-Zealot tradition. In this context, the author deals briefly with what he regards as the sovereign attitude adopted by Jesus towards the Mosaic Law. B.S.J.

955. C. Heubült, *"Mt*. 5:17-20. Ein Beitrag zur Theologie des Evangelisten Matthäus', *Zeitschrift für die neutestamentliche Wissenschaft* 71 (1980), 143-149. - These verses are largely redactional and show the evangelist's concern to oppose the Pauline view that the law was made obsolete by the death of Jesus. *Mt*. believes that every detail of the law must be observed till the *parousia*. G.J.W.

956. M.D. Hooker, "Beyond the Things that Written. St. Paul's Use of Scripture", *New Testament Studies* 27 (1981), 295-309. - Paul's *pesher* type of exegesis of *Ex*. 34 in *2 Cor*. 3 illustrates his understanding of the role of the law and its relationship to Christ. "Christ has replaced the Law in Paul's thinking as the expression of God's purpose, character and glory; but Paul cannot simply ditch the Law. He transfers to Christ his former beliefs about the Law without denying the law itself a role." "The Law's *true* role is to be a witness to Christ - that is why, when Christ comes, the Mosaic ministry is superseded." G.J.W.

957. Hans. Hübner, *Law in Paul's Thought*, trld. J.C.G. Greig, ed. J. Riches, Edinburgh: T. & T. Clark, 1984, ISBN 0567 09313 1, Pp. xi, 186, Price: £10.95 (Studies of the New Testament and its World). - The German original appeared as *Das Gesetz bei Paulus*, Vandenhoeck & Ruprecht, 1978; it is supplemented by new sections discussing subsequent English-language literature (including a reply to E.P. Sanders' *Paul, the Law and the Jewish People*, 1983). The author's thesis relates differences

between Paul's attitude to the law as found in Galatians and Romans to the development of his theology of justification. B.S.J.

958. L.E. Keck, "The Law and 'The Law of Sin and Death' *(Rom.* 8:1-4): Reflections on the Spirit and Ethics in Paul", in *The Divine Helmsman: L.H. Silberman Festschrift*, ed. J.L. Crenshaw and S. Sandmel (New York: Ktav, 1980), 41-57. - Though foundational for Paul's ethics, *Rom.* 8:1-4 poses various exegetical difficulties. Verse 2 is to be understood as a heading to the whole discussion in chapter 8. 'The law' mentioned by Paul in v.2 is not the torah mentioned subsequently in vv.3 and 7, but 'the law of the Spirit of life' is the life-giving power which the believer in Christ experiences through the gift of the Spirit. This brings freedom from 'the law of sin and death', i.e. the state of spiritual death brought about by sin. Paul is not opposed to the moral demands of the Torah, but he sees it as powerless to conquer sin which dominates the self until the Spirit comes. Then man can enjoy life, which is the goal of the Torah, here called 'the just requirement of the law' (v.4). G.J.W.

959. A. Lindemann, "Die Gerechtigkeit aus dem Gesetz. Erwägungen zur Auslegung und zur Textgeschichte von Römer 10:5", *Zeitschrift für die Neutestamentliche Wissenschaft* 73 (1982), 231-250. - L. Discusses the textual variants in *Rom.* 10:5, concluding that the usual reading is the best. 'Paul states that according to the testimony of Moses there is life through works and that Moses calls this the righteousness of the law. This righteousness, which involves doing, is not however God's righteousness (Scripture says this too), because God's righteousness only comes from faith' (author's summary). G.J.W

960. Wayne A. Meeks, *The First Urban Christians*, New Haven and London: Yale University Press, 1983, ISBN 0-300-02876-8, Pp. XII, 199, Price: £15. - In this important book, the author analyses the Pauline letters with a view to providing a social description of early Christianity. He focuses upon the urban environment of the first century, in terms of the social composition of the Greco-Roman City, the mobility of its population, the forms of association it contained (the household, the voluntary association, the synagogue, the School); he relates theological language to such social institutions. An instructive chapter is devoted to the internal discipline of the early Christian community, and the patterns of leadership within it: the norms of the Pauline communities are only rarely stated as rules; the impression is one of fluidity, of a complex, open-ended process of mutual discipline. Comparison is only occasionally made with rabbinic literature and Qumran; the posing of similar questions to these sources would undoubtedly be instructive. B.S.J.

961. P.W. Meyer, "*Rom.* 10:4 and the 'End of the Law'", in *The Divine Helmsman: L.H. Silberman Festschrift*, ed. J.L. Crenshaw and S. Sandmel (New York: Ktav, 1980), 59-78. - *Rom.* 10:4 'Christ is the end *(telos)* of the law' lies at a turning point in Paul's difficult discussion of the relationship of Christianity and Judaism in *Rom.* 9-11. It does not mean that the Torah has been terminated by Christ's coming, for Paul has a very positive attitude to the law. (Meyer suggests that the stone laid in Zion - *Rom.* 10:33 - is the law, not Christ.) Rather Christ is the goal to which the law aspired: through Christ and the Spirit the believer enjoys life and a right standing before God,

something the Torah looked for but was unable to deliver because of sin's dominating influence. Many commentators have wrongly followed Luther in supposing that Paul thought the law was made obsolete through the gospel. G.J.W.

962. U. Wilckens, "Zur Entwicklung des paulinischen Gesetzesverständnisses", *New Testament Studies* 28 (1982), 154-190. - Law is always important in Paul's theology. The development of his views is traced chronologically through his writings. In the earliest days of the Gentile mission he proclaimed total freedom from the law because the death of Christ had made a temple cult obsolete. In *I Cor.* Paul appeals to the law as Scripture, but is equivocal about keeping its injunctions. In *2 Cor.* Paul contrasts law and gospel. In *Gal.* 3 Paul argues from the law that Christians are free from the law. *Gal.* and *Phil.* were both written against opponents who insisted that Gentiles keep the law of circumcision. In *Rom.* Paul tries to deal with the accusation that he is a blasphemer in rejecting the law. For Paul, keeping the commandments, not possessing them, was important. The Spirit given in baptism enables a Christian to keep the law, while making it obsolete as a means of justification. G.J.W.

963. S.G. Wilson, *Luke and the Law*, Cambridge: Cambridge University Press, 1983, ISBN 0 521 25284 9, Pp. ix, 142, Price: £15.00 (Society for New Testament Studies Monograph Series, 50). - The author finds a discrepancy between the attitude to the law as found in Luke and Acts. The former is indifferent to the question, while the latter seeks to present Paul as one who in both word and deed was unfailingly obedient to the law. He suggests that Luke, when he wrote Acts, was responding to Jewish or Jewish-Christian attacks on Paul's reputation. The study commences with an analysis of the terminology used in Luke-Acts to refer to the law, with particular emphasis upon Luke's use of *ethos*, in the light of other Jewish Hellenistic sources. B.S.J.

See also 835, 872, 883, 904, 906, 907, 909, 1004, 1016, 1059, 1073.

OATHS

964. P.C. Albert, *The Jewish Oath in Nineteenth-Century France*, Tel-Aviv University, 1982, Pp. 43 (Spiegel Lectures in European Jewish History, 3) - This is a well-documented and fascinating lecture on the struggle of French Jewry in the 19th century for complete legal equality, and the final cessation of use of the oath *more judaico*. The matter was important, since the oath still had a variety of uses, not known in Common Law systems, for the purposes of proof; the significance of the issue lay in the fact that the special oath was not designed as a dispensation for those who objected on religious grounds to the normal procedure: it was not comparable to the modern substitution of the Old Testament for the Christian Bible, since in France at that time the normal oath involved no such religious affirmation, while the oath required *more judaico* was, at this time, prescribed specifically for Jews. Moreover, the author contends, it was of a deliberately humiliating character - sometimes being required to take place in the Synagogue, on the *sefer torah*. Professor Albert relates the issue to the history of anti-semitism in France, and to the struggle for full emancipation. The issue also throws interesting light on the internal divisions between the Jewish establishment,

in the form of the Central Consistory, and Jewish secularists. The author's account, based on archival sources, of the arguments and the course of litigation casts much light on an important area of legal and social history. B.S.J.

See also 950, 995.

OBLIGATIONS

See 885.

PARENT AND CHILD

965. I. Divon, "The Obligation of Child-Support in Adoption" (Heb.), *Diné Israel* 9 (1978-1980), 183-204. - Adoption in the sense that it is understood in Israeli law is not recognized by the *halakhah*. In terms of an obligation to support the adopted child, however, it would appear that the concept does exist in Jewish law. According to Divon, there is firm halakhic basis for transferring property in order to ground an obligation to support a child in circumstances similar to those of adoption, and adopting parents ought to sign a written obligation to undertake such support in accordance with the provisions of Israeli law. Y.S.K.

966. A.M. Rabello, "Les Effects Personnels de la Puissance Paternelle en Droit Hébraïque, à travers la Bible et le Talmud", *Mélanges ... Prévost (supra* no. 858), 85-101. - This is a French translation of the first Appendix of the author's book, *Effetti Personali della "Patria Potestas"*, of which an account was given in *Survey* no.742 *(JLA* V). B.S.J.

967. M. Shawa, "Maintenance of Minor Children in Jewish and Israeli Law" (Heb.), *Tel-Aviv University Law Review* 7 (1980), 316-344; 583-617. - Under s.3 of the *Family Law (Maintenance) Amendment Law* 5729-1959, the maintenance of all minor children is governed by the personal law of the party concerned. In the case of Jews resident in Israel, the relevant law is Jewish law. Shawa discusses the father's obligation to maintain his children until the age of fifteen, and the obligation to maintain under the laws of *tsedakah* (charity). The origin of these obligations, their substance and their scope in the *halakhah* are examined in the course of the article, and comparisons are drawn with Israeli law. Y.S.K.

See also 864, 898, 994.

PENOLOGY

968. E. Ben-Zimra, "The Aims of Punishment in Jewish Criminal Law as Reflected in the *Responsa* Literature" (Heb.), *Sinai* 88 (5741), - 239-259. - Both the generally accepted aims of punishment in the Criminal law, and the special role of punishment in terms of the Jewish religion, are reflected in the *Responsa* literature on this subject. In

the final analysis, all such aims are incorporated in the final goal of being "a holy people to the Lord your God." Ben-Zimra raises the issue of the influence of external factors on Rabbinic penology such as the limited jurisdiction of the Jewish courts to inflict punishment, the attitudes to the punishment of offenders in society at large and the internal strength of the Jewish communal governing body, and concludes that further research is necessary in this area. Y.S.K.

PROCEDURES

969. A.-M. Dubarle, "Le Jugement de Salomon: un coeur à l'écoute'" *Revue des Sciences Philosophiques et Théologiques* 63 (1979), 419-427. - The author discusses the story in *1 Kings* 3:16-28. He finds no adequate grounds for questioning its historicity and claims that it reflects the judicial practice of a fifty-fifty division between the two parties to a case, when the statements of the witnesses contradict each other without the possibility of a resolution. At the same time, great attention is paid to the human predicament, thus making it possible to go beyond the normal procedure. J.D.

970. A. Grossman, "Offenders and Violent Men in Jewish Society in Early *Ashkenaz* and their Influence upon Legal Procedure" (Heb.), *Shenaton* 8 (1981), 135-152. - The article describes the phenomenon of violent opposition to the rulings of the Jewish community and its courts in the early period of Ashkenazic Jewry. According to Grossman, this phenomenon was influential in the alteration of Jewish legal procedure in this period, which was undertaken in order to combat violence and strengthen communal authority over translucent offenders. Y.S.K.

971. G.T. Sheppard, "More on Isaiah 5:1-7 as a Juridical Parable", *CBQ* 44 (1982), 45-47. - S. argues that *Is.* 3:13-15 contains the missing parts of an original juridical parable preserved in *Is.* 5:1-7. He appeals to the fragmentary character of 3:13-15, its resemblance to 5:1-7, and evidence of similar displacement in *Is.* 1-12 (*Is.* 5:15-17 and 2:6-22; 9:8-21 and 5:25-30). He reconstructs the juridical parable as follows: parable, 5:1-2; judgment (implied on part of audience); interpretation, 3:13-14; indictment, 3:15; further interpretation, 5:7; summons to judge in light of interpretation, 5:3-4 *(cf. 2 Sam.* 14:15ff.); sentence, 5:5-6. 5:7 is placed after 5:1-6 to serve as a conclusion to a "love story" which trails suddenly into judgment. 3:15 supplies the missing rhetorical question appropriate to an indictment. This supports Yee's view that *Is.* 5:1-7 was originally a juridical parable. K.W.W.

See also 877, 895, 1042.

PROPERTY

972. Z. Ben-Barak, "Meribaal and the System of Land Grants in Ancient Israel", *Biblica* 62 (1981), 73-91. - The author examines the story of Meribaal *(2 Sam.* 9; 16:1-4; 19:17-18, 25-31) as the major piece of evidence that the system of royal land grants, which was widespread in the ancient Near East, was also practiced in Israel *(cf. 1 Sam*

8:14; 22:7). He traces the development of this process through a number of stages. The title to the paternal estate was transferred to the king as crown lands in the absence of an heir. The king was able to dispose of these as lands of grant in return for service to the crown. One of the important sources of land grant was the transformation to crown land of paternal estates which had been confiscated by the king on the grounds of treason.

K.W.W.

973. Z. Ben-Barak, "The Meribaal Story and Land-Grants in Ancient Israel", *BM* 25 (1980), 42-62 (Heb.). - Hebrew version of 972.

974. A. Cohen, "Shemitah", *BM* 24 (1979), 45-49, 120 (Heb.) - The sabbatical year of the land, it is here argued, was not observed in First Temple times due to the economic unfeasibility of neglecting vineyards for even one year. Only in the Second Temple period, when a large gentile population could supply agricultural products to the Jewish populace, and only in such northern areas as were no longer based on grape production, could the law be observed as prescribed. B.J.S.

975. Eryl W. Davies, *Prophecy and Ethics, Isaiah and the Ethical Traditions of Israel*, Sheffield: *JSOT* Press, 1981, ISBN 0 905774 26 4, Pp. 184, Price: £8.95 (subscribers: £6.50) (Journal for the Study of the Old Testament, Supplement Series, 16). - In this study of Isaiah's ethics, extracted from a doctoral dissertation, the author relates the prophet's work to earlier Israelite traditions on covenant and law, and pays particular attention to two passages, *Is*. 5:8-10 and 1:21-6, which concern abuses of the land-holding system, and of the administration of justice. The law in itself was incapable of preventing all such abuses; the prophet's concern for the maintenance of justice "in the gate" is related to that concerning land-holding, since the right to speak in the legal assembly was contingent upon the possession of property. B.S.J.

976. E. Lipinski, "Sale, Transfer, and Delivery in Ancient Semitic Terminology", in *Gesellschaft und Kultur im alten Vorderasien*, ed. H. Klengel (Berlin: Akademie Verlag, 1982), 173-185 (Schriften zur Geschichte und Kultur des Alten Orients, 15). - The author considers the semantic developments of the root *MKR* in Hebrew Ugaritic and Babylonian sources, and discerns a gradual shift in the direction of transfer of property, as opposed to mere transfer of possession. But the ancient semitic legal systems did not conceptualise the distinction between possession and ownership, as did the Romans; payment of the price and delivery of the goods were normally concurrent. B.S.J.

977. H. Möller, "Lösungsvorschlag für eine Crux interpretum (Lev. 25 33)", *ZAW* 90 (1978), 411-12. - Re *Va'asher yigal* in *Lev*. 25:33, Möller argues (1) that the verb *g'l* here also means "to redeem" and not "to acquire", (2) the introduction of a "not" is to be rejected, and (3) the *asher* relates not to the following *yig'al* but to the preceding *ge'ulat olam tihyeh laleviyyim.'* J.D.

978. J. Neusner, "Scriptural, Essenic, and Mishnaic Approaches to Civil Government: Some Comparative Remarks", *HTR* 73 (1980), 419-434. - Comparison of *Neziqin* with comparable collections of law in the Bible and at Qumran highlights the peculiar concerns of the Mishnaic editors. *B.K., B.M., Makk., Shebu., Hor.* are essentially

extensions of Scripture restating biblical facts. *Sanh.* and *A.Zar.* tend to develop new topics that could not be predicted on the basis of the Pentateuch. And *B.B.*, dealing with property law, and *Ab.* are completely independent of Scripture.

The Damascus Rule portrays a tightly-organised hierarchical community, whereas the Mishnah envisages a society governed by a consensus of the sages. It wishes to create a stable ongoing society on earth: it is not concerned with heroic efforts to bring in a new age. Heaven is created on earth when man obeys heaven's laws. This preoccupation with the present and property suggests that the framers of the Mishnah were property-owning householders. G.J.W.

979. U. Shtruzman, "The Significance of the Market Overt Enactment in Jewish Law" (Heb.), *Diné Israel* 9 (1978-1980), 7-50. - Under the provisions of Israeli law, the buyer of stolen goods, or a pawnbroker who receives a stolen object, will retain their respective rights in the stolen property, provided that they dealt in good faith, and various conditions specified in the relevant laws were fulfilled. In Jewish law, however, the buyer of stolen goods is under a religious obligation to restore them to the original owner, and the sole effect of the market overt enactment is to ensure that where the buyer acted in good faith, he is not required to endure any financial loss in order to restore the stolen goods. He may, therefore, demand compensation from the owner for any losses incurred in restoring his property to him. The writer believes that, this fundamental difference between Jewish and Israeli law notwithstanding, a fusion of the principles of both systems would provide a law which would be both efficient and just. In another article, "The Market Overt Enactment" (Heb.), *Hapraklit* 34 (1982), 353-374, the same author deals with different aspects of this topic in Jewish law, and compares it with Israeli law. J.S.K.

980. A. Sivan, "The Negotiations over the Cave of Machpelah", *Sivan*, 207-217 (Heb.). - This study is a Hebrew synopsis of recent articles by Melamed, Lehmann, Tucker, Westbrook, Speiser and Evans on Abraham's purchase of the Machpelah Cave. The various attempts by these scholars to elaborate on the ancient Near Eastern legal traditions underlying the narrative are presented and clarified. B.S.J.

See also 862, 864, 871, 895, 899, 935, 939, 991, 995, 1022, 1027.

PUBLIC LAW

981. J. Blidstein, "Medieval Public Law - Sources and Concepts" (Heb.), *Diné Israel* 9 (1978-1980), 127-164. - Since the *Talmud* does not provide detailed principles of Public Law, the Medieval scholars had to develop a legal basis for the authority of the Jewish community and its leaders on the basis of the few sources available to them. In the course of the article, the author discusses the rights of the individual *vis-à-vis* the community, the power of the public to override individual rights and the rights of the community not to accept a particular leadership. He analyses the dynamics of the concept of authority in Jewish communal life both in terms of its sources, and the different models for its exercise. He compares the concept of the *"Tsibbur"* with that of the Jewish court, and explores the question of whether a person absent during a public

meeting at which a piece of legislation was promulgated or a ban pronounced, was bound by decisions taken in his absence. Y.S.K.

982. H. Cazelles, "Droit public et droit privé dans l'Israel biblique", in *Mélanges ... Prévost (supra* no. 858), 17-22. - The author considers the public law elements in Biblical law, starting with the Noahide obligation to establish a legal system, and considering the public law content of the various biblical codes. B.S.J.

983. Daniel J. Elazar, ed., *Kinship and Consent, The Jewish Political Tradition and its Contemporary Uses,* Ramat Gan, Philadelphia, London, Montreal: Turtledove Publishing, 1981, ISBN 965-20-0014-X, Pp. xiii, 396, Price: $24.75. - Professor Elazar and his colleagues at the Center for Jewish Community Studies in Jerusalem have been working on the sources and development of the Jewish political tradition. This volume carries papers from a Colloquium held in 1975 under the sponsorship of the Kotlar Institute for Judaism and Contemporary Thought. The study of the Jewish political tradition necessarily involves the study of Jewish public law, and of the values which stand behind it. In this context, the following papers from the.volume are of especial interest: "The Covenant as the Basis of the Jewish Political Tradition" (Elazar), "The Rabbinic Understanding of the Covenant" (G. Freeman), "The Transition from Tribal Republic to Monarchy in Ancient Israel and Its Impression on Jewish Political History" (M. Weinfeld), "On Power and Authority: Halachic Stance in the Traditional Community and Its Contemporary Implications" (M. Elon), "Individual and Community in the Middle Ages" (G. Blidstein), "Halakhah as a Ground for Creating a Shared Political Dialogue Among Contemporary Jews" (D. Hartman). This is a pioneering work, which deserves to be widely read. It is now being distributed by The Jerusalem Center (12 Moshe Hess Street, Jerusalem 94185). B.S.J.

984. J.W. Flanagan, "Genealogy and Dynasty in the Early Monarchy of Israel and Judah", *Proceedings* VIII, A, 23-28. - In the face of fierce competition, upon what basis did the Davidic-Solomonic legitimacy rest? The author investigates possible clues in the genealogical tables, concluding that they indicate at least three views of the rule of monarchic succession. B.S.J.

985. Martin Goodman, *State and Society in Roman Galilee,* A.D. 132-212, Totowa, N.J.: Rowman & Allanheld, 1983, ISBN 0-86598-089-6, Pp. x, 305, Price: $36.95 (Oxford Centre for Postgraduate Hebrew Studies). - This is an important social and economic history of Galilee from the outbreak of the Bar Kochba revolt to the *constitutio Antoniniana* (which gave Roman citizenship to virtually all free inhabitants of the Roman Empire). The author draws on both classical and Jewish sources, and shows a particular interest in questions of legal organisation. A major part of the book is devoted to "Government and Law", with chapters on Rabbinic Authority in Galilee, Local Administration in Galilee, Roman Administration, and Conflicts of Jurisdiction. After the period of the revolt and its immediate aftermath, Roman administration - as elsewhere in the Empire - became relatively relaxed, with little interference in everyday matters of law. But Rabbinic authority only gradually developed within the period under study. Galilee had its own local courts, and acceptance of Rabbinic authority was conceded only at the price of relaxation by the Rabbis of some of the laws which bore

particularly harshly upon farmers. This is an important study, one which, in both conception and style, belies its origins in a doctoral thesis. B.S.J.

986. H. Jagersma, "The tithes in the Old Testament", *OS* 21 (1981), 116-28. - Tithes are first attested in the ancient near east about 2000 B.C. It is not possible to ascertain whether, either in the ancient near east or in the Old Testament, they originated from the temple or the royal state economy. Prior to the exile they were taken to the local sanctuary - often a royal sanctuary - but after the centralization of the cult they had to be brought to Jerusalem. In pre-exilic times tithes were thought of as related to a sacrificial meal, but afterwards they became obligatory taxes. The collection of tithes sharpened the contrast between town and country, causing poverty and destitution among the rural populations, whereas it brought privilege to those in close proximity to the king and the priesthood in Jerusalem. J.D.

987. Daniela Piattelli, "Riferimenti ed editti di sovrani achemenidi nella letteratura ebraica", in *Atti del secondo convegno tenuto a Idice Bologna, nei giorni 4 e 5 novembre 1981*, ed. F. Parente and D. Piattelli (Rome: Carucci, 1983), 89-94 (Associazione Italiana per lo studio del Giudaismo, Testi e Studi, I). - The author assesses the references to, and sometimes texts of, Achaemenid edicts in Jewish literature, including that mentioned in *Esther* 8:9 (especially as supplemented in the versions of the Septuagint and Jerome), *Daniel* 6:8, *Judith* 3:8, Josephus, and *Ant*. 12:142. The edict to which Esther, Daniel and Judith all refer is that of Antiochus Epiphanes, the monarch who, more even than other oriental sovereigns, claimed the respect owed to a god. B.S.J.

988. H. Reviv, "*Jabesh-Gilead* in I Samuel XI 1-4 - Features of the Israelite City in the Pre-Monarchic Period", *Zion* 43 (1978), xxix, 181-184 (Heb.). - The process of urbanization in Ancient Israel is tied to the rise of a juridical and political entity guided by decidedly local interests and of institutions capable of executing the decisions of the city, as well as the slackening of the tribal framework. B.S.J.

989. C. Saulnier, "Lois romaines sur les juifs selon Flavius Josèphe", *RB* 88 (1981), 161-198. - On the basis of Josephus' *Antiquities* 14.190-264, 306-323 and 16.160-172, the author provides a detailed examination of the Roman laws pertaining to the Jews. He concludes that Rome, in seeking to secure the political fidelity of Palestine, conferred on the Jewish communities of the empire religious privileges which in their own way consecrated the vitality of Judaism in the Diaspora. J.D.

990. B.E. Thiering, "Mebaqqer and Episkopos in the Light of the Temple Scroll", *JBL* 100 (1981), 59-74. - T. discusses the Temple Scroll and the development of the levitical class at Qumran. He argues that the *mebaqqer* or levitical priest at Qumran was an inferior minister who acted as priest to the laity in order to preserve the ruling authority and separateness of the senior priests, the sons of Aaron. In many of the essene settlements away from Qumran this minister acted as overseer for the laity, all new members came through him, and he was the first step in the judicial procedure. He also argues that the early Christian community adopted the office of bishop from the Essene lay communities. K.W.W.

991. Y. Zakovitch, "The Purpose of Narratives in Scripture Concerning Purchase of Possessions" (Heb.), *BM* 23 (1978), 17-21, 117. - As seen by rabbinic exegesis, the original purpose of the stories of Abraham's purchase of the Cave of Machpelah, Joseph's purchase of Shechem, David's purchase of the threshing-floor of Araunah and Omri's purchase of Samaria is to stress the Israelites'/Judaeans' full title to their lands. This is achieved by demonstrating that the four cities which served as capitals of Israel and Judah were acquired in keeping with full legal procedure, with full consent of the earlier inhabitants, at the agreed price and before witnesses. B.S.J.

See also 859, 930, 968, 1016, 1054, 1070.

RAPE

See 859.

REMEDIES

992. F.C. Fensham, "Das Nicht-Haftbar-Sein im Bundesbuch", *Journal of Northwest Semitic Languages* 8 (1980), 17-34. - The author discusses the laws in the Book of the Covenant concerning mitigated indemnity *(Ex.* 21:12-14, 18-19) and exemption from indemnification *(Ex.* 21:20-21, 28; 22:6-7, 9-10, 12, 13-14). He notes the characteristic expressions employed (e.g. *lo tsadah, nikah, shalah yad)* and discusses parallels in other ancient near eastern law codes with respect to indemnity. The Book of the Covenant dates from the pre-monarchical period, as is evidenced by the lack of references to the king or palace, which had important legal functions generally in near eastern law. In pre-monarchical Israel indemnity was generally determined by the elders. Indemnity was closely bound up with intention and premeditation. J.D.

993. A. Schenker, "Koper et expiation", *Biblica* 63 (1982), 32-46. - The author examines the use of *Kofer* in *Ex.* 21:28-32 and on the basis of the use of the verb in analogous contexts in *Gen.* 32:21 and *Prov.* 16:14 concludes that the noun means a "placating" or a "mollifying", or a means to mollify or placate. He distinguishes between a legal *kofer* and an illegal *kofer* (a synonym for *shohad),* and between *kofer* and *pidyon,* "ransom". He notes that dictionaries generally translate *kofer* as "ransom" or "indemnity". Expiation, understood theologically, means that God freely offers Israel the chance of an exchange to avoid definitive punishment. K.W.W.

RESPONSA

994. S. Spitzer, "The Decisions of Maharam Halevi of Vienna" (Heb.), *Sinai* 84 (5739), 37-46. - The article brings to light and analyses two *responsa* of this 14th century Ashkenazic scholar. Matters dealt with in the *responsa* are, *inter alia,* a father's right to marry off his daughter, and the taking of a pledge in order to secure payment of the debt at a particular date. Y.S.K.

995. D. Zafrani, "The *Sefer Hahokhmah* of R. Barukh of Mainz" (Heb.), *Sinai* 84 (5739), 245-265. - In this article, various *responsa* of R. Barukh of Mainz contained in his *Sefer Hahokhmah* are presented. These *responsa* deal, *inter alia*, with the right of a widow to her *ketuba* and those provisions under it which must be satisfied out of the estate; the general modes of acquisition in Jewish law, and conditions under which a litigant may be required to swear on an oath. Y.S.K.

See also 862, 914.

SALE

996. S.M. Passamaneck, *The Traditional Jewish Law of Sale*, Cincinnati: Hebrew Union College Press, 1983, ISBN 0-87820-408-3, Pp. ii, Price: $20.00 (Monographs of the Hebrew Union College, 9). - Professor Passamaneck here provides an English translation of chapters 189-240 of Shulhan Arukh Hoshen Mishpat, i.e. *hilkhot mekah umemkar* and *hilkhot ona'ah umekah ta'ut*, preceded by an Introduction which includes a survey of previous translations of the *Shulhan Arukh*, and of the history of the printed editions, commencing with that of Venice 1564, printed within a decade of the completion of the work. There is also a set of Lexicographical Notes, which usefully discusses the semantic range and criteria of translation of a number of crucial technical terms: *ona'ah, aharayut, asmakhta, kinyan*, and a lengthy Synopsis of the Jewish Law of Sale, which introduces the issues raised in the text and puts many issues in their context, through judicious use of comparative material from Roman and Canon law. There is also a substantial set of annotations to the translation, containing references to earlier rabbinic sources. The author points out the essential intelligibility of the laws of sale to the modern reader, and the contemporary relevance of the halakhic rules on fair prices. It is to be hoped that this book will not only assist students of Jewish law, but also attract the attention of comparative lawyers. The volume is distributed by Ktav Publishing House of New York. B.S.J.

See also 862, 878, 976, 991.

SANCTIONS

997. E. Ben-Zimra, "Considerations of Punishment in Jewish Criminal Law as Reflected in the *Responsa* Literature" (Heb.), *Shenaton* 8 (1981), 7-42. - In addition to the general aims of punishment found in every legal system, Jewish law also attaches religious significance to the penalties imposed by the Criminal law. This point emerges from the author's study of the *responsa* literature on this topic, as do the following criteria applied by the Rabbinic authorities in their administration of the various punishments available to them - severity of the offence, special circumstances of the time, place, and the individual concerned; character and weight of the evidence, and the frequency and results of the offence in question. Ben-Zimra emphasises the significance of moderation and impartiality in applying punishment and the sensitivity of the rabbis to the general circumstances surrounding the offence. He also describes the effects of the

policy of the secular governments of limiting the rights of punishment of Jewish courts, and the means employed by the latter to deal with this policy. Y.S.K.

998 L. Eslinger, "The Case of An Immodest Lady Wrestler in Deuteronomy XXV 11-12", *VT* 31 (1981), 269-281. - The writer argues that this is the only explicit example of a mutilative punishment in Israelite law and that *Deut.* 25:12 is a perfect example of talionic punishment. The key to understanding the meaning of *Deut.* 25:11-12 lies in understanding the Deuteronomist's legislative methods. He sees *Gen.* 32:25-33 as the basis of this law. *Kap* is used in *Gen.* 32:26,33 and *Cant.* 5:5 to refer to male or female genitalia which allows *Deut.* 25:11-12 to be seen as talionic. This passage is also a Deuteronomic comment upon Jacob's underhand action in the Jabbok wrestling match. K.W.W.

999. David Halperin, "Crucifixion, The Nahum Pesher, and the Rabbinic Penalty of Strangulation", *JJS* 32.1 (1981), 32-46. - Halperin examines some peculiarities of early rabbinic jurisprudence in the light of a philological observation from *4Q pNah* I:4-8. He observes that the reference in the pesher to hanging derives from the biblical lemma using the verb *hanneq*. He observes that crucifixion may have been regarded as a prolonged form of strangulation; and goes on to suggest that the long debated penalty of *heneq* in *M. Sanh.* VIII:1, which is not biblical, is a modification of an earlier penalty of crucifixion, derived from the Romans. Various legal traditions are adduced to show traces of older vestiges of this penalty among the old Rabbis; among these is the notable *Targum to Ruth* 1:17, which mentions crucifixion in the place normally occupied by strangulation. Halperin goes on to argue that the rejection of crucifixion in the Temple Scroll is not simply a polemic against other Jewish groups (Yadin), but that it reflects a development in the rabbinic materials as well. He notes that the changed attitude toward crucifixion is a major distinction between the pre-70 and post-70 Pharisaic group. M.F.

1000. N. Lifshitz, "Does a Man Not Receive Both the Death Penalty and Pay Damages? (On the origin of the Rule 'Kam leh Miderabah Minah')" (Heb.), *Shenaton* 8 (1981), 153-246. - According to this author, the general rule against multiplicity of punishments, .i.e. that a person is not to receive both the death penalty and payment of damages, nor is he subject to the death penalty and stripes *(makkot)*, nor to stripes and payment of damages, was not fully developed until the period of the Tannaim, and definitely not before the generation of R. Akiva and his disciples. Accordingly, there were conflicting views as to this rule amongst the Tannaim. Only later, when the lenient school of thought was generally accepted, did the broad principle of *"Kam leh Miderabah Minah"* emerge, and conflicting sources were interpreted in such a way as to support this lenient viewpoint. This process of interpretation resulted in certain restrictions of the originally very wide principle, and also provided the impetus for further development of related fields in Jewish law. The article also deals with the questions of the death penalty and corporal punishment *("makkot")*, and corporal punishment and payment of damages. Y.S.K.

SECURITY

1001. D. Piattelli, "Le Garanzie delle Obbligazioni nelle fonti ebraiche - Osservazioni in margine al problema dell'origine della Ketuba", *Mélanges .. Prévost (supra* no. 858), 105-122. - The author studies the clause of the Ketubah, attributed to Shimon ben Shetah, which placed a charge on the goods of the husband in order to guarantee payment of the *mohar*, in the light of the development of marriage contracts and documents of indebtedness. The theme is developed further in her *Concezioni giuridiche e metodi costruttivi dei giuristi orientali (infra,* no. 1070). B.S.J

See also 994, 1044.

SEXUAL OFFENCES

1002. P.W. Coxon, "A note on 'Bathsheba' in 2 Samuel 12, 1-6", *Biblica* 62 (1981), 247-250. - C. supports the LXX reading of *shivatayim* in *2 Sam.* 12:6 for *arbatayim* on the basis of an elaborate word play throughout *2 Sam.* 11 and 12 and the final irony of Nathan's judgment, *shivatayim*, as a word play on the name of David's mistress, *batsheva (cf. bt* in v.3). K.W.W.

1003. H. Mckeating, "A Response to Dr Phillips", *JSOT* 20 (1981), 25-6. - Mckeating offers a brief reply to the article by Phillips in *JSOT* 20 (1981), 2-25 *(infra,* no.1004). J.D.

1004. A. Phillips, "Another look at Adultery", *JSOT* 20 (1981), 3-25. - "In conclusion, then, this 'another look at adultery' in the Old Testament confirms the assertion of Greenberg, Paul and myself that the law covering adultery in Israel was unique in the ancient Near East, adultery being treated as a crime and not as a civil offence. Consequently it demanded community - not private - action leading to the execution of the adulterer, and, after the Deuteronomic reform, of the adulteress too. The husband could neither pardon the criminal(s), take any private act of revenge, nor settle for damages, since adultery was a crime and not a civil offence for which damages would properly be paid. The only thing which concerned him, as it did the community at large, was that the criminal(s) should be publicly tried, convicted and executed, though in the post-exilic period excommunication from the cult community replaced exaction of the death penalty. In my view this situation could only have arisen because ancient Israel came into being through accepting a distinctive law which, regardless of any covenant theology, made her a peculiar people among the other ancient Near Eastern peoples. This could only have been the Decalogue." J.D.

1005 A. Phillips, "A Response to Dr McKeating", *JSOT* 22 (1982), 142-3. - Phillips offers a brief reply to the criticisms levelled at his earlier article by H. McKeating in *JSOT* 20 (1981), 25-6. J.D.

See also 1057.

SELF-HELP

See 877.

SLAVERY

1006. M. Friedman, "Two *Responsa* from the Cairo *Genizah* Regarding the Marriage of Female Slaves" (Heb.), *Diné Israel* 9 (1978-1980), 165-181. - The practice of living with female slaves is recorded in Geonic literature, and is a result of the permissive attitude of Moslem society to this type of conduct. In many cases, the slave was freed, converted to Judaism and then married according to Jewish law. In this article, the writer publishes two *responsa* from the Cairo *Genizah* in which female slaves were married, and subsequently freed and converted to Judaism. Y.S.K.

1007. B. Lang, "Sklaven und Unfreie im Buch Amos (II 6, VIII 6)", *VT* 31 (1981), 482-488. - The writer suggests that Amos 2:6; 8:6, refer to the practice of debt slavery. He translates *bakesep* as "because of money (debt)". This is similar to the use of Akkadian *kaspu* which can mean "silver" or "money", but also has the special sense "money (debt)" (*PRU* IV 7, 238; *PRU* 17, 130). The sandal mentioned by Amos does not represent the purchase price of a slave, but rather the *reason* for the purchase. *Na'alayim* often has the transferred sense of "contract" (*cf. Ruth* 4:7f.; *Ps.* 60:10), and here in Amos has the special sense of "contract of debt". The context suggests that the poor were unable to repay fraudulent corn merchants for provisions or seed and were reduced to slavery. *Amos* 2:6 represents a particularly grievous crime of the sale of debtors into slavery abroad (*cf. Neh.* 5:8; *Joel* 4:6). The use of *tsadik* suggests a legal situation. The prophet denounces the execution of a wrongly imposed sentence which brings the rich plaintiff financial profit. There is little evidence for Israel to suggest under what circumstances the debtor either was reduced to personal service of his creditor or sold abroad for profit. K.W.W.

1008. S. E. Loewenstamm, "*Biqqoret Tihyeh*" (Heb.), *Shnaton Lamikra* 4 (1980), vii, 94-97. - The author rejects the recent claim that the noun *biqqoret* in *Lev.* 19:20 is to be explained in the sense of "indemnity", as the Akkadian *baqru* never has this meaning. The previously held "inquiry" is still the best interpretation for this crux in the law of the slave-girl. B.S.J.

1009. C. Osiek, "The Ransom of Captives: Evolution of a Tradition", *HTR* 74 (1981), 365-386. - Early Christian efforts to ransom fellow believers condemned to imprisonment or death for their faith are well documented. This tradition goes back to biblical injunctions encouraging the redemption of Hebrew slaves (*Lev.* 25:42,55; *Deut.* 15:15.). G.J.W.

See also 862, 864, 895, 912, 1021.

SOCIAL PROTECTION

1010. Léon Epsztein, *La Justice Sociale dans le Proche-Orient ancien et le Peuple de la Bible*, Paris: Editions du Cerf, 1983, Pp. 272, ISBN 2-204-01892-9, Price: F.69,50. - The author, whose earlier work on the content of social laws was noted in Survey no. 777 *(JLA* V), here adopts a broader approach to his subject. Part One surveys the legal documents of Mesopotamia and Ancient Egypt; Part Two is an historiographical essay, comparing the analysis of social justice in the bible by biblical exegetes, the rationalist tradition commencing with Maimonides, and more recent sociological approaches; Part Three discusses social justice in the light of nomadism and the prophetic movement, and surveys the social laws of the Pentateuch, making comparison with those of the Ancient Near East. A useful addition to the literature. B.S.J.

1011. M.H. Prévost, "L'oppression dans la Bible", in *Mélanges ... Prévost* (*supra* no. 858), 3-16. - This is a partially reconstructed posthumous article by Prévost, which first considers the term *ashak* in the Bible, proposes a typology of "oppression" in it (oppression by one people of another, internal political oppression, socio-economic oppression), and surveys protection of the oppressed in the Ancient Near East and in ancient Israel (where it receives a legal as well as an ethical appropriation). B.S.J.

See also 1032, 1077.

SOURCES OF LAW

1012. E. Berkowitz, "Rabbinical Authority" (Heb.), *Sinai* 87 (5740), 1-25. - In the course of this article, Berkowitz analyses the ways in which the Rabbis were able to override previous legislation. His main thesis is that the power of the Rabbis to enact legislation was limited by public acceptance. According to Berkowitz, a distinction must be drawn between *gezerot* and *takanot*: The former are measures taken in order to deal with a specific problem known to the public at large, whereas the latter are based upon reasons known only to the propounders of the enactment in question. Where the reasons for a *gezerah* no longer apply, a later court can annul it without special Rabbinical authority. A *takanah* however, cannot be revoked without such authority, even if it appears to the later court that the original reasons for its enactment no longer apply. This distinction is then employed in the discussion of the rule that a later court can only revoke the legislation of an earlier one if it "is greater in wisdom and numbers". Y.S.K.

1013. B.S. Jackson, "Jésus et Moïse: le statut du prophète à l'égard de la loi", *Revue historique de droit français et étranger* 59/3 (1981), 341-360. - The use of the "prophet like Moses" model *(Deut.* 18:15ff.) is examined in early rabbinics, Qumran and the New Testament. The powers of such a prophet in relation to the law, in terms of both legislation and adjudication, differed according to whether an eschatological or a non-eschatological view was taken of the prophet. The eschatological view is found at Qumran, the non-eschatological in early rabbinics, and traces of both are apparent in the New Testament. Jesus appears as a non-eschatological prophet like Moses, according to the rabbinic conception, when he seeks merely to suspend the law for all his followers, rather than abrogate it in general. A shortened version of this paper appears in Italian in *Atti del secondo convegno a Idice, Bologna, nei giorni 4 e 5 novembre 1981*, ed. F. Parente and D. Piattelli (Rome: Carucci, 1983), 95-100. B.S.J.

1014. B. Lifshitz, "Custom Overrides Law" (Heb.), *Sinai* 86 (5740), 8-13. - It is generally accepted that in matters of civil law, where custom is an independent normative category, custom overrides the law. In ritual matters, however, this is not the case. Consequently, any reference to this rule in the context of ritual law is problematic. Lifshitz analyses two passages in the Jerusalem *Talmud* which deal with this rule, and concludes that in neither instance was the *halakhah* actually overridden. In both cases a new situation arose in which the *halakhah* was simply no longer applicable. In this light, it is necessary to re-examine the concept of custom overriding *halakhah* in Jewish law. Y.S.K.

1015. S. Safrai, "Pluralism in the *Yavneh* Period" (Heb.), *De'ot* (1980), 166-170. - In the years between the rebellion which led to the destruction of the Temple and the Bar Kohba Revolt, the Jewish nation underwent a process of rehabilitation and succeeded in reconstructing its political structure. This article deals with the special problems encountered by the Rabbis of Yavneh and, in particular, with their decision that although both the opinions of Bet Shammai and Bet Hillel are "The words of the living God", nevertheless, the *halakhah* is in accordance with the lenient opinions of Bet Hillel.
Y.S.K.

1016. A. Steinfeld, "*'Tsibur'* (the public) and *'Rov tsibur'* (the majority of the public) in the Legislation of the Jewish Court" (Heb.), *Sinai* 85 (5739), 154-171 - Steinfeld discusses the following three principles which guide the court in imposing *gezerot*, i.e. directives of a negative nature aimed at prohibiting a specific act. The first one is consideration of the whole public and not only the majority, the second is whether or not a particular *gezerah* is beyond public endurance, and the third is the question of acceptance by the majority of the public after the *gezerah* has been promulgated. It is pointed out that in relation to the first two principles all the public must be taken into consideration and not only the majority. There is also a fundamental distinction between a *gezerah* accepted by all the public and one accepted by the majority. Y.S.K.

See also 865.

SOURCES - INTERTESTAMENTAL

1017. Philip R. Davies, *The Damascus Covenant*, Sheffield: JSOT Press, 1983, ISBN 0 905774 50 7 (cloth), 51 5 (paper), Price: £18.00 (cloth), £11.50 (paper) (Journal for the Study of the Old Testament, Supplement Series, 25). - The author provides a literary and historical analysis of the "Damascus Document", fragments of which were found by Schechter in the Cairo Genizah before the more complete text discovered at Qumran. After a source-critical investigation, the author concludes that the original Damascus Document (not including Cairo Ms. 2, which contains much more specifically legal content) is a coherent composition, which casts light upon the origins of the community in its pre-Qumran days. The *Admonition* section of the document must have been composed before the occupation of Qumran, possibly in the Diaspora, and the document has powerful ideological roots in the priestly Exilic literature, especially the Holiness Code and Ezekiel. B.S.J.

1018. Jacob Milgrom, "Further Studies in the Temple Scroll", *JQR* 71.1 (1981), 1-17, 71.4 (1981), 89-106. - These articles continue studies published elsewhere; *cf. JBL* 97 (1978), 501-23. Milgrom provides a variety of texual annotations and restorations of the Temple Scroll, based on Yadin's *editio princeps*. He primarily deals with cultic-legal phraseology and procedure, and seeks to clarify the Temple Scroll in its own right, and to compare it on occasion with the pertinent biblical materials. Forty-six topics are treated (Nos. 1-46). M.F.

1019. Michael E. Stone, ed., *Jewish Writings of the Second Temple Period,* Assen and Philadelphia: Van Gorcum and Fortress Press, 1984, ISBN 0-8006-0603-5, Pp. 23, 698, Price: $35.95 (Compendia Rerum Iudaicarum ad Novum Testamentum, Section Two: The Literature of the Jewish People in the Period of the Second Temple and the Talmud, II) - This volume seeks to provide an introduction to the sources of the intertestamental period which is both available to the non-specialist, yet not tautological to the scholar. To a large extent, it succeeds. I. Gafni's chapter sketches the historical background, and includes a section on Roman Rule in Judaea; G.W.E. Nickelsburg contributes chapters on "Stories of Biblical and Early Post-Biblical Times", and on "The Bible Rewritten and Expanded (1 Enoch, Jubilees, etc.)"; H.W. Attridge deals with Historiography and with Josephus; P. Borgen with Philo. Wisdom Literature is discussed by M. Gilbert, Testaments (of the Twelve Patriarchs, Moses, Job) and the Sibylline Oracles by J.J. Collins; Apocalyptic Literature by the Editor; Jewish Sources in Gnostic Literature by B.A. Pearson; Qumran Sectarian Literature (with separate sections on "Rules" and "Halakhah", the latter including the Temple Scroll) by D. Dimant; Psalms, Hymns Prayers by D. Flusser; and Epistolary Literature by P.S. Alexander. Some of these sources are of central importance to the historian of Jewish Law, especially the "legal" sections of Philo, Josephus and Qumran Literature. But relevant material may also be found widely scattered in this literature, and this book provides much useful background information. There is an extensive bibliography, and Indices of Sources, Names and Subjects. B.S.J.

1020. A.M. Wilson and L. Wills, "Literary Sources of the *Temple Scroll*", *HTR* 75 (1982), 275-288. - The Temple Scroll is not a homogeneous composition by a single author. "The source-critical and form-critical study of the *Temple Scroll* suggests that the work is a composite. The festival calendar, the collection of purity laws, and the Torah of the King can be distinguished on the basis of form, grammar, or syntax from the laws concerning the temple and its courts ... and they probably circulated as independent documents. These writings, along with the book of Deuteronomy, were utilized in the composition of the final work, a copy of which has been preserved at Qumran. The composite nature of the *Temple Scroll* should be considered in any discussion of its date and setting" (authors' summary). G.J.W.

SOURCES - OTHER

See 1033.

SOURCES - RABBINIC

1021. Z.W. Falk, "Four Glosses in Mishnah and Baraita", *Mélanges ... Prévost* (*supra* no. 858), 171-177. - The author analyses four texts where glosses or marginal notes appeared to have been incorporated into the text. They concern the use of illegal conditions in betrothal, manumission by deed, interpretation of a vow, and the use of an "old" deed of divorce. B.S.J.

1022. W.S. Green, The *Traditions of Joshua ben Hananiah,* Part One: The Early Legal Traditions, Leiden: E.J. Brill, 1981, ISBN 90 04 06318 8, Pp. xviii, 333, Price: Gld. 96 (Studies in Judaism in Late Antiquity, 29). - Originating as a doctoral thesis prepared at Brown University's Graduate Seminar, under the supervision of Professor Neusner, this study commenced as an attempt to write a biography of R. Joshua, but ultimately has focused upon the redactional processes by which his traditions are transmitted. The present volume analyses "the early legal traditions", as found in the Babylonian Talmud and sources parallel to them. Of particular interest to students of Jewish civil law will be the 30 or so passages from *Nashim* and *Neziqin* analysed in chapters IV and V, some of them attracting reasonably substantial commentary. Following the pattern of other works emanating from Brown, the general conclusions must be awaited until the whole corpus has been analysed. B.S.J.

1023. Irwin H. Haut, *The Talmud as Law or Literature. An Analysis of David W. Halivni's Mekorot Umasorot,* New York: Bet Sha'ar Press, Inc., 1982, distributed by Sepher Hermon Press, Pp. 83, Price $10.00 (cloth), $6.00 (paper). - The author first presents some basic concepts of Halivni's method of analysis, his theory of *Setam* and *Gemara,* and then analyses various *sugyot* from Eruvin (27d-29b), Pesahim (3b-10b), Gittin (77a, 88b), Kiddushin (2a), and Moed Katan (14a, 20b, 26b) in the light of Halivni's method. There is a somewhat more extended discussion of Halivni on Kiddushin 42b, a *sugya* on agency for delict *(shaliah lidvar averah).* His conclusion, in which he weighs the "literary" as against the "legal" elements in Halivni's method, includes an account of Gittin 32a, where the author sides with Elon as against Halivni, but looks for a rapprochement between their approaches. The book concludes with a brief (but remarkable) biography, and some bibliographical notes. Along with Halivni's own account of his method *(JJS* 30 (1979), 192-201; see *Survey* no. 526, *JLA* IV), and the Neusner collections on *The Formation of the Babylonian Talmud* (1970) and *The Modern Study of the Mishnah* (1973), this book will assist the reader towards an appreciation of some of the issues currently debated in modern scholarship on the Talmud. B.S.J.

1024. M. Hengel, J. Neusner, P. Schäfer, eds., *Übersetzung des Talmud Yerushalmi,* Tübingen: J.C.B. Mohr (Paul Siebeck), Band IV/1-3, *Bavot,* 1982, ISN 3-16-144490-6, Pp. xvii, 533, Price: DM 215; Band IV, *Sanhedrin,* 1981, ISBN 3-16-143092-1, Pp.

xiv, 341, Price DM 136; Band 1/7: *Avoda Zara,* 1980, ISBN 3-16-142662-2, Pp. xii, 192, Price: DM 78. - A German translation of the Jerusalem Talmud was commenced in 1975, with *Berakhot* translated by Charles Horowitz, and edited by the Institutum Judaicum der Universität Tübingen. The publisher now continues the series under new editorship. All three volumes are translated by Gerd A. Wewers. They are based on printed editions and manuscript sources, including published Genizah fragments. The translation is well annotated with references to both rabbinic parallels and modern literature. Indices of Biblical and rabbinic sources, the names of Rabbis mentioned in the text, and (in the case of Sanhedrin) place names, are provided. These volumes will considerably assist scholars in access to a difficult text, one of considerable importance - especially in the present Tractates - to the legal historian. B.S.J.

1025. Abraham Katch, "A Geniza Fragment of Talmud Yerushalmi in the Antonin Collection of the Saltykovshchedrin Library in Leningrad, *JQR* 71,3 (1981), 181-84. - A newly discovered fragment of *Yer. Shekalim,* Ch. 7, fol 31a, 31b, and 32a. These are not included in L. Ginzberg's *Yerushalmi Fragments from the Geniza* (N.Y., 1947). M.F.

1026. Hans Kvalbein, ed., *Blant skriftlærde og fariseere. Jødedommen i oldtiden,* Oslo: Verbum, 1984, ISBN 82-543-0248-0, Price: Dkr. 271,00. - In this textbook on Judaism a short chapter, pp. 193-206, gives an introduction to the history of the Torah. The author, Øyvind Moberg Wee, argues that *Mishnah* must be considered first of all as a kind of commentary to the *Torah.* K.N.

1027. Jacob Neusner, *A History of the Mishnaic Law of Damages,* Leiden: E.J. Brill, 1983-84: Part One - *Baba Qamma,* ISBN 90 04 06930 5, pp. 35, 164, Price. Gld. 80; Part Two - *Baba Mesia,* ISBN 90 04 06931 3, Pp. 30, 163, Price: Gld. 80; Part Three - *Baba Batra, Sanhedrin, Makkot,* ISBN 90 04 06853 8, Pp. 31, 293, Price: Gld. 148 (Studies in Judaism in Late Antiquity, XXV). - The author here continues the analysis of Mishnaic literature, noted earlier in *Surveys* nos. 267 *(JLA* II) and 780 *(JLA* V). The material treated in these volumes is of the greatest interest to the student of Jewish Civil Law, containing much of the regulation of Torts, Contracts, Property, Succession and Crime. The approach follows that adopted for the Orders on *Holy Things* and *Women.* A research assistant has compiled a useful bibliography, consisting largely of works with which the author, as he explains in the Preface, declines to engage. Further assessment of the series on *Damages* must await publication of the review of its concluding volumes. B.S.J.

1028. Nahum Rakover, *Guide to the Sources of Jewish Law* (Heb.: *Moreh-Derekh Bimkorot Hamishpat Haivri),* Jerusalem: Sifriyat Hamishpat Ha'ivri, 18-983, Pp. 89, Price: $16.00. - Prompted by the Foundations of Law Act, 1980, this volume seeks to provide a *Where to Look for Your Law* for Jewish Law. It provides brief introductions to the sources from the Bible to the Judgments of modern Rabbinical Courts in Israel, with sample texts from the law of bailment *(shemirah).* This is followed by a section on secondary literature (text-books, journals, encyclopaedias, indices to the responsa (including the Bar-Ilan Computer Project), biographies, bibliographies, manuals, dictionaries, anthologies and indices). There is an appendix of standard abbreviations and acronyms, a geographical and chronological chart of rabbinic authorities from the eleventh century, and an alphabetical index to that chart. The volume concludes with a general index of names, books and subjects. While the book is addressed primarily to Israeli practitioners without any previous grounding in Jewish law, the Appendices will serve the scholar as a convenient reference tool. B.S.J.

1029. F. Rosner, ed., *Maimonides' Commentary on the Mishnah, Tractate Sanhedrin*, New York: Sepher-Hermon Press, Inc., 1981, ISBN 0-87203-099-7, Pp. xix, 215, Price $14.95. - This is the first English translation of the whole of Maimonides' Commentary on Tractate Sanhedrin (as opposed to *Perek Helek*, which includes a very famous discussion of the nature of God, and the world to come). Dr. Rosner has based himself primarily upon Kafah's modern retranslation of the original Arabic into Hebrew. The current edition prints the Hebrew of the Mishnah (only), an English translation of the Mishnah, and a translation of Maimonides' Commentary. Each chapter is followed by notes, mainly of a text-critical character. The book will undoubtedly be of service to students studying the Mishnah as a classical Hebrew text, in giving them access to one of the classical commentaries. B.S.J.

1030. E.L. Segal, "Variant Traditions of Cases in the Babylonian Talmud", *JQR* 70 (1979), 1-27. - Segal seeks to identify "variant traditions" as opposed to textual variants, within TB. He identifies conflicting parallel *sugyot* in Nezikin that differ from cases whose meaning comes only from context. These independent literary units "take on the appearance of variant traditions." S.N.R.

1031. E. Shochetman, "*Kelale Hatalmud* of R. Bezalel Ashkenazi" (Heb.), *Shenaton* 8 (1981), 247-308. - This article is an analysis of the *Kelale Hatalmud* of R. Bezalel Ashkenazi, based upon a manuscript in the Jewish National and University Library of Jerusalem. The printed edition, published by A. Marx some seventy years ago, was based upon what he believed to be the sole manuscript of R. Bezalel's work, i.e. that of the Jewish Theological Seminary of New York. According to Marx, this work was mainly a preparatory and was not designed for publication. Shochetman argues that the Jerusalem manuscript is the later and more complete work, and he presents the additional *Kelalim* not found in the New York version in a special appendix at the end of the article. His main thesis, however, is that R. Bezalel did not intend to write a separate book of *Kelalim*, but intended his work to complement the *Sefer Keritut* of R. Samson of Chinon. Y.S.K.

See also 860, 908, 932, 936, 940, 944, 978, 996.

STATUS

1032. J.D. Amusin, "Die Gerim in der sozialen Legislatur des *Alten Testaments*", *Kilo* 63 (1981), 15-23. - The various allusions to the *gerim* "sojourners" in the social legislation of the Old Testament are noted, e.g. *Lev*. 19:9-10, 23:22; *Deut*. 14:28-9, 24:19, 20-21, 26-12. When we read of "the poor, the *ger*, the widow and the orphan" it is probable that "the widow and orphan" were those of dead *gerim*, whose position in foreign countries was especially precarious. So far as the laws in the Mishnah concerning the *gerim* are concerned, it is not impossible that some of them embody early material. The Old Testament contains a number of admonitions employing the negative imperative (e.g. "do not oppress ...") concerning the *gerim*, for the purpose of protecting them (e.g. *Ex.* 22:20-21, 23:9; *Lev.* 19:33-4; *Deut.* 24:14-15; *Exek.* 22:7; Ps. 94:6; *Mal.* 3:5). These remained only admonitions but the Talmud tried to introduce sanctions for their enforcement. Like native Israelites the *gerim* had the right of asylum (*cf. Num.* 35:15) and they were also on an equal footing with respect to the *lex talionis* (*cf. Lev.* 24:22). They lacked the right to own property, however. J.D.

1033. Michael Corinaldi, *The Personal Status of the Karaites* (Heb.), Jerusalem: Rubin Mass, 1984, ISBN 965-09-0036-0, Pp. 288 + 44, Price: $20.00. - This is a pioneering study of modern Karaite law, written by a lawyer expert in the subject from both the academic and practical points of view. An introductory chapter traces the history of the Karaites, and is written by a Karaite collaborator, with the author's assistance. Part One deals first with the arrangement of marriage, and then with divorce by judicial decree in Karaite *halakhah*. An English version of this last section, previously published in *Diné Israel* IX (1978-1980), 101-144, is conveniently provided in a pocket attached to the back cover. It traces the topic through the principal Karaite sources, in historical sequence, and thus serves also to introduce the reader to the classical sources of the Karite system. Part Two deals with intermarriage between Karaites and other Jews, from the viewpoint of rabbinic authorities. Particular attention is paid to the contemporary position in Israel, and Appendices reproduce a letter of Chief Rabbi Ovadya Joseph on the permission of intermarriage, and that of a rabbinical court in Haifa. Part Three deals with the personal status of the Karaites in Israel, including their status as a "religious community" and the millet system as received under the Mandate and later in Israel; and the question of the applicability of the Rabbinic Courts Jurisdiction (Marriage and Divorce) Law 1953, culminating in a parallel Bill for Karaite courts, presented to the Knesset in 1979 (and reproduced in an Appendix), a Bill which the Knesset decided to "refer back to the government". A further Appendix publishes for the first time a study of the Karaite problem by a 16th century scholar, Rabbi Shmuel Ibn Hakim Halevi. This is an invaluable work to both historians of Jewish law and those concerned with its modern application. B.S.J.

See also 856, 868, 1048, 1066.

STATUS-JEW

1034. R. Berg and M. Urbah-Bornstein, *Les Juifs devant le droit Français*, Paris: Les Belles Lettres, 1984, ISBN 2-905248-00-9, Pp. 282, Price: F.165 (Collection Franco-Judaïca, 11). - This is the first monographic study of the position of Jews in French law since 1903. The authors, both lawyers, take account of legislation and case-law from the end of the 19th century to date. The first part, by Berg, deals with the legal organisation of the Jewish religion, and its practice, in public law, including the status of the Consistories (Berg has served as Secretary-General of the Central Consistory). This section concludes with a documentary appendix, including extracts from the 1905

Law on the Separation of Church and State. The second part, contributed by Madame Urbah deals, with private law, and particularly problems of private international law, where immigrant Jews from North Africa have brought with them Jewish law as their personal law. There are chapters on nationality, legal capacity, marriage, divorce, and family property. Professor J. -P. Lévy contributes an elegant Introduction. B.S.J.

1035. Lawrence H. Schiffman, *Who was a Jew? Rabbinic and Halakhic Perspectives on the Jewish Christian Schism*, Hoboken, N.J.: Ktav Publishing House, Inc., 1985, ISBN 0-88125-053-8 (054-6, pbk.), Pp. xii, 131, Price: $14.95, $8.95 pbk. - This is an expanded version of a substantial paper contributed by Professor Schiffman to the second volume of the McMaster project on Jewish and Christian Self-Definition. The author considers the tannaitic definition of the Jew by birth, against its biblical background. He considers the various halakhic requirements of conversion to Judaism (acceptance of the Torah, circumcision, immersion, sacrifice), and the rules of heresy and apostasy. Against this background he considers the relationship between tannaitic Judaism and early Christianity, and traces the effects on Rabbinic attitudes of the changing balance within the daughter religion from Jewish Christianity to Gentile Christianity. B.S.J.

STATUS-WOMAN

1036. J.P. Brown, "The Role of Women and the Treaty in the Ancient World", *Biblische Zeitschrift* 25 (1981), 1-28. - Women's roles in ancient Israel, Greece and Rome developed along similar lines. Since the language of ancient treaties is similar in all these areas, it may be assumed women enjoyed a similar status in each centre. Three main stages in the development of women's roles can be discerned. Early (c. 1000-500 BCE) women had substantial prestige and authority within the patriarchal society. Then with the decline of the city state prostitution flourished and respectable women were forced to stay at home cut off from the centres of power. Finally the NT era sees the emergence of a feminine counter-culture reasserting women's equality in certain areas.
G.J.W.

1037. David Daube, "Johanan ben Beroqa and Women's Rights", *Zeitschrift der Savigny-Stiftung für Rechtsgeschichte, R.A.*, 99 (1982), 22-31. - D. seeks the characteristics of the halakhic view of Johanan ben Beroqa. He finds him moderate, a liberal disdaining excessive formalism, a helper of the underprivileged. In particular, he was dedicated to the improvement of the position of women, even where he extended the rabbinic duty to procreation to women. Women's liberation is relative to the mores of the times; it led to different results in R, Johanan's day from our own. B.S.J.

1038. Hans Jacob Hansen & Jakob Schow Madsen, eds., *Thi Gud er jeg, ikke mand. Studier over kvindebilleder i Det gamle Testamente*, FK-tryk, Aarhus, 1982, ISBN 87 7457 010 2, Pp. 100, Price: Dkr. 30. - Five female students have published their seminar papers on images of women in the Old Testament under the title *For I am God, and not man (Hos.* 11,9). In focus are texts like *Gen.* 1-3, the narratives about the patriarchs' wives, and the Song of Songs. These texts are analysed in their historical context, but from a female point of view. A special paper gives a systematic representation of female aspects of the image of God. Laws concerning women and the possible theological implications of these laws today are discussed in an appendix, a reprint of an article by their teacher, Kirsten Nielsen. K.N.

1039. Karin Friis Plum, *Kvindehistorie og kvindehistorier - i det gamle testamente*, Hans Reitzel, København, 1983, ISBN 87-412-3714-5, Pp. 144, Price: Dkr 138,50. - The title of the book indicates the main theme: the history of women as we know it through the stories about women in the Old Testament. According to the author, a woman herself, this history is a history of economic, sexual, and religious oppression. The author bases her thesis on legal texts like *Deut.* 25:11-12; *Ex.* 20-21; *Deut.* 24:1-4; 22-24.29, as well as stories like *Gen.* 3; 12; 19; 34; 38; *Judg.* 14-15, and *1 Sam.* 1. The authoress does not end up with this negative evaluation, but emphasises that alternatively read, from the point of a woman, the stories about woman often can be understood only as descriptions of misery, but as witnesses of women's courage and the will to transcend religious and political systems. K.N.

1040. Judith R. Wegner, "The Status of Women in Jewish and Islamic Marriage and Divorce Law", *Harvard Women's Law Journal* 5 (1982), 1-33. - The author compares the progress of women from the status of near-chattels to that of near-persons in Jewish and Islamic law, against the background of inhibitions against change in theocratic legal systems. B.S.J.

SUCCESSION

1041. G. Brin, "The Status of the First-Born in Genealogical Tables", *BM* 24 (1979), 255-259 (Heb.). - Examination of biblical genealogies reveals that the first-born son is not only the first mentioned but is frequently the only son whose own descendants are enumerated. This custom, as well as the right of the first-born son to inherit a double portion, is known in the Nuzu documents as well. B.S.J.

See also 863, 864, 881, 902, 921, 930, 938, 939, 995, 1027.

TERMINOLOGY

1042. Gunnel André, *Determining the Destiny. PQD in the Old Testament*, Lund: CWK Gleerup, 1980, ISBN 91-40-04759-8; Pp. 264, Price: SEK. 190. - This monograph purports to offer a semantic analysis of the verb *paqad* and its derivatives. Especially in the verb the author finds forensic connotations. The analysis is carried forth in a number of discrete steps. First, the "limited contexts" of *PQD* are dealt with; here grammatical constructions, related verbs and phrases, etc. are listed. Next, the author studies *PQD* in its "wider contexts". In this connexion the material is organized according to various *Gattungen* (oracles, psalms, narratives). It is argued that the verb *paqad* is anchored in a "judicial pattern", found in a wide variety of texts. We are here concerned with a lawsuit-pattern with YHWH playing the part of the plaintiff. The various elements of this pattern are described under the headings: A. "From the inception of the conflict to the appeal", B. "The appearance of the judge", and C. "From the accusation in court to the pronouncement of the sentence". In the next chapter the material is sifted according to the "larger units of contents". A categorisation is attempted according to what the author denotes as "conditional" and "unconditional act" respectively. The final chapter tries to answer the question: How are these two categories related to the alleged *PQD*-pattern? The book offers a lot of material, neatly organised but not properly evaluated. Almost no attention is paid to the modern discussions of semantic method. The relevant problem of how the alleged *PQD*-pattern is related to the well established *rib*-pattern will be dealt with in a separate study. T.M.

1043. G.J. Botterweck and H. Ringgren, eds., *Theological Dictionary of the Old Testament,* trld. D.E. Green, Grant Rapids: W.B. Eerdmans Publishing Company, 1980, ISBN 0-8028-2338-6, Pp. xix, 493. Price: £15.00. - The first three volumes of this series were noted in *Survey* no. 592 *(JLA* IV). The present volume extends from *zeev* to *hamets.* Of particular interest to the student of Biblical law are the entries on *zevul, zamam, zanah, haval, hag, hata, halal, halaf, halak, hamad, hamas.* B.S.J.

1044. L.R. Freedman ,"Studies in Cuneiform Legal Terminology with Special Reference to West Semitic Parallels", *Dissertation Abstracts International* 38 (1978), 6097-A. - This study applies the comparative lexicography of Landsberger and Held to legal terminology in order to make clear the institutions that they express within the context of the legal traditions of various localities or dialects. It aims to relate Biblical law to cuneiform common law traditions and claims to provide a key to unravelling the complex legal traditions of the Talmudic period, as the earliest evidence of how these Israelite traditions worked. It provides a study of ancient Israelite surety, including a study of the hand-gesture for suretyship, the relationship of Biblical Hebrew *' rb,* "to go surety", to its pseudo-homonyms, and of the nouns *'rbh,* "suretyship", and *'rbwn,* "pledge". K.W.W.

1045. S. Gervitz, "On Hebrew *sebet* = Judge", *The Bible World,* eds. G. Rendsburg et al, New York: KTAV, 1980, 61-66 (C.H. Gordon Festschrift) -*Sebet* and *sofet* are only apparent homonyms, deriving from different though related Proto-semitic roots. *Sebet* is an adjective used substantively while *sofet* is an active participle. Evidence comes from Ugaritic and Akkadian, especially names. G. concludes that MT's uses of *sebet* require neither consonantal nor vocalic emendation. S.N.R.

1046. A. Hurvitz, "The History of a Legal Formula: *kol aser hapes asah* (Psalms cvx 3, cxxxv 6)", *V.T.* 32 (1982), 257-267. - The phrase *kol aser hapes asah* is found twice in the Old Testament *(Ps.* 105:3, 135: 6), and in a slightly modified form in three other places *(Isa.* 46:10; *Jon.* 1:14, *Eccles.* 8:3). In all five instances it refers to either God *(Psalms, Isaiah, Jonah)* or to an earthly king *(Eccles.)* and denotes the unlimited power of the supreme authority which enables him "to do whatever he pleases". H. argues that this is an adapted legal formula from the realm of jurisprudence. He compares the biblical idiom with related phrases, mainly Aramaic, employed in strictly technical legal contexts from outside the Hebrew Bible. He concludes the formula emerges in the second half of the first millenium B.C. and that the phrase "he did whatever was good in his eyes" was a functional equivalent of the later "he did whatever he pleased". K.W.W.

1047. J. Shaviv, *"Shama Bekol - Shama Lekol"*, *BM* 23 (1978), 465-477, 521 (Heb.). - The two expressions are examined throughout the Old Testament and found to be distinct in usage. The former indicates obedience - to the law, authority, the divine, etc., while the latter denotes assent, acquiescence, to a plea or argument. The differentiation provides insight into aspects of hierarchical relations in Old Testament times. B.J.S.

1048. T. Wadsworth, "Is there a Hebrew Word for Virgin? *Bethulah* in the Old Testament", *Restoration Quarterly* 23 (1980), 161-171. - W. offers a refutation of the proposition advanced by Gordon Wenham (*VT* 22, 1972), that *betulah* means "a girl of marriageable age" and was never meant to connote a "Virgin". Of the fifty uses of *betulah* in Scripture those in *Deut.* 22:13-21 stand out. This passage is a key to W.'s acceptance of the equation *betulah* = "virgin". S.N.R.

See also 833, 842, 848, 873, 976, 993, 996.

THEFT

See 1002.

THEORY OF LAW

1049. J. Barton, "Ethics in Isaiah of Jerusalem", *JTS* 32 (1981), 1-18. - B. attempts to show that Isaiah (1-39) had developed an understanding of morality which has affinities with Western theories of natural law. He examines the basis of Isaiah's moral demands to illustrate what he assumed to underline the particular norms or transgressions he condemned. Isaiah sees God as creator and preserver of all things, occupying by right the supreme position over creation. The essence of morality is the maintenance of the ordered structure underlying God's guidance. This meant a proper submission to one's assigned place in the scheme of things and the avoidance of any challenge to God's supremacy or established order. Isaiah is an early example of a way of approaching ethics which begins with a hierarchically ordered universe whose moral pattern ought to be apparent to all men, and derived all moral offenses from the disregard of natural law. K.W.W.

1050. E. Berkovits, *Not in Heaven: The nature and Function of Halakha* , New York: Ktav Publishing House, Inc., 1083, Pp. vii, 131, ISBN 0-88125-003-1, Price: $12.50. - The author argues that *halakhah* is the application of Torah to life, and that historical circumstances have led to an exile of *halakhah* from real-life situations, combined with an exile into literature and codification. "The old principle of the acceptance of personal responsibility for halakhic decisions, which demanded that the *Dayan* ruled according to what his eyes see, has received a new meaning that reads: according to what he sees in some authoritative text" (p.91). It is this thesis which makes Berkovits, from within Orthodoxy, a more radical critic of contemporary *halakhah* than many Conservative writers, who often use the same sources to show the historical development of the *halakhah*, and the the human contributions to it. The latter use this as an argument to revise certain aspects of the content of Jewish law; Berkovits, by contrast, implies a quite different view of the very nature of Jewish law, and its formal development. These are readable and stimulating essays; specialists will wish to consult the author's more elaborate Hebrew work, *Halakah Kohah Vetafkidah,* published by Mosad Harav Kook. B.S.J.

1051. G.J. Blidstein, *Political Concepts in Maimonidean Halakhah* (Heb.), Ramat Gan: Bar-Ilan University Press, 1983, ISBN 965-226-040-1, Pp. 283, Price: $23.00. - This is an important book, in which the author considers various aspects of Maimonides' treatment of kingship, including the appointment of the king, the basis of his legitimacy, succession, his role in the legal system, his legislative power, and hs relation to the principle of *dina demalkhuta dina*. As such, it is of considerable interest not only to the Maimonidean scholar. but also to the student of the history of Jewish public law. An English translation would undoubtedly be well received. B.S.J.

1052. B. Dupuy, "Unité et tension de la Halakha et de l'Aggada", *Mélanges ... Prévost (supra* no. 858), 123-132. - The author considers the integral relationship between *halakhah* and *aggadah* in the light of both ancient sources and modern writings. B.S.J.

1053. Ze'ev W. Falk, *Law and Religion, The Jewish Experience*, Jerusalem: Mesharim Publishers, 1981, Pp. 238, Price: $10.00. - This is the text of a course of lectures delivered by Professor Falk at New York University in 1979/80. He writes in the preface: "Instead of engaging themselves in the intricacies of legal technique or in philological-historical niceties, Jewish scholars are called to study the meaning and justice of their culture against a broad comparative background." Succinct chapters are then devoted to Law and Religion, Values, Teleology, Democracy, Liberty, Human Rights, Equality, Disobedience, Generalization and Individualization, Validity and Efficacy, Authority, Legalism, Language, Logic, Human Nature, Faith and Proof, Acts and Duties; all of them are further sub-divided. The effect is to organise a wide variety of Jewish sources in relation to some of the major issues in contemporary legal philosophy and ethics. The value of such an approach for a student audience should not be underestimated. For the scholar, Professor Falk raises many interesting questions; he would be the last to believe that he has, within the present compass, gone very far in answering them. More substantial work along these lines would undoubtedly be rewarding. B.S.J.

1054. Ze'ev W. Falk, *Legal Values and Judaism, Towards a Philosophy of Halakhah* (Heb.), Jerusalem: The Magnes Press, 1980, ISBN 965-223-342-0, Pp. 193, Price: $8.00. - Professor Falk uses a wide range of comparative and philosophical sources in urging that we seek the values embedded in the *halakhah*, as part of an investigation into the philosophy of Jewish law. In so doing, he reflects an important trend which is gaining strength in contemporary legal studies, as reflected, for example, in Stein and Shand's *Legal Values in Western Society* (to which Falk refers). In Israel, this is a particularly apposite time for such a quest, given the incorporation into Israeli law, for some purposes at least, of what may be termed the values of the Jewish tradition by the Foundations of Law Act 1980. Professor Falk has sympathy for a version of natural law theory, and is anxious to use underlying values as a medium of critique of the law. He has interesting remarks on the law and spontaneity; procedure as reflecting the values of peace, law amd justice; law and state; interpretation; and the role of law. Parts of the book overlap with the author's *Law and Religion (Supra,* no. 1053). B.S.J.

1055. Jacques Goldstain, *Les Valeurs de la Loi,* Paris: Editions Beauchesne, 1980, Pp. 283, Price: F.165 (Théologie Historique, 56). - The author, a Catholic monk with special responsibilities for relations with Judaism, discusses Biblical law not as a set of binding rules but as a pedagogical instrument, a statement of the fundamental values which God sought to inculcate in his people. Drawing on a wide range of Jewish and Christian sources, he discusses the philosophy, the psychology and theology of the law, the Sinai narrative, the content of the law (including its terminology and classification), and cultic law, the festivals, sacrifice, purity, family and social life, and the administration of justice. A final section deals briefly with the attitude to the Law as described in Biblical history, from the patriarchal period down to Qumran. B.S.J.

1056. L.E. Goodman, *Monotheism, a Philosophic Inquiry into the Foundations of Theology and Ethics,* New Jersey: Allanheld, Osmun for the Oxford Centre for Postgraduate Hebrew Studies, 1981, ISBN 0-86598-068-3, Pp. 119. - In 1978, Professor Goodman delivered the David Baumgardt Memorial Lectures, sponsored by the American Philosophical Association, at the Oxford Centre for Postgraduate Hebrew Studies. The text forms one of the first volumes in the Oxford Centre's monograph series. The three lectures are entitled "The Logic of Monotheism", "The Existence of God", and "Monotheism and Ethics". The last will be of particular interest to those concerned with the theoretical basis of Jewish law and ethics. B.S.J.

1057. Basil F. Herring, *Jewish Ethics and Halakhah for our Time: Sources and Commentary,* New York: Ktav Publishing House Inc. and Yeshiva University Press, 1984, ISBN 0-88125-044-9 (145-7 pbk.), Pp.xiii, 243, Price: $15.00, $9.25 (pbk.) (The Library of Jewish Law and Ethics, vol. XI). - After an introductory chapter surveying traditional views on the relationship between law and morality, the author analyses 9 ethical problems: abortion, disclosure of a terminal illness to a patient, euthanasia, the lawyer's duty in respect of a client he knows to be guilty, civil disobedience, homosexuality, value conflicts between parents and children, smoking and drugs. A selection of the relevant traditional sources is translated at the beginning of each chapter (and reprinted in a booklet enveloped within the back cover). The text is addressed to the intelligent layman, with notes referring to both traditional and modern scholarly discussions. The format of the book will make it particularly useful for discussion groups. B.S.J.

1058. R.A. Horsley, "The Law of Nature in Philo and Cicero", *HTR* 71 (1978), 35-59. - Koester is wrong to argue that Philo created the concept of natural law. Philo and Cicero both discuss the law of nature in similar terms showing that they are drawing on a common tradition. This derives "ultimately from a Stoic tradition on universal law and right reason. But this Stoic tradition had been reinterpreted by a revived and eclectic

Platonism upon which both Cicero and Plato drew. The key figure in the Platonic revival upon whom Cicero and (probably) Philo depend was Antiochus of Ascalon, the head of the Academy in the first century, who devoted much of his energy to a reinterpretation of Stoic ethics. Through further analysis of their statements about natural law ... we can discern more clearly how these thinkers understood the law of nature and, more particularly, how they conceived of its transcendent basis in the mind of God, who is the lawgiver" (author's own summary, p.36). G.J.W.

1059. B.S. Jackson, "On the Tyranny of the Law", *Israel Law Review* 18/3-4 (1983), 327-347. - The author sketches a continuum representing the tension between formalist and existentialist attitudes to both law and theology. He notes the paradox that religious systems of law are often characterised as rigid and immutable, although in practice they admit of more flexible interpretation. Both rabbinic and New Testament texts contribute to a possible resolution of the conflict of values indicated by modern jurisprudence, in that flexibility applies to the act of adjudication, quite beyond that which applies to the interpretation of the rules *in abstracto*. B.S.J.

1060. B.S. Jackson, "Structuralism and the notion of Religious Law", *Investigaciones Semióticas* 2/3 (1982-83), 1-43. - In the context of a comparison between jurisprudential accounts of religious law, and anthropological/semiotic approaches, the author considers the classification of biblical law as "moral", "ceremonial" and "judicial" (Aquinas) and Neusner's analysis of the various Orders of the Mishnah, which appear to reveal differences in the semiotic processes involved in them. B.S.J.

1061. A. Kirschenbaum, "Categories of Morality in Jewish Law: Some Clarifications", *Mélanges ... Prévost (supra* no. 858), 158-170. - The author argues that there are clear differences between the moral categories *midat hasidut, ruah hakhamim* and *lifnim mishurat hadin*. The first of these standards is expected only of the saintly élite, while the second applies to men in general. *Midat hasidut* also comes to be conflated with *lifnim mishurat hadin*. *Midat hasidut* eventually lost its uniqueness: it ceases to be individual and spontaneous, and finds its place in the codified literature. B.S.J.

1062. M.R. Konvitz, "The Confluence of Torah and Constitution", in *Jews, Judaism and the American Constitution* (Cincinnati: American Jewish Archives, 1982), 5-19. - K. suggests an intriguing parallel between the structure of the American and the Jewish legal systems: constitutional interpretation by the Supreme Court stands as to the United States Constitution as does the Oral Law to the Written Law in *halakhah*. The American "oral constitution" was "in a manner of speaking, implicitly or potentially in the minds of the framers of the written constitution". In both systems, the interpretive process which allows the law to develop is protected from arbitrariness by its commitment to an ordered form of rationality, underpinned by the Biblical concept of covenant. In the United States, "the movement was from biblical covenant to congregationalism to constitution." B.S.J.

1063. J. Kraemer, "Alfarabi's Opinions of the Virtuous City and Maimonides' Foundations of the Law", *Studia Orientalia, Memoriae D.H. Baneth*, Jerusalem: Magnes, 1979, 107-153. - Maimonides' *Foundations of the Law*, Part One of his *Mishneh Torah*, wants to provide Jewish jurists and laymen with a scheme similar to that of Alfarabi. Thus, *Foundations*, like the *Guide of the Perplexed*, is a *kalam* work in terms of (some) techniques and methods despite M.'s criticisms of the Mu'tazillites. Alfarabi's work, in turn, shows some similarity with (knowledge of?) John of Damascus' *De Fida Orthodoxa*. S.N.R.

1064. J.D. Levenson, "The Theologies of Commandment in Biblical Israel", *HTR* 73 (1980), 17-33. - Attempting to rescue the theology of law from Wellhausen's charge of legalism, modern writers especially Eichrodt and Mendenhall have insisted that law is an aspect of covenant. Law is viewed as part of *Heilsgeschichte* rather than as an end in itself. By examining the motive clauses used to justify obedience to different commands and the explanations of the law found in the psalms and the prophets, L shows that although historical (covenantal) reasons are often adduced, other justifications of the law are also found. Law is seen as an aspect of wisdom, whose value may be perceived by human intelligence. It is also seen as inherent in nature (e.g. *Ps*.19) 'Biblical Israel believed the will of God to be known not only through history, but also through.. nature, not only through the word proclaimed, but also through thought and cognition' (32). These theologies of law are not contradictory but complementary. G.J.W.

1065. J. Neusner, *Judaism, The Evidence of the Mishnah*, Chicago and London: The University of Chicago Press, 1981, ISBN 0-226-57617-5, Pp. xix, 419, Price: $25.00. - This is the brilliant culmination of Professor Neusner's decade of single-minded devotion to the analysis of the Mishnah. It is a work of interpretation on the grand scale, based upon the results of detailed literary analysis. The development of the law is laid out in three periods: before the first Jewish revolt against Rome, between the destruction of the temple and the Bar Cochba rebellion, and subsequently up to the closure of the Mishnah at the end of the second century. We see the relative state of development of each tractate, and more generally of each *seder*, through these three periods. Of particular interest to legal historians are the results concerning *Nashim* and *Neziqin;* the latter, in particular, is shown to be non-existent in the first period, to remain extremely sketchy in the second, and to acquire any semblance of order and development only in the third. Neusner does not thereby seek to imply that there existed no Jewish civil law in these periods; rather that these areas were originally not of interest to the groups which contributed to the development of the *Mishnah*. He identifies three groups whose interests are represented in it: the Priests, the scribes, and the middle-class landowners *(ba'ale habayit);* it is, however, through the style and methodology of the Scribes that the document achieves a unity, based upon the consistent concern to show the interaction of principles and resolve their conflicts, just as the Priestly Code (regarded as a major influence upon the underlying thought-processes of the mishnaic Rabbis) had sought to resolve classificatory problems involving mixtures and opposed categories. But there are also substantive aspects to this unification: "The principal message of the Mishnah is that the will of man affects the material reality of the world and governs the working of those forces, visible or not, which express and effect the sanctification of creation and of Israel alike" (p.271). This is the world-view - a quite remarkable affirmation of the human spirit given the historical circumstances - which emerges from Neusner's holistic approach. In adopting it, he is closer to some forms of structuralism than he himself is prepared to admit.

Particularly, he shares the fundamental insight that everything found in a text is there as the result of a human choice, and that what is excluded (or omitted), and which we see - sometimes - in the choices made in other documents of the period (which Neusner briefly surveys, in order to set the scene), is significant not only as contributing to the message itself, but also as identifying the act of enunciation, the parties to it, and their interests. In all this, Professor Neusner has set his own objectives, and rigorously pursued them, putting aside the contributions which more traditional approaches may make to such questions. It would be sad if those more traditional disciplines were to return the compliment. The legal historian, for example, may well wish to compare Neusner's account of the arrangement of *Neziqin*, and its relation to Scripture, with Daube's elaborate study, "The Civil Law in the Mishnah: The Arrangement of the Three Gates", *Tulane Law Review* 18 (1943-44), pp. 351-407; philosophers of law may wish to bring the insights of the philosophy of action to bear upon the data which generate Neusner's conclusion regarding the centrality of human will; and theologians may wish to review the meaning of the doctrine of the Oral Torah in the light of the pattern of human choices revealed by the literary analysis of the document. B.S.J.

1066 David Novak, *Halakhah in a Theological Dimension*, Chico, Ca.: Scholars Press, 1985, ISBN 0-89130-757-5, Pp. xi, 174, Price $19.75, $16.25 pbk. (Brown Judaic Studies 68). - All but the last two of the essays here collected have been published before, although in some cases they are now revised. The contents are: "Can Halakhah Be Both Authoritative and Changing?", "The Conflict between Halakhah and Ethics: The Case of *Mamzerut*", "Annulment in Lieu of Divorce in Jewish Law", "Divorce and Conversion: Is a Traditional-Liberal Modus Vivendi Possible?", "Women in the Rabbinate?", "Alcohol and drug Abuse in the Perspective of Jewish Tradition", "Judaism and Contemporary Bioethics", "The Threat of Nuclear War: Jewish Perspectives", and "The Logic of the Covenant: An Essay in Systematic Jewish Theology". The essays reflect the author's "assumption of the *interpenetration* of Halakhah qua law and Aggadah qua theology throughout the history of Judaism"; they display his customary combination of traditional learning and sensitivity to theoretical issues. B.S.J.

1067. David Novak, *The Image of the Non-Jew in Judaism, An Historical and Constructive Study of the Noahide Laws,* New York and Toronto: The Edwin Mellen Press, 1983, ISBN 0-88946-975-X, Pp. xxi, 481, Price: $68.95 (Toronto Studies in Theology, vol.14). - The concept of Noahide Laws has played a number of different roles in Jewish thought: it corresponds to both the "speculative" and "practical" senses of the Roman *ius gentium,* the former representing the view of that law which is common to all mankind, the latter being the law practiced in relations between Roman citizens and non-citizens; it also indicates those norms binding on the Jewish people *before* the Sinaitic revelation. Rabbi Dr. Novak takes full account of these functions, but adds an important fourth: the Noahide Laws stand to revealed law as the Kantian *a priori* categories stand as presuppositions (but not sufficient grounds) of our experience. In this sense, Noahide Law represents the natural law contribution to Jewish positive law. In expounding these themes, the author deals in detail first with the institution of Noahide laws, with chapters on their origins (which he assigns to the circumstances of the Hadrianic persecution), and then severally on each of the seven laws, and their interpretations. In the second part, he deals systematically with the theory of Noahide Law, as it appears in the Jewish sources, with chapters on Aggadic Speculation, Maimonides, Albo, Late Medieval Developments, Moses Mendelssohn and his School, and Hermann Cohen and the Jewish Neo-Kantians.

This is a book of major importance, both for what it does and for the future possibilities which it indicates. It deserved far better than to be published by photo-reproduction of a typescript (hardly a cost-reducing measure, judging by the price charged for the book). It is to be hoped, nevertheless, that this work will achieve a wide distribution. B.S.J.

1068. Ch. Perelman, "Legal Ontology and Legal Reasoning", *Israel Law Review* 16/3 (1981), 356-367. - In this article, the author relates the "legal ontology" (meaning "the religious or philosophical view which is the basis of the system of law") of Jewish law, Continental European law and Common law with their different allocation of powers as between judge and legislator. Reviewing the sources of Jewish law, and the manner of its development, he regards it as "the extreme example of a system of law without a legislator other than Moses", and contrasts continental law since the French Revolution, as representing the other extreme, where the whole of the law is regarded as the expression of the will of the legislator. English common law, by contrast to both, is not the expression of will (either of god or the nation), but rather "assumes the existence of an objective, rational and just law which is evident in judicial decisions." In all three systems, the scholars and judges succeeded in liberating themselves from the baleful results of legal ontology, when "the felt necessities" of the legal situation demanded.
B.S.J.

1069. Ch. Perelman, "Ontologie juridique et sources du droit", *Archives de Philosophie du Droit* 27 (1982), 23-31. - In comparing the legal ontology reflected in the views on "sources of law" to be found in Jewish law, Anglo-American law and continental European law, the late distinguished Belgian legal philosopher takes note of the way in which the flexibility of the oral law was reconciled with the view that God's revelation to Moses was the sole source of law. B.S.J.

1070. Daniela Piattelli, *Concezioni giuridiche e Metodi costruttivi dei guiristi orientali*, Milan: Giuffrè, 1981, Pp. 194, Price: IL. 10,000 (Università di Roma, Pubblicazioni dell'Istituto di Diritto Romano e dei Diritti dell'Oriente Mediterraneo, LVIII). - The common theme of this wide-ranging series of studies is the tension revealed in Jewish sources between human political authority (indigenous or foreign) and the ideology of divine revelation. The traditional conception of the legal autonomy granted to the local population by Oriental monarchs is studied in the light of the evidence of the books of Ezra and Nehemia, Esther, Judith, and Daniel; knowledge of indigenous law is studied by reference to the Letter of Aristeas, the Books of Maccabees, the evidence of Josephus regarding Alexander the Great, the edict of Antiochus III, and Roman *senatus consulta* regarding the status of the Jewish community *(ethnos tôn Ioudaiòn)*. The rule of *Dina Demalkhuta* is studied, together with the claims of its inapplicability to Israelite kings, on the grounds that they are not true sovereigns. This leads to consideration of the divine legitimation actually claimed by Israelite kings. The influence of theological conceptions is pursued further in relation to the development of the substantive law, and

the process of Rabbinic interpretation, with particular reference to the *Ketubah* and the document of indebtedness *(shtar hov)*. This is a work which deserves far wider attention amongst historians of Jewish law than it is likely to attract, if published only in Italian.
B.S.J.

1071. E. Scheid, "The Authority Principle in Biblical Morality", *Journal of Religious Ethics* 8 (1980), 180-203. - "This article suggests a philosophical explication of the biblical demand that man should obey an outward authoritative commandment of God. As a starting point we claim that in Jewish traditional sources there is no "ethics" as a separate philosophical branch. The Hebrew '*musar*'' means authority in its action, or the act of authoritative deliverance of behavioral norms, and authority means in this context: a decided will directed so as to move the wills of others in its own direction ... We have shown that there are two complementary motivations to obey God's authority: (1) being moved by a superior, creative Will; and (2) The drive towards self-fulfillment. The first motivation is the source of the biblical morality of awe - or fear. In every situation which calls for a moral response, man should judge himself before God, as God is supposed to judge him. the principle of morality of awe is justice. The second motivation is the source of the biblical morality of love. One should relate to his fellows as extensions of his own being. The principle of morality of love is charity. But these two categories of biblical morality are complementary, love being the. hidden source of awe, and awe the hidden source of love" (from the author's abstract). J.D.

1072. J.J. Shepherd, "Man's Morals and Israel's Religion", *Expository Times* 92 (1981), 171-174. - L. Kohlberg has identified six main stages of moral development: the lowest being an 'obedience and punishment orientation' and the highest the 'universal ethical principle orientation.' S. finds within the Bible examples of moral thinking at various different levels, and implies that only those scriptural imperatives which conform to Kohlberg's highest categories need concern the modern believer. G.J.W.

1073. R. Smend and U. Lux, *Gesetz,* Stuttgart etc: Kohlhammer, 1981, Pp. 156, ISBN 3-17-002015-3, Price: DM 6.50 (Kohlhammer Taschenbücher, Biblische Konfrontationen 1015). - The authors describe different approaches to law to be found in various sections of biblical and intertestamental literature: the Decalogue, Deuteronomy, the Priestly Law, the Psalms, Wisdom, and the notion of a "new covenant" in Jeremiah 31; the approach of Jesus, Matthew, Paul, Luke. B.S.J.

1074. J.B. Soloveitchik, *Halakhic Man,* translated by L. Kaplan, Philadelphia: The Jewish Publication Society of America, 1983, ISBN 0-8276-0222-7, Pp. xi, 164, Price: $12.95. - This is the first English translation of Soloveitchik's classic Hebrew essay of 1944, in which he proposes "Halakhic man" as a combination of two personalities - "cognitive man", who seeks to uncover the secrets of the world by the imposition of intellectual order and the removal of mystery, and "religious man", who rather emphasises the mysteries of existence, including the very idea of lawfulness. Through Torah and Talmudic tradition, man is able both to rationalise and to experience the mysteries of divine creation. The book dips into religious psychology and phenomenology, and sketches a philosophy of Halakhah. S. is most sympathetic to a form of neo-Kantianism, but with significant qualifications; his legal philosophy is necessarily part of his theology, in that *halakhah* is a means of bringing transcendence down to earth. In the final paragraph, Rabbi Soloveitchik states his sole intention as having been to "defend the honour of the Halakhah and halakhic men, for both it and they have oftentimes been attacked by those who have not penetrated into the essence of Halakhah and have failed to understand the halakhic personality"; he describes the essay as "But a patchwork of scattered reflections, a haphazard collection of fragmentary observations...". It is, indeed, a tantalising but yet frustrating work, one which calls for that very creative capacity which the author attributes to halakhic. The translator is to be congratulated on a superb piece of work, through which not only the author's work but also many of the sources to which he refers will become known to a wider public.

B.S.J.

1075. S. Spero, *Morality, Halakha and the Jewish Tradition*, New York: Ktav Publishing House, Inc. with Yeshiva University Press, 1983, Pp. xv, 381, ISBN 0-87068-727-1, Price: $20.00 (Library of Jewish Law and Ethics IX). - The author states his aim as "to examine the moral teachings of Judaism so as to uncover their implicit structures in order to develop what might be called an ethical theory of Jewish morality". Ethical theory is understood as "a theory *about* morals and *about* moral systems .... It attempts to analyse the basic concepts and methods of a morality, to describe the types of phenomena involved such as a special feeling of "obligation" or perhaps certain ideal character traits, and to explain the relationship of the morality under study to other aspects of life, such as God and human nature and other moralities." S. is acquainted with a wide range of modern Jewish and philosophical writings, but expresses his arguments in the text of the book quite simply. He covers a wide range of topics: the nature of morality, its place in Judaism, the grounds of morality, its relationship to Halakhah and to the will of god, the law of love, freedom and responsibility, and the logic which binds the Jewish moral system. He finds a hierarchy of values which offer guidance in cases of conflict. Apart from *kiddush ha-shem*, human life and dignity set aside ritual obligations, love of God stands higher than fear of god, mercy higher than justice, and peace higher than truth. The book may serve as a useful introduction for students who lack a philosophical background. B.S.J.

1076. S. Talmon, "Torah as a Concept and Vital Principle in the Hebrew Bible", *Greek Orthodox Theological Review* 24 (1979), 271-289. - Jews do not sharply distinguish biblical views of the *Torah* and later attitudes. There is essential continuity between them despite Christian attempts to denigrate post-exilic Jewish religion as legalistic or ceremonial. *Torah* is not simply law, formal regulations, but a comprehensive approach to life involving a world view, practical regulations and advice. In the Bible laws are set within the history of Israel. Even ritual laws which are apparently arbitrary are related to historical events and are concerned to mould a whole way of life. It is through obedience to the *torah* that man abides in relationship with God and society is preserved from disintegration. G.J.W.

1077. A. Tambasco, "Jeremiah and the Law of the Heart", *Bible Today* 19 (1980), 100-104. - Jeremiah's call to reform is compared to the Second Vatican Council especially in matters pertaining to social justice. The article is intended for pastors - Jesus is the "answer" to *Jer.* 31:31 - and a catechesis of the prophet is promised in the future. S.N.R.

See also 837, 842, 850, 859, 860, 895, 931, 932, 934, 935, 949, 951, 954, 955, 956, 957, 958, 959, 961, 963, 975, 983.

TORT

See 848, 930, 935, 102, 1023, 1027.

UNJUST ENRICHMENT

See 867.

USURY

1078. M. Benayahu, "A Ban by the Rabbis of Constantinople Regarding Interest Payment between Jews and Italy" (Heb.), *Shenaton* 8 (1981), 43-111. - On the basis of the text of this Ban drawn up by the Rabbis of Constantinople in 1564, the author draws a comprehensive picture of the usurious dealings between Jews in the Ancora area, which threatened the whole of Italian Jewry in the period of the edicts issued by Popes Paul IV and Pius V. According to Benayahu, this document is one of the most important sources for the history of the Jews in 16th century Italy. The article contains both the relevant texts and an analysis of the historical material. Y.S.K.

1079. J. Gross, "Inflation Shock: The Linkage of Liabilities in Israel" (Heb.), *Hapraklit* 33 (1980), 53-80. - In this extensive discussion of liability linkage in Israeli law, the author also adverts to the position in Jewish law in which money paid as a result of linking an obligation to the Index may constitute a form of usury and may therefore be prohibited. Y.S.K.

See also 856, 862, 879.

For Product Safety Concerns and Information please contact our EU representative GPSR@taylorandfrancis.com Taylor & Francis Verlag GmbH, Kaufingerstraße 24, 80331 München, Germany

Batch number: 10725973

Printed by Printforce, the Netherlands